The World Crisis

Volume IV

TITLES IN THE BLOOMSBURY REVELATIONS SERIES

The Sexual Politics of Meat, Carol J. Adams

Aesthetic Theory, Theodor W. Adorno

Philosophy of Modern Music, Theodor W. Adorno

The Oresteia, Aeschylus

Being and Event, Alain Badiou

Infinite Thought, Alain Badiou

Theoretical Writings, Alain Badiou

On Religion, Karl Barth

The Language of Fashion, Roland Barthes

The Intelligence of Evil, Jean Baudrillard

Key Writings, Henri Bergson

I and Thou, Martin Buber

The Tomb of Tutankhamun: Volumes 1–3, Howard Carter

A History of the English-Speaking Peoples: Volumes I–IV, Sir Winston S. Churchill

Never Give In!, Sir Winston S. Churchill

The Boer War, Sir Winston S. Churchill

The Second World War, Sir Winston S. Churchill

The World Crisis: Volumes I–V, Sir Winston S. Churchill

In Defence of Politics, Bernard Crick

Intensive Science and Virtual Philosophy, Manuel DeLanda

Cinema I, Gilles Deleuze

Cinema II, Gilles Deleuze

Difference and Repetition, Gilles Deleuze

Logic of Sense, Gilles Deleuze

A Thousand Plateaus, Gilles Deleuze and Félix Guattari

Anti-Oedipus, Gilles Deleuze and Félix Guattari

Dissemination, Jacques Derrida

Origins of Analytical Philosophy, Michael Dummett

Taking Rights Seriously, Ronald Dworkin

Discourse on Free Will, Desiderius Erasmus and Martin Luther

The Theatre of the Absurd, Martin Esslin

Education for Critical Consciousness, Paulo Freire

Pedagogy in Process, Paulo Freire

Pedagogy of Hope, Paulo Freire

Pedagogy of the Heart, Paulo Freire

Marx's Concept of Man, Erich Fromm

To Have or To Be?, Erich Fromm

The Beginning of Knowledge, Hans-Georg Gadamer
The Beginning of Philosophy, Hans-Georg Gadamer
Truth and Method, Hans-Georg Gadamer
All Men Are Brothers, Mohandas K. Gandhi
Things Hidden Since the Foundation of the World, René Girard
Violence and the Sacred, René Girard
Among the Dead Cities, A.C. Grayling
Towards the Light, A.C. Grayling
The Three Ecologies, Félix Guattari
Mindfulness, Martin Heidegger
The Essence of Truth, Martin Heidegger
The Odyssey, Homer
Eclipse of Reason, Max Horkheimer
The Nazi Dictatorship, Ian Kershaw
Language of the Third Reich, Victor Klemperer
Everyday Life in the Modern World, Henri Lefebvre
Rhythmanalysis, Henri Lefebvre
Modes of Modern Writing, David Lodge
Libidinal Economy, Jean-François Lyotard
After Virtue, Alasdair MacIntyre
Time for Revolution, Antonio Negri
Apologia Pro Vita Sua, John Henry Newman
Film Fables, Jacques Rancière
The Politics of Aesthetics, Jacques Rancière
Course in General Linguistics, Ferdinand de Saussure
Philosophy, Roger Scruton
Understanding Music, Roger Scruton
The Five Senses, Michel Serres
The Precariat, Guy Standing
An Actor Prepares, Constantin Stanislavski
Building A Character, Constantin Stanislavski
Creating A Role, Constantin Stanislavski
My Life In Art, Constantin Stanislavski
States and Markets, Susan Strange
What is Art?, Leo Tolstoy
Interrogating the Real, Slavoj Žižek
The Universal Exception, Slavoj Žižek

Some titles are not available in North America.

The World Crisis

Volume IV: 1918–1928

The Aftermath

Winston S. Churchill

BLOOMSBURY ACADEMIC

LONDON • NEW YORK • OXFORD • NEW DELHI • SYDNEY

BLOOMSBURY ACADEMIC
Bloomsbury Publishing Plc
50 Bedford Square, London, WC1B 3DP, UK
1385 Broadway, New York, NY 10018, USA
29 Earlsfort Terrace, Dublin 2, Ireland

BLOOMSBURY, BLOOMSBURY ACADEMIC and the Diana logo are trademarks
of Bloomsbury Publishing Plc

First published by Charles Scribner's Sons 1929

Bloomsbury Revelations edition first published in 2015 by Bloomsbury Academic
Reprinted 2018 (three times), 2019 (four times), 2021 (twice), 2023
Reprinted with a new cover 2023

Cover Design by Ben Anslow

A catalogue record for this book is available from the British Library.

A catalog record for this book is available from the Library of Congress.

ISBN: HB: 978-1-4742-2341-6
PB: 978-1-4725-8695-7
ePDF: 978-1-4725-8697-1
ePub: 978-1-4725-8696-4

Series: Bloomsbury Revelations

Typeset by Deanta Global Publishing Services, Chennai, India
Printed and bound in Great Britain

To find out more about our authors and books visit www.bloomsbury.com
and sign up for our newsletters.

Contents

Maps, Charts etc.

PREFACE

This volume completes the task I undertook nearly ten years ago of making a contemporary contribution to the history of the Great War. As in previous volumes, the record and discussion of world-famous events is strung upon the thread of personal narrative. This method will justify itself to the reader who seeks to form his own opinion from a number of similar authentic accounts. It involves, however, considerable variation in the proportion of events. Thus episodes and transactions which I took part in myself, or had direct knowledge of, naturally obtain exceptional prominence. Wherever possible I have told the tale in my own words written or spoken at the time. The proper adjustments must be made in pages where this occurs. I tell the tale as I saw it unfold. But others saw it from a different angle, and there was much that I did not see.

I have been surprised in writing of the events with which this volume deals, to find the number of important affairs in which I was personally concerned which had utterly passed from my mind. In these years the press of business was extreme; developments succeeded each other in ceaseless transformation; the whole world was in flux at the same moment; one impression effaced another. It is only when I re-read the speeches, letters and memoranda of the time that these intense and exciting years live again for me. I am sure that there is scarcely any period about which more has been recorded, more has been forgotten and less is understood, than the four years which followed the Armistice. It may therefore be a serviceable act to present a general view of the scene—albeit from a personal angle—and still more to trace through a labyrinth of innumerable happenings the unique and inexorable sequence of cause and effect.

Most of the books written since the war have dealt with the Peace Conference in Paris, upon which a voluminous literature exists. My work during these years was concerned mainly with what happened outside the halls of Paris and Versailles, and with the consequences of the decisions—and not less of the delays—of the Plenipotentiaries upon great countries and millions of people. It is with these external reactions therefore that this volume mainly deals. It is unhappily for the most part a chronicle of misfortune and tragedy. Whether this tenor was inevitable or not the reader must judge. In no period of my official life, extending now over nearly a quarter of a century, was public business so difficult as in these post-war years. Events were crowded and turbulent. Men were tired and wayward. Power was on the ebb tide; prosperity was stranded; and money was an increasing worry. Not only therefore were the problems hard and numerous, but the means for coping with them continually diminished. Moreover it was not easy to adjust one's mind to the new dimensions. It was hard to realise that victory beyond the dreams of hope led to weakness, discontent, faction and disappointment; and that this was in itself a process of regrowth. I therefore wish to judge with special compunction the shortcomings and errors of those who at the summit filled the most difficult positions of all.

It is perhaps necessary for me to repeat here, as in the former volumes, that all the opinions expressed are purely personal and commit no one but myself. I have also to express my thanks to those who have so powerfully assisted me with advice and knowledge, or who have allowed their confidentially spoken or written opinions to be quoted.

Winston Spencer Churchill.
Chartwell.
January 1, 1929.

CHAPTER I
'THE BROKEN SPELL'

Four Centuries of Persistency—The Pageant of Victory—Rejoicing and Reaction—The Masters of the World—An Armistice Dream—The Rendezvous—Russia—Germany's Opportunity—The New Arm—The New Nobility—Abnormal Conditions—An Unforeseeable Situation—The Shock of Peace—The Broken Spell.

The conclusion of the Great War raised England to the highest position she has yet attained. For the fourth time in four successive centuries she had headed and sustained the resistance of Europe to a military tyranny; and for the fourth time the war had ended leaving the group of small States of the Low Countries, for whose protection England had declared war, in full independence. Spain, the French Monarchy, the French Empire and the German Empire had all overrun and sought to possess or dominate these regions. During 400 years England had withstood them all by war and policy, and all had been defeated and driven out. To that list of mighty Sovereigns and supreme military Lords which already included Philip II, Louis XIV and Napoleon, there could now be added the name of William II of Germany. These four great series of events, directed unswervingly to the same end through so many generations and all crowned with success, constitute a record of persistency and achievement, without parallel in the history of ancient or modern times.

But other substantial advantages had been obtained. The menace of the German navy was destroyed and the overweening power of Germany had been for many years definitely set back. The Russian Empire which had been our Ally had been succeeded by a revolutionary government which had renounced all claims to Constantinople, and which by its inherent vices and inefficiency could not soon be a serious military danger to India. On the other hand, England was united with her nearest neighbour and oldest enemy—France—by ties of comradeship in suffering and in victory which promised to be both strong and durable. British and United States troops had fought for the first time side by side, and the two great branches of the English-speaking world had begun again to write their history in common. Lastly, the British Empire had stood every shock and strain during the long and frightful world convulsion. The Parliamentary institutions by which the life of the Mother Country and the self-governing Dominions found expression had proved themselves as serviceable for waging war as for maintaining freedom and progress in times of peace. The invisible ties of interest, sentiment and tradition which across all the waters of the world united the Empire had proved more effective than the most binding formal guarantees, and armies of half a million Canadians, Australians and New Zealanders had been drawn by these indefinable and often imperceptible attractions across greater distances than any armies had travelled before, to die and conquer for a cause and quarrel which only remotely affected their immediate material safety. All the peoples and all the creeds of India during the years of crisis had made in their own way a spontaneous demonstration of loyalty, and sustained the war by arms and money on a scale till then unknown. The rebellion in South Africa in 1914 had been repressed by the very Boer generals who had been our most dangerous antagonists in the South African War, and who had signed with us the liberating treaty of Vereeniging. Only in parts of Ireland had there been a failure and a repudiation, and about that there was a lengthy tale to tell.

The pageant of victory unrolled itself before the eyes of the British nation. All the Emperors and Kings with whom we had warred had been dethroned, and all their valiant armies were shattered to pieces. The terrible enemy whose might and craft had so long threatened our existence, whose force had destroyed the flower of the British nation, annihilated the Russian Empire and left all our Allies except the United States at the last gasp, lay prostrate at the mercy of the conquerors. The ordeal was over. The peril had been warded off. The slaughter and the sacrifices had not been in vain and were at an end; and the overstrained people in the hour of deliverance gave themselves up for a space to the sensations of triumph. Church and State united in solemn thanksgiving. The whole land made holiday. Triple avenues of captured cannon lined the Mall. Every street was thronged with jubilant men and women. All classes were mingled in universal rejoicing. Feasting, music and illuminations turned the shrouded nights of war into a blazing day. The vast crowds were convulsed with emotions beyond expression; and in Trafalgar Square the joy of the London revellers left enduring marks upon the granite plinth of Nelson's column.

Who shall grudge or mock these overpowering entrancements? Every Allied nation shared them. Every victorious capital or city in the five continents reproduced in its own fashion the scenes and sounds of London. These hours were brief, their memory fleeting; they passed as suddenly as they had begun. Too much blood had been spilt. Too much life-essence had been consumed. The gaps in every home were too wide and empty. The shock of an awakening and the sense of disillusion followed swiftly upon the poor rejoicings with which hundreds of millions saluted the achievement of their hearts' desire. There still remained the satisfactions of safety assured, of peace restored, of honour preserved, of the comforts of fruitful industry, of the home-coming of the soldiers; but these were in the background; and with them all there mingled the ache for those who would never come home.

* * * * *

Along the British lines in France and Belgium eleven o'clock had produced a reaction revealing the mysterious nature of man. The cannonade was stilled; the armies halted where they stood. Motionless in the silence the soldiers looked at each other with vacant eyes. A sense of awe, of perplexity, and even of melancholy stole coldly upon men who a few moments before had been striding forward in the ardour of hot pursuit. It was as though an abyss had opened before the conquerors' feet.

'Unarm! Eros! The long day's work is done.'

The fighting troops seemed for a time incapable of adjusting themselves to the abrupt relaxation of strain. So quiet were the forward camps on the night of victory that one would have thought they belonged to brave men after doing their best at last defeated. This wave of psychological depression passed as quickly as the opposite mood in Britain; and in a few days Home had become the foundation of all desires. But here again were disillusion and hope deferred.

* * * * *

On the night of the Armistice I dined with the Prime Minister at Downing Street. We were alone in the large room from whose walls the portraits of Pitt and Fox, of Nelson and Wellington, and—perhaps somewhat incongruously—of Washington then looked down. One of the most admirable traits in Mr. Lloyd George's character was his complete freedom at the height of his power, responsibility and good fortune from anything in the nature of pomposity or superior airs. He was always natural and simple. He was always exactly the same to those who knew him well: ready to argue any point, to listen to disagreeable facts even when controversially presented. One could say anything to him, on the terms that he could say anything back. The magnitude and absolute character of the victory induced a subdued and detached state of mind. There was no feeling that the work was done. On the contrary, the realisation was strong upon him that a new and perhaps more difficult phase of effort was before him. My own mood was divided between anxiety for the future and desire to help the fallen foe. The conversation ran on the great qualities of the German people, on the tremendous fight they had made against three-quarters of the world, on the impossibility of rebuilding Europe except with their aid. At that time we thought they were actually starving, and that under the twin pressures of defeat and famine the Teutonic peoples—already in revolution—might slide into the grisly gulf that had already devoured Russia. I suggested that we should immediately, pending further news, rush a dozen great ships crammed with provisions into Hamburg. Although the armistice terms enforced the blockade till peace was signed, the Allies had promised to supply what was necessary, and the Prime Minister balanced the project with favouring eye. From outside the songs and cheers of multitudes could be remotely heard like the surf on the shore. We shall see that different sentiments were soon to prevail.

* * * * *

On that November evening the three men at the head of Great Britain, the United States and France seemed to be the masters of the world. Behind them stood vast communities organised to the last point, rejoicing in victory and inspired with gratitude and confidence for the chiefs who had led them there. In their hands lay armies of irresistible might, and fleets without whose sanction no vessel crossed the sea upon or beneath the surface. There was nothing wise, right and necessary which they could not in unity decree. And these men had been drawn together across differences of nationality and interest and across distances on land and sea by the comradeship of struggle against a dreaded foe. Together they had reached the goal. Victory absolute and incomparable was in their hands. What would they do with it?

But the hour was fleeting. Unperceived by the crowd as by the leaders, the spell by which they had ruled was already breaking. Other forms of authority would presently come into play and much might yet be done. But for the supreme tasks, for the best solutions, for the most serviceable policies NOW was the only time.

These men must come together. Geographical and constitutional obstacles are mere irrelevancies. They must meet face to face and settle swiftly after discussion the largest practical questions opened by the total defeat of the enemy. They must relegate to a lower plane all feelings of passion roused in conflict, all considerations of party politics in the countries they represent, all personal desire to continue in power. They must seek only the best arrangements possible for the brave nations that had followed them, for a tormented Europe and an awe-struck world.

If they could come together they would face realities and discern the proportion of events. The German, Austrian and Turkish Empires and all the mighty forces that had held the victors in check so long had yielded themselves helpless and disarmed. But the task was unfinished. Other foes remained in the field; other impulsions challenged the authority of the victors and barred a fair settlement of the world's affairs. Well might they have bethought themselves of the Roman motto 'Spare the conquered and war down the proud.'

* * * * *

The reader may perhaps at this point be willing to study some speculative questions in a purely imaginary form. Let us then for a few moments leave the region of 'What happened' for those of 'What might have happened.' Let us dream one of the many Armistice dreams. It is only a dream.

* * * * *

The victory produced an astonishing effect upon President Wilson. His responsibility and glory lifted him above the peace-time partisanship in which so much of his life had been lived. At the same time it exercised a sobering effect upon his judgment of foreign countries and their affairs. As soon as he received the joint message of Lloyd George and Clemenceau proposing a meeting in the Isle of Wight (or perhaps it was Jersey) before the end of November, he realized that he must go, and that whatever had happened in the past he must go as the representative of the whole of the United States. He asked himself what his position would be in history if he pledged the faith of his country without warrant, or if what he promised in his country's name was not made good. So, in the very flush of success, he appealed to the Senate of the United States to fortify him with a delegation of their strongest men, having due regard to the Republican majority in that body. 'I cannot tell,' he said, 'how party affairs will develop in the next few years, but nothing compares with the importance of our bearing our part in the peace as our soldiers have borne theirs in the war. We have been drawn against our wish, against our whole tradition into the affairs of Europe. We have not entered without reason, we will not quit without honour.'

Clemenceau said (to himself) : 'I have got to think of the long safety of France. Not by our own exertions alone but by miracles we have been preserved. The greatest nations in the world have come to our aid and we are delivered out of the deadly peril. Never again can we hope for such aid. A thousand years will not see such fortunate conjunctures for France. Now is the appointed time for making friends with Germany and ending the quarrel of so many centuries. We, the weaker, have got them down; we, the conquerors, will lift them up.'

As for Lloyd George, he said: 'History will judge my record and will not find it unworthy. In order to win through in this war I have destroyed every political foundation by which I rose and on which I stood. But after all, life is a brief span, and all that matters is not to fall below the level of events upon the greatest occasions. The British people have good memories, and I shall trust to them.'

So these three men met within three weeks of the Armistice in the Isle of Wight (or was it Jersey?) and settled together the practical steps which should be taken to set the world on its feet again in an enduring peace.

Meanwhile the Delegation from the Senate of the United States proceeded direct to Paris and visited their armies at the front.

When the three men met together they found themselves in complete agreement that a League of Nations must be set up not as a Super-State but as a Super-Function above all the valiant and healthful nations of the world. But they saw that they could only plant a tree which would grow strong enough as the years passed by, and at their first meeting, which might have occurred on December 1, 1918, they agreed that a League of Nations must embrace all the dominating races of the world. This was their first Resolution. Wilson said, 'I can answer for the United States, because I have behind me both the great parties, the Republicans as well as my own Democrats.' Lloyd George said: 'I speak for the British Empire and am sustained by the Prime Ministers of all the self-governing Dominions; and moreover both Mr. Asquith and Mr. Bonar Law have consented to support me till the settlement is made, when it is my inflexible resolve to withdraw (I will not say for ever) from public affairs.' Clemenceau said: 'I am seventy-five years old and I am France.'

So they said: 'It is no use setting up a League of Nations without Russia, and Russia is still outside our jurisdiction. The Bolsheviks do not represent Russia, they represent an international conception of human affairs entirely foreign and indeed hostile to anything we know of civilisation; but the Russians stood by us in the worst of the war and we owe it to them that they have a fair chance of national self-expression.'

They then agreed to their second Resolution: *The Russian people must be enabled to choose a national assembly before whom the present issues can be laid.*

So they sent for Marshal Foch and asked him, 'What can you do about Russia?'

Foch replied: 'There is no great difficulty and there need be no serious fighting. A few hundred thousand American troops who are longing to play a part in events, together with volunteer units from the British (I am afraid he said "English") and French armies can easily with the modern railways obtain control of Moscow; and anyhow we hold already three parts of Russia. If you wish your authority to embrace the late Russian Empire for the purpose of securing the free expression of the Russian wish, you have only to give me the order. How easy this task will be to me and Haig and Pershing compared with restoring the battle of the 21st March or breaking the Hindenburg Line!'

But the statesmen said: 'This is not a military proposition only, it is world politics. To lay hands on Russia, although no doubt physically practicable, is morally too big a task for the victors alone. If we are to accomplish this it can only be with the aid of Germany. Germany knows more about Russia than anyone else. She is at this moment occupying as sole guarantee of civilised life the richest and most populous parts of Russia. Germany let Lenin loose on Russia. Ought she not to play her part in clearing up this whole eastern battlefield like the others?' And they said, 'This will be the opportunity for Germany. This will enable a proud and faithful people to avoid all humiliation in defeat. They will slide by an almost unconscious transition from cruel strife to natural co-operation with all of us. Nothing is possible in Europe without Germany and everything will be easy with her.'

Then they passed the Third Resolution: *That Germany shall be invited to aid in the liberation of Russia and the rebuilding of Eastern Europe.*

But Foch said: 'How will you guarantee the life of France?' and the President and Mr. Lloyd George in their turn replied: 'Within the limits of the Fourteen Points the life of France will be guaranteed by the English-speaking peoples throughout the world and by all the states and races associated with them.'

Then, having settled all vital matters, the three chiefs turned for a moment to the expenses of the war. But this presented no difficulty. Evidently only one principle could rule, namely, *Equality of Sacrifice.* There were three factors to be fused,—loss of blood, loss of treasure, and on the other hand—rated very high—acquisition of territory. They laughed a little at the idea of appraising life in terms of money and deducting territorial gains therefrom. But they said: 'Though money is no doubt an inadequate token, it is the handiest we have in our present state of development. After all we only require a mathematical formula which experts can work out at the same time they are calculating the reparations of Germany and the defeated countries. Much has been destroyed that can never be repaired, but if we all stand together the burdens even on the vanquished need not be very great. We will have a world bank-note on the double security of Victory and Reconciliation. To the support of this, all will contribute on a basis which will recognise the difference between winning and losing. It might perhaps eventually become the foundation of a universal currency. Anyhow, so long as we are agreed upon the principle we can easily have the applications worked out.'

Then they went back to the League of Nations plan. No doubt once all the greatest nations were included, their moral force alone was an immense security for peace and justice. An almost universal trade and financial boycott, and total exclusion from the seas, were additional severe deterrents upon an aggressor. Credit, food, munitions were strong defences for the attacked. But surely the august authority of the League must not shrink in the last resort from the use of force!

It is not known which of the three chiefs first conceived the master-plan by which the peace of the world is now so well defended that national armaments are falling into increasing neglect. But history records the fact that on the second day of conversation it was decided that the new instrument of world-order should be armed with the new weapons of science. Nations great or small might, if they wished, for their own reassurance have battleships and cruisers, cavalry, infantry and artillery, and spend their money as they chose on these; but war from the air and war by chemical means were reserved to League and to international authority alone.

At the moment when science had produced weapons destructive of the safety and even the life of whole cities and populations, weapons whose action was restricted by no frontiers and could be warded off neither by fleets nor armies, a new instrument of human government would be created to wield them. Conversely, just as this new instrument was coming into being, the new weapons which it required were ready to its hand. But with that practical spirit which shone in these three experienced statesmen, they proclaimed at once the principle and its gradual application. Every state signatory of the Covenant would in the first instance dedicate to the League so many squadrons of aeroplanes. From these a new force would be formed. 'We are reviving, in fact,' said Clemenceau, 'the old Orders of chivalry like the Knights Templars and the Knights of Malta to guard civilisation against barbarism.' Here he made a remark of a somewhat irreverent character which has escaped the chronicler. 'There is certainly no lack,' said the President, 'of knights whose renown is deathless to found the Order. French, British, American, German, Italian aces have performed exploits for which there is no counterpart in human annals. Let these be the new nobility.' 'At any rate,' said Lloyd George, 'they are better than the profiteers who are sitting on my door-step every day.'

So it was agreed that in principle the power of the air should be reserved to the League of Nations for the purpose of maintaining world peace against aggression. No absolute veto was placed in the first instance upon national air forces, but the whole emphasis of the policy of the Great Powers would be laid upon building up the International Air Force, with the intention that as general confidence grew only commercial aviation should be developed nationally, and the military aspect should be reserved to international authority alone.

They thought the question of chemical warfare too difficult to settle at the moment further than by a universal decree forbidding any individual nation to practise it. 'Perhaps, however,' it was added, 'some day recalcitrant nations will be punished by being made to sneeze and if all else fails, to vomit.'

As they were going to bed on the third night of their talks someone inquired 'What will happen if our peoples will not take our advice?' Then they all said, 'Let them get somebody else. We shall have done our bit.'

It was at this moment that the spell broke. The illusion of power vanished. I awoke from my Armistice dream, and we all found ourselves in the rough, dark, sour and chilly waters in which we are swimming still.

* * * * *

Great allowances must be made for the behaviour of all the peoples and of all their governments—victors and vanquished alike—as they emerged from the furnace of fifty-two months' world war. The conditions were outside all previous experience. At the outbreak with all its unknown and measureless possibilities the flood of crisis flowed along channels which for some distance had already been prepared. The naval and military leaders and the staffs behind them assumed the immediate direction; and they had plans which, whether good or bad, were certainly worked out in the utmost detail. These plans of scientific havoc were put into execution; and the second series of events arose out of their clashings. Every War Office and every Admiralty emitted laconic orders, and for a while the consequences followed almost automatically. The immense forces of destruction, long gathered and stored, were released. When a battleship is launched the operation is short and simple. A few speeches are made; a few prayers are said; a bottle of champagne is broken; a few wedges are knocked away; and thousands of tons of steel swiftly gathering momentum glide irrevocably into the water. Very different are the problems of bringing that same ship, shattered in action, ripped by torpedoes, crowded with wounded, half full of water, safely back to harbour through storm and mist and adverse tides.

Of course, for more than a year before the war ended plans had been prepared for demobilisation and for reconstruction. Men had been withdrawn from the conduct of the war to study and elaborate the measures consequent upon an assumed successful peace. But they were not in any sphere the dominant figures. All other eyes were riveted on the war. The whole mind of the state, every energy which it could command, were concentrated on victory and self-preservation. This other field of interest—hypothetical, contingent, remote—was but dimly lighted. What had we to do with peace while we did not know whether we should not be destroyed? Who could think of reconstruction while the whole world was being hammered to pieces, or of demobilisation when the sole aim was to hurl every man and every shell into the battle?

Moreover, the governing minds among the Allies never expected the war to end in 1918. Behind the advancing armies all thought and preparation were concentrated upon the spring campaign on the Meuse or on the Rhine. It was to be the greatest campaign of all. More millions of men, more thousands of cannons, more tens of thousands of shells a week; aeroplanes by the hundred thousand and tanks by the ten thousand: new deadly engines, inventions and poisons of diabolical quality applied upon a gigantic scale: all were moving forward under the ceaseless impulse of the whole effective manhood and womanhood of every warring state. And then suddenly peace! The ramparts against which the united battering-rams of the strongest part of mankind were thundering disintegrated, leaving behind them only a cloud of dust into which the Allies and all their apparatus toppled headlong forward and lay sprawling.

The British Empire, apart from its navy, had only come gradually into the war. The armies had grown up division by division. The front had broadened a few miles at a time. The transformation of industry had taken years. Compulsion for national service and all the grinding codes of wartime had come into force by almost insensible degrees. We were in fact just approaching our maximum potential in every material sphere. The limits of our war effort in quantity and quality were everywhere in sight. How long those efforts could have been maintained at the highest pitch is unknowable, for at the culminating point every form of resistance simultaneously collapsed.

The dire need and the high cause which had cemented the alliance of twenty-seven states and held their workers and their warriors in intensifying comradeship, vanished in a flash. The scythe that shore away the annual swathes of youth stopped at the very feet of a new generation. Those who had braced themselves for the ordeal gazed stupefied rather than thankful at the carnage from which they had been withheld. The current of man's will and of his fate was suddenly, not merely stopped, but reversed. Therefore, I hold that for us at any rate the transition to peace was more violent than the entry into war, and that it involved a more complete and universal revolution of our minds.

The men at the head of the victorious states were subjected to tests of the most trying kind. They seemed all-powerful: but their power was departing. Although it was departing, the appearance of it remained for a space: and it might perhaps be recalled by great action. But time was paramount. With every day's delay it became more difficult to gather the fruits of victory. With every day the power not only of statesmen, but of the Allied nations themselves, and their unity, must decline. Their armies must come home; their electorates must regain their sway. Jealousies, factions, revenges long pent up now advanced on every side. Yet every day was so full of important and urgent business, and so disturbed by jostling personalities and events, that human nature could not cope with the task. Was it strange that these men should yield themselves to the illusion of power, to the relief of victory and to the press of business? Was it strange that they should wish to draw breath before beginning new tasks? They remained for some time under the impression that the same strenuous controls would continue in other forms and that equal powers and sanctions would be available for overcoming the new difficulties. In fact, however, just as the ship was coming into port more than half the rudder had dropped off without the men at the helm perceiving it.

The former peace-time structure of society had for more than four years been superseded and life had been raised to a strange intensity by the war spell. Under that mysterious influence, men and women had been appreciably exalted above death and pain and toil. Nothing had been too hard to bear or too precious to cast away. Unities and comrade-ships had become possible between men and classes and nations and grown stronger while the hostile pressure and the common cause endured. But now the spell was broken: too late for some purposes, too soon for others, and too suddenly for all! Every victorious country subsided to its old levels and its previous arrangements; but these latter were found to have fallen into much disrepair, their fabric was weakened and disjointed, they seemed narrow and out of date. The boundless hopes that had cheered the soldiers and the peoples in their tribulations died swiftly away. The vision of a sunlit world redeemed by valour, where work would be less and its recompense more, where Justice and Freedom reigned together through centuries of unbroken peace—that vision which had flickered over the battlefields and beckoned from behind the German or

Turkish trenches, comforting the soldier's heart and fortifying his strength, was soon replaced by cold, grey reality. How could it have been otherwise? By what process could the slaughter of ten million men and the destruction of one-third of the entire savings of the greatest nations of the world have ushered in a Golden Age? A cruel disillusionment was at hand for all. All men, all women, all soldiers, all citizens were looking forward to some great expansion, and there lay before them nothing but a sharp contraction; a contraction in material conditions for the masses; a contraction in scope and command for those who had raised themselves by their qualities—and they too were numbered by the hundred thousand—to stations of responsibility.

With the passing of the spell there passed also, just as the new difficulties were at their height, much of the exceptional powers of guidance and control. The triumphant statesmen, the idols of the masses, acclaimed as saviours of their countries, were still robed with the glamour of war achievement and shod with the sanctions of Democracy. But their hour was passing; their work was almost done, and Wilson, Clemenceau and Lloyd George were soon to follow into retirement or adversity the Kings and Emperors they had dethroned.

To the faithful, toil-burdened masses the victory was so complete that no further effort seemed required. Germany had fallen, and with her the world combination that had crushed her. Authority was dispersed; the world unshackled; the weak became the strong; the sheltered became the aggressive; the contrast between victors and vanquished tended continually to diminish. A vast fatigue dominated collective action. Though every subversive element endeavoured to assert itself, revolutionary rage like every other form of psychic energy burnt low. Through all its five acts the drama has run its course; the light of history is switched off, the world stage dims, the actors shrivel, the chorus sinks. The war of the giants has ended; the quarrels of the pygmies have begun.

CHAPTER II
DEMOS

Ministry of Munitions Problems—Work, Wages, and War-Material—Munitions Demobilisation—The War Unity—The Revival of Party Politics—Mr. Lloyd George and the Liberals—The Peace Conference and its Delegates—The General Election—The Hard Line—The National Temper—'Hang the Kaiser'—'Make them Pay'—Methods of Payment—How much?—Letters to Constituents—The Prime Minister on the Indemnity—Result of the Election—Its After-effects.

We must first of all unravel our own domestic affairs guided by the thread of personal narrative.

On the afternoon of November 11, I assembled the Munitions Council and directed their attention to the immediate demobilisation of British industry. The problems were intricate and perplexing. Nearly all the mines and workshops of Britain were in our hands. We controlled and were actually managing all the greatest industries. We regulated the supply of all their raw materials. We organised the whole distribution of their finished products. Nearly five million persons were directly under our orders, and we were interwoven on every side with every other sphere of the national economic life.

Certainly the organisation and machinery of which we disposed was powerful and flexible in an extraordinary degree. The able business men among us, each the head of a large group of departments, had now been working for a year and a half in a kind of industrial cabinet. They were accustomed to unexpected changes enforced by the shifting fortunes of war. Four or five of them, representing the departments involved in any project, would put their heads together in an intimate and helpful manner; and in a very few hours—at most in a few days—orders would be given which worked smoothly downwards through innumerable ramifications. There was very little in the productive sphere they could not at this time actually do. A requisition, for instance, for half a million houses would not have seemed more difficult to comply with than those we were already in process of executing for a hundred thousand aeroplanes, or twenty thousand guns, or the medium artillery of the American army, or two million tons of projectiles. But a new set of conditions began to rule from eleven o'clock onwards. The money-cost, which had never been considered by us to be a factor capable of limiting the supply of the armies, asserted a claim to priority from the moment the fighting stopped. Nearly every manifestation of discontent on the part of the munition workers had in the end been met by increases of wages—('Let 'em have it and let's get the stuff')—and the wage rates now stood at levels never witnessed in England before or since. The intensity of the exertions evoked by the national danger far exceeded the ordinary capacities of human beings. All were geared up to an abnormal pitch. Once the supreme incentive had disappeared, everyone became conscious of the severity of the strain. A vast and general relaxation and descent to the standards of ordinary life was imminent. No community could have gone on using up treasure and life energy at such a pace. Most of all was the strain apparent in the higher ranks of the brain workers. They had carried on uplifted by the psychological stimulus which was now to be removed. 'I can work till I drop' was sufficient while the cannon thundered and armies marched. But now it was peace; and on every side exhaustion, nervous and physical, unfelt or unheeded before, became evident.

The first question was what to do with the five million munition workers whose work and wages had to be provided week by week. It was clear that the majority of these would very soon have to find new occupations, and many hundreds of thousands would have to change their place of abode. More than one and a half million women were employed in the war industries, and had proved themselves capable of making nearly every conceivable commodity and of earning wages on piece work far in excess of what the strongest men had earned before the war. If the soldiers returning from the front were to find employment in any of the known industries, all these had in a few months to quit the factory for the home. How would they feel about this transformation of their life and outlook? In the meanwhile the main situation was still uncertain. An armistice is not a peace. The impression of the German might was still strong upon all of us. No orders of demobilisation had been issued or were imminent. At the best there would be an interval of months before large numbers of soldiers could return. Enormous programmes of war material were in every stage of completion. Were they all to be stopped at a stroke? Was a gun or a tank or an aeroplane, almost ready, to be scrapped as it stood? Obviously no new raw materials should be consumed. The tap could be turned off at the source. But the outflow of what was already pouring through the vast system could not be sealed up without throwing five million persons simultaneously into idleness. Could they be left without wages? Could they, on the other hand, be paid their inflated wages for doing nothing, while the armies were still on guard abroad on only soldiers' pay? Were there no dangers to social order in leaving these great numbers, whether paid or unpaid, to drift aimlessly about the cities and arsenals without any sense of guidance from the organisation which hitherto had gripped them all?

Fortunately an immense amount of work had been done. My predecessors, Mr. Montagu and Dr. Addison, had in 1916 and 1917 studied the subject. In the spring of 1917 the latter had appointed a Reconstruction Department to collect information, and in July this had been expanded into a Ministry of Reconstruction of which Dr. Addison became the head. This Ministry had the prime duty of making plans for demobilisation. For the special question of the liquidation of war contracts and the transition to peace production I had appointed in November, 1917, a standing committee of the Munitions Council under Sir James Stevenson. This body, with numerous sub-committees, had pursued its task in spite of all the distractions of war and a massive report had been completed by the beginning of October, 1918. The whole field had therefore been surveyed and we were able to take the decisions which the situation required with knowledge of what each step involved and how it could be carried out.

Compromise solutions were adopted. There was to be no immediate general discharge of munition workers; all who desired to withdraw from industry or to leave for any reason and all who could be absorbed elsewhere were at once to be released. Holidays were lavishly given. The production of guns and ammunition, aircraft and explosives was to be reduced by the abolition of overtime, by the suspension of systems of payment by results, and by a reduction of work hours to half the normal week. An elaborate scheme of unemployment donation prepared beforehand mitigated loss of wages. We were able to issue these instructions the same afternoon. They involved, however, the ruling that war material more than 60 per cent. advanced would generally be finished. The rest with all raw material on the spot was to be dispersed for removal by sea or rail and diverted to its probable peace-time destination. Thus for many weeks after the war was over we continued to disgorge upon the gaping world masses of artillery and military materials of every kind. It was certainly waste, but perhaps it was a prudent waste.

These arrangements worked smoothly and although the Ministry of Munitions was twice visited by mass deputations of ten or twelve thousand persons from Woolwich and other great establishments in London no serious hardships or discontents were caused. Large numbers of war volunteers employed as 'dilutees' and a considerable proportion of women workers dispersed to their homes in a steady flow. Day after day we continued to liberate industry. A catalogue of the commodities successively freed from control in their prearranged order would be an instructive treatise on modern industry. But I forbear. In two or three months the Ministry of Munitions had dispossessed itself of the greater part of its extraordinary powers and had cleared the path of peace-time industry. Credit is due to the group of able business men whose thought and action ensured this swift transition.

* * * * *

The removal of the paramount war motive made men conscious not only of exhaustion but of party politics. The gale no longer raged, and as the tide went out all the rocks and shallows, the stranded wreckage, the lobster-pots and local sewage outfalls became visible in detail from the esplanade. The outbreak of hostilities had found the British Isles plunged in an extremity of faction, not only fantastic but full of danger. The Conservative and Liberal masses, each under the impulse of their own Irish party— Orange or Green—charged against each other in hearty vigour and increasing disregard of national consequences. In Ireland both sides had begun unlawfully to arm and organise for lethal conflict; and it was cheerfully supposed that, even if actual bloodshed was confined to Irish soil, each side in Ireland would be reinforced from their respective partisans in Great Britain. The ordinary party strife between Right and Left provided a well-sustained accompaniment to the Irish chorus. In the midst of these festivities Armageddon arrived.

Under the new spell all political values and relationships were instantly transmuted; all that was deep and permanent in our island life became dominant: and it could then be perceived, had there been leisure for moralising, how many times over what we felt and cherished in common exceeded the importance of our quarrels. In the space at most of a few days party bitterness disappeared. The Conservative leaders hastened to support the Ministers they had so long denounced. The rival party machines became one pervasive recruiting agency. Except for a handful of unlucky politicians who committed themselves to pacifism before the issues were plain, all opposition to the war was obliterated. Ulster sent the smuggled rifles, on which she had believed her life depended, to arm the Belgians. The two Redmonds and the whole Nationalist Party proclaimed the accession of Ireland to the cause of the Allies; Dr. Clifford and the leaders of the Free churches manned the platforms of war meetings; the overwhelming majority of Trade Unionists earnestly endorsed the national action.

In the main all these forces had continued throughout the whole struggle, especially in its worst periods, in resolute and indissoluble accord. Neither the short-comings of Ministers and governments, nor military mistakes and disasters, nor the long weariness of years of slaughter, nor disappointment, nor just ground of complaint, nor loss, nor hardship had led to any falling away among those who had plighted their faith. They had endured together to the end. But now the end had come, and everywhere men drew breath and looked around them.

Since May, 1915, Coalition Governments had been in power, but the second Coalition of 1916 differed significantly from its predecessors. The Conservative Party although in a large minority in the House of Commons had obtained an obvious and decisive ascendancy. Mr. Lloyd George had secured as partners in his Government the official representatives of the Labour Party; but the leaders of the Liberal Party as well as a substantial majority of its members were under Mr. Asquith's control. The Liberal Ministers and members who adhered to the new Prime Minister might speak in the name of their individual constituencies but could not claim official and collective party status. No one had troubled about this during the war. Whatever differences had appeared in the House of Commons had been due not to party feelings but to divergent personal loyalties and for the rest were solely concerned with the question of how best to procure victory. From the hour of the Armistice, however, the situation in the Liberal Party became a matter of practical and urgent concern to the Prime Minister. He had wandered far from the orthodox paths of Liberalism; he was known to be the main author of conscription; he had raised his hand with noticeable animus against the conscientious objector; he had not hesitated in the public need to violate and trample upon Liberal sentiments; he had driven his old chief, the honoured leader of the Liberal Party, and nearly all his former colleagues from office and from all share in the conduct of the war. They naturally took a different view of his personal contribution to the victory from that of the cheering multitude. They were hostile, competent, extremely well informed and in possession of the party machine. The one significant division which had been taken against Mr. Lloyd George in war time had revealed one hundred and nine inveterate party opponents among the Liberal Members compared to seventy-three Parliamentary adherents. It was moreover certain that as soon as peace was signed the Labour Ministers would be formally recalled by the Labour Party from further participation in the Government.

There remained the Conservative Party, loyal and determined in their support of the Prime Minister, a very strong integral organisation, but entirely separate from him. Thus from the moment party politics began to rise again upon the threshold of political consciousness, Mr. Lloyd George's position at the height of his fame became one of singular insecurity.

For the moment, however, all eyes were turned upon the approaching Peace Conference and historical pictures of the Congress of Vienna rose in the political mind. Paris became the centre of the world, and thither as soon as the urgent domestic business could be dispatched all the leading statesmen of all the victorious countries were intending or eager to repair. The choice before Mr. Lloyd George was not free from embarrassment. His right-hand colleague must obviously be the Conservative leader, Mr. Bonar Law. Mr. Barnes must represent Labour. The limit provisionally imposed upon national delegations for the sake of convenience was three, and it was already complete. But two personages, very different in character and methods, and each with much to give or to withhold, had also to be considered. The first was Lord Northcliffe who, armed with *The Times* in one hand and the ubiquitous *Daily Mail* in the other, judged himself at least the equal of any political leader and appeared prepared to assert his claims or resent their disregard with a directness scarcely open to a statesman. A general election was imminent, and the wise and helpful behaviour of these great newspapers, obedient as they were to the orders of their proprietor, seemed to the Prime Minister a serious factor. The appointment of Lord Northcliffe as a principal peace delegate over the heads of Mr. Balfour, the Foreign Secretary and all the Prime Ministers of the British Empire was not, however, to be conceded.

The remaining figure was the leader of the Liberal Party. Mr. Asquith both at the moment and after his fall from power had steadily refused to contemplate serving under or even with Mr. Lloyd George; and he and his friends had been accustomed to treat any suggestion of that kind as highly offensive. Nevertheless, in the weeks which immediately followed the victory, it was indicated that he would not be unwilling to join as the head of his party in the national making of a peace. Such a development would in many ways have strengthened the Prime Minister's position. The peace negotiations must last for many months and the close co-operation between the Prime Minister and the Liberal leader could scarcely have failed to heal the breach between them. Mr. Asquith's own qualities would also have been of inestimable service at the Conference. On the other hand, his inclusion would still further have angered Lord Northcliffe. Weighing all these somewhat ill-assorted considerations, Mr. Lloyd George decided not to increase the size of the delegation beyond the limits already agreed upon with the other Powers.

I have no doubt that from his own point of view his decision was a mistake. He had no real knowledge of the Conservative Party; he must soon expect to lose the Labour Ministers; and here at hand was the opportunity of at once making amends to the chief to whom he had owed so much, and of reuniting the Liberal forces with which alone he could work contentedly in times of peace. But far above all personal and political considerations the association of all parties in the peace treaty was an object of national importance, and no one was more fitted than Mr. Asquith to enrich the councils of the

Allies. We should have had a more august delegation, a better treaty and a more friendly atmosphere at home.

While these delicate issues remained unsettled, except in his own mind, the Prime Minister resolved upon an immediate appeal to the country. He was armed with victory, complete, absolute, tremendous; victory beyond the dreams of the most ardent, the most resolute, the most exacting. The whole nation was eager to acclaim 'the pilot who weathered the storm.' Was it wonderful that that pilot should turn from aggrieved and resentful associates of former days who sourly awaited the hour of peace to call him to account, and from Conservatives with whom he had no real sympathy, to the vast electorate who sought only to testify their gratitude by their votes?

To this Election I was a consulted and consenting party. I thought we had need of all the strength we could get to face the problems of bringing home and disbanding our armies which then numbered at home and abroad nearly four million men, of reconstructing our industry, and making the treaty of peace. Moreover, I had in the stress of war resumed intimate contact with the Conservative Party and with the friends of my youth. Having seen so many implacable party quarrels swept away by the flood, I was in no mind to go back and look for them. The idea of methodically fishing up and revitalising all the old pre-war party controversies, and of fabricating disagreements even where none existed, was absurd and abhorrent. I therefore swam with the stream. If I had taken the opposite course it would not have made the slightest difference to the event. But candour compels acknowledgment of this measure of responsibility.

On constitutional grounds the case was overwhelming. The Parliament, elected for five, had lasted for eight years. The electorate was increased from eight to twenty millions by a newly passed Reform Bill. The people and the soldiers who had stubbornly maintained the war, had a right to a decision upon the use to be made of the victory. But the Election at once raised the party issue in its crudest form. The Conservatives had been for thirteen years in a minority in the House of Commons. They were in a minority of about 100 in the Parliament now to be dissolved. On the other hand, they were sure that their hour had come. They believed that the events and passions of the war had been withering in their effects upon Liberal principles and ideals; they held that these had been stultified or proved visionary by all that had occurred; they knew that the quarrels between Mr. Lloyd George and Mr. Asquith had split the Liberal Party from end to end; and finally they knew that in the personal prestige of the Prime Minister they had an overwhelming advantage. How then could they be asked to make an agreement to safeguard all Liberal seats? To do so was not only to condemn themselves to a minority in the new Parliament but to make the whole Election a farce. Conservative candidates were in the field throughout the constituencies. Evidently a hard line must be drawn through the midst of those who had in the main shared the efforts and the sorrows of the terrible years, and the decision to have an election inevitably involved the drawing of this line. Where then should it be drawn? The test adopted for sitting Members was their vote in April in the division on General Maurice's allegations. All who had followed Mr. Asquith on that occasion were considered opponents. Translated into the rough methods of electioneering this meant that even if such a Liberal Member or candidate had fought in the war, or been wounded, or lost his son, or two sons, or his brother, or had throughout in every way sustained loyally the national cause, he must be ruled out of any share in the victory, or even be accused of having impeded it. Letters were written by Mr. Lloyd George and Mr. Bonar Law, afterwards described in the jargon of war-time rationing as 'coupons,' to the avowed supporters of the Coalition. These included 158 Liberal Members and candidates who followed Mr. Lloyd George and were now described as National Liberals. The rest were attacked with vigour. All these consequences were inherent in the original decision to hold an election at this moment, and judgment need only be given upon the main issue.

But when the Election came it woefully cheapened Britain. The Prime Minister and his principal colleagues were astonished and to some extent overborne by the passions they encountered in the constituencies. The brave people whom nothing had daunted had suffered too much. Their unpent feelings were lashed by the popular press into fury. The crippled and mutilated soldiers darkened the streets. The returned prisoners told the hard tale of bonds and privation. Every cottage had its empty chair. Hatred of the beaten foe, thirst for his just punishment, rushed up from the heart of deeply injured millions. Those that had done the least in the conflict were as might be expected the foremost in detailing the penalties of the vanquished. A police report thrust under my eye at this time said:—'The feelings of all classes are the same. Even those who a few weeks ago were agitating for peace, now say, "The Germans should pay every penny of the damage even if it takes them a thousand years."' In my own constituency of Dundee, respectable, orthodox, life-long Liberals demanded the sternest punishment for the broken enemy. All over the country the most bitter were the women, of whom seven millions were for the first time to vote. In this uprush and turmoil state policy and national dignity were speedily engulfed.

Three demands rose immediate and clangorous from the masses of the people, *viz.* to hang the Kaiser; to abolish conscription; and to make the Germans pay the uttermost farthing.

Upon conscription the Prime Minister and the War Cabinet endeavoured at first to practise considerable reserve. With the lesson before our eyes of what we had suffered through not having a national army, it seemed imprudent in the last degree to cast away the weapon only just created at measureless cost, and to re-erect all those barriers against obligatory service which had been tardily and with difficulty overthrown. The idea of preserving a national militia on something like the Swiss system was certainly in the mind of the Government; but contact with the constituencies swept it out of existence before it was even mooted. Everywhere the cry was for the abolition of all compulsion, and everywhere candidates yielded readily to the popular wish. The Cabinet who had not committed themselves in any positive manner hastened to bury and forget the dangerous convictions with which they had toyed. Before the Election was a week old the people had settled that Britain should go back to the small professional army with which she had entered the war.

The demand to hang the Kaiser found great favour with the press and was voiced by Ministers. It was first raised in official circles by Lord Curzon: a piquant conjunction recalling Wilde's description of fox-hunting, 'The inexpressible in pursuit of the uneatable.' But unquestionably it also arose spontaneously from the great masses. For four years the Kaiser had been pilloried by every form of propaganda as the man whose criminal ambition and wicked folly had loosed the awful flood of misery upon the world. He was the man responsible for all the slaughter. Why should he not be punished for it? Why should the humble soldier who fell asleep through exhaustion at his post, or who broken with wounds and long service turned from the fighting line, be put to death, and this pampered miscreant who had darkened every home be allowed to scuttle off in wealth and luxury? We had armies; we had fleets; we had Allies; the arm of Britain was long, it could find him wherever he was and execute upon his person the justice of an outraged world. Quoth—in public speech—Mr. Barnes the official representative of the Labour Party in the War Cabinet. '. . .The Kaiser has been mentioned. . . . I am for hanging the Kaiser.'

The Prime Minister was from the first singularly affected by these opinions. He spoke with the utmost vehemence on both occasions when the topic was discussed in the Imperial War Cabinet. Not only at the Election but throughout the Peace Conference he showed himself ready to make persevering efforts to procure the surrender of the Emperor and to put him on trial for his life. Personally, I was not convinced that the responsibility of princes for acts of state could be dealt with in this way. It seemed that to hang the Kaiser was the best way to restore at once his dignity and his dynasty. The popular wish did not in its initial form apparently contemplate a trial. It was evident however that the lawyers would have to have their say, both on the validity of the proceedings and on the personal accountability of the accused. This also opened up a vista both lengthy and obscure.

I find that when my opinion was given officially (November 20), I urged circumspection. 'On the basis of Justice and Law, it would be difficult to say that the ex-Kaiser's guilt was greater than many of his advisers, or greater than that of the Parliament of the nation which had supported him in making war. It might well be that after an indictment had been laid against the ex-Kaiser, it would be found that it could not be sustained, and a serious *impasse* would be created.'

In the face however of the earnest and deep-seated demand from all classes and all parties in the city of Dundee that the Kaiser should be hanged, I was constrained to support his being brought to trial. I descanted upon the fundamental principles of British justice, that every man no matter how vile his crimes and obvious his guilt was entitled to a trial, and of course to a fair trial. We must not descend to his level by omitting this usual feature in the conviction and punishment of crime. This argument was accepted, though without much enthusiasm, as solid and valid. The Liberals drew a difference against the Coalitionists on the question of the Kaiser's punishment. He was, it appears from the *Daily News*, only to be 'incarcerated under the same conditions as any reprieved murderer.' But then they hastened to explain that this was really 'a harder penalty than execution.' These contortions were not successful from any point of view.

But the crux of the whole Election was the German indemnity. 'Hang the Kaiser' was a matter of sentiment, but 'make them pay' involved facts and figures. The first question was—How much could they pay? No General Election, no popular demand, no Ministerial promises could settle this. It was easy to sequestrate or surcharge all German property abroad and to require the surrender of all gold in German hands. But apart from this, payment from one country to another can only be made in goods or services. These goods or services may be rendered directly to the creditor country or they may be rendered to third parties who pass them on to their destination by roundabout routes and in a different form. Nothing however alters or can alter the simple nature of the transaction. Something that a German has made must be carried out of his country in a ship, or in a train, or in a cart, and must be accepted directly or indirectly in payment of his debt. Now the amount of goods which the Germans could make in a year exceeded the amount that could physically be carried out of the country by any vehicles then in existence, and this reduced amount again far exceeded what other countries, including the creditor countries, wished to receive. For instance, the Germans could and would readily have set to work to rebuild all the ships their submarines had sunk—but what was to happen to British shipbuilding if they did? They could no doubt make every form of manufactured article; but surely we had not fought the war in order to have all our native industries ruined by state-fostered dumping on a gigantic scale! They could export coal for nothing, and have done so regularly since, but the advantage to the British coal-fields has not been obvious. They could export to neutral countries only so far as they could tempt these countries with their wares, and the resulting credits would be transferable to the Allies in the form of other goods only by degrees as opportunity offered.

There remained the method of service. The Germans could, for instance, have manned all the merchant ships and carried everybody's goods at German expense till further notice, thus gaining the complete carrying trade of the world; or the Germans could go in scores of thousands into France and into Belgium and build up by their labour the houses that had been destroyed and recultivate the devastated areas. As, however, they had just been turned out of these very places at so much expense, and had left some unpleasant memories behind them, the inhabitants of these regions having at last got back to the ruins of their homes were not at all anxious to see the German face or hear the German tongue again so soon. Something might be done in all of these directions, but it was evident to anyone with the slightest comprehension of economic facts that the limits would very soon be reached and could not possibly be exceeded. They were limits not removable by ignorance and passion.

The bill for the damage was many months later scaled down to between six and seven thousand millions sterling. This figure was not known at the Election. Had it been known, it would have been scouted. Germany could, by lowering the wages and lengthening the hours of labour, and by limiting the profits of capital, undoubtedly pay very large sums; but then by this same process she would render herself the overmastering, if profitless, competitor in every market. Even so the result would be but a fraction of the damage done. In olden times a conquering army carried off in its own way all movable property in the territory which it ravaged, and in antiquity the conquerors drove along with them in a state of slavery all the men and women who were likely to be of use. Sometimes also a tribute was exacted for many years or in perpetuity. But what was now expected was on a scale utterly beyond these comparatively simple procedures. The payment of even the most moderate indemnity on a modern scale required the revival and maintenance of a superlative state of scientific production in Germany, and of the highest commercial activity. Yet those who clamoured for enormous figures were also the foremost in proposing every method by which German trade and industry could be crippled.

These arguments were unseasonable. Their mere statement exposed the speaker to a charge of being pro-German or at best a weakling. Not only the ordinary electors, but experts of all kinds, financial and economic, as well as business men and politicians, showed themselves unconsciously or wilfully blind to the stubborn facts.

No one understood the question better than the Prime Minister. His first statement to his colleagues on the subject (November 26) was a forceful epitome of the arguments recited above. A Committee of Treasury officials,[1] equipped with the profound knowledge of their Department, had already reported that spread over thirty years a total present value of £2,000 millions might be a reasonable and practicable sum for Germany to pay. This unwelcome figure was sharply challenged, and a new Committee of the Imperial War Cabinet was set up to test it. I was present with other Ministerial officials at the meeting where these statements were made. I held firmly to the Treasury estimate when I faced the electors of Dundee. I dressed it up as well as possible. 'We will make them pay an indemnity.' (Cheers.) 'We will make them pay a large indemnity.' (Cheers.) 'They exacted from France a large indemnity in 1870. We will make them pay ten times as much.' (Prolonged cheers.) '(200 millions $\times$ 10 = 2,000 millions).' Everybody was delighted. It was only the next day that the figures began to be scrutinised. Then came a hectoring telegram from an important Chamber of Commerce, 'Haven't you left out a nought in your indemnity figures?' The local papers gibbered with strident claims. Twelve thousand millions, fifteen thousand millions were everywhere on the lips of men and women who the day before had been quite happy with two thousand millions, and were not anyhow going to get either for themselves. However, adding under daily pressure 'Of course if we can get more, all the better,' I stuck to my two thousand millions, and this figure has not yet been impugned. But all over the country the most insensate figures were used. One Minister, reproached with lack of vim, went so far as to say 'We would squeeze the German lemon till the pips squeaked,' and many private candidates with greater freedom and even less responsibility let themselves go wherever the wind might carry them.

I cannot pretend not to have been influenced by the electoral currents so far as verbiage was concerned. But in order to establish my credentials for the further discussion of these issues, I print two letters to influential constituents which I wrote during the election.

November 22nd, 1918.

I am in sympathy with your feeling that we must not allow ourselves to be deprived of the full fruits of victory. But do you think that you are quite right in saying that we ought to impose upon Germany the same sort of terms as they imposed upon

---

[1]Headed by Mr. Keynes.

France in 1871? Surely the forcible annexation by Germany of Alsace-Lorraine against the will of the people who lived there and who wanted to stay with France was one of the great causes at work in Europe all these years to bring about the present catastrophe. If we were now to take provinces of Germany inhabited by Germans who wished to stay with Germany, and held them down under a foreign government, should we not run the risk of committing the same crime as the Germans committed in 1871 and bringing about the same train of evil consequences?

Again with regard to payment for the war, I am entirely in favour of making the Germans pay all they can. But payment can only be made in one of three ways. (A) Gold and securities. This would only be a drop in the bucket. (B) Forced labour, i.e. Germans coming to work for us and our Allies in a state of servitude. This would take the bread out of the mouths of our own people, and, besides, we would rather have these Germans' room than their company. Or (C) Payment in goods. We must be careful not to demand payment in goods from the Germans which would undercut our own trade here. Otherwise we shall be creating by Treaty that very dumping against which our own manufacturers are so much up in arms. The Allies have demanded from the Germans Reparation, i.e. payment by them for the damage which they have done. This may easily amount to more than £2,000,000,000. They have not asked them to pay for the expenses of the war which I see have been calculated at £40,000,000,000. The reason why they have not done so is because they believed that it was physically impossible for them to do so, and that a Treaty drawn up on that basis would be found afterwards to be valueless.

Speaking more generally, I think that the Government which has conducted this country to this astounding triumph and has compelled Germany to accept the hard conditions of the armistice, is entitled to claim some measure of confidence, and that the Allied Statesmen who are now going to meet together should be trusted, with their superior knowledge and experience, which cannot be shared by everybody, to do their best for the general future of the world. We must be very careful to stand firm upon those great principles for which we have fought and in whose name we have conquered.

And again:

December 9th, 1918.

If the peace which we are going to make in Europe should lead, as I trust it will, to the liberation of captive nationalities, to a reunion of those branches of the same family which have been long arbitrarily divided, and to the drawing of frontiers in broad correspondence with the ethnic masses, it will remove for ever most of the causes of possible wars. And with the removal of the *Cause, the Symptom*, i.e. armaments, will gradually and naturally subside.

I cannot but think we have much to be thankful for, and more still to hope for in the future.

With regard to Russia, you have only to seek the truth to be assured of the awful forms of anti-democratic tyranny which prevail there, and the appalling social and economic reactions and degenerations which are in progress. The only sure foundation for a State is a Government freely elected by millions of people, and as many millions as possible. It is fatal to swerve from that conception.

Mr. Lloyd George, having committed himself to the electoral scrimmage, played the part which circumstances enjoined. In his august station, national and European, he ought never to have been called upon to speak night after night upon the platform. The hardest test of all is to stand against the current of millions of rejoicing and admiring supporters. He ought to have been more sure of himself at this time, and of the greatness of his work and situation. He could well have afforded, as it turned out, to speak words of sober restraint and of magnanimous calm. More than this, it would only have been prudent to pour some cold water upon inordinate hopes and claims, and have on record a few sour statements, which however resented at the time, would have been precious afterwards. He tried his best. His speeches soon fell far behind the popular demand. On two occasions, one a great meeting of women, he was almost howled down. In the hot squalid rush of the event he endeavoured to give satisfaction to mob-feeling and press chorus by using language which was in harmony with the prevailing sentiment, but which contained in every passage some guarding phrase, some qualification, which afterwards would leave statesmanship unchained.

On the actual figure of the indemnity the Prime Minister was studiously vague. The Committee of the Imperial War Cabinet upon the German capacity to pay reported during the Election. Largely on the evidence of Lord Cunliffe of all people, the Governor of the Bank of England, they lent countenance to a maximum annual payment by 'the enemy Powers' (not Germany alone) of no less than £1,200 millions, i.e. the interest on £24,000 millions capital. Mr. Lloyd George had this staggering report before him when he made his Bristol speech. He did not accept it; and in spite of the public passion on the one hand and the Governor's opinion on the other, he delivered a restrained and cautious statement. Germany must be made to pay every penny, and a Commission would be set up to see how much she could pay. There was however an overflow, and the weary Prime Minister flung out this sentence to a rapturous crowd. 'They must pay to the uttermost farthing and we shall search their pockets for it.' This dominated all his qualifications. 'Search their pockets' became the slogan of the hour.

The actual decision which the Prime Minister recommended to, and obtained from, the Imperial War Cabinet will stand the test of time. 'To endeavour to secure from Germany the greatest possible indemnity she can pay, consistently with the economic well-being of the British Empire and the peace of the world, and without involving an Army of Occupation in Germany for its collection.'

Apart from these issues the Election resolved itself into an overwhelming vote of confidence in Mr. Lloyd George. Nearly every candidate who obtained his benediction was returned; nearly every one who did not seek or receive it was rejected. When the results, which were delayed for a month in order to collect the military votes, were announced, barely ninety of his Liberal and Labour opponents found seats in the House of Commons. Simultaneously the Irish Elections swept away the Nationalist Parliamentary Party and, as the Sinn Fein Members boycotted Westminster, the Irish representation in the Imperial Parliament disappeared.

The Prime Minister found himself, with a five-years' constitutional tenure before him, at the head of a majority, elected mainly upon his personal prestige and popularity, comprising nearly five-sixths of the whole House. But for this he had paid a heavy price. The Liberal Party was mortally injured. Those who opposed him were blotted out. The 136 Liberal members who supported him were cut from their party basis and in nearly every case were dependent upon Conservative support, and Mr. Lloyd George was thus sustained only by his transient personal prestige. So long as this lasted his position and authority were unchallengeable, but how long would it last?

Moreover, in the wider sphere of Europe the blatancies of electioneering had robbed Britain in an appreciable degree of her dignity. The national bearing, faultless in the years of trial—loyal, cool, temperate, humane amidst terrors and reverses—had experienced quite a vulgar upset. It was not from the majesty of the battlefield nor the solemnity of the Council chamber, but from the scrimmage of the hustings, that the British Plenipotentiaries proceeded to the Peace Conference. On the other side of the account there was, however, a solid and practical asset. We had a new Parliament, with a great majority, ready to sustain the Government in the labours and perplexities which lay before it.

CHAPTER III
DEMOBILISATION

'All the world over, nursing their scars
Sit the old fighting men, broke in the wars;
All the world over, surly and grim
Mocking the lilt of the conqueror's hymn.'

—Rudyard Kipling.

The Formation of the New Government—At the War Office—A Serious Situation in the Army—The Remedy—The New System—A Dangerous Interlude—Imponderabilia—The Calais Mutiny—On the Horse Guards' Parade—The Young Guard—Conduct of the ex-Soldiers—The Blockade—Lord Plumer's Despatch—The Territorial Army—The German Prisoners.

The new Administration was formed on the morrow of the Election results. I had obtained a promise beforehand from the Prime Minister that he would restore the old system of Cabinet Government at the earliest moment possible. This was not immediately achieved. The five members of the War Cabinet, who were alone responsible for all policy and to whose direction the Secretaries of State and other Ministers were in theory amenable, appeared reluctant to distribute their powers around a wider circle. It was indeed nearly a year before the normal constitutional practice was resumed. The principle was, however, conceded from the outset.

The Prime Minister reconstructed his Government with masterful despatch. At the end of a conversation on various topics he said to me in so many words, 'Make up your mind whether you would like to go to the War Office or the Admiralty, and let me know by to-morrow. You can take the Air with you in either case; I am not going to keep it as a separate department.'

I spent the night at Blenheim, and from there accepted the Admiralty together with the Air Ministry; but when I reached London the next afternoon I found the position had changed. The temper of the Army and the problem of demobilisation caused increasing anxiety. I could not refuse the Prime Minister's wish that I should go to the War Office. The new Ministry was announced on January 10, and I quitted the Ministry of Munitions and became responsible for the War Office on the 15th. I was immediately confronted with conditions of critical emergency.

In the summer of 1917 a draft scheme of demobilisation had been prepared partly in the War Office but mainly in accordance with civilian opinion. The prime object was naturally the re-starting of Industry, and questions of the feelings and discipline of the troops themselves were not accorded proper weight. In June, 1917, the scheme had been referred to General Headquarters and it was immediately criticised by Sir Douglas Haig as 'most objectionable and prejudicial to discipline.' The views of the Civil Departments were however generally sustained by the War Cabinet. The scheme lay in the background during the prolonged crisis of the War, and at the Armistice suddenly became vigorously operative.

According to the logic of this scheme the first men to be released were what were called 'key men,' *i.e.* men who were asked for by employers at home to restart the industries. These 'key men' were therefore being picked out by scores of thousands from all the units of the army and hurried back across the Channel. But these 'key men' who were to be the first to come home had been in many cases the last to go out. The important parts they played in war industry had retained them at home until the needs of the Army became desperate after March 21, 1918. In practice also the system lent itself to inevitable abuse. Those who were so fortunate as to be able to present letters and telegrams from employers at home offering them employment and claiming their services were immediately released. Influence was not slow to procure such credentials. Several thousands while on leave at home were actually excused from returning to the Army. The ordinary soldier without these advantages saw his lately joined comrade hurrying home to take his job, or somebody's job, in England, while he, after years of perils and privations on a soldier's pay, wounded and sent back to the carnage three or sometimes four times, was to be left until all the plums at home had been picked up and every vacancy filled. The fighting man has a grim sense of justice, which it is dangerous to affront. As the result the discipline of every single separate unit throughout the whole of our Army in all the theatres of war was swiftly and simultaneously rotted and undermined. For nearly two months this process had continued, and it had become intolerable to the fighting troops.

The study I gave to the matter in the five days which intervened between the acceptance and the assumption of my new office left me in no doubt upon the course to pursue. Mutinies and disorders had already taken place on both sides of the Channel. In particular a mutiny had occurred at Folkestone on January 3. Sir Eric Geddes had newly succeeded General Smuts in dealing with the restarting of Industry. A few days before I entered the War Office the approaches to the building were blocked by lorry-loads of insubordinate Army Service Corps men who had seized these vehicles and driven them up to London. On each lorry was painted the legend borrowed from a *Daily Express* cartoon, 'Get on or Get out Geddes.' A wave of intense impatience and resentment accompanied by serious breaches of discipline spread across the splendid armies which had never faltered in the direst stress of war.

If the cause was plain, so was the remedy. My only difficulty was to procure the assent of others; my only apprehension, whether we were not already too late. I had before taking up my new duties insisted that the Secretary of State for War should have the final word against all civilian departments in matters affecting the discipline of the troops. In the situation which had now developed this could hardly be denied, and was readily conceded.

I propounded forthwith the following policy—

First: Soldiers should as a general rule only be released from the front in accordance with their length of service and age. Those who had served the longest at the front were to be the first to be demobilised, and any man with three wound stripes or more was to be discharged forthwith. Everyone must take his turn in accordance with this order.

Secondly: The pay of the Army must be immediately increased to more than double the war rate, in order to lessen the gap between the rewards of military and civilian employment.

Thirdly: In order, whilst still maintaining the necessary forces in the field, to release the men who had fought in as large numbers and as quickly as possible, the 80,000 young lads who had been trained but had not quitted our shores, must be retained compulsorily for a period of two years and sent abroad.

Ardently supported by Sir Douglas Haig, whom I summoned from France, and amid the continued and growing demoralisation of the Army, I obtained the necessary authority from the War Cabinet. But this took some time. The Prime Minister was in France. Mr. Bonar Law, though exercising a wide measure of discretion, referred important matters to him. The War Cabinet were perturbed at the idea of presenting a new Conscription Bill to Parliament after the war was over, and after the electorate had shown such vehement repugnance to the idea. The Chancellor of the Exchequer was rightly concerned at the expenditure involved in the heavy cost of the increased pay to the Services. There was no time for ceremony. After consultation with the Adjutant-General, Sir George Macdonogh, an officer of brilliant attainments, I decided to take him over to Paris with me on the evening of January 23, to obtain the Prime Minister's approval to the scheme which had been proposed. We breakfasted with Mr. Lloyd George on the morning of the 24th, accompanied him to the Peace Conference at the Quai d'Orsay, returned with him to lunch and discussed the whole position. I instructed the Adjutant-General to draw up two Army Orders embodying the decisions which had been obtained from the Prime Minister, and to submit them to me at 6 p. m. Having approved these orders I directed the Adjutant-General to return to London by the midnight train and to get the Army Orders issued, with such departmental additions and Army Council Instructions as might be needed with the least possible delay. This he did, and on January 29 Army Order 54 (Extra Remuneration to those retained on Military Service) and Army Order 55 (Armies of Occupation) were issued. The title of the first of these Army Orders explains itself. The second announced the Government's intention about the maintenance of Armies of Occupation pending the reconstruction of the Regular Forces, and laid down the rules under which Officers and other Ranks would be retained or demobilised. Corresponding Royal Warrants were issued concurrently.

I wrote an explanation for the Armies of the whole position in language which they would understand and it was published officially at the same time as the Army Orders. It covered the whole field of War Office policy in relation to the troops during the year 1919. It was strictly and unchangingly carried into effect.

THE ARMIES OF OCCUPATION.

Explanatory Note by the Secretary of State for War.

1. On November 11, when the Armistice was signed, there were about 3,500,000 Imperial British officers and soldiers on the pay and ration strength of the British Army. During the two months that have passed since then, rather more than three-quarters of a million have been demobilised or discharged. The system of demobilisation which has been adopted aims at reviving national industry by bringing the men home in the order of urgency according to trades. There is no doubt that this is the wisest course, and it will continue to be followed in the large majority of cases. The time has now come, however, when military needs must be considered as well as industrial needs.

2. Unless we are to be defrauded of the fruits of victory and, without considering our Allies, to throw away all that we have won with so much cost and trouble, we must provide for a good many months to come Armies of Occupation for the enemy's territory. These armies must be strong enough to exact from the Germans, Turks and others the just terms which the Allies demand, and we must bear our share with France, America and Italy in providing them. The better trained and disciplined these armies are, the fewer men will be needed to do the job. We have, therefore, to create, in order to wind up the war satisfactorily, a strong, compact, contented, well-disciplined army which will maintain the high reputation of the British Service and make sure we are not tricked of what we have rightfully won. It will be an Army far smaller than our present Army. In fact, it will be about one-quarter of the great armies we have been using in the war.

3. Our Military Commanders, who know what Marshal Foch's wishes are, say that in their opinion not more than 900,000 men of all ranks and arms will be sufficient to guard our interests in this transition period. Therefore, when this new Army has been organised, and while it is being organised, over two and a half million men who were held to military service when the fighting stopped will be released to their homes and to industry as fast as the trains and ships can carry them and the Pay Offices settle their accounts. In other words, out of 3,500,000 it is proposed to keep for the present about 900,000 and release all the others as fast as possible.

4. How ought we to choose the 900,000 who are to remain to finish up the work? When men are marked for release they obviously ought to go home in the order which will most quickly restart our industries, for otherwise they would leave their means of livelihood in the Army and relinquish their rations and their separation allowance only to become unemployed in great numbers. But, when men are kept back in the Service to form the Armies of Occupation a choice cannot be made simply on trade grounds. It must be made on grounds which appeal broadly to a sense of justice and fair play. Length of service, age and wounds must be the

main considerations entitling a man to release. The new Army will, therefore, be composed in the first instance only from those who did not enlist before January 1, 1916, who are not over 37 years of age, and have not more than two wound stripes. If anyone has to stay, it must be those who are not the oldest, not those who came the earliest, not those who have suffered the most.

5. We, therefore, take these broad rules as our main guide. According to the best calculations which are possible they should give us about 1,300,000 men, out of which it is intended to form the Army of 900,000. If we find, as we shall do in all probability, that we have in the classes chosen more men than we actually require after dealing with a certain number of pivotal and compassionate cases, we shall proceed to reduce down to the figure of 900,000 first by reducing the age of retention to 36, to 35, next releasing the men with two wound stripes and then on to 34.

As the time goes on we shall not require to keep so large an Army as 900,000 in the field, and it will be possible to continue making reductions on the principle of releasing the oldest men by the years of their age. When, however, the results of the war are finally achieved, the Divisions which have remained to the end will be brought home as units and make their entry into the principal cities of Great Britain with which they are territorially associated.

Volunteers for one year's service at a time for the Armies of Occupation will be accepted from men who would otherwise be entitled to release if they are physically fit and otherwise suitable; and young soldiers now serving will be sent from home to take their turn and do their share. All these will be in relief of the older men. They will enable the age limit to be further reduced and the older men to be sent home. In particular the 69 battalions of young soldiers of 18 years of age and upwards who are now at home will be sent at once to help guard the Rhine Bridgeheads. They will thus enable an equal number of men, old enough to be their fathers, to come home, and they themselves will have a chance to see the German provinces which are now in our keeping and the battlefields where the British Army won immortal fame.

6. The new Armies of Occupation will begin forming from February 1, and it is hoped that in three months they may be completely organised. There will then be two classes of men in khaki, *viz.*, those who form the Armies of Occupation, and those who are to be demobilised. Everything possible will be done to send home or disperse the two and a half million men who are no longer required. But they must wait their turn patiently and meanwhile do their duty in an exemplary manner. Any of these men who are marked for home who are guilty of any form of insubordination will, apart from any other punishment, be put back to the bottom of the list. There are no means of getting these great numbers of men home quickly unless everyone does his duty in the strictest possible way. It is recognised, however, that service in the Armies of Occupation is an extra demand which the State makes in its need upon certain classes of its citizens. The emoluments of the

Armies of Occupation, will therefore be substantially augmented, and every man will draw bonuses from the date of his posting to these Armies with arrears from February 1.

. . . . . .

9. The Armies of Occupation will be as follows :—

Home Army.	Detachment of the Far North.
Army of the Rhine.	Garrisons of the Crown Colonies
Army of the Middle East.	and India.

. . . . . .

12. The above arrangements seem to be the best that can be devised for the year 1919. During this year, however, we must remake the Old British Regular Army so as to provide on a voluntary basis the Overseas Garrisons of India, Egypt, the Mediterranean Fortresses and other foreign stations.

It is believed that volunteering for the Regular Army will improve, as soon as the great mass of those who volunteered for the war against Germany in the early days have come back to the freedom of civil life, and have had a chance to look round. It is upon the steady rebuilding of this Army that the relief of the Territorial battalions in India and various detachments in distant theatres now depends. Every effort will therefore be made to hasten its formation both by recruiting and by re-engagement.

13. It is not necessary at this stage to settle the conditions on which the National Home Defence Army for after the War will be formed. There are many more urgent problems which should be solved first.

14. The entire scheme of the War Office for dealing with the many difficulties of the present situation and for safeguarding British interests is thus published to the Army and the Nation at large; it has been agreed upon between all the authorities and departments concerned. The consent of Parliament, where necessary, will be asked for at the earliest possible moment. It remains for all ranks and all classes to work together with the utmost comradeship and energy to put it into force, and thereby to safeguard the best interests of each one of us and the final victory of our cause.

But the time to prepare and decide upon these far-reaching measures and to procure the assent or submission of so many important personages, namely fourteen days, and the further time needed for the Armies to realise the new decisions was a very anxious period, marked by many ugly and dangerous episodes. Not only the armies but the peoples were profoundly affected by the sudden cessation of the war. The poise and balance even of Britain was deranged. In those days the Russian revolution had not been exposed as a mere organisation of tyranny, perverse and infinitely cruel. The events which had taken place in Russia, the doctrines and watchwords which poured out from Moscow, seemed to millions of people in every land to offer prospects of moving forward into a bright new world of Brotherhood, Equality and Science. Everywhere the subversive elements were active; and everywhere they found a response. So many frightful things had happened, and such tremendous collapses of established structures had been witnessed, the nations had suffered so long, that a tremor, and indeed a spasm, shook the foundations of every State.

Here in Britain we know our own people well. Millions of men and women have been accustomed for generations to take an active part in politics, and have felt that in their sphere and station they were constantly deciding and guiding the policy of their country. The political parties with all their organisations, associations, leagues and clubs afforded effective vehicles of popular expression. Moreover, the Constitution had itself grown up as the most thorough and practical mechanism yet devised in the modern world for bringing the force of public opinion to bear upon the conduct of affairs. Well was it that we were 'broad based upon the people's will' and newly authorised by their direct pronouncement.

Certainly there were factors which nobody could measure and which no one had ever before seen at work. Armies of nearly four million men had been suddenly and consciously released from the iron discipline of war, from the inexorable compulsions of what they believed to be a righteous cause. All these vast numbers had been taught for years how to kill; how to punch a bayonet into the vital organs; how to smash the brains out with a mace; how to make and throw bombs as if they were no more than snowballs. All of them had been through a mill of prolonged inconceivable pressures and innumerable tearing teeth. To all, sudden and violent death, the woeful spectacle of shattered men and dwellings was, either to see in others or expect and face for oneself, the commonest incident of daily life. If these armies formed a united resolve, if they were seduced from the standards of duty and patriotism, there was no power which could even have attempted to withstand them.

This was the testing time, if there ever was one, for the renowned sagacity and political education of the British Democracy.

In a single week more than thirty cases of insubordination among the troops were reported from different centres. Nearly all were repressed or appeased by the remonstrances of their officers. But in several cases considerable bodies of men were for some days entirely out of control. The chief offenders were the Army Service Corps in the Grove Park and Kempten Park Mechanical Transport Depots. Some units informed their officers that they had constituted themselves a Soldiers' Council and intended to march to the nearest township and fraternise with the workmen. Usually they were dissuaded by reasonable arguments. Sometimes the officers cycling by a circuitous route intercepted their men before the town was reached and induced them to return to their duty. The influence of the regimental officers was nearly always successful. Although the situation was very threatening in many places, almost the only spot where there was actual and serious rioting was at Luton, where owing to the weakness of the civic authorities, the Town Hall was burnt by the mob.

A regular mutiny broke out at Calais. Between the 27th and 31st of January the Army Ordnance detachments and the Mechanical Transport, which were the least-disciplined part of the army, had seen least of the fighting and were most closely associated with political Trade Unionism, refused to obey orders. They met the Leave-Boats and induced a large number of the returning soldiers to join them. In twenty-four hours the ringleaders were at the head of about three or four thousand armed men and in complete possession of the town. All the fighting divisions had moved on towards or into Germany, and there was no force immediately at hand to cope with the mutineers. The Commander-in-Chief accordingly recalled two divisions from their forward march, and placing them under the personal control of a most trusted and respected Army Commander, General Byng, directed them upon the scene of the disorders. The soldiers of these divisions were roused to indignation at the news that demobilisation was being obstructed by comrades of theirs who had in no wise borne the brunt of the fighting. By nightfall of the second day the disaffected soldiery were encircled by a ring of bayonets and machine guns. At daylight a converging advance was made upon them. In front officers, unarmed, called upon them to return to duty; behind them deadly overwhelming force was arrayed. Thus confronted, most of the men drifted to the rear, but several hundreds stood their ground with obstinacy. A shocking explosion would have been precipitated by a single shot; but self-restraint and good feeling triumphed. The ringleaders were arrested, and the rest returned to their obedience without the shedding of a drop of blood.

Simultaneously with this came the news of serious riots in Glasgow and Belfast. Both these riots were fomented by the Communists. The Army was called upon to aid the civil power. Two Brigades were moved into Glasgow. These were only second-line troops consisting of the least efficient soldiers or young recruits. They had not, like those at the front, been tempered in war nor had they tasted victory. However, officers and men discharged their duty faultlessly. Order was restored. Very few lives were lost, and when blood flowed, it was mostly from the nose.

The last incident that I shall record came under my personal notice. At half-past eight on the morning of February 8 I was summoned urgently to the War Office. As I drove thither I observed a battalion of Guards drawn up along the Mall. I passed through the Admiralty Arch and reached my office without remarking anything else unusual. Arrived there I received a disagreeable report: About 3,000 soldiers of many units and all arms of the service had gathered at Victoria Station to catch the early train for those returning from leave. The Director of Movements had failed to make adequate arrangements for the transport, feeding and housing of leave men coming in this case principally from the North. The poor soldiers, many of whom had waited all night on the platform, none of whom could obtain food or tea, felt it very hard to be going back to France now that the fighting was over and the war was won, while so many of their comrades were, as they had been told, snapping up the best billets in England. They had suddenly upon some instigation resorted in a body to Whitehall, and were now filling the Horse Guards' Parade armed and in a state of complete disorder. Their leader, I was informed, was at that very moment prescribing conditions to the Staff of the London Command in the Horse Guards building.

Sir William Robertson and General Fielding, commanding the London District, presented themselves to me with this account, and added that a reserve Battalion of Grenadiers and two troops of the Household Cavalry were available on the spot.

What course were they authorised to adopt? I asked whether the Battalion would obey orders, and was answered 'The officers believe so.' On this I requested the Generals to surround and make prisoners of the disorderly mass. They departed immediately on this duty.

I remained in my room a prey to anxiety. A very grave issue had arisen at the physical heart of the State. Ten minutes passed slowly. From my windows I could see the Life Guards on duty in Whitehall closing the gates and doors of the archway. Then suddenly there appeared on the roof of the Horse Guards a number of civilians, perhaps twenty or thirty in all, who spread themselves out in a long black silhouette and were evidently watching something which was taking place, or about to take place, on the Parade Ground below them. What this might be I had no means of knowing, although I was but a hundred yards away. Another ten minutes of tension passed and back came the Generals in a much more cheerful mood. Everything had gone off happily. The Grenadiers with fixed bayonets had closed in upon the armed crowd; the Household Cavalry had executed an enveloping movement on the other flank; and the whole 3,000 men had been shepherded and escorted under arrest to Wellington Barracks, where they were all going to have breakfast before resuming their journey to France. No one was hurt, very few were called to account, and only one or two were punished and that not seriously. A large portion of the blame lay upon the administration which had made no change in its routine at the railway stations since the fighting had stopped. For years men had gone back punctually and faithfully to danger and death with hardly any officers or organisation just as if they were ordinary passengers on an excursion train, and those responsible had not realised that much more careful arrangements were required in the mild reign of Peace.

The result of the new policy and of its explanation to the troops was almost instantaneous. A very few days sufficed to set back the evil currents which had begun to flow. The unfair trial to which our Army had been subjected was at an end. A system of demobilisation had now been instituted, the justice of which carried conviction to the soldier's mind. The principle that length of service, age and wounds counted before every other consideration and every form of influence commanded the immediate assent of all ranks. The increases of pay were accepted in a friendly spirit. As for the 80,000 lads of eighteen, they were eager to see the Rhine and set their fathers, uncles and elder brothers free after all the hardships these had gone through. The King reviewed a dozen of these fine young battalions in Hyde Park before their departure, and everyone was struck with their alert and confident bearing. Within a fortnight of the new Proclamation the discipline of our immense though melting armies all over the world had regained its traditional standards.

The new House of Commons met for the first time upon the heels of these events. It asked literally several thousand questions about the details of demobilisation, and special machinery had to be set up to cope with this unparalleled curiosity. But the Conscription Bill was passed by a very large majority. The Liberal and Labour Oppositions, animated by a sense of detachment from responsibility, fought it tooth and nail. It was lucky they were so few, for the essential services of the State might have been greatly obstructed, at a critical time.

Meanwhile the demobilisation of the armies proceeded on the greatest scale. For a period of nearly six months we maintained an average rate of 10,000 men a day discharged to civil life. This immense body, equal to a whole peace-time Division, was collected daily from all the theatres of war, disembarked, de-trained, disarmed, de-kitted, demobilised, paid off and discharged between sunrise and sunset. I regard this as an enormous feat of British organising capacity. The armies had grown up gradually; men had enlisted as individuals; they were dispersed in great masses, and somehow or other, at the outset, they nearly all found homes and employment. The history books boast of the way in which twenty or thirty thousand of Cromwell's Ironsides laid down the panoply of war and resorted to peaceful occupations. But what was this compared with the noble behaviour of nearly four million British soldiers who without confusion or commotion of any kind—once they were treated as they deserved—merged themselves unostentatiously in the mass of the nation and gathered together again the severed threads of their former lives? One had expected, after all the methodically inculcated butchery and barbarism of five years of war, that acts of murder and pillage, brutality and rapine, would for some years at any rate be rife in the land. On the contrary, such are the powers of civilisation and education, and such are the qualities of our people, that crimes of violence actually diminished and prisons had to be closed and sold, when four million trained and successful killers, or nearly one-third of the whole manhood of the nation, resumed their civic status.

* * * * *

Meanwhile, having halted for a week to allow the enemy to retreat, the armies of the Allies had advanced into Germany by easy marches. All the roads from France and Belgium which in 1914 had carried the invaders were now filled with endless columns marching in the reverse direction. The British troops were so good-humouredly received by the enemy population and got on so well with them that stringent and reiterated orders against 'Fraternisation' were required. By the end of November the heads of Sir Douglas Haig's columns had reached the Rhine and a few days later the occupation of the Bridge Head at Cologne was completed. In all almost a quarter of a million men representing the British Empire actually entered Germany and settled down in pleasant quarters and rest camps where their natural friendliness and good conduct speedily reassured the inhabitants.

But a hard story has here to be told. The Armistice conditions had prescribed that the blockade of Germany was to continue. At the request of the Germans a clause had been added that 'The Allies and the United States contemplate the provisioning of Germany to such an extent as shall be found necessary.' Nothing was done in pursuance of this until the second renewal of the Armistice on January 16, 1919. In fact the blockade of Germany was extended to the Baltic ports and was thus made more severe than before. The food situation in Germany became grave, and painful stories circulated of the hardship of mothers and children. During these months very few people in Germany, except profiteers and farmers, had enough to eat. Even as late as May members of the German Delegation at Versailles were suffering from the after-effects of want of proper food. There was in France and to some extent in England a deliberate refusal to face the facts.

In January, 1919, began a prolonged series of negotiations upon the conditions under which food might be imported into Germany. Public opinion in the Allied countries was callous. Their leaders were overwhelmed with business. A possible charge of "pro-Germanism" intimidated politicians. The officials into whose hands the arrangements fell thought they were doing their duty by haggling and stippling. Equally bad food conditions existed in other defeated States, for which partial provision was being made. There was also a general shortage of food and shipping throughout the world. But meanwhile the Germans under-went a period of extreme stringency equal to that of a besieged town.

It is remarkable that the sudden punch which destroyed this hateful deadlock originated with the British Army on the Rhine. In February the reports of military officers which reached the War Office of the food conditions in the occupied areas became increasingly disquieting. A note of anger began to mingle in the dry official chronicles. I made deliberately a rough exposure to the House of Commons on March 3. 'We are enforcing the blockade with rigour, and Germany is very near starvation. All the evidence I have received from officers sent by the War Office all over Germany show: first, the great privations which the German people are suffering; and secondly, the danger of a collapse of the entire structure of German social and national life under the stress of hunger and malnutrition.' Early in March the food negotiations at Spa appeared about to break down in glacial rigmarole. But Lord Plumer, who commanded the British Army of Occupation in Germany, sent a telegram to the War Office, forwarded to the Supreme Council, urging that food should be supplied to the suffering population in order to prevent the spread of disorder as well as on humanitarian grounds. He emphasised the bad effect produced upon the British Army by the spectacle of suffering which surrounded them. From him and through other channels we learned that the British soldiers would certainly share their rations with the women and children among whom they were living, and that the physical efficiency of the troops was already being affected. Armed with Lord Plumer's despatch and these details, Mr. Lloyd George took the Supreme Council by the throat. 'No one,' he remarked, 'can say that General Plumer is pro-German.' The officials were chidden, and the negotiations resumed. The difficulties and disorganisation of the world were however so great that it was not until May that substantial importations of food into Germany actually took place. The blockade, though according to the Peace Treaty in force until its ratification, disappeared altogether by the middle of July. But a great opportunity had been lost. The German people, on November 11, had not only been defeated in the field, they had been vanquished by world opinion. These bitter experiences stripped their conquerors in their eyes of all credentials except those of force.

*　*　*　*　*

A remaining task at the War Office was to get rid of the 250,000 German prisoners of war in British hands. For this we had to wait for many months. The French found it very difficult to release them. When they thought of all the slaughter represented by their capture, and of the depleted manhood of France, they could not bring themselves to let these hundreds of thousands of unlucky men go home. It was like surrendering captured cannon. But by the end of the summer the battlefields had all been cleared; every toil appointed to the prisoners had been performed. There was no longer excuse or reason for their retention. Yet as Pharaoh found it of old, it was hard 'to let the people go.' I determined to break this complex by direct action. The telegrams tell the tale.

Mr. Churchill to Mr. Balfour.

August 21, 1919.

After discussing the situation about German prisoners with General Asser, I am convinced that their repatriation should begin immediately.

Their work is done: they are costing us more than £30,000 a day. A fine opportunity of repatriating them is afforded by using the return trains which are bringing back the British Divisions from the Rhine to French ports. In addition they can proceed by march. I have therefore given directions to prepare plans for both these methods. The operation will begin at the earliest possible moment and at latest by September 1. May I urgently appeal to you to set the machinery in motion at your end which will ensure the reception of these prisoners in Germany. Eighty per cent of them belong to unoccupied Germany or our own area, and less than 20 per cent to territories under Allied control. I propose to begin with the German repatriations. Every day counts as every day trains are arriving with Rhine soldiers and going back empty.

Mr. Churchill to Sir Henry Wilson.

Please see my telegram about the German prisoners and do your utmost to facilitate immediate action. The whole economy of this army depends upon it. We should not hesitate to act independently of the French. Will you communicate direct with Asser, advising him when he may begin. He could fill every train returning to the Rhine from to-morrow onwards. 10,000 at Audricq for example could start at once. I am counting upon sanction being given within the next two or three days.

All went well. The French delayed no longer, and the process of repatriating the immense numbers of German soldiers who were eating their hearts out in captivity, once begun, continued without ceasing, until one more miserable relic of the war had passed out of daily life.

CHAPTER IV
RUSSIA FORLORN[1]

'He is no Socialist who will not sacrifice his Fatherland for the triumph of the Social Revolution.'

—Lenin.

'Ich bin der Geist der stets verneint.'
'I am the Spirit that evermore denies.'

—Mephistopheles in *Faust*.

The Absentee—The Nameless Beast—A Retrospect—The Revolution of March, 1917—The Grand Repudiator—The Liberal Statesmen—Kerensky—Savinkov—The Bolshevik Punch—The Dictatorship—Peace at any Price—Brest-Litovsk—Bolshevik Disillusionment—The German Advance—Effect of the Treaty.

From the circle of panoplied and triumphant states soon to gather from all over the world to the Peace Conference in Paris there was one absentee.

At the beginning of the war France and Britain had counted heavily upon Russia. Certainly the Russian effort had been enormous. Nothing had been stinted; everything had been risked. The forward mobilisation of the Imperial Armies and their headlong onslaught upon Germany and Austria may be held to have played an indispensable part in saving France from destruction in the first two months of the war. Thereafter in spite of disasters and slaughters on an unimaginable scale Russia had remained a faithful and mighty ally. For nearly three years she had held on her fronts considerably more than half of the total number of enemy divisions, and she had lost in this struggle nearly as many men killed as all the other allies put together. The victory of Brusilov in 1916 had been of important service to France and still more to Italy; and even as late as the summer of 1917, *after the fall of the Czar*, the Kerensky Government was still attempting offensives in aid of the common cause. The endurance of Russia as a prime factor, until the United States had entered the war, ranked second only to the defeat of the German submarines as a final turning-point of the struggle.

But Russia had fallen by the way; and in falling she had changed her identity. An apparition with countenance different from any yet seen on earth stood in the place of the old Ally. We saw a state without a nation, an army without a country, a religion

---

[1]For this and the next chapter see Map of Russia facing page 61.

without a God. The Government which claimed to be the new Russia sprang from Revolution and was fed by Terror. It had denounced the faith of treaties; it had made a separate peace; it had released a million Germans for the final onslaught in the West. It had declared that between itself and non-communist society no good faith, public or private, could exist and no engagements need be respected. It had repudiated alike all that Russia owed and all that was owing to her. Just when the worst was over, when victory was in sight, when the fruits of measureless sacrifice were at hand, the old Russia had been dragged down, and in her place there ruled 'the nameless beast' so long foretold in Russian legend. Thus the Russian people were deprived of Victory, Honour, Freedom, Peace and Bread. Thus there was to be no Russia in the Councils of the Allies—only an abyss which still continues in human affairs.

* * * * *

A retrospect is necessary to explain how this disaster had come upon the world, and to enable the reader to understand its consequences.

The Czar had abdicated on March 15, 1917. The Provisional Government of Liberal and Radical statesmen was almost immediately recognised by the principal Allied Powers. The Czar placed under arrest; the independence of Poland was acknowledged; and a proclamation issued to the Allies in favour of the self-determination of peoples and a durable peace. The discipline of the fleets and armies was destroyed by the notorious Order which abolished alike the saluting of officers and the death penalty for military offences. The Council of Soldiers and Workmen's deputies at Petrograd so prominent in the revolution, the parent and exemplar of all the soviets which were sprouting throughout Russia, maintained a separate existence and policy. It appealed to the world in favour of peace without annexations or indemnities; it developed its own strength and connections and debated and harangued on first principles almost continuously. From the outset a divergence of aim was apparent between this body and the Provisional Government. The object of the Petrograd Council was to undermine all authority and discipline; the object of the Provisional Government was to preserve both in new and agreeable forms. On a deadlock being reached between the rivals, Kerensky, a moderate member of the Council, sided with the Provisional Government and became Minister of Justice. Meanwhile the extremists lay in the midst of the Petrograd Council, but did not at first dominate it. All this was in accordance with the regular and conventional Communist plan of fostering all disruptive movements, especially of the Left and of pushing them continually further until the moment for the forcible supersession of the new government is ripe.

The Provisional Ministers strutted about the Offices and Palaces and discharged in an atmosphere of flowery sentiments their administrative duties. These were serious. All authority had been shaken from its foundation; the armies melted rapidly to the rear; the railway carriages were crowded to the roofs and upon the roofs with mutinous soldiers seeking fresh centres of revolt and with deserters trying to get home. The soldiers' and sailors' Councils argued interminably over every order. The whole vast country was in confusion and agitation. The processes of supply, whether for the armies or for the cities, were increasingly disjointed. Nothing functioned effectively and everything, whether munitions or food, was either lacking or scarce. Meanwhile the Germans, and farther south the Austrians and the Turks, were battering upon the creaking and quivering fronts by every known resource of scientific war. The statesmen of the Allied nations affected to believe that all was for the best and that the Russian revolution constituted a notable advantage for the common cause.

In the middle of April the Germans took a sombre decision. Ludendorff refers to it with bated breath. Full allowance must be made for the desperate stakes to which the German war leaders were already committed. They were in the mood which had opened unlimited submarine warfare with the certainty of bringing the United States into the war against them. Upon the Western front they had from the beginning used the most terrible means of offence at their disposal. They had employed poison gas on the largest scale and had invented the 'Flammenwerfer.' Nevertheless it was with a sense of awe that they turned upon Russia the most grisly of all weapons. They transported Lenin in a sealed truck like a plague bacillus from Switzerland into Russia. Lenin arrived at Petrograd on April 16. Who was this being in whom there resided these dire potentialities? Lenin was to Karl Marx what Omar was to Mahomet. He translated faith into acts. He devised the practical methods by which the Marxian theories could be applied in his own time. He invented the Communist plan of campaign. He issued the orders, he prescribed the watchwords, he gave the signal and he led the attack.

Lenin was also Vengeance. Child of the bureaucracy, by birth a petty noble, reared by a locally much respected Government School Inspector, his early ideas turned by not unusual contradictions through pity to revolt extinguishing pity. Lenin had an unimpeachable father and a rebellious elder brother. This dearly loved companion meddled in assassination. He was hanged in 1894. Lenin was then sixteen. He was at the age to feel. His mind was a remarkable instrument. When its light shone it revealed the whole world, its history, its sorrows, its stupidities, its shams, and above all, its wrongs. It revealed all facts in its focus—the most unwelcome, the most inspiring—with an equal ray. The intellect was capacious and in some phases superb. It was capable of universal comprehension in a degree rarely reached among men. The execution of the elder brother deflected this broad white light through a prism: and the prism was red.

But the mind of Lenin was used and driven by a will not less exceptional. The body tough, square and vigorous in spite of disease was well fitted to harbour till middle age these incandescent agencies. Before they burnt it out his work was done, and a thousand years will not forget it. Men's thoughts and systems in these ages are moving forward. The solutions which Lenin adopted for their troubles are already falling behind the requirements and information of our day. Science irresistible leaps off at irrelevant and henceforth dominating tangents. Social life flows through broadening and multiplying channels. The tomb of the most audacious experimentalist might already bear the placard 'Out of date.' An easier generation lightly turns the pages which record the Russian Terror. Youth momentarily interested asks whether it was before or after the Great War; and turns ardent to a thousand new possibilities. The educated nations are absorbed in practical affairs. Socialists and Populists are fast trooping back from the blind alleys of thought and scrambling out of the pits of action into which the Russians have blundered. But Lenin has left his mark. He has won his place. And in the cutting off of the lives of men and women no Asiatic conqueror, not Tamerlane, not Jenghiz Khan, can match his fame.

Implacable vengeance, rising from a frozen pity in a tranquil, sensible, matter-of-fact, good-humoured integument! His weapon logic; his mood opportunist. His sympathies cold and wide as the Arctic Ocean; his hatreds tight as the hangman's noose. His purpose to save the world: his method to blow it up. Absolute principles, but readiness to change them. Apt at once to kill or learn: dooms and afterthoughts: ruffianism and philanthropy: but a good husband; a gentle guest; happy, his biographers assure us, to wash up the dishes or dandle the baby; as mildly amused to stalk a capercailzie as to butcher an Emperor. The quality of Lenin's revenge was impersonal. Confronted with the need of killing any particular person he showed reluctance—even distress. But to blot out a million, to proscribe entire classes, to light the flames of intestine war in every land with the inevitable destruction of the well-being of whole nations—these were sublime abstractions.

'A Russian statistical investigation,' writes Professor Sarolea, 'estimates that the dictators killed 28 bishops, 1,219 priests, 6,000 professors and teachers, 9,000 doctors, 12,950 landowners, 54,000 officers, 70,000 policemen, 193,290 workmen, 260,000 soldiers, 355,250 intellectuals and professional men, and 815,000 peasants.'[2] These figures are endorsed by Mr. Hearnshaw, of King's College, Cambridge, in his brilliant introduction to 'A survey of Socialism.' They do not of course include the vast abridgments of the Russian population which followed from famine.

Lenin was the Grand Repudiator. He repudiated everything. He repudiated God, King, Country, morals, treaties, debts, rents, interest, the laws and customs of centuries, all contracts written or implied, the whole structure—such as it is—of human society. In the end he repudiated himself. He repudiated the Communist system. He confessed its failure in an all important sphere. He proclaimed the New Economic Policy and recognised private trade. He repudiated what he had slaughtered so many for not believing. They were right it seemed after all. They were unlucky that he did not find it out before. But these things happen sometimes: and how great is the man who acknowledges his mistake! Back again to wash the dishes and give the child a sweetmeat. Thence once more to the rescue of mankind. This time perhaps the shot will be better aimed. It may kill those who are wrong: not those who are right. But after all what are men? If Imperialism had its cannon food, should the Communist laboratory be denied the raw material for sociological experiment?

When the subtle acids he had secreted ate through the physical texture of his brain Lenin mowed the ground. The walls of the Kremlin were not the only witnesses of a strange decay. It was reported that for several months before his death he mumbled old prayers to the deposed gods with ceaseless iteration. If it be true, it shows that Irony is not unknown on Mount Olympus. But this gibbering creature was no longer Lenin.

---

[2]Sarolea, *Impressions of Soviet Russia* [1924], p. 81.

He had already gone. His body lingered for a space to mock the vanished soul. It is still preserved in pickle for the curiosity of the Moscow public and for the consolation of the faithful.

Lenin's intellect failed at the moment when its destructive force was exhausted, and when sovereign remedial functions were its quest. He alone could have led Russia into the enchanted quagmire; he alone could have found the way back to the causeway. He saw; he turned; he perished. The strong illuminant that guided him was cut off at the moment when he had turned resolutely for home. The Russian people were left floundering in the bog. Their worst misfortune was his birth: their next worst—his death.

* * * * *

With Lenin had come Zinoviev. Trotsky joined them a month later. It appears that it was actually at the request of the Provisional Government that he was allowed to leave Halifax, Nova Scotia, where he had been shrewdly intercepted by the Canadian authorities. Under the impulsion of these three the differences between the Soviet and the Provisional Government were soon brought to a head. During May and June the two powers faced each other in armed and brawling antagonism. But the Provisional Government had to maintain the daily life of the nation, to keep order and to produce military victory over the Germans, while the sole immediate aim of the Bolsheviks was a general smash. The eminent Liberal statesmen, Guchkov and Milyukov, well-meaning and unwitting decoy-ducks, soon passed from the scene. They had played their part in the astounding pageant of dissolution now in progress. With the best of motives they had helped to shake old Russia from its foundations; by their example they had encouraged many intelligent and patriotic Russians to put their shoulders to the work. They now found themselves destitute of influence or control. Venerable and in their own way valiant figures they slipped from the stage, a prey to tormenting afterthoughts. Said Guchkov, 'It is now to be proved whether we are a nation of free men or a gang of mutinous slaves.' But words had ceased to count in the universal chatter.

However, the agony of Russia did not find her without some last defenders. Among these with all his vanities and self-delusions Kerensky has his place. He was the most extreme of all the immature and amateur politicians included in the Provisional Government. He was one of those dangerous guides in revolutionary times, who are always trying to outvie the extremists in order to control them, and always assuring the loyal and moderate elements that they alone know the way to hold the wolf by the ears. Successively he forced changes of policy which moved his colleagues week by week further to the Left. There was a point beyond which Kerensky did not mean to go. Once that point was reached he was ready to resist. But when at last he turned to fight, he found he had deprived himself of every weapon and of every friend.

Kerensky succeeded Guchkov as Minister of War in the middle of May. He became Prime Minister on August 6. The tide of events which had carried him during a summer from a revolutionary to a repressive temper had been strengthened by two personalities. One was the General Kornilov, a patriotic soldier, resolute, popular, democratic; ready to accept the revolution; ready to serve the new Russian régime with the loyalty he would more gladly have given to the Czar. Trusted by the troops; not obnoxious to the politicians of the hour—he seemed to possess many of the qualities, or at any rate many of the assets, which a revolutionary government wishing to wage war and to maintain order required in a commander.

But a more dynamic figure had arisen in the background—Boris Savinkov, the ex-Nihilist, the direct organizer of the pre-war assassinations of M. de Plehve and the Grand Duke Serge, had been recalled from exile in the early days of the revolution. Sent as military commissar to the Fourth Russian Army, he had grappled with mutiny and dissolution with a quality of energy which amid these boorish Russian tumults recalls the tenser spirit of the French Revolution. In so far as comparisons are possible he seems in some respects to resemble in fiction Victor Hugo's Cimourdain, and to some extent in real life St. Just; but with this difference, that while second to none in the ruthlessness of his methods or the intrepidity of his conduct, his composed intellect pursued moderate and even prosaic aims. He was the essence of practicality and good sense expressed in terms of nitroglycerine. Above and beyond the whirling confusion and chaos of the Russian tragedy he sought a free Russia, victorious in the German war, hand in hand with the Liberal nations of the West, a Russia where the peasants owned the land they tilled, where civic rights were defended by the laws, and where parliamentary institutions flourished even in harmony perhaps with a limited monarchy. This man of extreme action and sober opinions had risen in two months to a position of central dominance in Russian military affairs. Assistant Minister for War to Kerensky, and in control of the Petrograd garrison, Savinkov had his hand on the vital levers. He knew all the forces at work; he had the root of the matter in him and he shrank from nothing. Would he be allowed to pull the levers, or would they be wrested from his grasp? Would they act or would they break?

Savinkov reached out for Kornilov, he pressed him upon Kerensky as the one indispensable sword. As the result of a prolonged internal struggle at the end of July, even the Petrograd Soviet agreed by a majority to the use of unlimited authority to restore discipline in the army. On August 1, Kornilov became Commander-in-chief; on September 8, the death penalty for breaches of discipline was restored. But meanwhile the German sledge-hammers were still beating in the front. The Russian summer offensive, Kerensky's supreme effort, had been repulsed with a woeful slaughter of the truest and best. In the middle of July the German counter-offensive had rolled forward, and the towns of Stanislau and Tarnopol were retaken by the Austro-German forces on July 24. The hostile advance continued. On September 1 the German Fleet in concert with their armies entered the Gulf of Riga. Riga fell on the 3rd. The forlorn nation had to bear simultaneously all that could be done by Ludendorff, and all that could be done by Lenin. At the culminating crisis the electric currents fused all the wires, physical and psychological alike. Kornilov revolted against Kerensky; Kerensky arrested Kornilov; Savinkov striving to keep the two together and to fortify the executive power was thrust aside. There was a fleeting interlude of Babel, of courageous hard-won Duma Resolutions, and of Russian Democratic Congress appeals for stability. The Duma, the Parliament of Russia, presented a large anti-Bolshevik majority. The Provisional Government issued manifestoes in favour of a liberal policy and loyalty to the Allies. So far as words and votes would serve, nothing was left undone. Meanwhile the German hammer broke down the front and Lenin blew up the rear.

Who shall judge these harassed champions of Russian freedom and democracy? Were they not set tasks beyond the compass of mortal men? Could any men or any measures have made head at once against the double assault? Politicians and writers in successful nations should not too readily assume their superiority to beings subjected to such pressures. Cæsar, Cromwell, Napoleon, might have been smothered here like Captain Webb in the rapids of Niagara. All broke, all collapsed, all liquefied in universal babble and approaching cannonade, and out of the anarchy emerged the one coherent, frightful entity and fact—the Bolshevik punch.

In the first week of November the Soviets, inspired by a Military Committee headed by Lenin and Trotsky, claimed supreme power to command the troops and arrest the Ministers. Mutinous warships steamed up the Neva, the troops deserted to the usurpers; the Duma, the All Russian Democratic Congress, the All Russian Congress of Soviets, still talking and all protesting by substantial majorities, were brushed into the void. The Provisional Government was besieged in the Winter Palace. Kerensky, rushing to the front to gather loyal troops, was deposed by Lenin's proclamation, and on his return was defeated in street fighting by the mutineers. His last defenders were the women and children. The battalion of women and the Cadets of the Military College held unflinching to their posts; the cadets were shot and the women were defiled so far as was judged necessary by the new ruling intelligences of Russia. The British Court of Appeal subsequently decided that for our domestic purposes the Soviet Government became the *de facto* authority in Russia as from November 14, 1917.

* * * * *

Gone for ever was the Empire of Peter the Great, and the long-dreamed-of liberal Russia, and the Duma, and the already summoned Constituent Assembly. Cast into outer darkness with the Czarist Ministers were the Liberal and Radical politicians and reformers. Social Revolutionaries, Mensheviks, many smaller groups of Socialists; all, especially the most extreme, those nearest in opinion to the Bolsheviks, were marked for destruction. The doctrinal left flank had been turned, and every gradation of political opinion known to men crumpled up almost simultaneously. One sect alone made a momentary stand. The Anarchists, strong in the traditions of Bakunin, conceived themselves unapproachable in extremism. If the Bolsheviks would turn the world upside down, they would turn it inside out; if the Bolsheviks abolished right and wrong, they would abolish right and left. They therefore spoke with confidence and held their heads high. But their case had been carefully studied in advance by the new authorities. No time was wasted in argument. Both in Petrograd and in Moscow they were bombed in their headquarters and hunted down and shot with the utmost expedition.

The Supreme Committee, sub-human or superhuman—which you will—crocodiles with master minds, entered upon their responsibilities upon November 8. They had definite ideas upon immediate policy—'Down with the War,' 'Down with Private

Property,' and 'Death to all internal Opposition.' Immediate peace was to be sought with the foreign enemy and inexpiable war was to be waged against landlords, capitalists and reactionaries. These terms were given the widest interpretation. Quite poor people with only a handful of savings, or a little house, found themselves denounced as 'Bourjuis.' Advanced Socialists found themselves proscribed as reactionaries. Pending more detailed arrangements, Lenin issued a general invitation to the masses to 'Loot the looters.' The peasants were encouraged to kill the landlords and seize their estates; and massacre and pillage, collective and individual, reigned sporadically over immense areas.

The domestic programme was thus initiated with remarkable promptitude. The foreign situation was more intractable. Lenin and his confederates began their task in the belief that they could appeal by wireless telegraphy to the peoples of every warring state over the heads of their governments. They did not therefore contemplate at the outset a separate peace. They hoped to procure under the lead of Russia and under the impact of the Russian desertion a general cessation of hostilities, and to confront every government, Allied and enemy alike, with revolt in their cities and mutiny in their armies. Many tears and guttural purrings were employed in inditing the decree of peace. An elevated humanitarianism, a horror of violence, a weariness of carnage breathed in their appeal—for instance the following:—'. . . Labouring peoples of all countries, we are stretching out in brotherly fashion our hands to you over the mountains of corpses of our brothers. Across rivers of innocent blood and tears, over the smoking ruins of cities and villages, over the wreckage of treasures of culture, we appeal to you for the re-establishment and strengthening of international unity.' But the Petrograd wireless stirred the ether in vain. The Crocodiles listened attentively for the response; but there was only silence. Meanwhile the new régime was sapiently employed in securing intimate and effectual control of the Czarist police and secret police.

By the end of a fortnight the Bolsheviks abandoned the plan of 'peace over the heads of the government with the nations revolting against them.' On November 20, the Russian High Command was ordered to 'propose to the enemy military authorities immediately to cease hostilities and enter into negotiations for peace,' and on November 22 Trotsky served the Allied Ambassadors in Petrograd with a note proposing an 'immediate armistice on all fronts and the immediate opening of peace negotiations.' Neither the Ambassadors nor their governments attempted any reply. The Russian Commander-in-Chief, the aged General Dukhonin, refused to enter into communication with the enemy. He was instantly superseded at the head of the Russian armies by a subaltern officer, Ensign Krilenko, who delivered the arrested general to be torn to pieces by a mutinous mob. The request for an armistice was then made to the Central Powers. These Powers also remained for a time plunged in silence. The promise of 'an immediate peace' had however to be made good at all costs by the Bolshevik Government, and orders were issued to the army at the front for 'compulsory fraternisation and peace with the Germans by squads and companies.' All military resistance to the conqueror thenceforward became impossible. On November 28 the Central Powers announced that they were ready to consider armistice proposals. On December 2 firing ceased on the long Russian fronts and the vast effort of the Russian peoples sank at last into silence and shame.

* * * * *

Three months' negotiations were required before the Treaty of Brest-Litovsk was signed. The Bolshevik leaders found this period filled with disappointing experiences. They asked for a six-months' armistice; all they could obtain was a month's respite denunciable at a week's notice. They wished to have the negotiations transferred to a neutral capital like Stockholm; this was refused. They sought to explain with their usual volubility to the conquerors, themselves desperate, the political principles on which human society should be conducted. 'But pray, dear Sirs,' asked the German General Hoffman, 'what do we care for your principles?' An inconsistent flicker of faith to the Allies led them to request that no German or Austrian troops should during the armistice be transferred from the East to the West. To this the Germans agreed, and at once began transporting their troops uninterruptedly to France. By the end of December such illusions as with singular credulity the Bolsheviks had nursed were at an end. They found themselves confronted with Force armed and resolute; and they knew that they had rendered Russia incapable of resistance.

Nevertheless, when the meaning of the Peace terms came home to this strange band of revolutionaries, a spasm of revolt, impotent but intense, shook their conclaves. The cruder spirits raved against Prussian Imperialism; the more subtle vented their bitterness in sarcastic newspaper articles. Trotsky and Zinoviev had indulged in imprudent mockery and empty threats. 'A time would come, Ha! Ha!' etc. 'The destiny of mighty peoples,' said Trotsky, 'cannot be determined by the temporary condition of their technical apparatus.' The Germans remained rigorously impassive. They received equally with the Bolshevik delegation representatives of a separate Ukraine Government. Vainly the Bolsheviks protested that they and they alone spoke for all the Russians. The Germans brushed their expostulations aside. Whatever else miscarried, the Central Powers meant to have the corn and the oil of the Ukraine and the Caucasus, and elaborate agreements to secure all they required without payment were presented to the new Ministers of the Russian people.

At the end of December the negotiations were suspended and the Bolshevik delegates returned home to consult with their confederates. Some details of this new debate in Pandemonium have been preserved. Trotsky, in the rôle of Moloch, urged the renewal of the war, and the majority of the secret Assembly seemed to share his passion. The calm sombre voice of Lenin rallied them to their duty in a Belial discourse of eighteen theses.

'I should be much for open war, O Peers,
As not behind in hate.' . . .

But how could they resist? The armies were gone, the Allies estranged, the fleet in mutiny, Russia in chaos! Even flight over the vast spaces still at their disposal could not last long. And was not something more precious than the fate of Russia at stake? Was there not the Communist Revolution? Could they fight the Bourjuis at home if they wasted their remaining strength upon withstanding the foreign invader? Geographical boundaries, political allegiances were not so important after all to Internationalists striving for world-wide revolution. Let them make themselves supreme and unchallengeable in whatever territories might still be left to Russia, and from this as a base spread the social war through every land. The arguments of Lenin prevailed. He did not even wait to hear rejoinders, but sat, according to an English eyewitness, cool and unconcerned in an ante-room while his followers frothed and raged inside. The most that Trotsky could obtain was the formula 'No war, no peace.' The Soviets would submit, but they would not sign. On February 10 Trotsky stated by wireless 'that in refusing to sign a peace with annexations Russia declares on its side that the state of war with Germany, Austria, Hungary, Turkey and Bulgaria has ended. The Russian troops are receiving at the same time an order for a general demobilisation on all lines of the fronts.'

But this was not good enough for the Germans; they allowed a week to pass in silence and on February 17 declared abruptly that the armistice was at an end and that the German armies would advance along the whole front at daybreak. Trotsky's ululations that they should have had at least a further week's notice were drowned in cannon fire. From Reval to Galatz on a front of a thousand miles, the German and Austrian armies rolled forward. There still remained a ragged line of troops in various stages of decomposition and of officers faithful to the end. All these were now swept away without the slightest difficulty. The whole front was destroyed, 1,350 guns were captured in a single day together with masses of material and prisoners in a German advance of about 20 miles. The town of Dvinsk, the principal objective, was captured the same evening and on the 19th the Soviets made absolute submission. Trotsky yielded the Foreign Office to the more pacific Chicherin and on March 3 the peace treaties were signed.

The Treaty of Brest-Litovsk stripped Russia of Poland, Lithuania and Courland; of Finland and the Aaland Islands; of Esthonia and Livonia; of the Ukraine; and lastly, in the Caucasus, of Kars, Ardahan and Batum.

'This is a peace,' said the Soviet wireless, 'not based upon a free agreement but dictated by force of arms . . . which Russia grinding its teeth is compelled to accept. . . . The Soviet Government being left to its own forces is unable to withstand the armed onrush of German Imperialism and is compelled for the sake of saving Revolutionary Russia to accept the conditions put before her.' Said Lenin some years later, 'We must have the courage to face the unadorned bitter truth, we must size up in full to the very bottom the abyss of defeat, partition, enslavement and humiliation into which we have been thrown.' It is not possible to better these descriptions of the first boon which Lenin conferred upon the Russian nation. In Mr. Buchan's well-weighed words 'They' (the Bolsheviks) 'lost for Russia 26 per cent. of her total population, 27 per cent. of her arable land, 32 per cent. of her average crops, 26 per cent. of her railway system, 33 per cent. of her manufacturing industries, 73 per cent. of her total iron production and 75 per cent. of her coalfields. So much for the policy of "No annexations." They had saddled themselves with a gigantic but as yet unassessed payment by way of war tributes, and had been compelled to grant free export of oils and a preferential commercial treaty. So much for "No Indemnities."

They had placed under German rule fifty-five millions of unwilling Slavs. So much for "Self-Determination." '

If to-day these consequences have been to any extent modified, and if the Soviet Republic is independent of German tutelage and systematic exploitation, it is because the democracies of the West and across the Atlantic, undismayed by Russian desertion, continued to uphold the common cause. It was upon them that the re-gathered might of Germany was now to fall.

CHAPTER V
INTERVENTION

Kornilov and Alexeiev on the Don—The Rise of the Russian Volunteer Army—The Munitions at Archangel—Grave Situation in the West—An American-Japanese See-Saw—A New Feature: Professor Masaryk—The Czecho-Slovak Army Corps—The Bolshevik Treachery—Astounding Retaliation—Allied Intervention in Siberia—The Omsk Government—A Surprising Transformation—The Baltic States—Finland—Poland—Pilsudski—The Ukraine—Bessarabia.

The Bolshevik truce and later peace with the Central Powers produced a far-reaching reaction in Russia. On the same day that hostilities were suspended (December 2, 1917), Generals Kornilov, Alexeiev and Denikin raised a counter-revolutionary standard on the Don. Each had made his way to this refuge among the loyal Cossacks by routes of various hazards. There among the rude surroundings of a primitive and loyal-hearted population these military leaders presented a rallying-point for all that was noblest in old Russia. What was their political authority? The Imperial régime was discredited with all classes. The Czar had abdicated and was already approaching the slaughterhouse of Ekaterinburg. Bolshevism still masqueraded as democratic progress carried in the pressure of events to a violent manifestation. In the domestic sphere nothing could stand against 'The land for the peasant,' 'Soviets for all.' But the safety and integrity of Russia against the invader, and the honour of the Russian name plighted to the Allies, were impulsive and commanding notes to sound. True, they appealed only to individuals, and these were scattered along the immense fronts and vast spaces of the interior. But the trumpet call was carried by the wind across the steppes and echoed by the mountains, and everywhere, in every class, in every town, in every village there were ears to hear it. If world revolution had reared its head, world civilisation was still in the field. More than twenty States and peoples spread over five continents were marching against the Central Empires that had laid Russia low. All the seas of the world bore their unimpedible ships to the Western battlefields. Mighty America, far across the ocean, resounded with a clang of reinforcing preparation. Statesmen, whose names were household words, stood at the head of vast organisations. Although Russia had been struck down and battered, the Cause continued. Despotic governments should be destroyed and not replaced by other tyrannies in other forms. For these Russian patriots there was also the honour of the Russian arms and the inheritance of Peter the Great to guard or to die in guarding.

The rise and achievements of the Russian Volunteer Army should certainly form the theme of an historical monograph to be read with gratitude by all their comrades in the British Empire, in France, in Italy and in the United States, as well as in the smaller States whose freedom is safe to-day. As news of the mutilations of the Russian Fatherland, and of the shame in which it had been involved, gradually permeated the enormous Empire the knowledge of disaster which appalled the many animated the few. Twenty unknown battles comparable to the fights of Garibaldi or Hofer or de Larochejaquelein against astounding odds marked the growth of a troop of desperate refugees into a substantial military entity. One by one the leaders fell. Kornilov was killed at the end of March. Kaledin, the leader of the Don Cossacks, committed suicide after a temporary defeat. The heaviest loss of all was Alexeiev, a strategist of the rank of Foch and Ludendorff, long versed in the highest affairs of the Russian State. He survived the hardships of the struggle only until September, 1918, when he was succeeded by Denikin who possessed both the qualities and limitations of a tough, sensible, steady and honourable military man. In the ups and downs of civil war the Russian Volunteer Army widely extended the limits of its authority during the latter part of 1918; but for a more detailed account of its adventures and achievements our retrospect can find no place. While all else was at first disputed and confused, a sense of association with the great world outside was a sure foundation upon which the authority of the counter-revolutionary leaders could rest, and this association was soon to take a practical form.

At the time of the Revolution, France, Britain and the United States were engaged in supplying munitions to Russia on a gigantic scale. These munitions had been purchased by Russia, Czarist and Revolutionary, upon loans. More than 600,000 tons of military material, apart from an equal quantity of coal, had been landed at Archangel and Murmansk. Thither, in the days of the Czar, a railway 800 miles long from Petrograd had been built by the unrecorded sufferings of multitudes of war prisoners. The munitions and supplies lay stranded on the quays. The Bolshevik Government had repudiated all the loans by which they had been purchased. They were therefore in equity the property of the Allies. But a far more urgent question was 'Into whose hands would they fall?' A similar situation obtained at Vladivostok, where enormous importations had been made by the Americans and Japanese. Was all this mass of deadly material to replenish the arsenals of the Central Powers and prolong the war in indefinite slaughter? Ought it even to enable a recreant Government, traitor to the Allies and the avowed foe of every civilised institution, to crush every form of opposition to its absolute sway? These issues arose in the winter of 1917; they became vital even before the Peace of Brest-Litovsk was signed.

The terms of the Treaty made it plain that the blockade of the Central Powers on which such immense naval efforts had been concentrated was to a large extent broken. The Germans obviously had Russia at their disposal. The granaries of the Ukraine and Siberia, the oil of the Caspian, all the resources of a vast continent could, it seemed to us, henceforth be drawn upon to nourish and maintain the German armies now increasing so formidably in the West, and the populations behind them. Germany had in fact achieved in the early months of 1918 all and more than she might have won two years before had Falkenhayn not imprudently preferred to break his teeth on the stones of Verdun. How far or how soon these reliefs could become effective was uncertain; but the subsidiary arrangements made with the Ukraine revealed the immediate German intention of overrunning that country and drawing from it the largest quantities of supplies. No one at this time saw any prospect of a speedy end to the war, and there seemed no reason to doubt that the Germans and Austrians would have the time—as they certainly had the power—to draw new life almost indefinitely from the giant Empire prostrated before them. Finally, the Germans were in process of transporting 70 Divisions, comprising more than a million men, and 3,000 guns with all their munitions from the Russian to the Western front. The Austrians had similarly reinforced their Italian front and further reinforcements were moving westward in a continuous stream. The French Army had scarcely recovered from the mutinies of 1917 and the British, in their efforts to take the pressure off the French and secure them a breathing space, had bled themselves white in ceaseless offensives from Arras to Paschendaele. Such was the dark situation on the morrow of the Russian collapse. It was soon to become even graver in the explosion of the greatest battles ever fought.

The reconstruction of an Eastern front against Germany and the withholding of Russian supplies from the Central Powers seemed even from the end of 1917 vital to win the war. The Military Representatives of the Supreme War Council accordingly recommended on December 23 that all national troops in Russia who were determined to continue the war should be supported by every means in our power. In Siberia one ally above all others could act with swiftness and overwhelming power. Japan was near, fresh, strong, ready, and intimately affected. The counter-argument was weighty. If Japan was loosed against Russia the Bolsheviks, with the support of the Russian people, might, it was said, actually join hands with Germany against the Allies. The Japanese showed themselves not unwilling to make exertions. They were prepared to take control of a considerable section of the Siberian railway. But they said that American participation would be unpopular in Japan. On December 31 the British Government opened these possibilities to President Wilson. The United States expressed themselves averse from either solitary intervention by Japan or combined intervention by America and Japan. The Japanese were offended by this attitude, which the British Government at first felt bound to endorse. They thought they ought to be entrusted with any intervention at Vladivostok which might be agreed upon, since the development of hostile German influence on the shores of the Pacific would be a peculiar menace to Japan. The British Government, with the support of the French, at the end of January decided to propose that Japan should be invited to act as the mandatory of the Allies. President Wilson remained adverse to all intervention and especially to isolated action by Japan. The Japanese, on the other hand, stipulated that if Japan were to act as mandatory for the Powers she must receive American aid in gold and steel.

The shock of the Treaty of Brest-Litovsk, Ludendorff's swiftly following onslaught in the West and the intense crisis which resulted, extorted from the two desperately struggling Allies increasingly vehement appeals. President Wilson however remained unconvinced. For four precious months a see-saw process between Japan and America continued in which one or the other successively demurred to every variant proposed by the French and British. However, the terrible conflict in France and Belgium and the increasing German exploitation of Russia presented arguments of inexorable force.

They were aided from an unexpected quarter. Trotsky was now Minister of War, and with remarkable energy was creating a Red Army to defend alike the Revolution and Russia. On March 28, he informed our Representative at Moscow, Mr. Lockhart, that he saw no objection to Japanese forces entering Russia to resist German aggression if the other Allies co-operated and certain guarantees were given. He asked for a British Naval Commission to reorganise the Russian Black Sea Fleet and for a British officer to control the Russian railways. Lastly, even Lenin was said to be not opposed to foreign intervention against the Germans, subject to guarantees against interference in Russian politics. Every effort was made by the British to obtain a formal invitation from the Bolshevik leaders. This would have been all important in overcoming the reluctance of the United States. Probably the Bolsheviks were only manœuvring to gain a measure of external sanction for their régime in its early days and to baffle and divide the patriotic antagonisms which were arming against them. Something else was needed to clinch the issue and bring the five great Allies into practical agreement. This new incentive was now to be supplied.

There suddenly appeared in Russia a foreign factor, unique in character and origin. On the outbreak of war a number of Czecho-Slovaks resident in Russia had voluntarily entered the Russian army. A body of Czecho-Slovak prisoners of war had enlisted in the Serbian voluntary division in the Dobrudja. Czecho-Slovaks had also deserted in considerable numbers and joined their compatriots in the Russian army both during the early months of the war and notably after Brusilov's victory on the Styr in 1916. These men had followed the guidance of the venerable Professor Masaryk who had lived in London during 1914, '15 and '16 as a refugee from Austrian animosity, and kept alive the conception not only of Bohemian nationality but of a considerable Czecho-Slovak state. The bond was purely of intellect and sentiment, but it proved in men of high morale superior to all the strains of this exceptional time. These soldiers, separated from their homes and families by immense distances, by a world of war and infinite confusion, and finally by the offences they had committed against the Austrian Government, preserved a disciplined comprehension of national and international causes and were entirely immune from all local Russian influence. The Czar's Government had embodied the Czecho-Slovaks as military units in the Russian army, but it had regarded with some misgiving the loyalty of foreigners who had denied the authority of their legal sovereign. After the outbreak of the Russian revolution, however, Professor Masaryk went to Russia, brought about the consolidation of all Czecho-Slovak units in one force, placed them under the red and white flag of Bohemia and procured for them in Paris the status of an Allied army. From the moment of the Treaty of Brest-Litovsk they held themselves fully armed at the disposition of the Allies for the general purposes of the war. On a much larger scale and with the necessary differentiations they resembled the Scottish Archers of Louis XI and the Irish Brigade of Sarsfield, or the Swiss Guard of Louis XVI, and like them, far from home and all that home means, surrounded by alien people whose passions did not stir and whose habits did not attract them, they lived a life by themselves. But in contrast to their forerunners they were linked with what had by now become almost a world cause in which they steadfastly persevered. By a continued collective study of the course of the war, by constant gymnastics and intense group-consciousness they held their heads high through all the welter: and in the crash of the Russian Empire remained

'Among innumerable foes unmoved,
Unshaken, unseduced, unterrified.'

When the Treaty of Brest-Litovsk ended the Russian resistance to Germany the Czecho-Slovak Army demanded to be transported to the Western front. The Bolsheviks were equally anxious that they should leave Russia. A free exit was promised to the Czechs by the Bolshevik Commander-in-Chief and embodied in a formal agreement between the Allies and the Soviet Government in Moscow on March 26. The Siberian Railway offered the safest route and the Czechs began their journey by Kursk, Penza, Cheliabinsk and Samara. They had started with 42,500 men, but their numbers were increased as they proceeded by fresh recruits from among the Czecho-Slovak prisoners of war to a total of about 60,000.

It was natural that the Germans should view these arrangements with disapproval. To prevent the manhood of two army corps of trustworthy troops from being transported round the world to the Western front became an object of urgent consequence to the enemy General Staff. Exactly what pressures they put upon the Soviet authorities is not yet known. At any rate they were effective. Lenin and Trotsky freed themselves from their engagements to the Czechs by treachery. Measures were rapidly taken under German direction to intercept and capture the Czech troops on their long journey. Many thousands of German and Austrian prisoners in Russian hands were hurriedly armed and under the supervision of German officers began to assume military formations. While Trotsky on the one hand was settling with Mr. Lockhart in detail the safe conduct of the Czechs through Russia, he was also moving his Red Guard forces to their appropriate stations. On May 26, the first echelon of Czecho-Slovak artillery arrived at Irkutsk. Their agreement with the Bolsheviks had left them only 30 carbines and some grenades for personal self-defence. When the trains steamed into the station the Czechs found themselves in the presence of a large and greatly superior force of Red Guards. They were ordered to surrender their few remaining arms within a period of 15 minutes. While the Czechs, nearly all of whom were unarmed, were discussing the situation on the railway-station platform, a machine gun fired upon them from the station building. The Czechs did not succumb. The training of the Red Army at this time had not progressed beyond a knowledge of Communism, the execution of prisoners and ordinary acts of brigandage and murder. In a few minutes with their 30 carbines and handgrenades the Czechs not only defeated but captured and disarmed their despicable assailants. Equipped with the captured weapons they overcame a few days later new forces sent against them by the local Soviet, and reported what had occurred to their army headquarters.

The whole of the Czech troops thereupon ceased to deliver up their arms and wherever they stood assumed an attitude of active self-defence which passed quite rapidly into a vigorous counter-attack. Their very dispersion now became the foundation of an extraordinary power. Eleven thousand had already arrived at Vladivostok, the rest were scattered all along the Trans-Siberian Railway and its subsidiary lines from a hundred miles west of the Ural Mountains to the Pacific Ocean. By June 6, 1918, they were in possession of all the railway stations between Omsk and Krasnoyarsk. Their comrades still in European Russia had gained corresponding successes. Their control of the vital communications rapidly extended eastward to Nijni-Udinsk and Penza in the west. On June 28 they assumed control of Vladivostok; by July 6 they were moving out of Nikolsk towards Harbin and Habarovsk. They took charge of Irkutsk on July 13. By the third week of July an immense area of Russia, several hundred miles broad and 3,000 miles long, including the backbone connections from the Volga River almost to Lake Baikal was in the effectual possession of these strangers thus foully attacked when seeking to leave the country in virtue of signed agreements. The pages of history recall scarcely any parallel episode at once so romantic in character and so extensive in scale.

We may anticipate the culmination of this effort. Those Czechs who had already reached and made themselves masters of Vladivostok determined to return to the rescue of their compatriots cut off in Central Siberia, and by about the middle of September, 1918, railway communication had again been established along the whole Trans-Siberian route. Thus, through a treacherous breach of faith, by a series of accidents and chances which no one in the world had foreseen, the whole of Russia from the Volga River to the Pacific Ocean, a region almost as large as the continent of Africa, had passed as if by magic into the control of the Allies. The message sent by the Czecho-Slovak Army to Professor Masaryk in the United States at the end of July epitomises the situation. 'In our opinion it is most desirable and also possible to reconstruct a Russian-German front in the East. We ask for instructions as to whether we should leave for France or whether we should stay here to fight for Russia at the side of the Allies and of Russia. The health and spirits of our troops are excellent.' The Czecho-Slovak National Council residing at Washington on this observed: 'Professor Masaryk has since then instructed the forces in Siberia to remain there for the present. . . . The Czecho-Slovak Army is one of the Allied armies and it is as much under the orders of the Versailles War Council as the French or American Army. No doubt the Czecho-Slovak boys in Russia are anxious to avoid participation in a possible civil war in Russia, but they realise at the same time that by staying where they are they may be able to render far greater service both to Russia and the Russian cause than if they were transported to France. They are at the orders of the Supreme Council of the Allies.'

* * * * *

These astonishing events as they proceeded were decisive upon the action of the great Allies. On July 2, 1918, the Supreme War Council had made from Versailles a further appeal to President Wilson to agree to the support of the Czech forces. The President thereupon proposed the dispatch of an international force of British, Japanese and United States troops, avowedly to restore and preserve the communications of the Czechs. The next day the British Government in concert with their Allies resolved to extend to them military help. On July 5 the United States announced that they had decided upon a limited intervention in Siberia 'for the purpose of rendering protection to the Czecho-Slovaks against the Germans and to assist in the efforts at self-government or self-defence in which the Russians themselves may be ready to accept assistance.' They also proposed to send a detachment of the Young Men's Christian Association to offer moral guidance to the Russian people.

Two Japanese divisions, 7,000 Americans and two British Battalions under the command of Colonel Johnson and of Colonel John Ward, a Labour Member of Parliament, 3,000 French and Italians, all under the supreme command of Japan were set in motion, landed as rapidly as possible at Vladivostok and proceeded westward along the railway. Concurrently with this an international force of 7,000 or 8,000 men, mainly British and all under British command, disembarked in June and July at Murmansk and Archangel. They were welcomed by the inhabitants, who expelled the Bolsheviks and formed a local administration. Agreements were signed between this Northern Government and the British commander whereby the local authorities undertook to assist the Allies to defeat German aggression and the Allied Governments became responsible for finance and food.

In Siberia within the widespread picket line—for it was little more—of the Czecho-Slovaks, an Anti-Bolshevik Russian Government began to organise itself at Omsk. Broadly speaking, Siberia bore the same relation to Russia as Canada does to Great Britain. The apparition of the Czechs, their sudden extraordinary activity and success, their manifest personal superiority to the armed political rabble of Bolshevism had created an enormous enclave in *Sovdepia*, within which a Russian administration and military organisation could be set on foot on a considerable scale.

In the summer of 1918 a provisional Government was formed at Omsk, aiming primarily at the convocation of a constituent assembly for all Russia. This Government passed through various transformations during its tenure. It reflected the chaos reigning throughout Russia when everybody was eager to talk and many were ready to kill, and no large body of persons could be got to agree upon anything for any reasonable space of time. Even before the Armistice cast its fatal depression upon all anti-Bolshevik movements, the tide of Siberian fortunes had begun to ebb. The Czechs were already wearying somewhat in well-doing. Their toils were ceaseless and their dangers increasing. Their own political opinions were of an advanced character, and accorded ill with White Russian views. They were, moreover, exasperated by constant contact with Russian instability and mismanagement. Their far-spread Southern line in October, 1918, had been forcibly contracted by Red pressure in front and around them.

Already also by September, 1918, there were two governments functioning side by side at Omsk—one for Siberia and the other claiming to be an all-Russian body. Meanwhile, Cossack and anti-Bolshevik officers had been energetically raising armed forces. As these forces grew in size and influence they overshadowed both these mushroom administrations. It became increasingly evident that all would have soon to fight for their lives, and in these straits the military point of view quickly became predominant. The original Omsk Government yielded readily to this new pressure; its brother government, on the contrary, became a hotbed of socialist conspiracy.

The rival administrations counterworked each other. The futility of these proceedings in the face of impending slaughter led to a military *coup d'état*. On November 17, a week after the Armistice, the leaders of the new armies forcibly appropriated one government and arrested the principal members of the other. They decided, probably wisely in the desperate circumstances, to concentrate all power in the hands of one man. They found this man in Admiral Kolchak, the former commander of the Black Sea Fleet.

At the same time, far to the south in the Province of the Don, the Russian Volunteer Army, now under Denikin, had already made itself master of a large and fertile area, and before the end of the year was destined to advance to Ekaterinodar after an operation in which over 30,000 Bolsheviks were made prisoners.

Such was the surprising transformation of the Russian situation which followed the Treaty of Brest-Litovsk. The snows of winter war had whitened five-sixths of Red Russia, but the springtime of Peace, for all others a blessing, was soon to melt it all again.

* * * * *

To the preoccupations which these developments caused the Allies another set of problems was added. The Treaty of Brest-Litovsk had formally detached from the Russian Empire all her western provinces. The Germans evidently had in mind the creation of a chain of buffer states carved out of the Russian Empire to guard their eastern marches. We saw reproduced in the twentieth century, and five hundred miles farther east a new version of Napoleon's plan for a Confederation of the Rhine. Finland, Esthonia, Latvia, Lithuania, Russian Poland, the Ukraine, Bessarabia, the Caucasus, were all to exercise under the guidance of a victorious Germany, and in repulsion from a defeated and Communist Russia, the power of self-determination. They were to owe their liberty, if not their independence, to Germany, and the Russian Empire was to be stripped, by one sabre-cut drawn across the map of Europe from Helsingfors to Batoum and Baku, of all the conquests of Peter and Catherine the Great. Lenin and Trotsky had agreed to this.

Imperial Germany had now disappeared; the mighty centre of the whole new system had been destroyed. Germany had yielded herself, disarmed and helpless, at the disposal of the conquerors, and her part for the time being was punctually to obey the orders they might give. Therefore all these states were released almost at a stroke alike from their old allegiance and from their new. For several months the light of coming events had shone with increasing plainness. From August, 1918, onwards the defeat of the Central Powers was certain; the only questions were how complete it would be and how long delayed. Everyone wanted to get out of Bolshevik Russia, and to the desire for racial or national independence was added resolve to escape from a frightful reversion to barbarism and terror. The movement of opinion in every one of these countries was passionately decisive. Esthonia declared independence on November 28, 1917; Finland on December 6; the Ukraine on December 18; Latvia on January 12, 1918; Lithuania on February 16, 1918. On April 9, Bessarabia contracted a union with Roumania subject to autonomy; on April 22 the Transcaucasian Council declared the complete independence of its Federal Republic and claimed to place its territory outside the operation of the Treaty of Brest-Litovsk. At the end of May the Transcaucasian Federal Government dissolved into its constituent elements; Georgia formed an independent national government; the Armenian National Council assumed charge in Armenia; the Tartar National Council proclaimed the independence of Azerbaijan. All these movements may be said to have originated in the prospect of a war settlement in which Germany would have been the greatest power in Europe. They were now stimulated by the growing fear of Bolshevik aggression, which Germany was no longer likely to hold in check.

As therefore the power of Germany waned and when she suddenly collapsed entirely, every one of these states transferred their hopes and their loyalty to the league of victorious democracies which from across the Atlantic Ocean and the English Channel, and over the battle lines in France and Italy, poured an irresistible avalanche of flame and steel upon the recoiling German-Austrian fronts. And when in the end all resistance fell in one stupendous crash, it was to the triumphant western allies that all these peoples and embryo governments rallied with joy and conviction.

However, this transition did not take place without opposition. The Bolsheviks who, on January 4, had joined with the French and Swedish Governments in recognising the independence of Finland, invaded Finland and captured Helsingfors on January 28, 1918. This was no ordinary war of troops and cannon. The Soviet Red Guards advanced by mob-like methods, and before them, more deadly than carnal weapons, sprang up the local forces of Communist propaganda and revolt. Two horrible pages in Finnish history were successively written. On March 1 a treaty of peace and amity was signed between the Finnish Republic and the Soviet. A Red Terror followed in Finland. But here the Germans intervened as rescuers. On April 3 a German division landed in Finland under the command of General Von der Goltz; and the anti-Communist Finns under General Mannerheim, an ex-officer of the Russian Imperial Guard, joined them in large numbers. The Soviet forces and local Communists were scattered like chaff, and on April 13, Generals Von der Goltz and Mannerheim reoccupied Helsingfors.

Less than three months of Communist rule had made an impression upon public opinion which a generation will not efface. The Communist flight from the Finnish capital had been hurried; the corpses of the executed bourgeoisie cumbered the courtyards and corridors of the public offices. This dour, northern people, roused to fury, took a merciless revenge upon their late oppressors. They were resolved to give them a lesson as lasting as that which they themselves had learned. A White Terror, certainly not less bloody, succeeded the Red. May 7 is regarded as the end of the Finnish civil war, but it was by no means the end of the punishment inflicted not only upon the Finnish Communists but upon many harmless socialists and radicals in the unmeasured and undiscriminating resentment of the victors. So much for Finland.

Immediately south of Finland the three Baltic States of Esthonia, Latvia and Lithuania found themselves in a peculiarly unhappy position. They were close neighbours on the East to Petrograd and Kronstadt, the nurseries of Bolshevism; on the West to the birthplace and stamping-ground of those Prussian landowners who had proved themselves to be the most rigid element in the German system and one of the most formidable. During the winter of 1918 and the early summer of 1919 the Baltic States were subjected alternately to the rigours of Prussian and Bolshevik domination.

Immediately after the Armistice the retiring Germans mischievously yielded their military material to the Bolsheviks, who quickly overran Esthonia and a large part of Latvia and Lithuania. Assisted by Finnish volunteers and British war material the Esthonians drove back the Bolsheviks at the beginning of February, 1919, but the Letts and Lithuanians were not so successful. While these events were in progress, the Germans under Von der Goltz organised an unauthorised partisan force ultimately numbering 20,000 men which was intended to turn out the Russians and establish in their stead, and in spite of anything the Peace Conference might decide, a refuge for the distressed nobility of East Prussia. They were temporarily successful and exercised like the 'free companies' a fierce and adventurous licence until the arrival in July of an Allied military mission. In these circumstances it is not surprising that the independence of Esthonia, Latvia and Lithuania existed for the time being only in the aspirations of their inhabitants and the sympathies of the allied and associated Powers.

Let us turn to Poland. In March, 1917, the Russian Provisional Government had, as we have seen, declared that Poland should be 'an independent state attached to Russia by a free military union.' At Brest-Litovsk Trotsky proposed the independence of Poland, and this was embodied in the treaty. But the Polish troops in the Russian army were anti-Bolshevik, and the Polish Legion in the Ukraine soon revolted against the Russian Soviet Commissariat supervision of Polish national affairs. The representative in Moscow of the Polish Regency Council was also at once in full clash with the Soviet Government. One of those rugged figures which come to the succour of peoples in tribulation now appeared upon the scene—Josef Pilsudski.

Pilsudski was born in Lithuania in October, 1867, and he was therefore brought up amongst peasants who had a first-hand recollection of the atrocities committed after the insurrection of 1863. At the age of 22 he became involved with Russian revolutionaries and was condemned to five years' deportation to Siberia. He returned to Vilna in 1892 and four years later was again arrested for sedition, but escaped. During these years he was intermittingly linked with Boris Savinkov, and a life-long friendship was formed between the two men. Pilsudski, in consequence of these events, naturally looked on Russia as the principal enemy of his country. At the outbreak of war in 1914 he devoted himself to raising a volunteer force for use against Russia and made Galicia the base of his operations: but he entered into no engagement with either Germany or Austria. He had no illusions as to what the fate of Poland would be if the Central Empires emerged victorious from the war. While fighting under their ægis against Russia and her allies, he remembered always the ancient Greek saying, 'Love as if you shall hereafter hate, and hate as if you shall hereafter love.' The Russian revolution changed the scene, Czardom disappeared, and the implicit conflict between Pilsudski and the Central Powers became manifest. At the end of July, 1917, he refused to swear allegiance to them. He was imprisoned at Magdeburg. On regaining his liberty immediately after the armistice of November, 1918, Pilsudski was acclaimed as leader not only by the patriotic military associations which had been growing up during the German occupation, but by the Polish nation as a whole. He proceeded to Warsaw, disarmed the German soldiers left there, and assumed with profound national assent all the powers of the Regency Council.

At the end of January, 1919, Pilsudski, retaining in fact dictatorial authority, entrusted the formation of the Government to Paderewski, the great pianist. But the Polish nation had now risen again to its feet. The ancient state, torn into three pieces by Austria, Prussia and Russia, had been liberated from its oppressors and reunited in its integrity after 150 years of bondage and partition.

In the Ukraine the Bolsheviks had from the first taken up the challenge of separation. The Germans had signed their separate peace treaty with the Ukrainian Government centred upon Kharkov. But another Ukrainian Government at Kiev, in sympathy with the Bolsheviks, carried on armed resistance, both against counter-revolutionary Kharkov and the arriving Germans seeking corn and oil. The Ukrainian population was distracted by the double collision between anti-Germanism and anti-Communism, between the foreign invader and the domestic infection. These conflicting lines of pitiless quarrel ran through every town, street, village, and family, and even individuals were often at a loss to tell which side of their changing partisanships they hated most.

But German efficiency and discipline pushed steadily through all these feeble-passionate cross-currents. With small bodies of good soldiers they rapidly occupied most of the regions necessary to their replenishment. On March 13, 1918, they occupied Odessa; on the 17th Nikolaev; on April 8 they took Kherson. On the 28th they established a military dictatorship in the Ukraine under their local nominee, General Skoropadski. On May 1 they occupied Sevastopol, seizing part of the Russian Black Sea fleet; on May 8 they took Rostov on the Don. In all these operations, resulting in the effective acquisition of a rich, fertile area the size of a considerable country, not more than 5 reserve divisions of the German Army were employed. Everything is relative. Everyone remembers (and tries to forget) the German occupation of Belgium. Here in the Ukraine these same Germans came as deliverers and were spontaneously recognised as such, not only by the general population, but by those patriotic elements most hostile to the invaders of Russia. A dose of Communism induces a desire in any population to welcome any other form—even the harshest—of civilised authority. With the arrival of the German 'steelhelmets' life again became tolerable. One had only to submit, keep quiet, and obey: thereafter everything was smooth and efficient. Better the iron heel of the foreign soldier than unresting persecution by a priesthood of blackguards and fanatics.[1]

The situation in Bessarabia was curious and painful in a different way. The remnants of the Roumanian army and leading elements of the Roumanian people found a refuge on Russian territory after the conquest of their native land. They were sheltered by the Czar. The revolution and the negotiations of Brest-Litovsk rendered their position desperate. The old affinity between Roumania and Bessarabia, and the unceasing quarrel between Russia and Roumania about this province since the Russo-Turkish War of 1878, revived simultaneously. On the same day (January 28) that the Red Guards entered Helsingfors in the north, the Bolsheviks declared war upon Roumania. The Roumanians were in no condition to resist, but German authority intervened and a peace was signed six weeks

---

[1]A moving account of this phase is found in *Once I had a Home, The Diary of Madejda, Lady of Honour to the late Empress of Russia.*

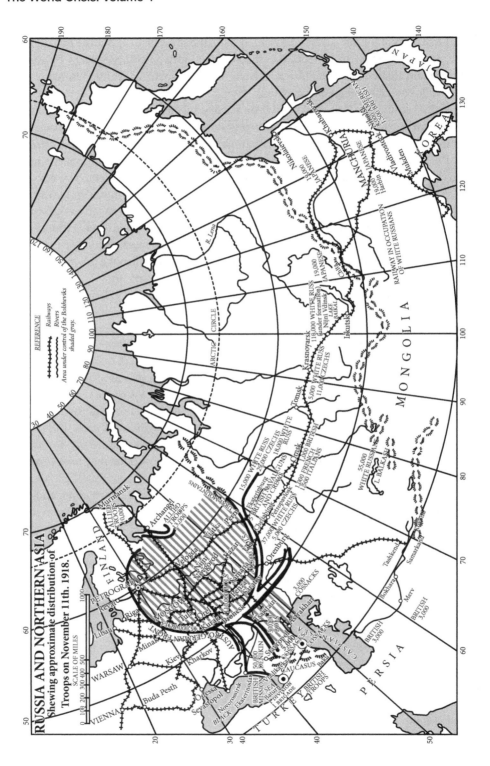

later. Then in the depth of her suffering, Roumania, captive and ruined, attained her heart's desire. On April 9 Bessarabia proclaimed her unity with Roumania subject to autonomy. The ceaseless advance of the German forces in southern Russia forced the Soviet to content themselves with an empty protest.

Such was the vast panorama of anarchy and confusion, of strife and famine, of obligation and opportunity presented to the western conquerors on Armistice Day.

CHAPTER VI
THE FOURTEEN POINTS

President Wilson—The Fourteen Points—The Armistice Negotiations—Colonel House's Commentary—The Meeting of October 29—Mr. Lloyd George's Refusal— Colonel House's Threat—The Prime Minister Obdurate—Allied Reservations—The Freedom of the Seas—Agreement Reached—The French Plan—The Preliminaries of Peace—Wilson's Mission—Dangers of Delay—The Gap.

President Wilson reached at the Armistice the zenith of his power and fame. Since the United States had entered the War in its thirty-second month he had proclaimed more vehemently, and upon occasion more powerfully, than anyone else the righteousness of the Allied cause. Coming into the struggle fresh and cool, he had seemed to pronounce the conclusions of an impartial judge upon the terrible and frantic disputation. High above the swaying conflict, speaking in tones of majesty and simplicity, deeply instructed in all the arts of popular appeal, clad with power unmeasured and certainly unexhausted, he had appeared to the tortured and toiling combatants like a messenger from another planet sent to the rescue of freedom and justice here below. His words had carried comfort to every Allied people, and had been most helpful in silencing subversive peace propaganda in all its forms.

From time to time during the war the various Allies had declared their war aims. In the bleak January of 1918 both Great Britain and the United States had sought to restate their case in the most reasonable terms. In particular on January 8 President Wilson had delivered a speech to Congress in which he had mentioned fourteen points which should in his opinion guide American aspiration. These 'Fourteen Points,' admirably, if vaguely, phrased, consisted in the main of broad principles which could be applied in varying degrees according to the fortunes of war. They included however two perfectly definite conditions, the reconstitution of an independent Poland, and the retrocession to France of Alsace-Lorraine. The adhesion by the United States to these profoundly important war-objectives, involving, as it did, a fight to a finish with Germany, was very satisfactory to the Allies. None of them was concerned to examine the whole speech meticulously or felt committed except in general sympathy. In the meanwhile the President's declaration played an important part in holding the Western Democracies firmly and unitedly to the prosecution of the war, and also encouraged defeatist and subversive movements among the enemy populations.

When on October 1 Ludendorff made his panic demand that the German Government should immediately ask for an armistice, it was on the basis of these Fourteen Points that Prince Max of Baden addressed himself to President Wilson. Wilson seized the opportunity of keeping the negotiations in his own hands in their first and all-important phase. He exploited the advantages of his position energetically both against the enemy and against the Allies, so as to engross to himself the whole task and its responsibility. He refused to transmit the appeals of the despairing enemy to the Allies until he was himself satisfied of their sincerity. He dealt with the suppliant Germans in the sternest manner. He used the weapon of delay with masterly skill. No armistice was possible, he declared, without 'absolutely satisfactory safeguards and guarantees of the maintenance of the present military supremacy of the armies of the United States and of its Allies.' The terms of the armistice must be settled by the Allied Commanders. There could be no question of discussing peace until Germany had deprived herself of all power of resuming the war. The Germans were to deliver themselves naked and defenceless to the discretion and judgment of their conquerors. The month occupied by these parleyings had been one incessant gigantic battle on the whole front. The armies of the United States had lost over 100,000 men killed and wounded, and the French, British and Italians about 380,000. Their advance had been continuous. German resistance had crumpled under the double pressure of the terrors of war and the hopes of peace. At the end they had fallen prostrate at the Presidential footstool.

Wilson's conduct of these negotiations had been so strong and skilful that France and Britain, though at first startled by his self-assertion, were content to leave them in his hands. Even the most rigorous against the enemy could find no fault with his sword-play. He had thus been in the closing stages of the war the spokesman, for all purposes, not only of the United States but of the Allies. He had enunciated the highest principles; he had driven the hardest of bargains. It was now important to see exactly what this bargain was.

When it became evident that the Central Powers were actually in dissolution and were stretching desperate hands towards the Fourteen Points these propositions suddenly acquired intense practical significance. It became imperative towards the end of October to make sure what the Fourteen Points meant and would be understood to mean by friend and foe. Had the Germans, instead of asking for an armistice, sought a peace by negotiation and meanwhile fought on, the interpretation placed upon the Fourteen Points by them and by each of the Allies might have been reduced to an exact and concrete form. But their collapse was so rapid that they could only sue for an armistice, and in the mere process of the correspondence they became utterly prostrate and finally submitted to conditions which left them henceforward helpless. This development, which far transcended the highest expectation of the Allies, left the victors sole judges of the interpretation which should be placed upon the Fourteen Points, while the vanquished naturally construed them in their most hopeful and generous sense.

Through the foresight of Colonel House a Commentary on the Fourteen Points was prepared by the American Representative in Paris and approved by the President. This has now been published by Colonel House. It was the brief from which he spoke on all occasions and certainly an accommodating document.

Point III for instance prescribed '*the removal so far as possible of all economic barriers, and the establishment of an equality of trade conditions among all the nations.*'

The American Commentary prudently explained that this was not intended to prevent tariffs or special railroad rates or port restrictions, so long as they were equally maintained against all. Upon Point IV, *'Adequate guarantees given and taken that national armaments will be reduced to the lowest point consistent with domestic safety,'* it was explained that 'domestic safety' clearly implied not only internal policing but the protection of territory against invasion. Point V prescribed *'A free, open-minded, and absolutely impartial adjustment of all Colonial claims, based upon a strict observance of the principle that in determining all such questions of sovereignty the interests of the populations concerned must have equal weight with the equitable claims of the Government whose title is to be determined.'* On this it was made clear that the German colonies would not be returned to Germany, but that whatever Power managed them, must act as *'trustee for the natives'* and be subject to the supervision of the League of Nations. Point VI, *'The evacuation of all Russian territory'* and *'an unhampered and unembarrassed opportunity for the independent determination of her own political development and national policy.'* However, it was explained that 'Russian territory' did not mean all the territory belonging to the former Russian Empire. And so on.

A meeting was held at the Quai d'Orsay in the afternoon of October 29, between the Representatives of France, Great Britain, Italy and the United States. The principals were M. Clemenceau, Mr. Lloyd George, Mr. Balfour, Baron Sonnino and Colonel House. The question was how the Allies should reply to President Wilson's note.

Mr. Lloyd George said that there were two closely connected questions. First there were the actual terms of an armistice. With this was closely related the question of terms of peace. If the notes which had passed between President Wilson and Germany were closely studied, it would be found that an armistice was proposed on the assumption that the peace would be based on the terms in President Wilson's speeches. The Germans had actually demanded an armistice on these conditions; consequently, unless something definite was said to the contrary, the Allies would be committed to President Wilson's peace terms. Hence, the first thing to consider was whether these terms were acceptable. He asked Colonel House directly whether the German Government were counting on peace being concluded on the basis of President Wilson's Fourteen Points and his other speeches. Colonel House said this was undoubtedly so. Mr. Lloyd George said that unless the Allies made their attitude clear, they would in accepting the armistice be bound to these terms.

M. Clemenceau asked whether the British Government had ever been consulted about President Wilson's terms. France had not been. If he had never been consulted, he did not see how he could be committed. He asked if the British Government considered themselves committed. Mr. Lloyd George replied that they were not committed yet, but if he accepted an armistice without saying anything to the contrary, he would undoubtedly regard the British Government as committed to President Wilson's terms. Mr. Balfour confirmed this. Then said Clemenceau, 'I want to hear the Fourteen Points.'

The first Point was read.

'Open covenants of peace, openly arrived at, after which there shall be no private international understandings of any kind, but diplomacy shall proceed always frankly and in the public view.'

Colonel House then read an extract from a later speech made by President Wilson, pointing out that this would not prohibit secret conversations on confidential and delicate matters, provided that the final results were made public. Mr. Balfour said this really amounted to a prohibition of secret treaties rather than secret conversations.

The second Point was then read.

'*Absolute freedom of navigation upon the seas, outside territorial waters, alike in peace and in war, except as the seas may be closed in whole or in part by international action for the enforcement of international covenants.*'

This point about what is called the 'Freedom of the Seas' naturally aroused British concern. It sounded well intentioned, but what did it mean? Did it mean that the right of blockade in time of war was abolished? We were emerging from a struggle in which blockade had played an important part in preserving the liberties of Europe and the rights of the United States. The British Navy had just crushed the submarine. British ships had just carried the greater part of the American army to Europe. We had saved ourselves from invasion and maintained our population unstarved by sea power. It certainly seemed hard to be told, in the moment of common victory by the friend we had aided, that this great weapon of defence was to be blunted if not broken. It did not follow that the conditions which would prevail in the future would not require and also render possible a review of the whole question of belligerent rights at sea. But now that the enemy's front was being battered down by French and British armies after horrible cost in life and blood, now that Britain under the shield of the Royal Navy was coming safely out of the greatest convulsion of mankind, was hardly the moment when we should be asked, at a few days', almost a few hours' notice, to subscribe to a formula in a matter of life and death which might mean everything or nothing.

Mr. Lloyd George said he could not accept this clause under any condition. If it had been in operation at the present time we should have lost the power of imposing a blockade. Germany had broken down almost as much from the effects of the blockade as from that of the military operations. . . . He would like to see the League of Nations thoroughly established and proved before any discussion on Clause II took place. Even after the establishment of the League of Nations he would only be prepared to begin discussing it. He was not prepared to discuss this question with Germany. It was impossible to make an armistice, if doing so committed us to these conditions.

Clemenceau and Sonnino agreed with Lloyd George.

Colonel House then said that the discussions were leading to this, that all the negotiations up to this point with Germany and Austria would have to be cleaned off the slate. The President would have no alternative but to tell the enemy that his conditions were not accepted by his Allies. The question would then arise whether America would not have to take up these questions direct with Germany and Austria.

M. Clemenceau asked if Colonel House meant to imply that there would be a separate peace between the United States and the enemy. Colonel House said it might lead to this. It would depend upon whether America could or could not agree to the conditions put up by France, Great Britain and Italy.

Now this was assuming a great responsibility for the United States. The armies were still in full battle. Even in this month of extreme American effort, nearly four British, French and Italian soldiers were falling every day to one American. The stake of the United States in the European scene was incomparably small, yet here was a direct threat that if Great Britain, France and Italy did not swallow the Fourteen Points whole, whatever they might be, or be claimed to be, the United States would withdraw from the line, make a separate peace with Germany and Austria, leave the scene in perfect confusion and condemn the world to another year of war. It is a measure of Lloyd George's quality when acting for his country that he did not quail before this unwarrantable pressure.

The Prime Minister replied that it was impossible for the British Government to agree to Point II. If the United States were to make a separate peace we should deeply regret it, but nevertheless should be prepared to go on fighting. (Clemenceau here interjected 'Yes.') 'We could never give up the one power which had enabled the American troops to be brought to Europe. This was a thing we were prepared to fight for and could not give up. Great Britain was not really a military nation; its main defence was its Fleet. To give up the right of using its Fleet was a thing no one in England would consent to. Moreover, our sea power had never been exercised harshly. . . . Apart from the question of Freedom of the Seas, there was no word in President Wilson's speech about reparation for the wanton destruction of property in Belgium and France, and the sinking of ships. Otherwise he had no objection to the President's Fourteen Points. He suggested that a reply should be sent to the President in the sense, that the Fourteen Points must include reparation; that we believed reparation was included in the President's speeches, but that we wished to be perfectly clear about it, and that we could not accept the interpretation which we understood Germany put upon the point about the Freedom of the Seas.'

Colonel House agreed that the first step was for the Allied Governments to get together and make their exceptions to President Wilson's terms. He said later, after other points had been mentioned, that the President's conditions were couched in very broad terms. In the case of Alsace-Lorraine, for example, he did not say specifically that it would go back to France, but he intended it positively. M. Clemenceau said the Germans certainly did not place that interpretation on it. Colonel House continued that the President had said so much [i.e. made this clear] on other occasions. He had insisted on Germany accepting all his speeches and from these you could establish almost any point that anyone wished against Germany. Reparation for Belgium and France was certainly implied in Clauses VII and VIII, where it was stated that these invaded countries must be evacuated and 'restored.' The same principle applied to illegal sinkings at sea, and to the sinking of neutrals.

It was then agreed that the reservations of the Allies should be formulated.

Nearly a week passed in tension. President Wilson armed Colonel House with an ultimatum which his representative decided to hold in reserve. On October 30: 'I feel it my duty to authorise you to say that I cannot consent to take part in negotiations of a peace which does not include the Freedom of the Seas, because we are pledged to fight not only Prussian militarism but militarism everywhere. Neither could I participate in a settlement which does not include the League of Nations because such a peace would result within a period of years in there being no guarantee except universal armaments which would be disastrous. I hope I shall not be obliged to make this position public.'[1]

Meanwhile a British draft of reservations was prepared.

'The Allied Governments have given careful consideration to the correspondence which has passed between the President of the United States and the German Government. Subject to the qualifications which follow, they declare their willingness to make peace with the Government of Germany on the terms of peace laid down in the President's address to Congress of January 8, 1918, and the principles of statements enunciated in subsequent addresses. They must point out, however, that Clause II, relating to what is usually described as the Freedom of the Seas is open to various interpretations, some of which they could not accept. They must therefore reserve for themselves complete freedom on this subject when they enter the Peace Conference.'

'Further in the conditions of Peace laid down in his address to Congress of January 8, 1918, the President declared that the invaded territories must be restored as well as evacuated and freed. The Allied Governments feel that no doubt should be allowed to exist as to what this provision implies. They understand that compensation would be made by Germany for all damage done to the civilian population of the Allies and their property by the forces of Germany, by land, by sea and from the air.'

The Italians had other reservations, but it was pointed out that the present negotiation only applied to Germany, and did not govern the treatment of Austria-Hungary. M. Clemenceau accepted the British draft, and this became the crucial document.

A third meeting was held on November 3 in Colonel House's residence when House read a message from President Wilson in conciliatory amplification of the formula 'Freedom of the Seas.'

'The President says that he freely and sympathetically recognises the necessities for the British and their position with regard to the seas both at home and throughout the Empire. Freedom of the Seas, he realises, is a question upon which there should be the freest discussion and the most liberal exchange of views. The President is not sure, however, that the Allies have definitely accepted the principle of the Freedom of the Seas and that they are reserving only the limitation and free discussion of the subject. . . . The President insists that Terms I, II, III and XIV are essential American terms in the programme and he cannot recede from them. The question of the Freedom of the Seas need not be discussed with the German Government provided we have agreed amongst ourselves beforehand. . . . Blockade is one of the questions which has been altered by developments in this war and the law governing it will certainly have to be altered. There is no danger, however, that it will be abolished.'

---

[1]House, *Papers*, Vol. IV, p. 173.

Mr. Lloyd George said that the formula adopted by the Allies simply provided for free discussion [on Point II] and did not challenge the position of the United States who were perfectly free to go into the Conference and urge their own point of view.

Colonel House asked if Mr. Lloyd George could not accept the principle of the Freedom of the Seas. The Prime Minister replied that he could not. 'It had come to be associated with the idea of the abandonment of the blockade. He did not want to bind the American Government in their discussion, he only wanted to have a free hand for the British Government.' On Colonel House again asking that the principle should be accepted Mr. Lloyd George repeated his refusal. 'Were he to accept,' he said, 'it would only mean that in a week's time a new Prime Minister would be here who would say that he also could not accept the principle. The English people would not look at it. On this point the nation was absolutely solid. Consequently it was no use for him to say that he could accept when he knew he would not be speaking for the British nation.' And again, according to Colonel House (whether at this meeting or at some other is not clear), Mr. Lloyd George said that 'Great Britain would spend her last guinea to keep her navy superior to that of the United States or any other Power, and that no Cabinet Official could continue in the Government in England who took a different position.'[2]

Colonel House then modified his position; all that he wanted was 'the principle that the question could be discussed.' No one could object to that. Mr. Lloyd George replied at once, 'We are quite willing to discuss the Freedom of the Seas in the light of the new conditions which have arisen in the course of the present war.' According to House the actual conversation was—

'I wish you would write something I could send to the President,' said House.

'Will he like something of this kind?' returned Lloyd George—'We are quite willing to discuss the Freedom of the Seas and its application.' He confirmed this by letter to Colonel House the same afternoon. House contented himself with this, and has rather naïvely informed us that he reported a diplomatic victory to the President.[3]

These matters being adjusted, President Wilson on November 5 forwarded to the Germans the Allied Memorandum accepting with reservations the Fourteen Points as the basis of peace, and informed them that Armistice terms could be received from Marshal Foch. The Germans had therefore a right to claim that they surrendered and disarmed themselves on President Wilson's Fourteen Points and other speeches except in so far as these were modified by the formal reservations of the Allies. They were not, however, accorded—nor were they in a position to request—any share in the interpretation. This left a latitude to the victors certainly wide enough for misunderstanding and reproach in after years.

* * * * *

The sharp interchanges which had taken place within the councils of the Allies, the vague character of many of the Fourteen Points and the President's speeches which were

---

[2] House, *Papers*, Vol. IV, p. 190.
[3] House, *Papers*, Vol. IV, p. 188.

to be read with them, to say nothing of the Commentary, made it especially desirable to frame without delay a more precise instrument. But nothing was possible for some weeks. The slaughter had to stop. The drawing up of the Armistice terms for land and sea, the vast surrender by Germany of her whole remaining powers of self-defence, the internal convulsions in Germany and in other defeated countries, and the celebrations of victory by the Allies filled the compass of human nature. When these overwhelming events and emotions had passed, one fact dominated the scene. It was above all things important to make Peace soon.

M. Clemenceau as usual had clear-cut plans. On November 29 the French Ambassador in Washington laid these in writing before Mr. Lansing.

'The arrival of President Wilson in Paris in the middle of December will enable the four Great Powers to agree among themselves upon the conditions of the peace preliminaries to be imposed severally on the enemy without any discussions with him.'

'The examination will first apply to Germany and Bulgaria. . . .'

'After reaching an agreement as to the peace preliminaries, the representatives of the Great Powers will have to come to an agreement on the principles of the representation of the several belligerent, neutral, and enemy states at the Peace Congress. . . . The great victorious powers alone will attend all its sessions, the small powers being called only to sessions designated for their special affairs. As for the neutrals and states in formation, they may be called when their own interests are at stake. . . .'

'It seems that the labours of the Congress should be divided into two main series: the settlement of the war properly so-called, and the organization of the Society of Nations. The examination of the second question no doubt calls for the settlement of the first. Furthermore, the settlement of the concrete questions should not be confounded with the enforcement of the stipulations of general public law. Besides, that distinction is made necessary by the fact that the enemy has no right to discuss the terms that will be imposed upon him by the victors, and that the neutrals will only be called in exceptional cases to attend the sessions where the belligerents will fix the peace terms, while all the peoples, whether belligerents, neutrals or enemies, will be called to discuss and take part in the principle of the Society of Nations.'

'The procedure of the Congress will also be determined at the preliminary meetings in the second half of December. . . .'

'The Congress finally could place itself as has sometimes been done in the past under the invocation of some of the great principles leading to justice, morals and liberty, which would be proclaimed at its very opening and even before fixing the procedure (concerning which an unofficial agreement only would have been reached): right of self-determination of the peoples, right of [the] minorities, *suspension of all previous special agreements arrived at by some of the Allies only, with a view to the fullest freedom*[4] of [the] examination by the Congress, declaration that the metropolitan and colonial territory held by the Allies on August 1, 1914, shall not be touched, solemn repudiation of all [the] violations of international law and of humane principles, and disqualification of enemy delegates who have signed violated instruments or are personally guilty of violations of the law of nations or of [the] crimes against humanity.'

There is no doubt that the French plan was at once logical, practical and speedy. It placed the settlement of all main questions and all procedure definitely in the hands of the four great victorious powers who had made the chief exertions in the war; it drew a line between the past and the future; above all by the 'suspension of all previous special agreements arrived at by some of the Allies only,' it swept away the whole network of secret treaties contracted in the stress of the war. It brought together the four authorities who alone could settle everything, and secured for them an absolutely free hand.

The mature reflections of Colonel House have led him to believe that a preliminary peace should have been negotiated with Germany at the earliest moment. There would have been no difficulty in grafting on to the foundation proposed by the French a preliminary peace. This was a device which had often been found helpful in the past. In a preliminary peace only the main essentials are settled between the belligerents, and they then meet together no longer at war to argue at leisure about details and their application. Nothing in the French procedure would have prevented President Wilson from striving, had such been his inclination, for the most lenient terms towards the conquered enemy, or for any disposition of the captured territories which he thought would in the long run be best. Grave conflicts of opinion were inevitable in any case. But they would have arisen in their natural order and each decision would have made the treatment of secondary problems easier. And agreement between the 'Big Four,' as they afterwards came to be called, was the indispensable prelude to a smooth and speedy peace.

The French plan, however, did not at all commend itself to Mr. Wilson. It thrust on one side all the pictures of the peace conference which his ambition and imagination had painted. He did not wish to come to speedy terms with the European Allies; he did not wish to meet their leading men around a table; he saw himself for a prolonged period at the summit of the world, chastening the Allies, chastising the Germans and generally giving laws to mankind. He believed himself capable of appealing to peoples and parliaments over the heads of their own governments, and he had as we have seen already hinted a willingness to try.[5] No doubt the French proposal was injudiciously framed; in parts it wore an air almost of cynicism. It seemed to treat high ideals as if they were a mere garnish to agreements on sound policy. The President understood that the overstrained European Allies would be above all things anxious for swift settlement; and that delaying procedure would increase his bargaining power. So no answer was

---

[4] Author's italics.
[5] P. 68.

returned either by him or by Mr. Lansing to the French Note of November 29; and no notice whatever was taken of the French proposal to sweep away the secret treaties. All Old World affairs therefore hung in suspense; and instead of leaders meeting together in good-will and good faith to make a lasting settlement, the governing forces in each country drifted into an intensive development of their own points of view.

The French soon began to reconcile themselves to this delay. If President Wilson was coming to Europe not only to punish the Germans but to discipline them, it perhaps was not regrettable that their armies were getting a firm grip on the Rhine and that the peace conference, whenever it should assemble, would be confronted with accomplished facts. Great Britain was still in the throes of the Election, the results of which were not yet known. The Imperial War Cabinet sat almost daily and surveyed the whole future field of the peace. The only inter-Allied discussion which took place in this interval was the meeting in London on December 2 and 3 between Lloyd George, Clemenceau and Orlando, House being absent through illness. This meeting, apart from various matters arising out of the Armistice, decided only that an inter-Allied commission should be set up to report on the amount the enemy countries could pay for reparations and indemnities; that the Kaiser and his accomplices should be brought to trial before an international court, and that before preliminaries of peace should be signed an inter-Allied conference should be held in Paris or Versailles and the date thereof be settled after the arrival of President Wilson.

Here when time is vital and strength in all its forms is ebbing from the victors, we have a ready acceptance of delay. No doubt all these leading men were too easily persuaded that the world would remain at their feet indefinitely and that they could settle its future fortunes at leisure. Most of all did this illusion dwell with President Wilson. He now wished to preside himself over the Peace Conference. When House tactfully explained that only a Frenchman could preside over a conference held in Paris, he made it clear that he would sit as a delegate. His best friends in the United States advised him strongly not to descend into the arena. To visit Europe to discuss the main issues in private with the European statesmen was permissible and even desirable; but to quit the lofty isolation of his Presidential chair for the rough and tumble of a prolonged peace conference, was to sacrifice solid advantages. This American advice was at first strongly reinforced by the wishes of the three European Prime Ministers. They were disturbed at the idea of the head of a state, a personage of sovereign rank, sitting with them nominally on equal terms but with inalienable superiority of status. They were alarmed by much that they had heard of Wilson's autocratic temper and airs. But the desires of the President overrode his own advisers, and the Allied chiefs gradually realised that perhaps the President's mistake would conduce to their advantage. If he chose to step down from his pedestal, why were they the losers? House assured them that he was affable in personal relations. So the President had his way.

In these discussions and in the immense press of events, November and December soon slipped away, and it was not until the middle of January that the representatives of the Twenty-Seven States which had either fought the war or ultimately joined the winning side assembled in Paris. The most cumbrous procedure had been adopted. But the one feature which would have redeemed it had somehow or other been omitted. All depended upon a serious discussion at the outset between Great Britain, France, Italy, Japan and the United States, at which the main principles could be settled. But this discussion never took place. The two months that followed the Armistice had produced no progress of any kind towards the systematic discussion of the peace settlement. By the beginning of January the world was restive; everyone asked what had happened to the Peace; the representatives of all the smaller states were already congregated in Paris where they found assembled all the journalists of the world. The second stage, or general meeting of all the Powers, overtook and overwhelmed the first. Further delay could not be tolerated and the conference sprang into being before the fundamental questions had even been surveyed in common by those who alone had the power to decide.

CHAPTER VII
THE PEACE CONFERENCE

1814–1919—The Literature—A Film Production—Wilson at his Zenith—The Congressional Elections—The Adverse Senate—Wilson's Misconceptions—The Consequences—The 'Plain People'—The Secret Treaties—Under Duress—The Disclosure—The True American View—The Defence of the Allies—The British Peace Delegation—The British Empire Delegation—The Composition of the Conference—President Wilson's Compromise—The Press—The Official Languages—Europe in Convulsion.

How wide is the contrast between the conditions of the Peace Conference in 1919 and those in which the Congress of Vienna had met in 1814! In 1814 the victorious Allies were in effective possession of practically the whole of Europe. They had the physical power to impose their will. In 1919 the dangers were more acute and the victors were much more exhausted; large regions and cardinal factors remained outside their control. In 1814 a group of Aristocrats, life-trained as statesmen or diplomatists, utterly wearied of war and hating change, met together in elegant and ceremonious privacy to re-establish and fortify, after twenty years of tumult, a well-understood conservative system of society. In 1919 the orators and mass leaders who had risen to the dizzy summits of power and victory in the rough and tumble of the struggle all balanced themselves precariously upon the unsure shifting platform of public opinion, and claimed to be guiding mankind to higher destinies. Public opinion was, it is true, focussed and steadied to some extent by the Parliaments. But it was also vehemently swayed by the Press. In 1814 calm, deliberate conclaves of comfortable and firmly established personages: in 1919 a turbulent collision of embarrassed demagogues who were also great men of action, each of whom had to produce a triumph for himself and his Party and give satisfaction to national fears and passions well founded or not. In these circumstances the historian of the future must judge, much less their shortcomings and failures, than their substantial achievements.

＊ ＊ ＊ ＊ ＊

The literature upon the Peace Conference, represented in almost every known language, is large, and that upon the Peace itself far larger. The first place must be assigned to Dr. Temperley's monumental work. Although Dr. Temperley did not feel at liberty to publish all the information and documents at his disposal, his six volumes hold their place as the unique and indispensable guide for any student. Of French books, M. Tardieu's *The Truth about the Treaty* is the most important, partly because he was one of those who acted for France at the Conference, and partly because he publishes many documents which have not appeared elsewhere. M. Mermeix has also in his *Combat des Trois* printed important extracts from the secret minutes of the Supreme Council and from those of the Council of Four. The principal Italian contribution is comprised in three volumes from Signor Nitti. The American point of view is represented first by Mr. Stannard Baker's *Woodrow Wilson and the World Settlement*, of which more later; secondly, in Colonel House's Papers, edited by Mr. Seymour; and thirdly by Mr. Lansing's *Peace Negotiations*. There is also the admirable and scholarly *Drafting of the Covenant*, by Mr. David Hunter Miller; and on the Russian aspect Dennis's *Foreign Policy of Soviet Russia* and *Russian-American Relations*, compiled by Messrs. Cumming and Pettit.

Mr. Stannard Baker's work is distinguished from all these publications, both by the wealth of secret information at his disposal and the peculiar manner in which he has used it. President Wilson at the end of 1920 placed at the disposal of this gentleman, formerly the head of his Press Bureau while in Paris, two trunks and three steel boxes containing all his records of the Peace Conference. 'I plunked them into the trunk in Paris,' he wrote, 'and have not had time or physical energy even to sort or arrange them.' Mr. Baker lost little time in presenting these treasures to the world in the form of a sustained defence of the President's conduct and policy. In his object of vindicating his honoured chief, Mr. Baker will be supported by the sympathy of the Allied nations; and certainly it is not from them that much harsh criticism has come. Everyone recognises the high motives which inspired Mr. Wilson's actions, his remarkable abilities, his comprehensive goodwill and his readiness to arrive at practical solutions. He was a good friend, not only to the Allies but to Europe. He faced the real facts as he gradually got to know them, not only with lofty idealism but with sympathy and common sense. The part he played in the making of the treaties was marked by the strictest loyalty and good faith; and the last remnants of his life and strength were freely expended in trying to make good the obligations into which he had entered and to which he had pledged his country. His memory should long command the sympathy of Europe.

But Mr. Baker detracts from the vindication of his hero by the absurd *scenario* picture which he has chosen to paint. Wilson's share in the Peace Conference, his hopes, his mistakes, his achievements, his compromises and his disasters are worthy of something better than the Hollywood setting with which we are provided. In conventional film style all the lights are heightened and all the shadows darkened. The apparatus of lurid contrast is lavishly employed. A plot suited to the more fruity forms of popular taste is chosen; and the treatment of facts, events and personalities is compelled to conform to its preconceived requirements. For this purpose the President is represented as a stainless Sir Galahad championing the superior ideals of the American people and brought to infinite distress by contact with the awful depravity of Europe and its statesmen. Mr. Baker's film story is, in short, the oldest in the world. It is nothing less and nothing more than the conflict between good and evil, between spiritual conceptions and material appetites, between generosity and greed, between moral earnestness and underhand intrigue, between human sympathy and callous selfishness.

The plot is certainly sensational, but it hardly represents what actually happened. It is difficult to believe that the European emigrants by whom America has been populated took away with them all the virtues and left behind them all the vices of the races from which they had sprung; or that a few generations of residence on the other side of the Atlantic Ocean is sufficient to create an order of beings definitely superior in morals, in culture, and in humanity to their prototypes in Europe. The American sense of humour, it is hoped, will itself supply to such claims the necessary correctives. It would seem probable that on both sides of the Atlantic men find it easy to be disinterested upon questions which do not affect them directly; that they are often inclined to prescribe high principles for others to follow; that they can resist austerely other people's temptations.

However, let us allow Mr. Stannard Baker to open his tale in his own fashion:

'Three weeks and three days after the last victorious shots of the Great War had been fired by Yankee doughboys in the French Argonne, the American peace argosy—the *George Washington*, with accompanying warships—dropped down through the bedecked and beflagged harbour of New York, a new *Santa Maria* on its extraordinary voyage of discovery to an unknown world. The great ship passed majestically out through the Narrows, with airplanes cutting the sky above and the forts on either hand roaring with unprecedented salutes of twenty-one guns; for never before had a President of the United States set sail for a foreign land.'

Modern technical conditions have given so great an extension to publicity that comparisons with other times are vitiated. It seems probable that no human being has ever centred in himself more hopes or enjoyed a greater, if transient, prestige than President Wilson as he paced the decks of the 'American peace argosy.' But the reverse of the medal bore sinister emblems. Mr. Baker has depicted the difficulties which awaited the President in Europe, and the tragic contrast between his noble outlook and the degradation of the old diplomacy. He has not dwelt sufficiently upon the difficulties he left behind him in the United States. Here, too, the old Adam manifested itself in recalcitrant forms, and the spirit of Party politics had raised its unregenerate head. But for this aspect we must turn to other authorities.

The Republican Party view has been explained by Mr. Hollis[1] in terms which, though disfigured by bias, undoubtedly described a widespread American opinion.

'The world was before him like a class. The sight of it turned the head of the pedagogue made prince. In November, 1918, took place the elections to Congress. As the summer drew to an end there began to trickle in from Democratic candidates throughout the country requests that the President give them a letter of endorsement. It was decided that the best plan would be for him to make a speech at some central Middle Western town such as Indianapolis, in which he would appeal to the country not to favour one Party rather than the other but to give him a Congress which would support him in his leadership of the national effort of war. . . . Burleson, the Postmaster-General, had advised this plan, and went off

[1] *The American Heresy*, by Christopher Hollis. Sheed and Ward, Paternoster Row.

to Texas for ten days at the end of September assured that his advice would be followed. On his return he found that behind his back the party politicians had brought pressure upon Wilson to cancel his speech at Indianapolis and instead to write a letter appealing for a Democratic Congress. This letter Burleson found had already been given to the Press. It was interpreted, as Burleson foresaw that it would be, as an abominable slur upon the loyalty of Republicans; and its publication made certain an overwhelming Democratic defeat. Wilson was at the time, according to Mr. White's explanation, "in the upper spiritual zones of idealism," and therefore not at leisure to correct the popular impression that the letter was sent on Burleson's responsibility.'

European opinion upon this episode is not important. But its consequences were formidable. The Republican party, who had given much patriotic support to the President's war policy, deemed themselves 'gratuitously and outrageously insulted.' The November election gave them a majority in Congress, and they already possessed a substantial majority in the Senate. The American Constitution requires the ratification of all treaties by the Senate. It seemed to British and French eyes very curious that in the war crisis President Wilson did not seize the opportunity of becoming a National rather than a Party leader. It is still more remarkable that, confronted with the fact of a hostile majority in the Senate, he did not endeavour to associate that body as a whole with the Treaty negotiations. It would have been impossible, if the President had forced the issue, for Republican senators to refuse to form part of a Senatorial delegation to the Peace Conference; on the contrary, they would probably have been delighted to go; and Wilson could then have been assured that what he promised would not be repudiated. His strong Party feeling and his sense of personal superiority led him to reject this indispensable precaution. The 'American peace argosy' wended on across the waters bearing a man who had not only to encounter the moral obliquity of Europe, but to produce world salvation in a form acceptable to political enemies whom he had deeply and newly offended. Upon him centred the hopes of the world. Before him lay the naughty entanglements of Paris; and behind him, the sullen veto of the Senate.

Nevertheless, it was with no sense of personal inadequacy that the President surveyed his task.

'Three days before the *George Washington* sailed into Brest Harbour in a blaze of glory the President called together a group of the delegation for a conference. There were two members of the Peace Commission itself on the ship, Secretary Lansing and Mr. White (Colonel House and General Bliss being already in Europe), but the great body of the delegation was made up of geographers, historians, economists, and others upon whom the President was to depend for the basic facts to be used in the coming discussions.'[2]

---

[2] *Woodrow Wilson and the World Settlement*, by Ray Stannard Baker, Vol. I, p. 9.

'After a few introductory remarks to the effect that he was glad to meet us,' writes Dr. Isaiah Bowman, who alone kept a record of this meeting, '…the President remarked that *we would be the only disinterested people* at the peace conference, and that *the men whom we were about to deal with did not represent their own people*.'[3]

The first of these two statements can best be judged in the light of ultimate events. The second reveals an undoubted misconception. The European statesmen whom President Wilson was about to meet represented only too well, in the assertion of national claims and in severity to the beaten enemy, the views and wishes of their own peoples. They ceased and failed to represent them only in so far as they diverged from these hard standards, and guided by experience, tolerance and detachment sought to mitigate the misfortunes of the vanquished, or to disappoint their own national expectations. Orlando, in making the most extreme claims, fell short of Italian aspirations. The iron Clemenceau, the prop of France, was throughout and is to-day condemned by the French for weakness in championing his country. As for Lloyd George, he was not only fortified by an overwhelming majority but actually embarrassed by the demands of the multitude for the unsparing punishment of the guilty. So far from these national leaders thrusting forward upon their own impulse a ruthless claim against the defeated, they were every one of them in danger of censure for lukewarmness. The Parliaments and Press of every country stood vigilant to detect the slightest symptoms of tender-heartedness or philosophic indifference. Even the prestige which sprang from absolute victory did not protect them from constant scrutiny and suspicion. In every victorious State there rose the cry: 'Our soldiers have won the war; let us make sure our politicians do not throw away the peace.' These European leaders represented their democracies best in all in which they differed from President Wilson most.

And where was he? He had pledged and was about to recommit the United States to the service of mankind. 'We have no selfish ends to serve. We desire no conquest, no dominion. We seek no indemnities for ourselves, no material compensation for the sacrifices we shall freely make. We are but one of the champions of mankind. We shall be satisfied when those rights have been made as secure as the faith and the freedom of nations can make them.'[4] And again, on the deck of the *George Washington* to Mr. Creel: 'It is to America that the whole world turns to-day, not only with its wrongs, but with its hopes and grievances. The hungry expect us to feed them, the roofless look to us for shelter, the sick of heart and body depend upon us for cure. All of these expectations have in them the quality of terrible urgency. There must be no delay…. Yet you know, and I know, that these ancient wrongs, these present unhappinesses, are not to be remedied in a day or with a wave of the hand. What I seem to see—with all my heart I hope that I am wrong—is a tragedy of disappointment.'[5]

The misgiving was justified. The American populace fell as far short of their Chief in disinterested generosity to the world, as the peoples of the Allied countries exceeded

[3] *The Drafting of the Covenant*, by David Hunter Miller, p. 41. The italics are Mr. Miller's.
[4] Speech, April 2, 1917.
[5] *The War, the World and Wilson*, by George Creel, p. 163.

their own leaders in severity to the enemy. The President himself was without a majority both in the Senate and in the newly elected Congress. Already Ex-President Roosevelt had brutally proclaimed, 'Our Allies and our enemies and Mr. Wilson himself should all understand that Mr. Wilson has no authority whatever to speak for the American people at this time.' Much lower and cruder views than his were to prevail on both sides of the Atlantic. The Allies were destined to settle their affairs among themselves. The agreements to which President Wilson sought to commit the United States, for which the Allies would be asked to concede many grave things, were to be swiftly repudiated by the American Senate and electors. After immense delays and false hopes that only aggravated her difficulties, Europe was to be left to scramble out of the world disaster as best she could; and the United States, which had lost but 125,000 lives in the whole struggle, was to settle down upon the basis of receiving through one channel or another four-fifths of the reparations paid by Germany to the countries she had devastated or whose manhood she had slain.

To write thus is not to blame peoples or their leading men. It is only to recognise the comparatively low level upon which the intercourse of vast communities can proceed at the present stage in human development. How could the peoples know? Through what channel could they receive their instruction? What choate and integral conviction could they form? How could they express it? Vague, general ideas, some harsh, some noble, attracted them from day to day. But in the main they were so glad the war had stopped that each individual family was thinking of nothing so much as reunion, and building up again the home, the business, the old life. Wilson created world democracy in his own image. In fact, however, the 'plain people' of whom he spoke so much, though very resolute and persevering in war, knew nothing whatever about how to make a just and durable peace. 'Punish the Germans,' 'No more War,' and 'Something for our own country,' above all 'Come Home,' were the only mass ideas then rife.

If Wilson had been either simply an idealist or a caucus politician, he might have succeeded. His attempt to run the two in double harness was the cause of his undoing. The spacious philanthropy which he exhaled upon Europe stopped quite sharply at the coasts of his own country. There he was in every main decision a party politician, calculating and brazen. A tithe of the fine principles and generous sentiments he lavished upon Europe, applied during 1918 to his Republican opponents in the United States, would have made him in truth the leader of a nation. His sense of proportion operated in separate water-tight compartments. The differences in Europe between France and Germany seemed trivial, petty, easy to be adjusted by a little good sense and charity. But the differences between Democrat and Republican in the United States! Here were really grave quarrels. He could not understand why the French should not be more forgiving to their beaten enemy; nor why the American Republicans should not expect cold comfort from a Democratic Administration. His gaze was fixed with equal earnestness upon the destiny of mankind and the fortunes of his party candidates. Peace and goodwill among all nations abroad, but no truck with the Republican Party at home. That was his ticket and that was his ruin, and the ruin of much else as well. It is difficult for a man to do great things if he tries to combine a lambent charity embracing the whole world with the sharper forms of populist party strife.

* * * * *

The first shock which the President and his Delegation is said to have received was confrontation with the secret Treaties made between the Allies during the war. Mr. Baker in lurid pages has gloated upon their unmoral character. 'The old diplomacy—what it stood for'; 'The Secret Treaties'; 'The Turkish Empire as booty'; 'The Slump in Idealism', form the headings of chapters which reveal to the American public European baseness and their own correctitude. But let us see what had actually occurred. The American thesis after the United States entered the war was that the Germans represented the most violent form of military aggression recorded by history. England and France had been fighting against this monster since August 4, 1914. In the spring of 1915 Italy had shown a disposition to come and help them. The accession to their side of a nation of thirty-five millions mobilising an army one and a half millions strong seemed to be a matter of the highest consequence. But Italy appeared to have a move either way; and the Germans were eagerly displaying to Italian eyes the advantages to Italy of playing a true part in the Triple Alliance. Instead of seeking the Trentino from Austria, why not take Savoy from France? And so on; bid and counter-bid. We should wrong the Italians by suggesting that their decision was taken on these material grounds. But who can blame the Allied statesmen for dwelling upon the superior advantages which Italy could obtain at the expense of Austria and of Turkey? The Treaty of London, upon which Italy entered the war on the Allied side, embodied the belief that to France and Britain the aid of Italy spelt speedy victory, and that her hostility might mean their total defeat.

In the same way Roumania, who had equally great prizes to gain by adhering to either combination provided it emerged victorious, was the subject in 1916 of every form of threat and inducement which States at desperate leaguer could present. Such were the secret Treaties entered into by the Allies in their distress and jeopardy in order to secure reinforcements.

Another series of secret agreements had been made among the Allies themselves—to keep themselves in good temper with each other. In 1914, 1915 and 1916 Russian assistance was vital. France was bleeding to death; the British armies were only just becoming a prime factor in the field. To keep the struggling Russian Colossus in good heart, to avoid all excuses for estrangement, was the first duty of British and French diplomacy. Turkey, which had been offered territorial integrity on the guarantee of France, Britain and Russia, had joined the Germans and had made an unprovoked assault upon Russia. No one was going to shed many tears about the break-up of the Turkish Empire or the end of Turkish domination over Christian or Arab races. The assignment of spheres of interest over the non-Turkish provinces of Turkey became at once a necessity and a convenience to the Allies. England, abandoning the policy of generations, consented to the prospect of a Russian Constantinople and dwelt upon her own interests in the

Persian Gulf and in Mesopotamia. France asserted her historic claims to Syria. Italy was assured that none of her Allies would obstruct her ambitions in Adalia nor indeed upon the Alps and in the Adriatic. An understanding about Persia had for many years been an indispensable foundation of good Anglo-Russian relations. These arrangements had to be recast on the assumption of a general victory in which the Turkish Empire would have disappeared. Mr. Baker pretends that all these inter-Allied agreements represented the inherent cynical wickedness and materialism of old-world diplomacy. They were in the main simply convulsive gestures of self-preservation.

The greater part of these secret Treaties was found to be conformable to the principles laid down by President Wilson in his Fourteen Points and was consented to by him in the ultimate settlement. There were features in all of them which nothing but duress could explain and excuse; but Mr. Baker and the United States Delegation had no grounds for taking a lofty and judicial view of these transactions. If the United States had entered the war—a war, as they subsequently described it, of right and justice against unspeakable wrong and tyranny—on the 4th of August, the world would never have come into this plight. American statesmen could have judged for themselves in concert with the ministers of England, France, and Russia what conditions, if any, might fittingly be offered to procure the adherence of Italy. If the United States had entered the war after the sinking of the *Lusitania*, they could have judged for themselves how far it was right to go to prevent Roumania being drawn into the orbit of the Central Powers. If even two years after the outbreak of war they had joined the Allies, they could have regulated at their pleasure any arrangements made with Japan about Shantung and China generally. One has a right to stand on the bank; but if one has exercised the right for a prolonged and agonising period without even throwing a rope to a man struggling in the rapids, some allowance should be made for the swimmer who now clutches at this rock and now at that in rough or ungainly fashion. It is not open to the cool bystander, who afterwards becomes the loyal and ardent comrade and brave rescuer, to set himself up as an impartial judge of events which never would have occurred had he outstretched a helping hand in time.

Mr. Baker produces his first film tableau when he shows us the hearty, whole-souled American Delegation suddenly confronted on their arrival with this 'labyrinth' of secret Treaties. The President had never heard of their existence. Mr. Lansing, with all the resources of the State Department at his disposal, had never dreamed of them. But here they were, naked and horrible, now flung on the table of the Peace Conference and blotting the fair lay-out of the Fourteen Points. Can we wonder that the moral sense of the American people recoiled? No such effect had been produced since Fatima opened the secret chamber of Bluebeard.

In fact, however, the Government of the United States (we cannot speak for individuals) had been made aware of the gist of each of these secret Treaties, and could at any time after their entry into the war have obtained every detail by merely asking. Most remarkable of all, in their memorable despatch of November 29, 1918, the French Government as we have seen had formally proposed to the American State Department that all secret agreements should be abrogated forthwith before any Peace negotiations were begun. And Mr. Lansing had left this note without an answer. But here Mr. Baker shall speak for himself. He speaks very fairly.

'. . .In America we knew little and cared less about these European secret Treaties. Our national interests were at no point affected by them. . . . Everyone knew indeed that Italy had driven a hard bargain when she came into the War on the side of the Allies. But this was war, and in war anything may be necessary. . . . Even the State Department of the United States, which is the organisation especially charged with the duty of knowing about foreign affairs, seems to have had no interest in these secret Treaties, and if Secretary Lansing is to be believed, little or no knowledge of them. . . . While the President must have known in general of these secret agreements, for he often excoriated the practice of "secret diplomacy," he apparently made no attempt to secure any vital or comprehensive knowledge. . . .'

'. . . When Mr. Balfour came to Washington as the British Commissioner in 1917 he explained certain of these Treaties to Col. House. Col. House, however, said he was not particularly interested, because it seemed to him more important to bend all energies to the winning of the war; and he finally told Mr. Balfour that they were "dividing the bear-skin before the bear had been killed." The President's advisers thus underestimated the importance of the whole matter, and felt that to waste any time on it would only interfere with the energetic prosecution of the war, which they believed was the most important consideration of the moment. They trusted, as did the whole country, that all would come right in the end once we had "licked the Kaiser.". . .'

.   .   .   .   .

'. . . If our diplomatic service lacked a background of comprehension of the significance of the secret Treaties, what should be said about public opinion? Venturing into a totally unfamiliar scene, driven blindly by a blast of war feeling, a few leaves of secret engagements in the wind meant absolutely nothing to it. . . .'

But surely all this was masculine good sense. And if these excuses for carelessness or indifference are valid for the United States Government and people, how much more do they protect the Allies? If America can be pardoned for being 'driven blindly by a blast of war feeling' into underrating or ignoring the significance of such transactions, surely England and France, streaming with blood, seared in the flame of battle, with their dearest dead and national life at stake, may be excused for setting them in a similar twilight.

It is at once silly and unjust to pretend that these partitions of possible war gains had any substantial relation to the causes for which the Allies were fighting the war. When wars begin, much is added to the original cause of quarrel and many results follow never aimed at or cared for at the beginning. When the United States in 1898 declared war upon Spain, it was with no thought of taking the Philippine Islands and subjugating the Philippine Islanders; yet both these events followed inevitably or incidentally from their victory. It is no less a calumny upon France and England to say that they fought 'for the booty of Turkey' than to say that the United States picked a quarrel with Spain in order to annex and conquer the Philippines; and it is perhaps a good thing to clear these calumnies out of the way even if it somewhat mars the film effects in which Mr. Stannard Baker delights. However, here were the secret Treaties to which the faith of great countries was pledged and their signatures appended; and they ran criss-cross, not in the main, but in some important instances, to the broad and simple theories of the Fourteen Points.

* * * * *

Mr. Lloyd George and the British Peace Delegation had crossed the Channel on January 10. They were accompanied by naval and military authorities. They had been preceded by a large and elaborate staff of experts and officials who filled to overflowing one of the largest hotels in Paris. The competence of this staff, the fund of knowledge of history, law and economics which it commanded, and its methods of conducting business have gained the respect both of Ally and enemy observers. 'As for the slim white booklets of the English experts,' says a German writer, 'dealing with Belgian neutrality, with the Rhine problem, with the Danube, with the possible future of little Luxemburg, and Heaven knows what besides, the number of these books was legion. Of all the rival guides to the maze of the troubled earth which awaited reshaping, the English collection was the amplest and was generally felt to be more systematically and concisely arranged than either the American or the French. Even members of the American and French delegations frequently consulted the little white books in their search for enlightenment on obscure subjects on which they were called upon to pronounce or prophesy.'[6]

The great machine was directed and focussed for business by the comparatively small instrument of the War Cabinet Secretariat which had been perfected during the preceding four years by the organising insight and measureless industry of Maurice Hankey. This officer of Marines, while still a young Captain, had become in 1912 the Secretary of the Committee of Imperial Defence. He had been responsible for the War Book which had been the key to the whole transition of Britain from peace to war in 1914. He had kept and arranged the records of all the great business which had come first before the War Committee of the Cabinet and later before the War Cabinet during the war and the Armistice. He knew everything; he could put his hand on anything; he knew everybody; he said nothing; he gained the confidence of all; and finally he became by the natural flow of their wishes the sole recorder for the decisive six weeks of the conversations between President Wilson, M. Clemenceau and Mr. Lloyd George by which the Peace was settled.

The British Plenipotentiaries were reinforced by the British Empire Delegation consisting of the Prime Ministers of the self-governing Dominions, the representatives of India, and four or five Ministers in charge of the great executive Departments, of whom I was at this time one. This body was purely consultative. It assembled in Paris only when required by the Prime Minister, and its members were widely dispersed in

---

[6]Nowak, *Versailles*, p. 34.

other activities. In contrast to President Wilson's isolation from the Senate, it was Lloyd George's policy to fortify himself at important moments by the counsel and agreement of the leaders of the whole British Empire. This was *his* Senate, and he moved through the darkness and confusion of the Paris firmament always surrounded by numerous and shining satellites. At his side, with matchless experience and a calm imperturbable wisdom, stood Arthur Balfour; and (must we not add?) Louis Botha. Were Labour questions raised, Barnes, the veteran Trade Unionist, could speak as a working man. Did he require exponents of the Liberal creed in international affairs, General Smuts and Lord Robert Cecil could meet President Wilson on his own ground and speak his language to Wilson's surprise and gratification. Was there a moment when the robust instincts of youthful conquering pioneer states deserved expression, Mr. Hughes of Australia and Mr. Massey of New Zealand were at hand, with Sir Robert Borden of Canada not far away. If the panorama of the East or Middle East should be lighted, Maharajas and Emirs of a thousand years' historic descent advanced in glittering gravity. Himself singularly free from that perversion of the historic sense which degenerates into egotism, the Prime Minister parcelled out great functions and occasions among his colleagues and those whom he wished to persuade or conciliate; and by modesty in good fortune preserved intact his own controlling power. Thus he was well fitted in himself for the impending ordeal and equipped with a fine apparatus.

On the other hand he reached the Conference somewhat dishevelled by the vulgarities and blatancies of the recent General Election. Pinned to his coat-tails were the posters, 'Hang the Kaiser,' 'Search their Pockets,' 'Make them Pay'; and this sensibly detracted from the dignity of his entrance upon the scene.

* * * * *

The actors had arrived: the stage was set: and the audience already clamoured for the curtain to rise. But the play and its method of presentation were still unsettled. We have seen how President Wilson had rejected the original French plan of November 29, 1918, for a preliminary settlement upon essentials by the four or five principal partners in the war, and how he had wished for a general assembly of the victors, over which he should himself preside and before which he could lay his schemes for the better government of mankind. His mere unspoken dissent from the French proposals had been sufficient to delay all prior consultation between the Allied Powers. But now everyone met face to face and practical decisions must forthwith be taken. The President came immediately into contact with personalities who were certainly his equals in force and experience, and who guarded the vital interests of mighty nations which in the long-drawn-out struggle had staked their all and won. The glowing if nebulous ideas he may have cherished of haranguing the Old World into a nobler way of life and of marshalling to his support—if necessary over the heads of their own chosen leaders—the public opinions of the various countries, must now give place to silk and steel conversations with Clemenceau and Lloyd George.

From January 12 onwards meetings were held of the five principal Powers, each with two representatives. These meetings were at first intended only to settle procedure and inaugurate the Plenary Conference; but as they succeeded one another day after day, the body assumed an impressive shape and came almost at once to be called 'The Council of Ten.'

The Council of Ten first discussed the constitution of the Peace Conference and its control. Wilson was in favour of the whole twenty-seven States meeting together upon more or less equal terms. Clemenceau demurred:

'Am I to understand from the statement of President Wilson that there can be no question, however important it may be for France, England, Italy or America, upon which the representative of Honduras or of Cuba shall not be called upon to express his opinion? I have hitherto always been of the opinion that it was agreed that the five Great Powers should reach their decisions upon important questions before entering the halls of Congress to negotiate peace. If a new war should take place, Germany would not throw all her forces upon Cuba or upon Honduras, but upon France; it would always be upon France. I request then that we stand by the proposals which have been made, proposals to the effect that meetings be held in which the representatives of the five countries mentioned shall participate, to reach decisions upon the important questions, and that the study of secondary questions be turned over to the commissions and the committees before the reunion of the Conference.'

He was supported by Mr. Lloyd George, and evidently commanded the agreement of Italy and Japan. Lansing thought that Wilson should insist. He contemplated apparently the President forming a block or lobby of small States and out-voting the Great Powers. Wilson's inherent good sense saved him from this folly. He proposed as a compromise that informal conversations should be held among the Great Powers simultaneously with the Plenary Conferences of all the nations. This was no compromise at all. It was a recognition of facts. The Council of Ten were to converse and not to confer, but they were to continue. This was readily agreed to.

The next problem was the Press. No less than five hundred special correspondents had gathered in Paris—the most able, competent writers in every country, representing the most powerful newspapers and the largest circulations. The sense of history was strong upon all of these men, and also the importance of getting it in first. Every day the cables and the wireless had to be charged with tens of thousands of words directed to every printing office in the globe, describing how the great peace was going to be made. Except from the French Press, which was carefully looked after, all the gag of war censorship had been removed. The whole five hundred stood together in the truest comradeship and the keenest rivalry; and all chanted aloud in chorus the first of the Fourteen Points which seemed specially drafted for their benefit, namely, 'Open covenants of peace openly arrived at.' Mr. Wilson was seriously embarrassed at this application of his doctrine. He hastened to repeat that he had not intended that every delicate matter must at every stage be discussed in the newspapers of the world. Obviously one had to draw the line somewhere. But this made no impression. The people of the United States must have news, or at least copy, day by day; and the British and French could scarcely be expected to be fed only through American channels. The great question was, said Mr. Stannard Baker, 'What would democracy do with diplomacy?' On the one hand, one hundred million strong, stood the young American democracy. On the other cowered furtively, but at the same time obstinately, and even truculently, the old European diplomacy. Here young, healthy, hearty, ardent millions, advancing so hopefully to reform mankind. There, shrinking from the lime-lights, cameras and cinemas, huddled the crafty, cunning, intriguing, high-collared, gold-laced diplomatists. Tableau! Curtain! Slow music! Sobs: and afterwards chocolates!

'Open covenants of peace openly arrived at'! If this meant anything it surely meant a vast world debate upon the war settlement; and that all the 'plain people' in all the lands, the plain blacks as well as the plain whites, should consciously and intelligently participate in the grand solution. But how to bring this about? The plain people were busy getting their daily bread. They had no time to listen to all the frantic pleadings and protests which arose. One tale was good until another was told, and probably both were untrue and certainly very difficult to understand. Nevertheless, here were the plain people represented by a highly coloured Press; and here was Point One of the Fourteen, which said that the covenants of peace were to be 'openly arrived at.'

However it is curious that the Press fared a good deal worse in the peace than they had in the war. In fact their fortunes were unexpectedly reversed. They had begun the war brushed contemptuously aside by the Generals, excluded from the war zone, and strait-jacketed by the Censorship. They had soon compelled generals and politicians to come to heel. They emerged from the war at the highest point of their power and influence. They were still in the mood to break Governments and dictate policy. But war conditions had passed; and as the Parliaments and the platform revived, the newspapers and their proprietors were gradually brought to a more reasonable view of their function. Their first experience of the horrors of Peace was to learn that none of the Fourteen Points applied to them; and that the Council of Ten would meet in secret.

* * * * *

A discussion at times rather heated then took place upon what was to be the official language. France claimed that French was by long custom the official language of diplomacy, that the French were the hosts of the Conference and that France had suffered more than anyone else. Britain, with her Dominions, and the United States, all acting together, said as opportunity offered that they represented a hundred and sixty millions of English-speaking people and were in a large majority. Neither side would agree to abate its claims, so both languages were declared official; and an Italian attempt for the recognition of a third language was not successful. The way was then clear for business; and on January 18 the first Plenary session of the Peace Conference opened.

It was time. More than two months had passed since the Armistice. The interval had been filled by the British General Election, by President Wilson's journey to Europe and by the French preparations—certainly not unduly hurried—for the greatest international gathering that has ever taken place. Meanwhile the armies had advanced into Germany and taken possession of the Rhine bridgeheads. Allied officers and missions, clad in the brand-new authority of conquest, had moved freely about through Austria, Turkey and Bulgaria, giving such directions as they thought necessary or thought fit to these entirely submissive populations. The French, with the Greeks at their side, had landed at Odessa (of which more later). British divisions had occupied the railway across the Caucasus, and British flotillas rode the Caspian as well as the Rhine. Allenby's armies had effectively occupied all Syria and joined hands with the Anglo-Indian armies in Mesopotamia. But these purely military measures, although for the moment they seemed effective, only masked the deepening chaos in which so many vast defeated communities were involved. The greater part of Europe and Asia simply existed locally from day to day. Revolutions, disorders, the vengeance of peoples upon rulers who had led them to their ruin, partisan warfare, brigandage of all kinds and—over wide areas—actual famine lapped the Baltic States, Central and Southern Europe, Asia Minor, Arabia and all Russia in indescribable confusion. These were fearful months for a large proportion of mankind; nor was the end in sight.

But behind these tribulations new and often inordinate hopes and ambitions everywhere reared their heads. The Baltic States sought their independence, and each strove desperately to erect some form of ordered government. Germany was in actual revolution. A Communist uprising, eventually choked in blood, taught Munich a lesson never to be forgotten. Hungary was soon to fall under the oppression of Bela Kun, an offshoot of the Moscow fungus sprouting independently at Buda-Pesth. The Austrian Empire was in utter dissolution. Poland was rising again out of the wreck of the three Empires by whom she had been partitioned a hundred and fifty years before. Bohemia, under the shield of Masaryk and Benes, was accepted as an ally by the victors. The remnants of Roumanian society and army which had straggled back to their devastated country after the withering Treaty of Bucharest, now rapidly overran Transylvania. The Italians poured into the Tyrol, and passing the Adriatic soon came face to face with fierce, gaunt, unconquerable Serbs who now called themselves Yugo-Slavs. The Arabs under Feisal, with the fiery Lawrence bound in blood brotherhood to their cause, had settled down in Damascus and dreamed of a great Arabia from Alexandretta to Aden, and from Jerusalem to Bagdad. Not only the victors but the vanquished, not only the peoples but parties and classes, proclaimed their ambitions. Appetites, passions, hopes, revenge, starvation and anarchy ruled the hour; and from this simultaneous and almost universal welter all eyes were turned to Paris. To this immortal city—gay-tragic, haggard-triumphant, scarred and crowned—more than half mankind now looked for satisfaction or deliverance.

CHAPTER VIII
THE LEAGUE OF NATIONS

Three Phases—A Defective Procedure—The Supreme Council—A Dual Association—The League of Nations Commission—Origin of the Covenant—The British Contribution—Scepticism—The President's Credentials—The Question of Mandates—The Dominions' View—The President and the Dominions Prime Ministers—The Period of Commissions—'Make them Pay'—Mr. Keynes's Book— The Solution—War Criminals—The Ladder of Responsibility—The Kaiser— Growing Impatience—The Covenants Achieved—The Foundation Stone.

The story of the Peace Conference divides itself naturally into three well-marked phases which the reader would do well to keep in mind as the narrative proceeds.

First, the Wilson period, or the period of Commissions and of the Council of Ten, culminating in the drafting of the Covenant of the League of Nations. This lasted for a month, from the first meeting of the Council of Ten on January 14 down to the first return of President Wilson to America on February 16. Secondly, the Balfour period, when President Wilson had returned to Washington and Mr. Lloyd George to London, and when M. Clemenceau was prostrated by the bullet of an assassin. In this period Mr. Balfour, in full accord with Mr. Lloyd George, induced the Commissions to abridge and terminate their ever-spreading labours by March 8 and concentrated all attention upon the actual work of making peace. Thirdly, the Triumvirate period, when the main issues were fought out by Lloyd George, Clemenceau and Wilson in the Council of Four and finally alone together. This Triumvirate, after tense daily discussions lasting for more than two months, framed preliminaries of peace which were accepted by all the Allied States great and small and then presented to the enemy in the Treaties of Versailles, St. Germain, Trianon, and Neuilly.

To understand the Conference the reader must grasp both the procedure and how it arose. The logical French scheme of November 29 had not been accepted by President Wilson. Nevertheless there was general if tacit agreement that in the first instance the victors should meet together alone. They would then draw up preliminary peace terms, and after thrashing these out among themselves would present draft treaties unitedly to the enemy. The French had proposed and the British, Italians and Japanese expected that from among the victors the leaders of the five Great Powers would confer privately beforehand and would settle all the largest questions and principles among themselves before the crowd of small states were admitted to the discussion. However, except for the questions of procedure mentioned in the last chapter, this all-important, and as it proved indispensable stage never had its proper place. The main Conference overlapped and overlaid the vital preparatory discussions. The first Plenary Session of January 18 saw the whole twenty-seven States represented and no agreement on any fundamental matter among the five principal Allied Powers.

Of course the five Great Powers from the beginning to the end settled everything as they chose; and nothing could have prevented them from doing so. But these primordial facts only became apparent and dominant after a prolonged period of uncertainty and confusion. Decisions were taken not as the result of systematised study and discussion, but only when some individual topic reached a condition of crisis. Throughout there was no considered order of priority, no thought-out plan of descending from the general to the particular. All sorts of thorny, secondary questions were discussed and fought over by chiefs who had not agreed upon the primary foundations. There was no mutual confidence between the five Great Powers, and no achievement of a common point of view. Two months of discussion took place while all the burning issues were hidden in the breasts of the leading plenipotentiaries. In fact, so far as I have been able to ascertain, right down to the end of March there never was any heart-to-heart and frank conversation between the three men on whom ultimately everything rested: Mr. Lloyd George, M. Clemenceau and President Wilson. This is the dominating fact of the Wilson and Balfour stages.

These chiefs were, however, continually in official contact. Not only were there frequent sessions called 'conversations' of the Council of Ten, but the same men (or some of them) often sat together as the Supreme War Council.[1] This instrument had reached a very high development during the concluding months of the war. The meetings of the Supreme War Council were not concerned with the terms of peace. Many practical and urgent matters pressed upon them from week to week: for instance, the whole economic situation; the continuance of the terms of the Armistice; the relations with Russia. And then from time to time the disorders of Europe rose to explosion-point. The newly founded Republic of Poland found itself in a state of war with the people of East Galicia; and the Supreme War Council had to interfere. They sent out a special Commission to Poland, and we saw the spectacle of an international train starting on an adventurous journey with its five heavily guarded carriages each for a separate nation. In spite of hazards the international Commission reached Warsaw and patched up some kind of truce between the Poles and the Ukrainians. Then similar difficulties arose in Teschen. The Allies had to intervene to prevent the outbreak of fighting between the Poles and the Czecho-Slovaks. In April again they had to intervene in consequence of the Bolshevik revolution of Bela Kun in Hungary and the great dangers which it involved. The situation was indeed difficult and dangerous in the last degree.

There was serious peril that the whole continent might lapse into anarchy. Everyone turned to the principal Allies, looking for help; but in many cases the help could not be given. They wanted food, but there was still a shortage of food even in the Allied countries. They wanted military occupations; but the British, whose soldiers were in the greatest demand as pacifiers, could not spare many troops and could not risk

---

[1] The word 'war' was gradually dropped.

sending small detachments to remote districts far from the sea. All these consequential war measures occupied during the first months much of the time and the energy of the principal Powers.

This dual association exercised an irresistible effect upon the making of the Peace. The five Great Powers found themselves continually together for one cause or another. In the morning they 'conversed' as a Council of Ten about the Peace settlements; in the afternoon they sat as a Supreme Council taking important executive decisions. The rest of the twenty-seven States, who according to the fiction originally adopted were of equal status, were from time to time assembled in Plenary Sessions where under conditions of the fullest publicity nothing of any importance could ever be done. President Wilson yielded himself inevitably and almost insensibly to these developments. He saw that they did not arise from the evil nature of European diplomacy, but from practical and physical causes against which it was vain to strive. How could any thorny question affecting the main interests of nations, great or small, be helpfully debated by twenty-seven Powers in public? If platitudes and honeyed words alone were used, the proceedings would be a farce. If plain speaking were indulged in, they would become a bear-garden. Even the Council of Ten, solely composed of the leading statesmen of the greatest Powers and meeting in secret, was too unwieldy. With its attendant experts it rarely numbered less than fifty persons of very various rank and status. Even secrecy was doubtful, apart from calculated leakages. We shall see the President presently, guided by common sense and the force of facts, lock himself up with Clemenceau and Lloyd George, and with only Maurice Hankey to record and give precise shape to the decisions, settle every question of crucial importance. If such meetings had taken place in December or even in January, the whole course of the Peace Conference would have been smooth and coherent. He had begun by rejecting the obvious and the easy. He welcomed them warmly when they returned to him upside down after many days.

The moment at length came for the President to launch his main policy. He declared that a League of Nations must become an integral part of the Treaty of Peace and must have priority over all territorial or economic settlements. It was upon the structure of the League that the whole Treaty should be built, and with its general principles all must be in harmony. This would have been admirable if a preliminary understanding had been reached on the main issues between the leading men, and if they had known where they stood with one another in essentials and had not felt that very serious conflicts impended. But now it seemed that the Conference was to dive into interminable academic discussions upon a new Constitution for mankind, while all the practical and clamant issues had to drum their heels outside the door.

It was agreed that a special Commission upon the Constitution of the League of Nations should be appointed by a Plenary Session of the Conference. The discussions in the Council of Ten, at which this procedure was settled, are instructive reading. President Wilson, hitherto the champion of the smaller Powers, had already realised that no business would be done if any large number of them were allowed to sit upon the Commission of the League. He therefore argued for the smallest possible body composed of representatives of the highest responsibility. Clemenceau and Lloyd

George, on the other hand, somewhat ironically voiced the claims of the smallest nations. The League was to be their shield and buckler. Ought they not to be there? Would this not open to them a useful sphere of activity instead of leaving them to loaf morosely about Paris waiting for the decisions of the Council of Ten? All the Great Powers except the United States were profoundly disquieted at the total lack of progress, and their representatives had to face a rising menace of impatience at home. While the main questions were unsettled, every aspect of the League of Nations' Constitution would have to be vigilantly scrutinised. They regarded with despair the prospect of so many weeks' or even months' delay.

In the end a very good Commission was appointed which included some of the smaller nations and yet was not unmanageable in numbers. The two foremost British champions of the policy, Lord Robert Cecil[2] and General Smuts, were appointed delegates. Wilson himself decided to preside, and the immense task was vigorously taken in hand.

The history of the Peace Conference, edited by Dr. Temperley and published under the auspices of the Institute of Foreign Affairs, attributes the origin of the League of Nations to three reasons. First, the need of some settled Council of Nations which would be responsible for the maintenance of peace; secondly, the need for a more comprehensive guarantee of the safety of small nations, as proved by the fate of Belgium; and thirdly, a growing belief in the advantages of economic co-operation. An additional argument might be found in the fact that twenty million men had been blowing each other to pieces for more than four years, that this process had now stopped, and most people hoped it would not begin again.

It is sometimes pretended that the League of Nations was an American inspiration forced and foisted upon Europe against its froward inclination. The facts are different. The idea had stirred in most civilised countries during the last three years of the war, and various societies had been formed to propagate it both in America and in England. Lord Robert Cecil was the first Englishman to put something down in writing, and he wrote a paper on this subject at the end of 1916. His thesis, though necessarily undeveloped, amounting indeed only to a rough draft of what now forms Articles XV and XVI of the Covenant, provided a basis for a Committee set up in 1917 under Lord Phillimore's presidency to work upon. This Committee produced draft statutes of a League in a document circulated to the United States among other Governments early in 1918. In the summer of 1918 President Wilson deputed Colonel House to work upon the Phillimore draft and House's suggestions reached him on July 16. The main addition made by House was the positive guarantee of the territorial integrity and independence of the States members of the League. Phillimore's draft had been content merely to provide guarantees for the execution of arbitration agreements. When Wilson came to revise this he omitted the clause providing for an International court but added tremendous words, indeed such words as Lord Robert Cecil had advocated in his early draft, that violation should be punished by lethal force.

---

[2]Now Viscount Cecil of Chelwood.

Meanwhile General Smuts produced independently on December 16, 1918, his own draft of a League which embodied detailed suggestions of an organisation, proposed to set up a Council as well as the Assembly, included a provision for the abolishment of conscription and for the limitation of military equipment and recommended a mandatory system for backward territories or states in tutelage.

Of Wilson's share in the task his chronicler, Mr. Baker, says 'Practically nothing, not a single idea, in the covenants of the League was original with the President. His relation to it was mainly that of editor or compilist, selecting or rejecting or compiling the projects which came in to him from other sources.'[3]

This is no wise detracts from the magnitude of Wilson's contribution. He embodied all helpful amendments in his own draft, and also added one draft Article designed to ensure fair hours and humane conditions for labour, and another requiring new States to grant equal rights to minorities. This was the draft which the Americans presented on January 10, 1919, at the Peace Conference, and ten days later the British Delegation also produced the most up-to-date version of the British ideas on the subject. The British and American drafts, which in all essentials 'meant the same thing,' were consolidated by Sir Cecil Hurst representing Great Britain and Mr. Hunter Miller the United States. They were considered and amended by the League Commission during the latter part of January and beginning of February, and eventually laid before a Plenary Session of the Conference on February 14. Thus the League of Nations was an Anglo-Saxon conception arising from the moral earnestness of persons of similar temperament on both sides of the Atlantic.

President Wilson had made this great idea his own, and when all the vexations of these days and his own mistakes are forgotten it is in the establishment and ascendancy of a new international society that his memory will be enshrined. The British were throughout his chief supporters. In our island all liberal elements clung and cling to the plan. All other right-minded persons realised the advantages which such a League might confer upon the widely dispersed communities of the British Empire. Criticism arose only from scepticism. Was it not too good to be true? Could it be a substitute for national armaments? Might it not turn out in the hour of need to be an illusion and those who had counted on it perish in some future earthquake? It seemed to these critics more prudent to retain the old proved safeguards while the new were a-building. But the support given by Great Britain to President Wilson's League of Nations plan was whole-hearted, positive, and above all, practical. Without it he could never have succeeded. It was natural that the smaller or weaker States of the world should acclaim a Reign of Law which would protect them from over-lordship or aggression. France and Italy and, on the other side of the globe Japan, received the new gospel with goodwill; but being much closer anchored to the grim realities, they reproduced in more stubborn forms the misgivings of British sceptics. The real opposition came from the United States. The whole tradition of the American people had been separation from the tribulations and antagonisms of the Old and Older Worlds. The Atlantic pleaded three thousand

---

[3]Vol. I, p. 242.

and the Pacific seven thousand reasons against entanglements in these far-off affairs. All the teachings of the Fathers of the American Union from Washington to Monroe had ingerminated Non-intervention. Science has to march perhaps another fifty years before the gulfs of ocean space are rendered politically meaningless. This is no long period in human history, but it far exceeded the life of the Paris Conference in the Year of Grace 1919.

Moreover, as has been seen, President Wilson had taken no measures to conciliate or disarm the inveterate and natural aversion of his own countrymen. It was as a Party not as a National leader that he sought to rule the United States and lecture Europe. His native foundations broke beneath him. While his arm was lifted in rebuke of the embarrassed and respectful Governments of the old world he was unceremoniously hauled out of the pulpit by his hefty Party opponents at home. Some of the most gifted Americans whom I have met—'men of light and leading'—as the saying goes, have said 'European politicians ought to have understood the Constitution of the United States. You ought to have known that the President without the Senate could do nothing. You have only yourselves to blame if you have suffered through counting on his personal decisions or undertakings. They had no validity.'

There were from the very beginning serious doubts about the credentials of President Wilson. The supreme efficacy of the League of Nations depended upon the accession of the United States. Here was the great new external balancing factor. Was it at the command of President Wilson? If it were not, no surge of liberal sentiment in the various countries could replace it. It would, on the other hand, have been highly imprudent to canvass his credentials. What would have happened if, for instance, Lloyd George and Clemenceau had said across the table: 'We know we speak for the overwhelming mass of our two countries. Test it any way you will. But is it not true that nothing but your fixed and expiring tenure of office prevents you from being thrown out of power? Your constitutional authority is not complete. Where is the Senate of the United States? We are told that you have lost control both of the Senate and Congress. Are you just a well-meaning philosopher, eager to reform others; or do you carry the faith and will of the American nation?' Probably the Americans would have been deeply offended. They would have replied: 'You were glad enough to have our troops and money on President Wilson's authority. Now that you are out of your troubles you flout the supreme magistrate of the Republic. Whatever Party we belong to, we resent that. It is an insult to suggest that we shall not make good all our undertakings; and in the face of that insult, we will quit the scene.' So no one questioned the President's title. Moreover, in spite of a hundred irritations and anxieties, there was an underlying and true conviction in English and French minds that he was the most forthcoming friend of Europe who up to that moment had crossed the Atlantic.

The composition of the League of Nations Commission was determined by a meeting of the Council of Ten on January 22 and by a Plenary Session of the Peace Conference on January 25. It began its labours on February 2. But meanwhile an acute tension had developed between Great Britain and the Dominions upon the question of the mandatory principle in regard to conquered territory. This principle owed its birth to

General Smuts. Its application has now to be extended to limits the General had not contemplated. The theory that the conquered German colonies, or parts of Turkey, would be held by the victors not as their own property but in trust for all mankind under the League of Nations and with formal international supervision of the treatment of the natives seemed to meet all requirements. It was welcomed by President Wilson on the highest grounds.

But the General had only intended it to apply to ex-Russian, ex-Turkish or ex-Austro-Hungarian territory. He had never thought it suited to the regions conquered in the course of the war by the various British Dominions. Least of all had he expected it to be applied to the case of German South-West Africa, which the Union Government had occupied and intended to annex. This was carrying a sound principle too far. The self-governing Dominions all took the view that the Mandatory principle should not apply to the places they had taken.

The British Government could not be indifferent to territorial gains. The nation looked for some compensation for its awful losses. As the result of long and costly campaigns the British Armies held Palestine, Mesopotamia, the Cameroons and German East Africa. The mandatory system imposed no conditions which had not for many years been strictly observed throughout the British Colonial Empire. Alone among all the Colonial possessions of the Great Powers, the immense tropical domains of the British Crown had been free to the trade of all nations. The ships of all countries used British Colonial ports as freely as their own. There had never been any discrimination in favour of British nationals. As for our treatment of the natives, we had nothing to fear from fair International scrutiny. On the contrary we were proud to explain and expose our system.

Mr. Lloyd George therefore stood forward at once and declared the British acceptance of the mandatory principle unreservedly for all territory which the British fleets and armies had wrested from the Turks or the Germans. We could not however speak for the self-governing Dominions. Australia, New Zealand, South Africa were to us precious entities from which we could not separate ourselves, but which we could not control. Of course, the King was supreme. Cession or annexation of territory like peace or war resided in the Crown. But what Minister, except in the face of unutterable wrong, would invoke this abstract and almost mystic function against a beloved member of the family? Australia had captured New Guinea; New Zealand, Samoa; and the Union, German South-West Africa. They did not mean to give them up. Nor ought they to be pressed to do so. To speak of these places as 'communities shoved hither and thither as pawns in a diplomatic game' is an abuse of language. These territories, sparsely populated by primitive races, had been part of the brand-new outfit of less desirable Colonies which Great Britain had in the nineteenth century willingly seen accorded to the growth of the German power. Every one of them presented to each of these remote Dominions an inroad upon their own Monroe Doctrine; and every one had been found to be a menace and the cause of bloodshed in the recent conflict. They had taken them; they would not give them up. But their title-deeds did not depend on local conquests. They were consecrated by sacrifice in the common cause. These three Dominions, aggregating together less than a twelfth of the white population of the United States, had lost nearly as many lives on the battlefields of Europe—six, eleven or twelve thousand miles from home—in a cause which the United States had made its own. Whatever happened, we could not quarrel with them.

Accordingly, on January 23, Mr. Lloyd George introduced to the Council of Ten the Prime Ministers of Canada, Australia, New Zealand and South Africa. There they stood, armed in the panoply of democracy, of war service, and of young nationhood. Borden with wide Canada—French and English—behind him; Massey of New Zealand, fearless and faultless in all that touched the common cause; Hughes the vibrant Australian Labour Premier; the grand and rugged Botha; the gifted, philosophical, persuasive Smuts. There they stood, and with them stood not only the modern age but the future. These figures and what they represented were not to be lightly put aside. No George the Third England this; no smooth-phrased European diplomatists; no benighted Old World aristocrats! Here were the Pilgrim Fathers, with tongues as plain in speech and lands as vast to till. Wilson was not unmoved by their insignia. This at any rate was not what he had crossed the Atlantic to chastise. But he had his cause to defend; and it was a great one.

A jagged debate ensued. Australia, New Zealand and South Africa said they meant to keep the colonies they had taken from the Germans; and Canada said she stood with them. 'And do you mean, Mr. Hughes,' said the President, 'that in certain circumstances Australia would place herself in opposition to the opinion of the whole civilised world?' Mr. Hughes, who was very deaf, had an instrument like a machine gun emplaced upon the table by which he heard all he wanted; and to this challenge he replied dryly, 'That's about it, Mr. President.' The statesmanship of Borden and of Botha behind the scenes eventually led the Dominion leaders to agree to veil their sovereignty under the name at any rate of Mandate; and this Mr. Wilson was willing to accept.

This discussion had been very gratifying to M. Clemenceau; and for the first time he had heard the feelings of his heart expressed with unbridled candour. He beamed on Mr. Hughes, and punctuated his every sentence with unconcealable delight. 'Bring your savages with you,' he said to Mr. Lloyd George beforehand; and to the Australian, 'Mr. 'Ughes, I have 'eard that in early life you were a cannibal.' 'Believe me, Mr. President,' said the Commonwealth Prime Minister, 'that has been greatly exaggerated.' This day's meeting was an event in the proceedings of the Council of Ten.

The Ten now entered the period—indispensable but undefinable—of Commissions. Here were the crucial questions, here were the real differences; but first let us know the facts. Accordingly Commissions were appointed. At one time or another fifty-eight Commissions were formed to find out all about everything; and to enable the masters of the world—if masters they remained—to decide wisely and justly and tolerably how the maps of the world should be redrawn and how its depleted riches should be apportioned. In this domain the most effective step was probably the creation as an executive department of the Supreme Council of the Supreme Economic Council, to which was later assigned for instance the feeding of Austria and all such matters. Thus was averted in Vienna and elsewhere the final catastrophe of mass deaths from starvation which was otherwise imminent. But besides this vital executive function, Commissions were set up in every sphere to prepare proposals for the Treaty: Commissions upon the Financial Arrangements; upon the Economic Clauses; upon Reparations; upon the punishment of War Criminals and Hanging the Kaiser; upon all the territorial issues, the frontiers of Poland, Roumania, Czecho-Slovakia, Yugo-Slavia; upon the future of Turkey and Arabia; upon Colonies in Africa and Asia and islands in the Pacific Ocean. In all fifty-eight Commissions, great and small, upon objects wise or foolish!

Even at the cost of some anticipation of the narrative it will be convenient to dispose of some of the less serious of these topics at this stage.

* * * * *

We have seen to what extent Mr. Lloyd George had yielded to the newspaper and popular demand that he should use the strongest language about 'Make them pay'; and how he had tried to do this while at the same time safeguarding himself as far as possible by 'ifs' and 'buts.' For instance, in effect, 'They shall pay to the utmost farthing—if they can do so without delaying the economic revival of the world.' Or, 'They shall pay the maximum possible—but what is the maximum possible must be ascertained by financial experts.' When the Election was over and I had asked the Prime Minister how he was going to meet the expectations of the public that all the damage of the war would be paid for by Germany, he had replied: 'It will all have to be settled by an Inter-Allied Commission. We will put on this Commission the ablest men we can find, men not mixed up in politics or electioneering; they will examine the whole matter coolly and scientifically, and they will report to us what is feasible.' Now that the time had come, he chose Mr. Hughes, the Prime Minister of Australia; Lord Cunliffe, the Governor of the Bank of England; and Lord Sumner, one of the ablest judicial authorities and greatest legal intellects at our disposal.

It was to be expected that the Inter-Allied Commission with its powerful American element would reduce the clamour of the election and the claptrap of the popular press to hard matter-of-fact business. But the Commission on Reparations was never able to reach agreement. Lord Cunliffe's Sub-Committee on capacity to pay, which reported in April, cautiously avoided any figure. The Governor had begun apparently to feel some misgivings. At any rate he did not wish to be committed publicly. His Sub-Committee declared that the factors were too fluctuating to render a forecast possible. Enormous figures, however, still continued to rule in authoritative circles. Mr. Lamont, one of the American representatives, has in a published article stated that subject to certain important conditions, he was willing to go as high as a capital sum of seven thousand five hundred millions, that the French asked for ten thousand millions, and that the British would not accept less than twelve thousand. The Prime Minister was not therefore ever to receive that substantial but at the same time reasonable figure, vouched for by the highest authority, of which he stood greatly in need. His various semi-official conversations with the British representatives gave him no comfort. They spoke always in extremely optimistic terms of German capacity to pay; and on no occasion was any lower figure mentioned than £8,000 millions. Invited formally on March 6 to name a figure 'on the assumption that it was to be insisted on even at the point of breaking off the

Peace negotiations,' they promised to report separately by March 17. But of this report there is no record. The oracle was mute; and the embarrassed Prime Minister was left to bear the burden himself with the choice either of infuriating the public by mentioning a low figure for which no authority could be cited or a high figure which his instinct and reason alike convinced him could never be obtained. So no figure of German Reparations was fixed by the Allied and Associated Powers.

Other Commissions laboured upon the economic clauses of the Peace, and whole chapters of the Treaty were filled with provisions—mostly temporary in character—for making sure that the trade of the Allies would be restarted ahead of that of enemy countries. This separate work was never brought into relation with the financial clauses. Thus the draft Treaty imposed upon Germany at one and the same time an unspecified and unlimited liability and every conceivable impediment upon the means of payment. Mr. Keynes, a man of clairvoyant intelligence and no undue patriotic bias, was a member of the staff which Great Britain transported to Paris for the Peace Conference. Saturated in the Treasury knowledge of the real facts, he revolted against the absurd objectives which had been proclaimed, and still more against the execrable methods by which they were to be achieved. In a book[4] which gained a vast publicity, particularly in the United States, he exposed and denounced 'a Carthaginian Peace.' He showed in successive chapters of unanswerable good sense the monstrous character of the financial and economic clauses. On all these matters his opinion is good. Carried away however by his natural indignation at the economic terms which were to be solemnly enacted, he wrapped the whole structure of the Peace Treaties in one common condemnation. His qualifications to speak on the economic aspects were indisputable; but on the other and vastly more important side of the problem he could judge no better than many others. The Keynes view of the Peace of Versailles, justified as it was on the special aspects with which he was acquainted, greatly influenced the judgment of England and America on the whole Settlement. It is however of high importance for those who wish to understand what actually happened, that the economic and general aspects of the Treaty of Versailles should be kept entirely separate.

When Mr. Lloyd George was reproached or rallied in private during the Peace Conference upon the economic and financial clauses he was accustomed to make the following answer: 'It is too soon to expect the peoples who have suffered so much to regain their sanity. What does it matter what is written in the Treaty about German payments? If it cannot be carried out, it will fall to the ground of its own weight. We have to give satisfaction to the view of the multitude who have endured such frightful injuries. We will however insert in the Treaty clauses which provide for the recurrent review of these provisions after a few years have passed. It is no good fretting about it now; we must let them all calm down. All I am trying to do now is to insert the machinery of revision in the text of the Treaty.'

This may not have been heroic, but it is very largely what has come to pass. The main economic clauses of the 'Carthaginian Peace' have either lapsed or have been revised

---

[4] *The Economic Consequences of the Peace.*

under the machinery provided in the Treaty; and in fact, the Dawes Agreement claims no more from Germany than the 2,000/2,500 millions indemnity which the well-instructed British Treasury mentioned as a reasonable figure on the first occasion when their opinion was invited.

* * * * *

Another Commission laboured upon the punishment of War Criminals. Horrible things had been done in the war, and while it raged the fighting fury of millions had been inflamed by the tale. The victors were now in a position to lay down their own view of these events. Certainly in military executions, in organised 'frightfulness' as distinct from spontaneous or uncontrollable brutality in actual fighting, the case was black against the Germans. They had stood throughout the war on conquered soil. The Allies had with difficulty defended their own invaded lands. Germany had held for four years writhing populations in her grip. To British minds the execution of Edith Cavell, and still more of Captain Fryatt, were crimes for which somebody should be held rigorously accountable. But France and Belgium had long and hideous indictments to unfold. A thousand atrocious acts committed by privates, by sergeants, by captains, by the orders of generals, marshalled behind them a cloud of witnesses. There were also dark tales from the sea—not wholly one-sided; but here also was the German submarine campaign— sinking merchant ships at sight; and the *Lusitania* with some munitions but also with its forty babies; and hospital ships with their helpless, nerve-shattered patients and faithful nurses, sinking and choking in the cold sea. This found no counterpart in any of the reprisals, fierce and ferocious as some of them were, which these deeds extorted from seafaring men.

The conduct of the Bulgarians in Serbia excited the extreme indignation of the investigators. As for Turkish atrocities: marching till they dropped dead the greater part of the garrison at Kut; massacring uncounted thousands of helpless Armenians, men, women, and children together, whole districts blotted out in one administrative holocaust—these were beyond human redress.

But a passionate demand arose in Belgium, France and England that certain definite deeds, contrary to such laws of war as men have tried to make and keep, should be brought home to individuals. No one could deny that this held justice. But how was it to be carried out? The submarine lieutenant could plead the orders of his superiors; these he had to obey upon his life. Whether hospital ships should be sunk or not was a matter for governments. A naval lieutenant could only do what he was told. The executions had behind them whatever sanctions the military tribunals of warring nations could give. As for the brutality in the zone of the armies, obscure people could be indicated who had done vile things; but they said they had not; or alternatively, that their officers had told them to do it. The officers said they had not, or would have said so if they could have been found. Or thirdly, that they could match these incidents with others done against themselves which they had seen and in respect of which there was no lack of testimony.

Commissions were appointed to probe these matters. Material was plentiful, but where lay the responsibility? The captain had ordered the platoon to fire the volley.

He had received his orders from the military governor. The military governor had acted under the authority accorded him by his commission. The corps commander could say he obeyed the Army Group, and the Army Group was but the servant of main Headquarters. Above all was the German Government supported by the German People, and at the summit, the Emperor. Led on by logic the commission climbed this ladder. How could they condemn the sergeant or the captain for actions for which the general bore responsibility? How could they condemn the general when the Government and the Parliament had approved, or at least acquiesced? So if anyone was to be punished it must not be the small people, but the big. Thus after months of toilsome argumentation, a list was drawn up which included all the greatest men in Germany; all the Army Commanders; all the most famous Generals; most of the Princes; and above all, the Kaiser. An article of the Peace Treaty obliged the Germans to stigmatise all their greatest men and potentates as War Criminals. The mere inscribing of all these names upon the list was sufficient to bring the whole business to futility.

The one practical measure was to hang the Kaiser, who was the 'All-Highest' and who was constitutionally responsible for everything that his armies had done. Much vitality still remained in the trial of the Kaiser. Mr. Lloyd George persisted and persevered. He was not only committed to this aim; he was ardent for it. The Americans disinterested themselves in the matter; the French mildly scandalised, but at the same time amused, gave a gay assent. The law officers elaborated their processes. However, the Kaiser was outside Allied Jurisdiction. He had been driven out of France; he had fled from Germany; he had found refuge in Holland. A demand for the extradition or surrender of the Kaiser was formally made to Holland. Mr. Lloyd George at the height of his triumph after the signature of the Treaty of Versailles announced to Parliament that the Kaiser was to be tried by an international tribunal in London. What followed might have been foreseen. Field-Marshal von Hindenburg declared that he took full personal responsibility for all the acts done by the German armies from 1916 onwards and offered to deliver himself to judgment. All the Kaiser's sons wrote by the hand of Prince Eitel Fritz, offering themselves collectively as rams taken in the thicket. The fugitive at Doorn saw before him a martyr's crown without much likelihood of the usual physical inconveniences. There can hardly have been a moment in history when martyrdom stood at so high a premium.

But the Dutch are an obstinate people and, more important still, Holland is a small country. Small countries were very much in fashion at the time of the Peace Conference. 'Gallant Little Belgium' was being evacuated, reparated, compensated and congratulated. The war had been fought to make sure that the smallest state should have the power to assert its lawful rights against even the greatest, and this will probably be for several generations an enduring fact. Holland came to the rescue of the Allies—she refused to surrender the Kaiser. Whether or not the subterranean intrigues of old world secret diplomacy may have conveyed to the Dutch Government some assurance that they would not be immediately fallen upon with armed violence by all the victorious nations, will never be ascertained. Mr. Lloyd George was genuinely indignant, but by this time among responsible people in England he was alone. The victorious States therefore submitted to the Dutch refusal, and the Kaiser still dwells in Holland.

* * * * *

We have now disposed of a number of much-talked-of issues which beset the Peace Conference. None of them, excepting the League of Nations and the disposal of German colonies, touched essentials, and the rest dispersed themselves in a comparatively short time. Many people will be quite surprised to remember how strongly they once felt about them. The idealism of America has now definitely made its contact with the wickedness of Britain and of Europe. Absurd ideas about what the Germans should pay are being embodied in clauses which will never be put into execution and which indeed are safeguarded by other clauses from ever being put into execution. The War Criminals have found shelter under the shields of the most renowned warriors of Germany, and the Dutch will not give up the Kaiser for Lloyd George to hang. Having thus cleared the ground of many encumbrances and trivialities, we are free to approach the central problems of race and territory, of the balance of power in Europe and of the foundations of a world state. These dominate the future, and there is no cottage or hut in which a white, brown, red, black or yellow family is now dwelling which may not some day find itself directly and quite unpleasantly affected by them.

Meanwhile, temper was rising in all the countries. The British public demanded to know when peace was going to be signed and how soon Germany would be made to pay and what had happened about the Kaiser. The Republican Party in America spoke in scornful terms of the President's scheme for world improvement, and stridently called for the return of the American troops and the collection of the American debts. The Italians clamoured for a settlement of their territorial and colonial requirements; and France was boiling with rage and anxiety about her future security. Behind all, the defeated nations waited paralysed with anxiety and incertitude to learn their fate.

It had been hoped that the acceptance by the British Dominions of the mandatory principle, and the agreement reached with President Wilson on this issue, would clear the way for practical decisions about frontiers and jurisdictions. But he remained determined that the drawing-up and adoption of the Covenant of the League of Nations should precede all territorial settlements. The Council of Ten was spurred to action by the fears and growing impatience of the countries they represented; and in the earliest days of February there occurred the first crisis of the Peace Conference. Mr. Lloyd George, voicing the opinion of all, demanded that practical issues should no longer be shelved. How was it possible to frame this new world instrument while everyone was waiting for the answers to urgent questions? An immense task lay before them. It was their duty to make peace. They had gathered together for that. They would fail in their duty if they did not give it speedily to the world. It was known that the President had to return to the United States on February 14 in order to discharge certain imperative constitutional duties. How was it possible to decide the Covenant of the League before then? The President however declared to an audience at once incredulous and relieved that all should be settled by that date. This was in fact accomplished. The Commission was driven forward at break-neck speed; and by an extraordinary effort, in which the British Delegation staff played a decisive part, the draft Covenant of the League was actually finished and presented in full Conference on February 14. Three months had now passed since the firing stopped, and so far no agreement had been reached on any one of the definite and all-important issues upon which the immediate peace and recovery of Europe depended. In many regions the power of the victors to enforce their decisions had obviously diminished. A heavy price in blood and privations was in the end to be paid by helpless and distracted peoples for the long delay. But here at last was a majestic constitution to which all the Allied States had given provisional but earnest assent.

Many minds had made their contribution to the Covenant of the League. Phillimore, Robert Cecil, Smuts and Hurst are names which for ever link the British Empire with its institution. Some errors and imperfections arose inevitably from the haste and pressure under which the Covenant was prepared. Nevertheless the base of the new building was set upon the living rock; and the mighty foundation stone, shaped by the innumerable chisellings of merciful men the world over and swung into position by loyal and dexterous English pulleys, will bear for all time the legend: 'Well and truly laid by Woodrow Wilson, President of the United States of America.' Who can doubt that upon and around this granite block will ultimately be built a dwelling-place and palace to which 'all the men in all the lands' will sooner or later resort in sure trust?

CHAPTER IX
THE UNFINISHED TASK

'Bolshevism threatened to impose by force of arms its domination on those populations that had revolted against it, and that were organised at our request. If we, as soon as they had served our purpose and as soon as they had taken all the risks, had said, "Thank you, we are exceedingly obliged to you, you have served our purpose. We need you no longer. Now let the Bolsheviks cut your throats," we should have been mean—we should have been thoroughly unworthy ....'

[Lloyd George, *Speech House of Commons*, April 16, 1919.]

'If Russia is to be saved, as I pray she may be saved, she must be saved by Russians. It must be by Russian manhood and Russian courage and Russian virtue that the rescue and regeneration of this once mighty nation and famous branch of the European family can alone be achieved. The aid which we can give to these Russian Armies—who we do not forget were called into the field originally during the German war to some extent by our inspiration and who are now engaged in fighting against the foul baboonery of Bolshevism—can be given by arms, munitions, equipment, and technical services raised upon a voluntary basis. But Russia must be saved by Russian exertions, and it must be from the heart of the Russian people and with their strong arm that the conflict against Bolshevism in Russia must be mainly waged.'

[Churchill, *Speech Mansion House*, Feb. 19, 1919.]

Commitments at the Armistice—Lord Balfour's Memorandum of November 29—British and French Spheres of Interference—The French at Odessa—At the War Office—Prinkipo—The Conference in Paris—My Proposals—Correspondence with the Prime Minister—The Bullitt Mission—The Situation Worsens—Kolchak—Advance of the Siberian Army—The Big Five Question Kolchak—Note to Kolchak—His Reply—Decision of the Great Powers to Support Him—Too Late.

President Wilson's departure and the interlude which followed at Paris afford the opportunity for placing the reader once more in contact with the gaunt realities which prowled outside.

The Armistice and the collapse of Germany had altered all Russian values and relations. The Allies had only entered Russia with reluctance and as an operation of war.

But the war was over. They had made exertions to deny to the German armies the vast supplies of Russia: but these armies existed no more. They had set out to rescue the Czechs; but the Czechs had already saved themselves. Therefore every argument which had led to intervention had disappeared.

On the other hand, all the Allies were involved physically and morally in many parts of Russia. The British commitments were in some ways the most serious. Twelve thousand British and eleven thousand Allied troops were actually ice-bound in North Russia at Murmansk and Archangel. Whatever was decided, they must stay there until the spring. Naturally the position of such detachments against whom the Bolshevisks might concentrate very large forces was not free from anxiety. Colonel John Ward, M.P., and the two British battalions, together with some sailors from the cruiser *Suffolk*, were in the heart of Siberia playing a remarkable part by arms and counsel in sustaining the Omsk Government. The new Siberian army was being rapidly created. It had received from British sources alone 100,000 rifles and 200 guns. It was largely dressed in British uniforms. Training schools under British management had been established at Vladivostok, and were in process of turning out 3,000 Russian officers of indifferent quality. In the South, Denikin, who had succeeded to the command when Alexeiev died, had been encouraged to expect the help of the Allies at the earliest possible moment. With the opening of the Dardanelles and the entry of the British Fleet into the Black Sea, it had become possible to send a British military commission to Novorossisk. On the reports of this commission the War Cabinet decided on November 14, 1918, to assist Denikin with arms and munitions; to send additional officers and military equipment to Siberia and to grant *de facto* recognition to the Omsk Government.

Lord Balfour, the Foreign Secretary, in a Memorandum of November 29 set forth to the Cabinet the policy which should be pursued.

'This country,' he wrote, 'would certainly refuse to see its forces, after more than four years of strenuous fighting, dissipated over the huge expanse of Russia in order to carry out political reforms in a State which is no longer a belligerent Ally.

'We have constantly asserted that it is for the Russians to choose their own form of government, that we have no desire to intervene in their domestic affairs, and that if, in the course of operations essentially directed against the Central Powers we have to act with such Russian political and military organisations as are favourable to the *Entente*, this does not imply that we deem ourselves to have any mission to establish or disestablish any particular political system among the Russian people.

'To these views His Majesty's Government still adhere, and their military policy in Russia is still governed by them. But it does not follow that we can disinterest ourselves wholly from Russian affairs. Recent events have created obligations which last beyond the occasions which gave them birth. The Czechoslovaks are our Allies and we must do what we can to help them. In the South-east corner of Russia, in Europe, in Siberia, in Transcaucasia and Transcaspia, in the territories adjacent to the White Sea and the Arctic Ocean, new anti-Bolshevik administrations have grown up under the shelter of Allied forces. We are responsible for their existence and must endeavour to support them. How far we can do this, and how such a policy will ultimately develop, we cannot yet say. It must largely depend upon the course taken by the associated Powers who have far larger resources at their disposal than ourselves. For us no alternative is open at present than to use such troops as we possess to the best advantage; where we have no troops to supply arms and money; and in the case of the Baltic provinces, to protect as far as we can the nascent nationalities by the help of our Fleet. Such a policy must necessarily seem halting and imperfect to those who on the spot are resisting the invasion of militant Bolshevism, but it is all that we can accomplish or ought in existing circumstances to attempt.'

On November 30 our representatives at Archangel and Vladivostok were informed that the general lines of policy towards Russia which the Government proposed to follow were:

'To remain in occupation at Murmansk and Archangel for the time being; to continue the Siberian Expedition; to try to persuade the Czechs to remain in Western Siberia; to occupy [with five British brigades] the Baku-Batum railway; to give General Denikin at Novorossisk all possible help in the way of military material; to supply the Baltic States with military material.'

This was a far-reaching programme. It not only comprised existing commitments, but added to them large new enterprises in the Caucasus and in South Russia. Of these some account must be given.

A year before, on December 23, 1917, an Anglo-French Convention had been agreed at Paris between Clemenceau, Pichon and Foch on the one hand, and Lord Milner, Lord Robert Cecil, and British military representatives on the other, regulating the future action of France and Britain in southern Russia. This Convention contemplated the support of General Alexeiev, then at Novo Tcherkask, and divided geographically the spheres of action of the two Powers so far as they might be able to act at all. French action would develop to the north of the Black Sea 'against the enemy,' i.e. Germany, and hostile Russians; that of England to the east of the Black Sea against the Turks. It followed from this, as set out in Article 3, that the French zone would consist of Bessarabia, the Ukraine, and the Crimea; and the English zone, of the Cossack territories, the Caucasus, Armenia, Georgia, and Kurdistan. The War Cabinet on November 13, 1918, reaffirmed their adherence to these limitations.

In consequence the British landed at Batum and rapidly occupied the Caucasian railway from the Black Sea to the Caspian at Baku. Here our troops found a friendly and on the whole a welcoming, though agitated population. They settled down along the 400-miles' stretch of railway and acted as 'big brothers' to the inhabitants and their various fluctuating governments, and developed a flotilla which soon secured the effective command of the Caspian Sea. This sea is larger than the British Isles. The British forces, about 20,000 strong, were by the end of January, 1919, in possession of one of the greatest strategic lines in the world, and both flanks rested securely on superior naval power on the two inland seas. What the British Government was going to do with it was never clearly thought out. Behind this shield the peoples of Georgia, of Armenia, and of Azerbaijan were to be free to develop their independent existence; and incursions by the Bolsheviks, whether into Turkey (at that time entirely submissive), or Kurdistan, or Persia, were prevented. There was never any fighting and no lives were lost; but it was with the greatest difficulty, on account of our diminishing forces, that this protecting line was maintained intact for about a year.

Disastrous fortunes attended the French incursion into their assigned sphere. A condition of the Armistice had prescribed the immediate evacuation by the Germans of the Ukraine. This seemed reasonable enough to those whose minds were inflamed by the conflict with the Central Powers, and the Germans themselves had no wish but to comply and go home. In fact, however, it withdrew from South Russia the only strong, sane, effective element by which the daily life of twenty or thirty million people was maintained. As the once-hated and dreaded 'steelhelmets' swiftly evacuated the towns and cities of South Russia, the Red Guards followed apace, and rousing the dregs of the population against the bourgeoisie and against all who had been friendly either to the German invader, or to the cause of the Allies, celebrated their assumption of power by horrible massacres and prolonged, insatiate proscriptions.

While these lamentable events were in progress, the French on December 20 landed with about two divisions, supported by a powerful fleet, at Odessa. Their strength was swelled by two Greek divisions furnished by Venizelos, at the request of the Supreme Council of the Allies. Thereupon occurred the first real collision between the victors and the Bolsheviks. It was not decided by the ordinary implements of war. The foreign occupation offended the inhabitants: the Bolsheviks profited by their discontents. Their propaganda, incongruously patriotic and Communist, spread far and wide through the Ukraine. On February 6, 1919, they reoccupied Kiev, and the population of the surrounding districts rose against the foreigners and the capitalists. The French troops were themselves affected by the Communist propaganda, and practically the whole of the fleet mutinied. Why should they fight now that the war was over? Why should they interfere in Russian affairs? Why should they not go home? Why should they not indeed assist those Russian movements which sought to level all national authority and establish the universal régime of soldiers, sailors, and workmen? The well-tempered weapon which had served with scarcely a failure in all the clashes of Armageddon now broke surprisingly in the hands which turned it to a new task. The mutiny in the French fleet was suppressed, and its ringleaders were long in prison; but a shock was sustained in Paris which promptly terminated the whole adventure. On April 6 the French evacuated Odessa, and the Greek divisions, which had been unmoved by these occurrences, were simultaneously withdrawn to their own country. Hard on their heels the Bolsheviks entered the city and inaugurated a second fierce revenge.

This brief recital of the salient episodes is necessarily incomplete. The same kind of ebullitions and confusions were repeated with varying features wherever Bolshevik and anti-Bolshevik forces were in the field. A welter of murder and anarchy, of pillage and repression, of counter-revolt and reprisal, of treachery and butchery, of feeble meddling and bloody deeds, extended in a broad belt from the White Sea to the Black. In all this zone no one knew what to do or whom to follow. No organisation seemed proof against the universal decomposition, and cruelty and fear reigned in chaos over a hundred million people.

Marshal Foch had on January 12 brought the Russian-Polish situation before the Supreme War Council. He proposed to add to the Armistice terms, then requiring to be renewed, a condition that the Dantzig-Thorn railroad should be put in good order by the Germans, and should, together with the port of Dantzig, be available for the movement of Allied troops. He contemplated forming a considerable army principally of American troops, together with Polish forces and well-disposed Russian prisoners of war, for the protection of Poland and operations against the Bolsheviks. The Americans had however no intention of being used for such a purpose however desirable. It was certain that no British troops would be available. The Marshal therefore fell back on minor expedients, and the statesmen took refuge in platitude.

* * * * *

I entered the War Office as Secretary of State on January 14, 1919, and became an heir to the pledges and tragedies of this situation as well as to those domestic difficulties recounted in a previous chapter. Up to this moment I had taken no part of any kind in Russian affairs, nor had I been responsible for any commitment. I found myself in the closest agreement on almost every point with Sir Henry Wilson, the Chief of the Imperial General Staff, and the policy which we advised and, so far as we had the power, pursued to the end, had at any rate the merit of simplicity. Our armies were melting fast. The British people would not supply the men or the money for any large military establishment elsewhere than on the Rhine. It was highly questionable whether any troops raised under compulsion for the war against Germany would consent to fight anybody else in any circumstances, or even to remain long in occupation of conquered territory. We therefore sang one tune in harmony: contract your commitments; select your obligations; and make a success of those to which you are able to adhere.

We then urged the following measures: first, to wind up the Batum-Baku adventure in the Caucasus and bring our substantial forces out of danger and responsibility without delay: secondly, to make a peace with Turkey that would show her that England was her friend: thirdly, to discharge our pledges faithfully and fully by arming and equipping the anti-Bolshevik forces from our own immense surplus of munitions, and help them with expert officers and instructors to train efficient armies of their own. Naturally it followed that we should try to combine all the border States hostile to the Bolsheviks into one system of war and diplomacy and get everyone else to do as much as possible. Such was the policy we consistently pursued—and such were its limitations.

But an alternative policy of which there were powerful advocates competed and clashed with these simple conceptions. The British Government had enquired as early as December, 1918, of its allies and associates whether some sort of peace proposals could not profitably be made to Russia.[1] Although this scheme was frowned upon by the French, and its rumour caused an outcry in England, Mr. Lloyd George,[2] raised the question again on January 16, 1919, and suggested that representatives of Moscow and of the various generals and states with which Moscow was at war should be summoned to Paris 'in the way that the Roman Empire summoned generals of out-lying tributary states to render an account of their actions.'

President Wilson adopted Mr. Lloyd George's suggestion, and on January 21, 1919, it was decided that the United States should draft the invitations. But the *rendezvous* was changed. Instead of Paris, the island of Prinkipo in the Sea of Marmora was chosen. Very near to Prinkipo lay another island to which the Young Turks before the war had exiled all the *pariah* dogs which had formerly infested the streets of Constantinople. These dogs, shipped there in tens of thousands, were left to devour one another and ultimately to starve. I saw them with my own eyes, gathered in troops upon the rocky shores, when I visited Turkey in 1909 in a friend's yacht. The bones of these dogs still whitened the inhospitable island, and their memory noisomely pervaded the neighbourhood. To Bolshevik sympathisers the place seemed oddly chosen for a Peace Conference. To their opponents it seemed not altogether unsuitable.

The invitation was accepted by the Bolsheviks in ambiguous terms on February 4. The white Governments of Siberia and Archangel, as well as Nabokov, Sazonov and other representatives of the anti-Bolshevik groups, refused it with contempt. The whole idea of entering into negotiations with the Bolsheviks was abhorrent to the dominant elements of public opinion, both in Great Britain and in France.

It was at this stage that I was for the first time involved in the Paris discussions about Russia. Having directly on my hands the Archangel, Kolchak and Denikin military commitments, I had repeatedly pressed the Prime Minister for a definite policy. In long anxious conversations he showed his customary patience and kindness in dealing with the anxieties of a colleague. He finally suggested that I should go to Paris and see what could be done within the scope of our limited action.

Accordingly on February 14, I crossed the Channel on this mission, and sat in the seats of the Mighty. Then I saw the scene which has been so often described of the Peace Conference at work: Clemenceau presiding, grim, rugged, snow-white, with black skull-cap; opposite him Marshal Foch, very formal, very subdued, grave, illustrious, lovable. On either hand, in sumptuous chairs, sat the representatives of the victorious Powers. Around Gobelin tapestries, mirrors, gilding and glittering lights! This was the only occasion when I had any official contact with President Wilson, and I shall recount what occurred.

---

[1] *The Foreign Relations of Soviet Russia*, by A. L. P. Dennis.
[2] *The Foreign Relations of Soviet Russia*, by A. L. P. Dennis, p. 76.

The Conference had sat long that day, and it was past seven o'clock when the Russian item on the agenda was reached. It was the very night that President Wilson was leaving on his first return journey to the United States. He had only a short time to get his dinner and catch his train to Cherbourg. He had actually risen from his place to leave the Conference, and there could not have been a less propitious moment for raising an extra, disagreeable and baffling topic. However, with the persistence born of my direct responsibilities upon the various Russian fronts, and with all sorts of cruel realities, then proceeding, present in my mind, I stood up and made my appeal. 'Could we not have some decision about Russia? Fighting was actually going on. Men were being killed and wounded. What was the policy? Was it peace or was it war? Were we to stop or were we to go on? Was the President going away to America leaving this question quite unanswered? What was to happen while he was away? Was nothing to go on except aimless unorganised bloodshed till he came back? Surely there should be an answer given.'

The President, contrary to my expectation, was affable. He turned back to the table and, resting his elbow on Clemenceau's chair, listened without sitting down to what I had to say. Then he replied frankly and simply to the following effect: 'Russia was a problem to which he did not pretend to know the solution. There were the gravest objections to every course, and yet some course must be taken—sooner or later. He was anxious to clear out of Russia altogether, but was willing, if necessary, to meet the Bolsheviks alone (i.e. without the National Russians) at Prinkipo. Nevertheless, if Prinkipo came to nothing, he would do his share with the other Allies in any military measures which they considered necessary and practicable to help the Russian armies now in the field.' Then he left us.

It seemed to me obvious that whatever the Russian policy of the Allies might be or by whatever measures it might be executed, some central body should be set up to study and concert it. To the fifty-eight commissions there might at least be added a fifty-ninth for Russia.

Next day, at a special meeting at the Quai d'Orsay on the Russian situation, I proposed, with Mr. Balfour's approval, the setting up of an Allied Council for Russian Affairs with political, economic and military sections, and with executive power within the limits of the policy defined for it by the Allied Governments; and that the military inquiry into what resources were available and how they could best be co-ordinated should proceed forthwith.

I reported the course of the discussion to the Prime Minister and added:

'If Prinkipo fell through, the Supreme War Council could be presented immediately with a complete military plan and an expression of opinion from the highest military authorities as to whether within the limits of our available resources there is a reasonable prospect of success. The Supreme War Council would then be in a position to take a definite decision whether to clear out altogether or to adopt the plan.'

The following were the actual proposals:

Draft Wireless Message

Feb. 15, 1919.

The Princes Island proposal of the Allied Powers has now been made public for more than a month. The Bolsheviks have replied by wireless on the 6th instant offering to meet the wishes of the Allied Powers as regards the repayment of loans, the grant of concessions for mineral and forest rights, and to examine the rights of eventual annexation of Russian territories by the Entente Powers.

The Allies repudiate the suggestion that such objects have influenced their intervention in Russia. The supreme desire of the Allies is to see peace restored in Russia and the establishment of a Government based upon the will of the broad mass of the Russian people.

It is solely with this object that the Princes Island proposal has been made. It is not essential to that proposal that any conference should be held or that representatives of the various Russian forces in the field should meet around a common table. But what is imperative is that fighting should stop, and stop forthwith. The Bolshevik Government while verbally accepting the invitation to Princes Island have, so far from observing a truce of arms, taken the offensive in many directions and are at the present time attacking on several fronts. In addition they have called up new classes and expedited and expanded their military preparations.

It is therefore necessary to fix a precise time within which the Princes Island proposal must be disposed of. Unless within 10 days from the 15th instant the Bolshevik forces on all fronts have ceased to attack and have withdrawn a distance of not less than 5 miles from the present position of their adversaries' outpost lines, the Princes Island proposal will be deemed to have lapsed. If, however, within 5 days a wireless notification is received from the Bolshevik Government that they have so ceased attacking, so ceased firing and so withdrawn, and if this is confirmed by the reports received from the various fronts, a similar request will be addressed by the Allies to the forces confronting them.

It is in these circumstances only that a discussion at Princes Island can take place.

Proposal for a Committee of the Associated Powers to Examine the Possibilities of Allied Military Intervention in Russia.

In anticipation of the Soviet Government refusing to accept the allied terms and continuing hostilities, it is suggested that suitable machinery should be set up forthwith to consider the practical possibilities of joint military action by the Associated Powers acting in conjunction with the independent border States and pro-Ally Governments in Russia.

The machinery in question might take the form of a Commission comprising military representatives of the American, British, French, Italian and Japanese

Governments. This Commission would make it its business, among other things, to examine competent representatives of Russia, Finland, Esthonia, Poland and the other border States, in order to form an estimate of the actual military assistance which these States and Governments are in a position to supply, and to prepare a plan for the utilisation of the joint resources.

It is considered that the existing organisation at Versailles, with certain necessary additions, would be suitable for the purpose, but in this case it should be understood that the military representatives would be acting as the mouthpieces of the Chiefs of the Staff of their respective nationalities.

The Committee should endeavour to furnish their report within 10 days, or whatever time limit is set in the ultimatum that it is now proposed to send to the belligerent Governments in Russia.

Mr. Lloyd George's view is well set forth in the following telegram:

Prime Minister to Mr. Philip Kerr.

February 16, 1919.

See Churchill and tell him I like the cable which it is proposed to send Bolsheviks. As to alternative programme. I trust he will not commit us to any costly operations which would involve any large contribution either of men or money. The form of his cable to me looks rather too much like this. I had understood from his conversation with me that all he had in mind was to send expert details who volunteer to go to Russia together with any equipment we can spare. I also understand our volunteer army has not to be drawn upon for that purpose and that effort made to secure volunteers would not be on such a scale as to arouse vehement opposition in this country involving us in heavy expenditure and interfere with growth of our own volunteer army.

All these things ought to be made clear to all the other Powers before an agreement is arrived at otherwise they might either depend too much on us or subsequently upbraid us with having failed in our promises. The main idea ought to be to enable Russia to save herself if she desires to do so; and if she does not take advantage of opportunity, then it means either that she does not wish to be saved from Bolshevism or that she is past saving. There is only one justification for interfering in Russia—that Russia wants it. If she does, then Kolchak, Krasnov and Denikin ought to be able to raise much larger force than Bolsheviks. This force we could equip, and a well-equipped force of willing men would soon overthrow Bolshevik army of unwilling conscripts especially if whole population is against them.

If, on the other hand, Russia is not behind Krasnov and his coadjutors, it is an outrage on every British principle of freedom that we should use foreign armies to force upon Russia a Government which is repugnant to its people.

I replied that in accordance with his views the limited character of our assistance would be clearly stated. It was not however possible to obtain any measure of agreement between the Powers. Perhaps if President Wilson and Mr. Lloyd George had both been present, some conclusion either in one sense or the other might have been reached.

Mr. Churchill to the Prime Minister.

This afternoon I proposed the formation of a military commission to enquire into what measures were possible to sustain the Russian armies we had called into being during the war with Germany and to protect the independence of the border States.

Fears were expressed that even setting up a commission to enquire into the military situation might leak out and cause alarm.

Mr. Balfour therefore proposed that no formal commission should be set up, but that the military authorities might be allowed informally to talk together and, instead of presenting a report to the Conference as a whole, might individually hand to their respective representatives on the Conference a copy of the results of their informal and unofficial conversations.

After Clemenceau had commented on the strange spectacle of the victorious nations in this great struggle being afraid even to remit to the study of their military advisers at Versailles a matter admittedly of vital importance to Europe, this project was agreed to.

You are therefore committed at some date in the near future to receiving an informal document embodying certain military opinions bearing upon Russia. You are committed to nothing else....

In the circumstances it was useless for me to remain in Paris, and I therefore returned to London on the 18th. I am sure the procedure I proposed was reasonable and practical. The one chance of success and safety for the National Russians lay in the united countenance of the Allies, and the proper concerting of any action they could take. The Allies had not much to give them, but they might at least have given it in a manner likely to be useful.

* * * * *

Both the Prinkipo proposals and the study of the military and diplomatic possibilities having been reduced to nullity, the Americans with the assent of Mr. Lloyd George sent a certain Mr. Bullitt to Russia on February 22. He returned to Paris in a week or two with proposals for an accommodation from the Soviet Government in his pocket. The moment was unpropitious. Kolchak's armies had just gained notable successes in Siberia, and Bela Kun had raised his Communist rebellion in Hungary. French and British indignation against truckling to the Bolsheviks was at its height. The Soviet proposals to Mr. Bullitt, which were of course in themselves fraudulent, were treated with general disdain; and Bullitt himself was not without some difficulty disowned by those who had sent him.

Thus again we reached the void.

The Prime Minister, nettled by repeated War Office requests for decisions of policy, retorted by demanding exact estimates of the cost in money of the various alternatives open.

Mr. Churchill to the Prime Minister.

Feb. 27, 1919.

I send you herewith a statement of British assistance given to Russia, which, as you will see, is considerable. The criticism that may be passed is that it is related to no concerted policy, and that while it constitutes a serious drain on our resources it is not backed with sufficient vigour to lead to any definite result. There is no 'will to win' behind any of these ventures. At every point we fall short of what is necessary to obtain real success. The lack of any 'will to win' communicates itself to our troops and affects their morale: it communicates itself to our Russian allies and retards their organisation, and to our enemies and encourages their efforts.

With regard to your complaint that the War Office have not furnished you with information, I must point out to you that the War Cabinet have long been accustomed to deal direct with the Chief of the Staff and other military authorities, and they know as well as I do the difficulties of obtaining precise plans and estimates of cost from military men in regard to this Russian problem. The reason is that all the factors are uncertain and that the military considerations are at every point intermingled with political decisions which have not been given. For instance, to begin with what is fundamental, the Allied Powers in Paris have not decided whether they wish to make war upon the Bolsheviks or to make peace with them. They are pausing midway between these two courses with an equal dislike of either....

And a fortnight later:

Mr. Churchill to the Prime Minister.

March 14, 1919.

The four months which have passed since the Armistice was signed have been disastrous almost without relief for the anti-Bolshevik forces. This is not due to any great increase in Bolshevik strength, though there has been a certain augmentation. It is due to the lack of any policy on the part of the Allies, or of any genuine or effective support put into the operations which are going on against the Bolsheviks at different points in Russia.

Prinkipo has played its part in the general discouragement and relaxation which has set in. The fact that the German troops were commanded to withdraw from the Ukraine without any provision being made to stop the Bolshevik advance, has enabled large portions of this rich territory full of new supplies of food to be overrun, and the Bolsheviks are now very near the Black Sea at Kherson. There are many signs of weakness in Kolchak's forces, and, as you have observed, many Bolshevik manifestations are taking place behind the Siberian front, in one of which the Japanese have had quite severe fighting.

* * * * *

It will be convenient at this stage somewhat to anticipate the fortunes of Admiral Kolchak and the march of events in Siberia.

Kolchak, a vigorous man in the early forties, was in many ways the naval counterpart of Kornilov. On the outbreak of the revolution, after a mutiny of his fleet in which he had proved his personal courage and physical strength, he had been advised by the Provisional Government to take refuge in Japan, for they would probably have need of him at a later stage. On their fall he had entered Siberia from the East and had for some months been serving in the curious rôle of Minister of Marine in the Omsk Government, which was at no point less than 1,000 miles from the sea. Kolchak was honest, loyal and incorruptible. His outlook and temperament were autocratic; but he tried hard to be liberal and progressive in accordance with what he was assured was the spirit of the times. He had no political experience, and was devoid of those profound intuitions which have enabled men of equal virtue and character to steer their way through the shoals and storms of revolution. He was an intelligent, honourable, patriotic admiral. He took no part in the movement or conspiracy which overthrew the civil power; but when the necessities of the time and the general demand of those with whom he was in contact thrust upon him the responsibilities of dictatorship, he accepted the duty. He proclaimed himself 'Supreme Ruler' and Commander-in-Chief for Siberia, the Cossack territories, and Orenburg. He stated that his chief aims were "the revival of the fighting power of the army, the triumph over Bolshevism, and the restoration of law and order so that the Russian people may without hindrance select its own form of government." There is no doubt that this programme met the needs of the moment. In practice, any vigorous policy involved the total exclusion of the anti-Bolshevik Socialists from the Siberian government. These auxiliaries, hampering in council, feeble to help but powerful to embarrass, became henceforth definite opponents. On the other hand, the principal trading and industrial circles, the co-operative societies, the municipal institutions, and above all the indispensable military power, rallied at once and increasingly in Kolchak's support. The mass remained sunk in Russian apathy and fatalism. He was the best man available; his programme was the right programme; but he possessed neither the authority of the Imperial autocracy nor of the Revolution. He was destined to fail in investing with fighting strength those intermediate conceptions which are the commonplaces of civilised society.

Under his direction General Gaida, now commanding the Siberian army, numbering about 100,000 men, for the time being advanced rapidly, reforming the whole front from which the Czechs had been withdrawn. By the end of January they had reconquered a belt of territory 150 miles wide. On March 1, encouraged by these successes, they resumed the offensive, with the object of gaining in the centre and south the line of the Volga, and in the north of joining hands through Viatka and Kotlas with the Russian and inter-allied forces at Archangel. An advance on a front of 700 miles with only 100,000 men could not succeed if any serious resistance was encountered. Nevertheless, by the 1st of May the Siberians had further advanced on their enormous front to a depth of 125 miles in the north and 250 miles in the centre. In the south also they had achieved appreciable successes. Meanwhile, in the Black Sea region, the Russian volunteer army under Denikin, now joined to Krasnov's 100,000 Cossacks, had become a considerable military factor, less imposing but more solid than the Siberian forces. In this theatre there was much more real fighting, and actual trials of strength took place from time to time between the combatants.

Such was the position on which the Supreme Council of the Allies in the end of May, 1919, came at last to take its decision.

Clemenceau, Lloyd George, President Wilson, Orlando, and the Japanese delegate, Saionji, set forth their views on May 26 in a note addressed to Admiral Kolchak. This document is so important that it must be printed textually.

Note From the Supreme Council to Admiral Kolchak, May 26th, 1919.

The Allied and Associated Powers feel that the time has come when it is necessary for them once more to make clear the policy they propose to pursue in regard to Russia.

It has always been a cardinal axiom of the Allied and Associated Powers to avoid interference in the internal affairs of Russia. Their original intervention was made for the sole purpose of assisting those elements in Russia which wanted to continue the struggle against German autocracy and to free their country from German rule, and in order to rescue the Czechoslovaks from the danger of annihilation at the hands of the Bolshevist forces.

Since the signature of the Armistice on November 11th, 1918, they have kept forces in various parts of Russia. Munitions and supplies have been sent those associated with them at a very considerable cost. No sooner however did the peace conference assemble than they endeavoured to bring peace and order to Russia by inviting representatives of all the warring governments within Russia to meet them in the hope that they might be able to arrange a permanent solution of the Russian problem.

This proposal and the later offer to relieve the suffering millions of Russia, broke down through the refusal of the Soviet government to accept the fundamental condition of suspending hostilities while negotiations for the work of relief were proceeding.

Some of the Allied and Associated Governments are now being pressed to withdraw their troops and to incur no further expense in Russia on the ground that continued intervention shows no prospect of producing an early settlement. They are prepared, however, to continue their assistance on the lines laid down below, provided they are satisfied that it will really help the Russian people to liberty, self-government, and peace.

The Allied and Associated Governments now wish to declare formally that the object of their policy is to restore peace within Russia by enabling the Russian people to resume control of their own affairs through the instrumentality of a freely elected constituent assembly, and to restore peace along its frontiers by arranging for the settlement of disputes in regard to the boundaries of the Russian State and its relations with its neighbours through the peaceful arbitration of the League of Nations.

They are convinced by their experience of the last twelve months that it is not possible to attain these ends by dealing with the Soviet Government of Moscow. They are therefore disposed to assist the government of Admiral Kolchak and his associates with munitions, supplies, and food to establish themselves as the government of all Russia, provided they receive from them definite guarantees that their policy has the same object in view as the Allied and Associated Powers.

With this object they would ask Admiral Kolchak and his associates whether they would agree to the following as the conditions under which they would accept continued assistance from the Allied and Associated Powers.

In the first place as soon as they reach Moscow that they will summon a constituent assembly elected by a free, secret, and democratic franchise, as the supreme legislature for Russia, to which the government of Russia must be responsible, or, if at that time order is not sufficiently restored, they will summon the Constituent Assembly, elected in 1917, to sit until such time as new elections are possible.

Secondly—that throughout the areas which they at present control they will permit free elections in the normal course for all free and legally constituted assemblies, such as municipalities, Zemstvos, etc.

Thirdly—that they will countenance no attempt to revive the special privilege of any class or order in Russia. The Allied and Associated Powers have noted with satisfaction the solemn declaration made by Admiral Kolchak and his associates, that they have no intention of restoring the former land system. They feel that the principles to be followed in the solution of this and other internal questions must be left to free decision of the Russian Constituent Assembly. But they wish to be assured that those whom they are prepared to assist stand for the civil and religious liberty of all Russian citizens and will make no attempt to re-introduce the régime which the revolution has destroyed.

Fourthly—that the independence of Finland and Poland be recognised, and that in the event of the frontiers and other relations between Russia and these countries not being settled by agreement, they will be referred to the arbitration of the League of Nations.

Fifthly—that if a solution of the relations between Esthonia, Latvia, Lithuania, and the Caucasian and Trans-Caspian territories and Russia is not speedily reached by agreement, the settlement will be made in consultation and co-operation with the League of Nations, and that until such settlement is made, the government of Russia agrees to recognize these territories as autonomous and to confirm the relations which may exist between their *de facto* Governments and the Allied and Associated Governments.

Sixthly—that the right of the Peace Conference to determine the future of the Roumanian part of Bessarabia be recognised.

Seventhly—that as soon as a government for Russia has been constituted on a democratic basis, Russia should join the League of Nations and co-operate with other members in the limitation of armaments and military organisation throughout the world.

Finally—that they abide by the declaration made by Admiral Kolchak on November 27th, 1918, in regard to Russia's national debt.

The Allied and Associated Powers will be glad to learn as soon as possible whether the government of Admiral Kolchak and his associates is prepared to accept these conditions, and also whether in the event of acceptance they will undertake to form a single government and army command as soon as the military situation makes it possible.

G. CLEMENCEAU.

LLOYD GEORGE.

ORLANDO.

WOODROW WILSON.

SAIONJI.

Naturally Kolchak did not delay his reply. 'I should not retain power one day longer than required by the interests of the country; my first thought at the moment when the Bolsheviks are definitely crushed will be to fix the date of the election of the Constituent Assembly.... I shall hand over to it all my power in order that it may freely determine the system of government; I have, moreover, taken the oath to do this before the Supreme Russian Tribunal, the guardian of legality. All my efforts are aimed at concluding the civil war as soon as possible by crushing Bolshevism in order to put the Russian people in a position to express its free will.' He then proceeded to answer satisfactorily all the specific questions which the Council of Five had asked.

This answer was dated June 4, and on June 12 Lloyd George, Wilson, Clemenceau, and the representative of Japan, welcomed the tone of the reply which seemed to them 'to be in substantial agreement with the proposition they had made, and to contain satisfactory assurances for the freedom and self-government of the Russian people and their neighbours.' They were therefore 'willing to extend to Admiral Kolchak and his Associates the support set forth in their original letter.'

If this far-reaching and openly proclaimed decision was wise now in June, would it not have been wiser in January? No argument existed in June not obvious in January: and half the power available in January was gone by June. Six months of degeneration and uncertainty had chilled the Siberian Armies and wasted the slender authority of the Omsk Government. It had given the Bolsheviks the opportunity of raising armies, of consolidating their power and of identifying themselves to some extent with Russia. It had provided enough opposition to stimulate and not enough to overcome the sources of their strength. The moment chosen by the Supreme Council for their declaration was almost exactly the moment when that declaration was certainly too late.

CHAPTER X
THE TRIUMVIRATE

To you all three,
The senators of this great world.

—Antony and Cleopatra, II, 6.

Wilson and Preliminary Terms—Mr. Baker's Second Film Effect—A German Version—The Garbled Extract—President Wilson's Second Voyage—A Change of Mood—Mr. Balfour's Achievement—The Polish Report—End of the Council of Ten—The Threatened Exodus—Mr. Lloyd George's Memorandum of March 25—M. Clemenceau's Rejoinder—Mr. Baker's Blunder—The Triumvirate—The German Revolution—Germany's Survival.

It is pleasant to return to Paris after these Russian snows. Unluckily we have also to return to Mr. Stannard Baker.

Before President Wilson had departed, the question of the renewal of the armistice on February 12 had directly raised the issue of a preliminary peace. How much longer were we all to go on officially bound to hate the Germans, and indeed, since the blockade was still in operation, to starve them? How much longer were schemes for regenerating the world and the daily round of business to take precedence of the commonplaces of good sense and humanity? There must be peace, the armies must demobilise and the troops come home. It was therefore necessary to fix the final limits of German martial power while time remained. It was agreed that a preliminary treaty, containing military, naval and air terms, should be drafted forthwith by an expert committee. The records show that Wilson said 'He did not wish his absence to stop so important, essential and urgent a work as the preparation of a preliminary peace. He hoped to return by March 13 or 15, allowing himself only a week in America; but *he did not wish that during his unavoidable absence such questions as the territorial questions and questions of compensation should be held up*. He had asked Colonel House to take his place while he was away.' This statement was inconvenient for Mr. Stannard Baker. It threatened to spoil his second film effect, which was as follows:

'No sooner had the President left Paris, on February 15, than the forces of opposition and discontent began to act. On February 24, resolutions were adopted by the Council of Ten which, if carried through, would wreck the entire American scheme for the peace.

'It was exceedingly shrewd strategy these skilled diplomatists played. They did not like the League as drafted and they did not want the Covenant in the Treaty, but they made no direct attack on either proposal. The League was scarcely mentioned in the conferences until just before the President returned.

'Their strategy was as simple as it was ingenious. They had been left . . . with resolutions which the President had strongly supported, to make quickly a preliminary peace treaty, including only military, naval and air terms. What was easier or more obvious than to generalize that treaty, put into it also all the other terms that really mattered to them—boundaries, reparations, colonies: in short crowd the whole peace into the preliminary treaty without any reference to the League…. If the League got squeezed out in the process, or was consigned to some innocuous future conference after all the settlements were made, who cared?

'Thus while it is too much to say that there was a direct plot, while Wilson was away, to kill the League or even cut it out of the Treaty, one can affirm with certainty that there was an intrigue against his plan of a preliminary military and naval peace—which would have indirectly produced the same result.

'It seemed that every militaristic and nationalistic force came instantly to the front when Wilson had departed. Lloyd George had gone home, but instead of leaving the liberal leaders in control in Paris, men who were imbued with the purposes laid down in the League—Cecil, Smuts, and Barnes—who were indeed Lloyd George's associates on the British Peace Commission, he sent over Winston Churchill, the most militaristic of British leaders. Churchill was not a member of the peace delegation and had had nothing before to do with the Peace Conference. Moreover, he was a rampant opponent of the League….'

He proceeds to argue that Lloyd George, who 'began to think he had gone too far with this League business,' gave instructions to Mr. Balfour to take advantage of President Wilson's temporary absence for the purpose of rupturing the policy of the League of Nations, and to further these evil ends he sent specially to Paris the very wicked author of this book.

This charge has had a wide currency. The German writer Novak repeats it.

'Lord Balfour had actually forestalled President Wilson in proposing that the Armistice terms should be renewed without laying fresh obligations on the Germans. But that was already a week ago. Since then Winston Churchill had arrived in Paris, Churchill the Bolshevik-hater, still filled with thoughts of war, filled with the same ideas as Marshal Foch for a promising campaign in the East; full also of contempt for the League of Nations, which, he declared with conviction, was useless to his country and no substitute for a navy…. Subsequently there had been an interchange of views between Winston Churchill and Marshal Foch, and now Lord Balfour proposed that after all it would be better at once to incorporate the essentials of the peace terms in the Preliminaries of Peace.'[1]

The correspondence printed in the last Chapter will have sufficiently apprised the reader of the reasons which sent me to Paris. They were the only reasons. The only matter which concerned me at the three sessions which I attended of the Supreme Council was the quest for some policy in Russia. Absorbed in my own work, I was never even aware of these more spacious issues. I went to Paris on Russian business, and when it was clear no business could be done, I went home.

Mr. Stannard Baker's mettle is, however, best judged from his own pages. It is necessary to his effect that President Wilson should be depicted as leaving Europe in the sure confidence that territorial and reparations questions would not be dealt with in his absence, and that such dealing would be a breach of faith. Yet there in the *procès verbal* of February 12 stood the awkward words of President Wilson, 'He did not wish that during his unavoidable absence such questions as the territorial questions and questions of compensation should be held up.' But what of that? A stroke of the pen will cut it out. It does not fit the story. High ideals must be supported at all costs and by all methods. So the man to whom President Wilson entrusted all his most secret papers, with leave to publish as he pleased, in breach of all faith between the parties concerned, first garbles the record by omitting the vital sentence and last perverts it by inserting after the words preliminary peace 'as to military, naval and air terms.' The American author of 'Colonel House's Papers' has summed up this discreditable performance in some salt sentences.

'The papers of Colonel House, like the British Foreign Office Memorandum, furnish clear indication that in making his charge of an intrigue, Mr. Baker has advanced assumptions and insinuations without a tittle of evidence. The House papers show Wilson discussing with House the very plans which Mr. Baker asserts "would wreck the entire American scheme for the Peace." They show House cabling to Wilson the progress of those plans through the Balfour resolutions, and in his cables of February 27 and March 4 (cited above) explaining how he hoped to push the future of the League. They show that in order to maintain a semblance of probability in his charges against the British Mr. Baker has been forced to omit essential passages from the official record.'[2]

* * * * *

It was a different President Wilson that crossed the Atlantic in the *George Washington* for the second time. He had had a rough time in the United States. The White House Dinner to the Senate Foreign Relations Committee had revealed to him the implacable Party rancour which he had provoked and by which he was pursued. 'Senators Knox and

[1] *Versailles*, p. 84.
[2] Mr. D. Hunter Miller also writes of Mr. Baker's thesis, 'The effort to prove a plot where none existed could not well go further.'—The Drafting of the Covenant 1, 98.

Lodge remained perfectly silent, refusing to ask any questions or to act in the spirit in which the dinner was given.[3] The Republicans had raised the spirit of Monroe against the League of Nations. If a quarrel arose between Spain and Brazil, or between England and Venezuela, and the League of Nations said Brazil or Venezuela were in the wrong, were the United States to be compelled to take sides with a European Power, simply because of impartial justice? This was a hard blow, and the President bent under it. He felt like General Smuts, who saw clearly that the Mandatory System for colonies was of universal application except in regard to German South-West Africa.

At the Opera House in New York, the President, vexed by the unpitying opposition which he knew he must encounter, had used an almost naked threat. The Covenant of the League of Nations, he had suggested, would be so intertwined with the Treaty that the two could not be separated. The American reaction to this had been distinctly hostile. The *George Washington* this time carried to Europe a man who had learned much. He now knew that the wicked Old World statesmen were backed by even more deplorable Old World nations and that the American idealist would be repudiated by his own. The 'Teach the world' theme was over; the immediate need was to emerge without discredit from exceedingly delicate and responsible transactions. On his first voyage all his moral indignation had been concentrated upon the Old World, on the second at least two-thirds of it was generously distributed to the New. Then his purpose had been to compel the policies of Europe to his views; now it was the Senate of the United States which stood in need of discipline. Indeed he had almost a fellow-feeling for those European Statesmen and diplomatists who, like him, were at grips with unfair intractable forces. Was it not time they should help each other? How could any solutions of world affairs be reached if mobs and senates and five hundred gifted journalists interfered? Three or four men talking quietly on the dead-level might avert breakdown and chaos if they acted quickly. After all, Lloyd George and Clemenceau, the trusted, acclaimed leaders of immense Parliamentary and Democratic majorities, were not unworthy comrades. He had met them now and he understood their quality and the causes of their strength. He envied them their national credentials. They were conciliatory, considerate, earnestly desirous of his goodwill, and yet resolute in their countries' cause. He might not be able to give Justice to the world, or even to define it in set terms, but the three of them together could give Peace.

There is no authority for saying that these were the reflections of President Wilson on his voyage; it is mere surmise; all that is known is that on his arrival he was far from pleased with Colonel House. House had already adapted himself to the relaxing atmosphere of Europe. All sorts of hitherto unauthorised ideas like 'We *must* settle something,' 'We *must* face facts,' 'Everyone must concede a lot,' had laid hold of the Colonel's calm, benevolent, and extremely practical mind. Wilson had not wished to see on his second arrival at Brest, House's finger pointing the path which he had probably already himself resolved to tread. So he said to House 'Your Dinner' [*i.e.* the Dinner you suggested] to the Senate Foreign Relations Committee was a failure as far as getting together was concerned.'

---

[3] House, p. 401.

* * * * *

What had happened while he had been away? Mr. Lloyd George had gone home. M. Clemenceau was, on February 19, fired at and wounded by an Anarchist. He was for some weeks incapacitated.

The commission appointed in February, on President Wilson's motion, to draw up preliminary naval, military and air terms for Germany had been expected to report 'within 48 hours.' They had, however, found the task vastly more difficult than the President had expected. A whole month had passed and the Generals and Admirals were still in the midst of their labours. Meanwhile, however, Mr. Balfour who in the absence of the three Heads of Governments became naturally the leading figure at the Conference had made an immense effort to hasten and conclude the work of the Commissions upon the rest of the Peace Treaty. On February 22 he told the Supreme Council that 'a general feeling of impatience was now becoming manifest in all countries on account of the apparent slow progress the Conference was making in the direction of final peace.' Supported by Lansing and House and with the assent of the still prostrate Clemenceau he obtained from the Conference a resolution of which the first clause ran:

i. 'Without prejudice to the decision of the Supreme War Council to present naval, military and air conditions of peace to Germany at an early date, the Conference agrees that it is desirable to proceed without delay to the consideration of other preliminary peace terms with Germany and to press on the necessary investigations with all possible speed.'

He also carried a motion that the work of the Territorial Commissions should be completed and presented by March 8.

The whole of the real work of the Conference, driven forward insistently from above, now began to advance with remarkable rapidity. The Commissions which in the lack of steady control had hitherto been ambling off indefinitely into inquiries and discussions, now rallied to precise commands to produce conclusions forthwith. From every quarter early in March they began to present reports. By the time Wilson returned (March 13), most of the great territorial issues had reached the point when final decisions could be taken by the chiefs. But the military terms which were to have been so speedily disposed of were still lagging on the road. It therefore became possible again to contemplate bringing the whole of the work on the treaty to a common and simultaneous conclusion. There is no doubt that Mr. Balfour had during his three weeks of virtual ascendancy achieved an extraordinary transformation in the whole position. Whereas in the middle of February the work of the Conference was drifting off almost uncontrollably into futility, all was now brought back in orderly fashion to the real. The decks were cleared for action and the long-looked-for conflict of wills could now at last begin.

President Wilson at no time challenged the decisions taken in his absence. On the contrary he approved with increasing cordiality the work of the 'Balfour period'; he saw how scrupulously his own position had been safeguarded by the steady and dexterous hands into which the Conference had fallen. He realised that all the main issues were now presented uncompromised, intact, and ripe for decision.

But the Council of Ten (or Council of Fifty as it had become) was no instrument to settle or even discuss the crucial questions between the Great Powers. An organism more compact, more secret, more intimate, was imperatively demanded, and to this the minds of all the chiefs were driven by the steady pressure of facts. The actual crisis arose upon the report of the Commission on the future frontiers of Poland and Germany. The Commission among other things had assigned the whole of Upper Silesia to Poland as well as Dantzig and the Polish corridor. Mr. Lloyd George at once stigmatised the report as 'unjust', since according to the statistics of the Commission itself the number of Germans to be assigned to Polish sovereignty was too great. He therefore moved that the report should be sent back to the Commission. The Commission reconsidered it, but refused to alter their recommendations. The French championed the Commission. Tension rose and leakage followed. Lord Northcliffe bitterly attacked the Prime Minister in the Paris *Daily Mail*, urging that he had no right to override the opinion of the experts upon the Commission and revealing passages from his statements in the secret discussions of the Council of Ten. According to present-day opinion, Mr. Lloyd George was, of course, entirely in the right. The proposals of the Commission were indefensible. The members of the Commission were not in any real sense of the word experts; but whether or no, it is for experts to advise and for Ministers and Heads of Governments to decide. Angered by the leakages and Lord Northcliffe's attacks, the Prime Minister successfully broke up the Council of Ten. From March 20, President Wilson, Mr. Lloyd George, M. Clemenceau and Signor Orlando met regularly in secret conversations, at which not even secretaries were present. For the first time since the conclusion of the armistice there began that thorough and frank discussion which should have taken place three months before. The Council of Ten (or Fifty) was now reduced to the Five Foreign Ministers and still continued for a while to meet; but deprived of all important business and of all the men who had the power to settle, it perished painlessly of inanition.

We now reach a page of the Peace Conference story which may well be called Exodus. As a prelude to acceptance of the brutal fact that they must agree, every one of the 'Big Four' threatened to quit the Conference. Mr. Lloyd George was first and far the most artistic. He assigned no specific point of disagreement. He was distressed at the slow progress of the Treaty. He feared he was merely wasting his time in Paris. Meanwhile he had direct and urgent responsibilities in England. The Cabinet, the House of Commons, the industrial situation—all required his immediate personal attention. Since no progress seemed likely in Paris, he must return home and get on with his job. He could come back later if there was any sign of some practical work being done upon the Treaty. He fixed March 18 as the date of his departure. This prospect and the suggestion that there was more important work to be done in London than in Paris, filled his compeers with alarm. They knew well that no progress could be made in his absence. Yet the ground he had chosen was unassailable. Every effort was made to persuade him to remain. But it was not until he had received on March 17 a joint letter (since published by Colonel House) signed by Wilson, Clemenceau and Orlando, begging him to remain if only for another two weeks, that he was pleased to yield. He consented to remain, but in a strengthened position.

Clemenceau and Wilson had long been ripening for a trial of strength. House has made us aware of the striking interchange which arose on March 28 out of the discussions about the Saar Valley coalfields. ' "Then if France does not get what she wishes," said the President, "she will refuse to act with us. In that event do you wish me to return home?" "I do not wish you to go home," said Clemenceau, "but I intend to do so myself," and left the house.' In this rough fashion did the Tiger deal with his opponent. Moreover, he had only to go round the corner. But Wilson's position was very different. To recross the Atlantic was final and irrevocable. Nevertheless, in the face of Clemenceau's continued threat to withdraw the French delegation from the Conference, and in the despondency following an attack of influenza, the President telegraphed on April 7 for the *George Washington* to return to France. His faithful secretary, Mr. Tumulty, who remained on guard at home, warned the President in the bluntest terms that his exodus would be looked upon by his friends and foes in America as 'an act of impatience and petulance . . . not accepted here in good faith . . . most unwise and fraught with most dangerous possibilities . . . a desertion.' This was decisive. He could not quit; he must go through with it. And meanwhile Clemenceau had said no more about withdrawal and continued his daily attendances upon the Conference.

The last exodus was that of Orlando. When upon the question of Fiume President Wilson threatened to appeal over his head to the Italian people, and on the strength of his three-days' visit to Italy exclaimed, 'I know the Italian people better than you do,' Orlando went straight to the railway station and actually departed in voluble indignation to Rome. He at least carried out his threat. But this only consolidated the others. The Triumvirate found a common ground in standing together against him. After waiting a fortnight for appeals to his higher nature which never arrived, he came back of his own accord in time to sign the Treaty.

* * * * *

Mr. Lloyd George had remained in France, but while the Council of Ten were fading away and the meetings of the Four were gradually assuming a formal character, he paid a brief visit to Fontainebleau.[4] There he wrote his famous Memorandum of March 25. This document has already been published, but since it expresses more completely and explicitly Mr. Lloyd George's sentiments about the Peace Settlement, and since the views he expressed corresponded very fairly with those of the people in whose name he spoke, it will be well to give some typical extracts here:

'*Some considerations for the Peace Conference before they finally draft their terms.*'

'When nations are exhausted by wars in which they have put forth all their strength and which leave them tired, bleeding and broken, it is not difficult to patch up a

---

[4]Actually 24 hours only.

peace that may last until the generation which experienced the horrors of the war has passed away. Pictures of heroism and triumph only tempt those who know nothing of the sufferings and terrors of war. It is therefore comparatively easy to patch up a peace which will last for thirty years.

'What is difficult, however, is to draw up a peace which will not provoke a fresh struggle when those who have had practical experience of what war means have passed away....

'To achieve redress our terms may be severe, they may be stern and even ruthless, but at the same time they can be so just that the country on which they are imposed will feel in its heart that it has no right to complain. But injustice, arrogance, displayed in the hour of triumph, will never be forgotten or forgiven.

'For these reasons I am, therefore, strongly averse to transferring more Germans from German rule to the rule of some other nation than can possibly be helped. I cannot conceive any greater cause of future war than that the German people, who have certainly proved themselves one of the most vigorous and powerful races in the world, should be surrounded by a number of small States, many of them consisting of people who have never previously set up a stable government for themselves, but each of them containing large masses of Germans clamouring for reunion with their native land. The proposal of the Polish Commission that we should place 2,100,000 Germans under the control of a people which is of a different religion and which has never proved its capacity for stable self-government throughout its history must, in my judgment, lead sooner or later to a new war in the East of Europe. What I have said about the Germans is equally true of the Magyars. There will never be peace in South-Eastern Europe if every little state now coming into being is to have a large Magyar Irredenta within its borders. I would therefore take as a guiding principle of the peace that as far as is humanly possible the different races should be allocated to their motherlands, and that this human criterion should have precedence over considerations of strategy or economics or communications, which can usually be adjusted by other means. Secondly, I would say that the duration for the payments of reparation ought to disappear if possible with the generation which made the war....

'The greatest danger that I see in the present situation is that Germany may throw in her lot with Bolshevism and place her resources, her brains, her vast organising power at the disposal of the revolutionary fanatics whose dream it is to conquer the world for Bolshevism by force of arms. This danger is no mere chimera. The present Government in Germany is weak; it has no prestige; its authority is challenged; it lingers merely because there is no alternative but the spartacists, and Germany is not ready for spartacism as yet. But the argument which the spartacists are using with great effect at this very time is that they alone can save Germany from the intolerable conditions which have been bequeathed her by the war. They offer to free the German people from indebtedness to the Allies and indebtedness to their own richer classes. They offer them complete control of their own affairs and the prospect of a new heaven and earth. It is true that the price will be heavy.

There will be two or three years of anarchy, perhaps bloodshed, but at the end the land will remain, the people will remain, the greater part of the houses and the factories will remain, and the railways and the roads will remain, and Germany, having thrown off her burdens, will be able to make a fresh start.

'If Germany goes over to the spartacists it is inevitable that she should throw in her lot with the Russian Bolsheviks. Once that happens all Eastern Europe will be swept into the orbit of the Bolshevik revolution and within a year we may witness the spectacle of nearly three hundred million people organised into a vast Red army under German instructors and German generals equipped with German cannon and German machine guns and prepared for a renewal of the attack on Western Europe. This is a prospect which no one can face with equanimity. Yet the news which came from Hungary yesterday shows only too clearly that this danger is no fantasy. And what are the reasons alleged for this decision? They are mainly the belief that large numbers of Magyars are to be handed over to the control of others. If we are wise, we shall offer to Germany a peace, which, while just, will be preferable for all sensible men to the alternative of Bolshevism. I would, therefore, put it in the forefront of the peace that once she accepts our terms, especially reparation, we will open to her the raw materials and markets of the world on equal terms with ourselves, and will do everything possible to enable the German people to get upon their legs again. We cannot both cripple her and expect her to pay.

'Finally, we must offer terms which a responsible Government in Germany can expect to be able to carry out. If we present terms to Germany which are unjust, or excessively onerous, no responsible Government will sign them; certainly the present weak administration will not . . . .

'From every point of view, therefore, it seems to me that we ought to endeavour to draw up a peace settlement as if we were impartial arbiters, forgetful of the passions of the war. This settlement ought to have three ends in view. First of all it must do justice to the Allies by taking into account Germany's responsibility for the origin of the war and for the way in which it was fought. Secondly, it must be a settlement which a responsible German Government can sign in the belief that it can fulfil the obligations it incurs. Thirdly, it must be a settlement which will contain in itself no provocations for future wars, and which will constitute an alternative to Bolshevism, because it will commend itself to all reasonable opinion as a fair settlement of the European problem. . . .

'To my mind it is idle to endeavour to impose a permanent limitation of armaments upon Germany unless we are prepared similarly to impose a limitation upon ourselves. . . .

'I should like to ask why Germany, if she accepts the terms we consider just and fair, should not be admitted to the League of Nations, at any rate as soon as she has established a stable and democratic Government. Would it not be an inducement to her both to sign the terms and to resist Bolshevism? Might it not be safer that she should be inside the League than that she should be outside it?

'Finally, I believe that until the authority and effectiveness of the League of Nations has been demonstrated, the British Empire and the United States ought to give to France a guarantee against the possibility of a new German aggression. France has special reason for asking for such a guarantee. She has twice been attacked and twice invaded by Germany in half a century. She has been so attacked because she has been the principal guardian of liberal and democratic civilisation against Central European autocracy on the Continent of Europe. It is right that the other great Western democracies should enter into an undertaking which will ensure that they stand by her side in time to protect her against invasion, should Germany ever threaten her again or until the League of Nations has proved its capacity to preserve the peace and liberty of the world.

'If, however, the Peace Conference is really to secure peace and prove to the world a complete plan of settlement which all reasonable men will recognise as an alternative preferable to anarchy, it must deal with the Russian situation. Bolshevik imperialism does not merely menace the States on Russia's borders. It threatens the whole of Asia and is as near to America as it is to France. It is idle to think that the Peace Conference can separate, however sound a peace it may have arranged with Germany, if it leaves Russia as it is to-day. I do not propose, however, to complicate the question of the peace with Germany by introducing a discussion of the Russian problem. I mention it simply in order to remind ourselves of the importance of dealing with it as soon as possible.'

Clemenceau replied with asperity in writing. He suggested that Lloyd George's magnanimity was achieved exclusively at the expense of France and the continental States, while England had received all the advantages and securities which were of interest to her.

'But what would be the results of following the method suggested by the note of March 26? A certain number of total and definitive guarantees will be acquired by maritime nations which have not known an invasion. The surrender of the German colonies would be total and definitive. The surrender of the German navy would be total and definitive. The surrender of a large portion of the German merchant fleet would be total and definitive. The exclusion of Germany from foreign markets would be total and would last for some time. On the other hand, partial and temporary solutions would be reserved for the continental countries; that is to say, those which have suffered most from the war. The reduced frontiers suggested for Poland and Bohemia would be partial solutions. The defensive agreement offered to France for the protection of her territory would be a temporary solution. The proposed régime for the coal-fields of the Saar would be temporary. Here we have a condition of inequality which might risk leaving a bad impression upon the after-war relations between the Allies, more important than the after-war relations between Germany and the Allies.'

Mr. Stannard Baker had the Lloyd George Memorandum before him when he wrote his History. He admired it greatly. 'A peace resting upon military coercion could never,' he felt, 'be anything but a curse to the world.' 'No finer expression of this feeling,' he wrote, 'based on a farsighted perception of the verities of the situation can be found than in a memorandum sent to President Wilson by General Tasker H. Bliss on March 25. It was called 'Some Considerations for the Peace Conference before they finally draft their Terms.' A few pregnant sentences may be quoted, etc. . . . . 'General Bliss,' he continues, 'was one of the few Members of the Conference that never lost his sense of perspective and who saw that there was a great danger of ruining the whole work of peace if the Conference should produce a treaty against which the mass of German opinion would at once revolt.'

This is probably the most astonishing blunder which any man claiming to write a standard history, and armed for that purpose with a mass of exclusive official and authentic information, has ever committed. Little did Mr. Baker dream when he penned his tributes to General Bliss that they should really have been directed to another address. Bitter must have been his chagrin when he realised that his praise belongs not to the distinguished American soldier whom all respect, but to an unregenerate Old World politician.

This is the concluding specimen of Mr. Baker's fidelity in the search of Truth with which the reader will be troubled. I have dwelt upon his work with attention because of the solemn character of the mission entrusted to him and the stream of precious knowledge placed in his charge by President Wilson. It is disquieting to think how many conscientious citizens of the United States must have drunk from his infected fountain. But fortunately it has not been left to English writers to discredit Mr. Baker. The pages of Dr. Hunter Miller and of the Editor of Colonel House's Papers have remorselessly exposed his errors, and indeed vices, to the alert, critical faculty of the American public and to their inherent desire for Truth and Justice.

* * * * *

It is not the purpose of these Chapters to re-tell the story of the Peace Conference, but only to guide the reader to some of its salient features. We have, nevertheless, surveyed the general scene and its actors. Nearly five months have passed since the fighting ended and it is only now that the real making of the Peace begins. Four men, for a time to be reduced to three, each the responsible head of a great victor State, are all that are left. The five hundred gifted journalists, the twenty-seven eager nations, the Council of Ten (or Fifty), the fifty-eight Commissions, so rich in eminent personages, have all melted down to three men. Henceforward they will stand together. They have learned to respect each other and to trust each other; they have become colleagues and comrades in an adventure of much danger and unequalled difficulties. Each knows he must make serious concessions to reach agreement. Each knows that agreement must be reached; and all resolve to give a speedy peace to the world and answer unitedly, promptly, and to the best of their ability, for good or for ill, the hundred hard questions which stand open.

We shall see in the next chapter what some of these questions were and how they were decided. For a month (March 20–April 19) they argue and consult alone, all speaking English. Much common ground is won: but it is not entrenched each night. Even the rendezvous of the Four sometimes fail. One goes to M. Clemenceau's rooms and one to President Wilson's. Organisation now alone is needed. Then they admit as secretary, Maurice Hankey. He listens to all that is said and keeps his record and tells them at the end of every day what they have settled. From that moment their decisions flow out to jurists and officials in a swiftly growing stream. By May 7 the Treaty of Versailles is printed and on the 9th a Plenary Session of the Conference accepts with resignation or resentment the accomplished fact.

*　*　*　*　*

It was now time to summon the enemy. Early in May the German envoys presented themselves in the Palace of Versailles to receive the volume in which the preliminary terms of Peace were incorporated; and at the end of June, peace in substantial accordance with these terms was duly signed.

Meanwhile Germany had been travelling fast. German writers are prone to dwell upon the humiliations their people endured at the hands of the conquerors in this period. But their own country was all the while the scene of events most important and helpful to them and to civilisation. Some brief account has been given in these pages of the Russian revolution. The German revolution was the paroxysm of an incomparably stronger and more highly nerved organisation. It passed across our anxious, satiated, jaded consciousness with no more attention than surviving troops just withdrawn into rest quarters after battle would pay to a distant cannonade. The story requires a book to tell. The interest is enhanced by comparison with what happened in Russia. So many of the conditions and episodes and their sequence are exactly reproduced. The nation is beaten in war, the Fleet and Army mutiny and dissolve, the Emperor is deposed, and Authority bankrupt is repudiated by all. Workmen's and soldiers' councils are set up, a Socialist Government is hustled into office; upon the famine-stricken homeland return millions of soldiers quivering from long-drawn torment, aching with defeat. The Police have disappeared; industry is at a standstill; the mob are hungry; it is winter. All the agencies which destroyed Russia are ready. They are organised; each individual knows his task; the whole procedure of Communist revolution is understood and scheduled. The Russian experiment stands as a model. In Karl Liebknecht, in Rosa Luxemburg, in Dittmann, in Kautsky and a score of others are the would-be Lenins and Trotskys of the Teutonic agony. Everything is tried and everything happens; but it does not happen the same way.

The Communists seize the greater part of the capital; but the seat of government is defended. The would-be constitutional assembly is attacked; but the assailants are repulsed. A handful of loyal officers—loyal to Germany—disguised as privates, but well armed with grenades and machine-guns, guard with their lives the frail nucleus of civic government. They are only a handful; but they win. A naval division infected with Bolshevism seizes the Palace; they are expelled, after bloody fighting, by faithful troops.

In the mutinies which overturned authority in almost every regiment, the officers were derived of their épaulettes and swords; but not one was murdered.

In the midst of all we discern a rugged, simple figure. A Socialist workman and Trade Unionist—Noske by name. Appointed Minister of National Defence by the Social-Democratic Government, furnished by them with dictatorial powers, he does not fail the German people. A foreign opinion of German heroes is necessarily very detached and can only be expressed with diffidence; but in the long line of kings, statesmen and warriors which stretches from Frederick to Hindenburg it may be that Noske has his place—a son of the people, amid universal confusion acting without fear in the public cause.

The fibre and intellect of 'all the German tribes' enabled the Provisional Government to hold elections. Always the reader will see in these pages the same tactics by the same forces: their one object—to prevent the people from choosing a Parliament. In Russia they have succeeded: in Germany they fail. Presently we shall see them fail in Ireland.

Representative government being still alive, thanks to shot and steel, machine-guns, trench mortars, and *flammenwerfer*, thirty millions of German men and women, 90 per cent of the electorate, recorded their votes, and from that hour a free and supreme Parliament became the central fact in German life.

It was therefore as a united nation which in the hour of disaster had risen superior to despair, that Germany came to Versailles.

CHAPTER XI
THE PEACE TREATIES[1]

Though we had Peace, yet 'twill be a great white ere things be settled. Though the Wind lie, yet after a Storm the Sea will work a great while.

—Selden's *Table Talk*.

The Territorial Settlements—The Outstanding Features—National Self-determination—Its Application—Alsace-Lorraine—Schleswig—The Rebirth of Poland—The Eastern Frontier of Germany—Upper Silesia—The British Empire Delegation—Its Moderation—Mr. Lloyd George's Handicap—The Upper Silesian Plebiscite—What Britain Risked—The Case of France—The French Demand for Security—The Rhine Frontier—The Disarmament of Germany—The Demilitarised Zone—The Joint Guarantee—Its Sequel—The Fate of Austria-Hungary—The Innocent and the Guilty—Czechoslovakia: The Czechs—Czechoslovakia: The Slovaks—Jugo-Slavia—Rumania—Hungary—Austria—The Anschluss—Bulgaria—The General Design.

However keen may be the feelings excited by the distribution of tropical colonies, of compensation in money or in kind and of retributive justice; high as are the hopes centred in the League of Nations, it is by the territorial settlements in Europe that the Treaties of 1919 and 1920 will finally be judged. Here we are in contact with those deep and lasting facts which cast races of men into moulds and fix their place and status in the world. Here we stir the embers of the past and light the beacons of the future. Old flags are raised anew; the passions of vanished generations awake; beneath the shell-torn soil of the twentieth century the bones of long dead warriors and victims are exposed, and the wail of lost causes sounds in the wind.

The treaties with which we now have to deal take their place in the great series which includes the Treaty of Westphalia, the Treaty of Utrecht and the Treaties of Vienna. They are at once the latest and the largest link in the chain of European history. They will be memorable for three events of the first magnitude: the dissolution of the Austro-Hungarian Empire; the rebirth of Poland; and the preservation of united Germany. Even the short distance we have travelled since the Conference in Paris reveals the scale of these monarch-peaks, and how they tower above the range and dominate the wide regions of mountainous and hilly country. Already through the clearer air we can discern the proportions of the vast landscape and its massive simplicity. The Empire of

---

[1]See map of Europe facing page 150.

Charles V, and with it the Hapsburg Monarchy, the survivor of so many upheavals, the main structure of central and southern Europe, is represented only by a chasm. The three sundered parts of Poland are re-united into a sovereign independent Republic of thirty million souls; and Germany, beaten and disarmed upon the field of battle, defenceless before her outraged conquerors, rises the largest and incomparably the strongest racial mass in Europe.

These dominant facts in the life of Europe did not spring solely, or even mainly, from the volcanic violence of the war. They were the result of the methodical application of a principle. If the treaty makers of Vienna in 1814 were ruled by the principle of Legitimacy, those of Paris in 1919 were guided by the principle of Self-determination. Although the expression 'Self-determination' will rightly be forever connected with the name of President Wilson, the ideal was neither original nor new. The phrase itself is Fichte's '*Selbstbestimmung.*' The conception has never been more forcefully presented than by Mazzini. Throughout the British Empire it had long been known and widely practised under the somewhat less explosive precepts of 'Self-government' and 'Government by Consent.' During the nineteenth century the rise of Nationalism made it increasingly plain that all great Empires must reckon with this principle and increasingly conform to it, if they were to survive united and vital in the modern world. The almost complete exclusion of religion in all its forms from the political sphere had left Nationalism the most powerful moulding instrument of mankind in temporal affairs.

The Fourteen Points embodied and proclaimed the principle of Self-determination. In his speeches the President had declared that 'national aspirations must be respected. Peoples may now be dominated and governed only by their own consent. Self-determination is not a mere phrase.' 'Peoples and provinces are not to be bartered about from sovereignty to sovereignty. . . . Every territorial settlement must be made in the interest and for the benefit of the populations concerned. . . . All well-defined and national aspirations shall be accorded the utmost satisfaction that can be accorded them without introducing new or perpetuating old elements of discord and antagonism.' The Allies had earnestly identified their war aims with this declaration. The Germans had accompanied their requests for an armistice by the conditions that the peace settlement should be based upon the Fourteen Points of President Wilson and his other speeches. They had even claimed that they laid down their arms and rendered themselves defenceless upon this understanding. Therefore the principle of Self-determination was at once what the victors had fought for and the vanquished claimed.

Here was one clear guiding principle upon which all the peoples so cruelly sundered, so torn with wounds and hatreds, were united, and to which all were bound both by faith and interest. The main and imperative duty of the Peace Conference, in all matters comprised in their task of making peace between the belligerents, was to give effect to this principle; or in words which I venture to requote, 'to liberate the captive nationalities, to reunite those branches of the same family which had long been arbitrarily divided, and to draw frontiers in broad accordance with the ethnic masses.'

All being agreed upon the fundamental principle, it remained to apply it. But if the principle was simple and accepted, its application was difficult and disputable.

What was to be the test of nationality? How were the wishes of 'national elements' to be expressed and obtained? How and where were the resulting frontiers to be drawn amid entangled populations? To what extent should the main principle override every other consideration—historical, geographical, economic or strategic? How far could the armed and vehement forces which were everywhere afoot be brought to accept the resulting decisions? Such were the problems of the Peace Conference, and in particular of the Triumvirate.

In the main it was decided that language should be adopted as the proof of nationality. No doubt language is not always its manifestation. Some of the most nationally conscious stocks can scarcely speak their own language at all, or only with the greatest difficulty. Some oppressed races spoke the language of their oppressors, while hating them; and some dominant breeds spoke the language of their subjects, while ruling them. Still matters had to be settled with reasonable dispatch, and no better guide to the principle of nationality in disputed cases could be found than language; or, as a last resort, a plebiscite.

It was inherent in the realities that the scheme of drawing frontiers in accordance with nationality as defined by language or with the wish of the local inhabitants could not in practice be applied without modification. Some of the new States had no access to the sea through their own populations, and could not become effective economic units without such access. Some liberated nationalities had for centuries looked forward to regaining the ancient frontiers of their long vanished sovereignty. Some of the victors were entitled by treaty to claim, and others of the victors bound by treaty to accord them, frontiers fixed not by language or the wish of the inhabitants, but by Alps. Some integral economic communities lay athwart the ethnic frontier; and at many points rival and hostile races were intermingled, not only as individuals but by villages, by townships and by rural districts. All this debatable ground had to be studied and fought over mile by mile by the numerous, powerful and violently agitated States concerned.

Nevertheless all these reservations and impingements upon the fundamental principle affected only the outskirts of peoples and countries. All the disputable areas put together were but a minute fraction of Europe. They were but the exceptions which proved the rule. Fierce as were and are the irritations which have arisen wherever these sensitive and doubtful fringes of nationality have been roughly clipped by frontier scissors, they do not impair the broad essence of the treaties. Probably less than 3 per cent. of the European population are now living under Governments whose nationality they repudiate; and the map of Europe has for the first time been drawn in general harmony with the wishes of its peoples.

*　*　*　*　*

Let us now test these assertions by examining the actual frontiers of Germany fixed by the Treaty of Versailles. Let us begin with the western and northern frontiers.

Point VIII of the Fourteen stated that '*the wrong done to France by Prussia in 1871 in the matter of Alsace-Lorraine, which has unsettled the peace of the world for nearly fifty years, should be righted.*' This had become one of the prime objects of the Allies after the war had broken out. It was explicitly accepted by Germany when she asked for peace on the basis of the Fourteen Points and signed the Armistice accordingly. There was therefore no dispute about Alsace-Lorraine. These two provinces, after being French for nearly two hundred years, had been wrested from France in 1871 against the wishes of their inhabitants. They had been, to use the words embodied in the Treaty, 'separated from their country in spite of the solemn protests of their representatives at the Assembly of Bordeaux. The retrocession of Alsace-Lorraine was the repairing of a breach in the principle of Self-determination committed within living memory.

Apart from an insignificant alteration of the Belgian frontier around Eupen and Malmédy, no other change was made in the Western frontiers of Germany. The French had vehemently claimed in addition to Alsace and Lorraine the annexation of the district of the Saar with its very valuable coalfields. They founded their claim at first upon historical grounds. President Wilson's refusal to endorse it, against the reputed wish of the inhabitants, led to one of the notable crises in the discussions of the Triumvirate. The French then fell back upon a demand for the temporary use of the coalfields in the Saar Valley to compensate them for the destruction of the French mining districts at Lens and Valenciennes. They themselves proposed that the ultimate destination of the Saar Valley should be determined by the vote of the inhabitants themselves taken in the year 1935. There are no grounds whatever of principle upon which the resulting agreement of the Conference can be assailed.

Upon the northern or Danish frontier one other cession of territory was required of Germany. When, after the defeat of Denmark by Prussia in 1864, Schleswig and Holstein were surrendered by Denmark to Prussia and Austria, a clause had been inserted at the instance of Napoleon III in the Treaty, that the inhabitants of Northern Schleswig should be consulted upon whether they desired to be Danish or German. This only accorded with justice. The Duchy of Holstein was and had always been purely German. The south of Schleswig had been gradually Germanised, but the north remained Danish in speech and Danish in sentiment. The stipulation of the Treaty had never been carried out. The inhabitants of Northern Schleswig were never consulted, and Prussia had at a later date freed herself from the legal obligation. Now was clearly the time to repair this injustice and the permanent estrangement between Denmark and Germany which had resulted from it. There were some who would have desired that the whole of Schleswig should be separated from Germany, in order so to arrange the frontier that the Kiel Canal should cease to run entirely through German territory. The prudence of the Danish Government set all such designs on one side. They desired to receive into the Danish nation only those districts whose people felt themselves to be Danes. They rejected all suggestions that a German-speaking population should be unwillingly incorporated in Denmark. Accordingly it was agreed that the future frontiers should be drawn by the free vote of the population given in a plebiscite.

Let us now turn to the eastern frontier of Germany. Here we encounter one of the great new facts. Only a prodigy could have brought about the rebirth of Poland. Before that event could come to pass, it was necessary that every single one of the three military Empires which had partitioned Poland should be simultaneously and decisively defeated in war, or otherwise shattered. If the Powers which had devoured Poland stood together in a *Drei-Kaiserbund*, there was no force in the world which would or could have challenged them. If they warred on opposite sides, at least one would emerge among the victors and could not be despoiled of its possessions. But the astounding triple event had occurred: Russia had shattered Austria; the Bolsheviks, aided by Germany, had destroyed Russia; and Germany herself had been overpowered by France and the English-speaking world. So all three parts of sundered Poland were free at the same moment; and all their chains—Russian, German, and Austrian—fell to the ground in a single clash. The hour of Destiny had struck; and the largest crime of European history, triumphantly persisted in through six generations, was now to pass away. Point XIII had declared that '*an independent Polish State should be erected, which should include the territories inhabited by indisputably Polish populations, which should be assured a free and secure access to the sea.*' Germany had accepted this. Indeed her own claim for ethnic integrity was based upon the very principle which recreated the ancient State of Poland.

But with the best will in the world the drawing of a frontier between Germany and Poland could not be free from anomaly and injustice. The great plain which stretched from Warsaw to Berlin was marked by no physical barrier. Along a belt of four hundred miles the population was mixed in varying proportions. It had been the policy of Germany to colonise Poland with German settlers. German capital, science and ability had created a vigorous industrial life. Their culture, thrust forward with the power of an armed and militant Empire, had everywhere made its impression upon the conquered and partitioned population. The Germans pointed to the obvious benefits which their rule had conferred on Prussian Poland; the Poles declared this was the mere usufruct of a stolen inheritance. It was the task of the Peace Conference, of the Poland Commission, and finally of the Triumvirate to draw the line.

The problem divided itself into three sections: the centre, the north and the south. The task of the Poland Commission was to determine which districts were inhabited by an indisputably Polish population. Plebiscites were convenient for well-marked districts, but no plebiscite was possible throughout this great belt of country whose boundaries were indefinite. To seek such a plebiscite would have involved occupying the whole area by impartial British, French and American troops. But the Americans were going home; the British had demobilised so fast that they could scarcely spare half a dozen battalions; and the French avowed themselves Polish champions. In the centre, therefore, which broadly comprised the Prussian province of Posen, the only basis was the German statistics. No doubt these were more than discounted by the not unnatural anti-German bias of the victors. But upon the whole the line was drawn with the desire to assign to Germany the fewest possible number of Poles, and to Poland the fewest possible number of Germans.

More difficulty arose in the north. The province of East Prussia, though originally in the nature of a German colonial conquest, had become a purely German land whose population was animated above all other parts of Germany by the spirit of intense Nationalism. This province was separated from the rest of Germany by a strip or corridor running down to the sea, in which from all accounts there appeared to be a Polish-speaking majority. The Poles demanded large portions of East Prussia from Germany, and for the rest suggested that 'this small island of German people should be made a republic with its capital at Königsberg.' This demand was rejected. But the Polish-speaking corridor was joined to Poland, not only on grounds of language but as the most obvious means of giving Poland that access to the sea which had been accepted by all parties to the Fourteen Points.

Adjoining the corridor was the great city of Dantzig inhabited by two hundred thousand Germans, which was the natural outlet to the sea for the whole trade of the Valley of the Vistula. The Commission originally proposed to transfer Dantzig absolutely to Polish sovereignty, so that the inhabitants of Dantzig would be subject to Polish legislation and to compulsory service in the Polish Army. Through Mr. Lloyd George's exertions a solution was found by which Dantzig was restored to the old position it had held for five hundred years as a self-governing civic State, united by close ties with Poland but with autonomous sovereign control over its whole internal administration and government. Dantzig was to be a free city, but it was to enter the Polish Custom system and the Poles were to have the administration of the great harbour. This ingenious and complicated expedient did not give complete satisfaction to either side. But it is not easy to see what better method could have been adopted.

In this northern section of the frontier two minor points of difficulty must be mentioned. East Prussia had been preserved to Germany, but certain districts on its southern borders contained considerable Polish-speaking populations and were claimed by Poland. For these districts of Allenstein and Marienwerder a plebiscite was prescribed. The majority voted to remain with Germany, and their wish was law. Lastly the small port and district of Memel, situated on the other side of the river Niemen, was the only means by which Lithuania could obtain that outlet to the sea without which it could not exist as an independent State. It was hoped that the Lithuanians would voluntarily join themselves once more to Poland. This they refused, and could not be compelled. Thus eventually Memel, a German town of about 30,000 inhabitants, surrounded by rural districts largely Lithuanian-speaking, was assigned to Lithuania, under elaborate securities for local autonomy.

We have still to consider the southern section of the German-Polish frontier; and here upon the question of Upper Silesia another of the great disputes of the Conference occurred. The draft Treaty presented to the Germans prescribed the absolute cession of Upper Silesia, after the Ruhr the richest iron and coal district in the German Empire, to the Poles. This was the greatest blot upon the draft Treaty with Germany. The rest was implicit in the acceptance of the Fourteen Points; but the enforced cession of the whole of Upper Silesia was received with vehement German resentment and indeed with general surprise.

* * * * *

The conflicts of the Triumvirate, now rejoined by Italy, which had marked the framing of the preliminary peace terms did not end with their presentation to Germany. The

Germans protested by every means in their power against the Financial and Economic clauses, against the clauses compelling their avowal of war guilt and the surrender of war criminals. In the territorial sphere they complained chiefly of the cession of Upper Silesia. It seemed possible that they would refuse to sign the treaty, and thus force the Allies into a military occupation of Berlin and other important centres, or a prolongation of the blockade, or both. Such a course presented no immediate military difficulty but very grave political dangers. No one could tell how long an occupation would last. Until it ended very large numbers of soldiers must be kept under arms and further demobilisation indefinitely suspended.

On June I Mr. Lloyd George, wishing to strengthen himself in his efforts to obtain a mitigation of the peace terms, convened a meeting in Paris of the British Empire Delegation. The whole Empire was represented together with the principal British Departments of State. General Smuts made a powerful appeal for clemency. When my turn came, I supported him by arguments of a different character. As Secretary of State for War I had a special point of view.

I stated that

'there were the most serious difficulties either in re-imposing the blockade or in governing the whole territory of Germany and undertaking the solving of local political problems. A foreign garrison would never make the Germans work unitedly and effectively. The weapons of blockade and occupation were mutually exclusive. If you occupied the country, you would have to feed the people in the territory held and this could not be done under blockade. If the Allies entered Germany and occupied the country, it would be necessary to have conscription indefinitely. It was impossible to control the internal life of Germany without maintaining compulsory service [for Great Britain]. The pressure to obtain the release of men from the army was already indescribable. The very classes who were calling most loudly for extreme terms to be imposed upon Germany were those who were the most anxious to get men out of the army.'

Accordingly I urged that further negotiations should take place and 'implored the Delegation to cast their opinion in the direction of giving their plenipotentiaries the greatest possible liberty to make a "split the difference" Peace' [on the points outstanding]. The Chancellor of the Exchequer, Mr. Chamberlain; the Lord Chancellor, Lord Birkenhead and others spoke to the same purpose.

Although there were many gradations of opinion the will of the Delegation was unanimous. It was resolved that the Prime Minister in his negotiations should press for concessions to be made to the enemy in the treaty of peace. In particular: Amendment of the proposals for the Eastern frontier of Germany, leaving to Germany districts preponderantly German and providing for a plebiscite in doubtful cases: Extension to Germany of the right to enter the League of Nations at an early date: Reduction in the numerical strength of the Army of Occupation: Modification of the reparation clauses and the fixing of the German liability at a definite amount.

The Delegation in a mood of strong conviction further authorised the Prime Minister in the event of resistance on the part of any of his colleagues on the Council of Four, 'to use the full weight of the entire British Empire even to the point of refusing the services of the British Army to advance into Germany, or the services of the British Navy to enforce the blockade of Germany.'

This seemed to be a memorable occasion.

Mr. Lloyd George was thus strongly armed for all the future discussions: and he would probably have succeeded in improving the treaty in an even greater degree but for his burden of reparation pledges. The crazy echoes of the General Election were a humiliating handicap both to the Prime Minister and Great Britain. Clemenceau, Wilson and Orlando understood the position perfectly. When Wilson was rallied with placing Germans under Polish, Czechoslovak or Italian rule; when Clemenceau was reproached for vindictiveness or Orlando for territorial appetite, each had his retort. A sarcastic smile, a shrug of the shoulders, some reference to the difficulties of democratic electioneering were quite sufficient to place the Big Four upon an equality, and at a lower level.

All the time the odd fact was that however many thousand millions Germany paid, Great Britain was only to receive a very small fraction, less than half the share of France and subject to Belgian priority; and that, scarcely two years later, she was to proclaim the principle, revived from the wisdom of an aristocratic past, that all war debts ought to be simultaneously extinguished by universal consent with consequent reactions upon reparations.

A prolonged conflict ensued about Silesia. President Wilson and the French championed the claims of Poland. England asserted the rights of Germany and invoked the principle of Self-determination. The President's bias in favour of Poland was as marked as his prejudices against the Italians. Cynics pointed to the fact that Italian emigrants to America usually return to Italy without acquiring voting rights, while the Polish vote was a formidable factor in the domestic politics of the United States. Be this as it may, Mr. Wilson had made up his mind that Poland should have Upper Silesia and he resented all opposition. However in this field Mr. Lloyd George was unhampered by British electioneering and in spite of the persistent attacks of the Northcliffe Press his efforts and persuasion prevailed. The principle of a plebiscite was conceded to the Germans in the final Treaty, which is thus cleared from reproach in this respect.

It is worth while to describe briefly the outcome.

A plebiscite was eventually held in 1920 under the authority of British and French troops. While these were occupying the disputed zones and preparing for the voting, a violent incursion of Poles under one Korfanty, a former Polish deputy of the Reichstag, was organised with the object of preventing the election. The Germans were not slow to retaliate with a similar inroad. A sort of civil war broke out in which British troops sympathised with the Germans and the French with the Poles. Matters thus came to a dangerous and ludicrous pass. However, law and good sense prevailed. The plebiscite was duly taken, and a German majority of 6 to 4 declared itself. When these results were brought before the Supreme Council no agreement could be reached. The Americans had gone home, and England and France were in obstinate equipoise. The deadlock was resolved by an agreement to refer the issue to the Council of the League of Nations. This was the first occasion upon which a dispute between two of the greatest Powers had been relegated to the new instrument. The Council, sundered by the differences between England and France, in its turn devolved the decision upon a Commission consisting of the representatives of the smaller states, who though on the Council of the League were not involved in the discussions of the Supreme Council of the Allies. A Belgian, a Spaniard, a Brazilian and a Chinese were entrusted with this delicate and thorny problem. Under all the pressures which were brought to bear this body took refuge in a compromise. Their decision was bitterly resented by Germany, but accepted as binding by England and France. It is not easy to see what other procedure could have been followed.

Judged by Gladstonian standards, Germany issued from the war and the peace with many positive advantages. She had in fact realised all the main objectives of British Liberal policy in the Victorian era. Defeat has given the German people effective control of their own affairs. The Imperialist system has been swept away. A domestic self-determination has been achieved. A parliamentary system based on universal suffrage to which the rulers of Germany are effectively responsible may be some consolation for the loss of twenty-two kings and princes. The abolition of compulsory military service has always seemed to British eyes a boon and not an injury. The restriction of armaments enforced by treaties upon Germany is to-day extolled as the highest goal to which all nations should aspire. The absurd and monstrous economic and financial chapters of the Treaty of Versailles have already been swept almost entirely into limbo; they have either lapsed or have been superseded by a series of arrangements increasingly based on facts, on good sense and on mutual agreement. The sufferings of the German bourgeois and rentier classes, the humble pensioner, the thrifty annuitant, the retired toiler, the aged professor, the brave officer—which resulted from the act of repudiation involved in the destruction of the mark largely by the German Government themselves—are piteous. They may affront the justice of the German State; they have not weakened the pulsations of the German heart, nor the productive vitality of German industry, nor even the credit and saving power of the German people. Germany has lost her colonies, but she was a late-comer on the colonial scene. She possessed no territory over-seas in which the German race could live and multiply. 'Foreign plantations,' to quote the old-fashioned English phrase, in tropical lands might be a source of pride and interest and certainly of expenditure. They were in any case hostages to a stronger sea-power. Their alienation in no way impaired the German strength and very doubtfully improved the fortunes of their new possessors.

Contrast for a moment the position which Germany occupies to-day with the doom which would have fallen upon the British Empire and upon Great Britain itself had the submarine attack mastered the Royal Navy and left our forty millions only the choice between unconditional surrender and certain starvation. Half the severity meted out by the Treaty of Versailles would have involved not only the financial ruin of our ancient, slowly built-up world organisation but a swift contraction of the British population by at least ten million souls and the condemnation of the rest to universal and hopeless poverty. The stakes of this hideous war were beyond all human measure, and for Britain and her people they were not less than final extinction. When we consider the fate of the Austro-Hungarian Empire, of Austria itself, and of the overcrowded city of Vienna, we may measure in miniature the risks we were forced to run.

In these blunt paragraphs there is an appeal to the intellect of Germany.

* * * * *

How stood the case of France?

The disproportion of national power between Germany and France was and is the main problem of the Peace. A stationary population of forty millions under-inhabiting the fairest portion of the globe, in contact along hundreds of miles of land frontier with a multiplying, progressing German race and State of sixty or seventy millions, is a proposition inherent with explosive quality. It is well always to talk about peace and to strive and suffer for peace; but it is better at the same time to understand the causes which lead to wars. How is a forty million France to be defended from invasion and destruction in the next generation against a sixty, seventy, eighty million Germany? There was the root problem of the Peace Conference. We need not dive into elaborate statistics. It should be sufficient to state that after 1940 Germany will have about twice as many men of military age as France. How was France to find security against that? France was victorious. Germany was utterly defeated. But every intelligent Frenchman and German knew that though these conditions might rule for twenty or thirty years, they embodied no finality. It would have been impossible for France to fight Germany without the aid of Russia; but Russia had gone. No one could say whether, when, or in what mood Russia would reappear. It seemed at least as likely as not in the days of the Peace Conference that the resurgence of Russia would find her on the German side. England had the Channel, and the United States the Ocean between them and these issues. 'There is nothing in the long run,' said the French, 'to stand between us and Invasion, but the bayonets and breasts of our soldiers.'

Here was the fear and the peril. It broods over Europe to-day. Even as I write, we see the French devoting fifty millions of their thriftily accumulated money to building a line of concrete and steel defences to preserve their country against a renewal of what happened in August, 1870, and in August, 1914. Here was the root issue of the Peace Conference: the fear of France that she would be destroyed by Germany and her evident determination not to be guilty of imprudence in a matter of life and death.

But, it was said, the growing moral sense of mankind will prevent such a downfall of civilisation ever happening again. The Covenant of the League of Nations guarantees to each member State the independence and integrity of its territory. To which the French replied, 'Did treaties protect Belgium?' But, it was urged, the world has learned its lesson; the Germans have learned their lesson. No one is going to fight any more. To which the French said, '*We* have already had enough.' Finally it was asserted that men had become wiser, nobler, more humane in consequence of four years of butchery and impoverishment; that one had only to look around to see how much better all were than their fathers. Trust to Democracy. Trust to the mass mind. Trust to Parliamentary institutions. Trust to the sting of old wounds. But the French continued mournfully to reiterate, 'We want Security.' On this the United States, being perfectly safe, and England, being fairly safe, remarked philosophically, 'There is no such thing as absolute security.' And the French said, 'In that case we will have the best we can get.'

Marshal Foch, with the laurels of unfading splendour on his brow and recent experiences being present in all minds, declared, 'We must have the left bank of the Rhine. There is no English or American help which could be strong enough and which could arrive in sufficient time to prevent disaster in the plains of the north; preserve France from defeat; or, if she wants to spare her Armies from this, to free her from the necessity of drawing them back behind the Somme or the Seine or the Loire in order to await help from her Allies. The Rhine remains therefore to-day the barrier which is indispensable to the safety of Western Europe and thereby the safety of civilisation.'

Then the English and the Americans said, 'But the Germans live on both sides of the Rhine, and how can you rule over them?' So Marshal Foch went back to Napoleon and his Confederation of the Rhine. 'It would be the duty,' he said (March 31), 'to settle the political condition of the left bank of the Rhine and to endow this district with a conception that would be compatible with the freedom of nations. As a matter of fact these countries have never been anything but independent states or odd parts of states of Central Germany.' The discussion was tense. Mr. Lloyd George asked two questions: 'If the Germans knew that Great Britain and the United States of America were bound to support France, do you think they would nevertheless attack?' Marshal Foch answered that if they were assured that there was no danger from Russia, they would not hesitate to do so. Again, 'If the German Army had been reduced to the same size as the British Army, would they attack?' Foch replied that they would, because in fact the German Army would not be reduced. He also said that the existence of a Channel Tunnel would not make much difference.

At the same time it was apparent that the population who dwelt by the Rhine would far rather belong to defeated Germany than to victorious France. Neither did they wish to be made into a buffer state. So that at the very outset the Conference was at a complete deadlock.

Both President Wilson and Lloyd George were deeply conscious of the dangers and fears of France. Wilson had hoped that the League of Nations would give France with all other nations security against invasion. But the French, while quite willing to have the League's protection for what it was worth, sincerely disbelieved in its power. When the sanction of armed force was withdrawn from the draft of the covenant and financial and economic boycott of the aggressor alone remained, French scepticism could hardly be challenged. President Wilson's visit to the United States and the reservations which he had felt himself forced by American public opinion to make, still further weakened the resources of the League. Thenceforward it became clear that if France was to be induced to withdraw from the Rhine, some other additional assurance of safety must be found for her. Mr. Lloyd George had for some time foreseen that this was inevitable. He was even more convinced than Wilson of the dangers of subjecting German populations to alien rule. Both he and Wilson refused to contemplate confining Germany behind the Rhine; both felt increasingly the obligation to find alternative securities.

The first and most obvious precaution was the disarmament of Germany. Marshal Foch and the French military men were curiously apathetic on this point. In the armistice terms the Marshal had not included any provision for the demobilisation of the German army nor for its disarmament except the surrender of a large number of guns. It has been stated on his behalf that he did not believe that any general disarmament could be enforced for a prolonged period, and that he did not wish to put his name to terms the execution of which he could not guarantee. He profoundly distrusted all German assurances, and believed that whatever promises were made, Germany would as soon as she recovered her freedom of action in some way or other create and arm new military forces.

Under the vigorous impulsion of the Prime Minister the British delegates on the Disarmament Commission pressed for the most drastic measures. Mr. Lloyd George insisted that the German army should not be stronger than the British; that it should not be raised by compulsion and should not be maintained upon a short service basis. It was to be a volunteer, professional army, each soldier serving on a minimum engagement of twelve years. Thus it would not have the power of developing a mass of trained reserves. The total strength of those serving with the colours was not to exceed 200,000 men. Similar proposals were made for the German Navy. The French yielded themselves with some hesitation to this strong initiative. The scheme was entirely contrary to all continental ideas. It seemed to impugn the principle of 'a nation in arms' which was the inheritance of the Revolution and the supreme guarantee of the life and liberties of the French Republic. Nevertheless, they saw its merits so far as Germany was concerned. They stipulated that if the German Army was to be thus highly professional, it should not exceed 100,000 men. To this Mr. Lloyd George raised no objection.

The military terms finally agreed to are astonishing. A nation of sixty millions, hitherto the first military power in the world, was forbidden for all time to have an army of more than 100,000. The whole basis of the former military organization by which the German nation had been built up was swept away. The General Staff which had so powerfully swayed the policy of the German State was abolished. Rifles, machine guns, and field artillery were strictly limited; and the making of armoured cars, tanks or poison gases was prohibited. No military aeroplanes or airships were to be made or kept, and the manufacture of arms, munitions and war material was limited to a small number of named factories. The work of destroying the surplus munitions was pressed forward with singular energy by the Prime Minister. I received at the War Office his repeated directions to enforce and accelerate it. In all 40,000 cannon were blown to pieces and all other military materials destroyed in like proportion. Thus mainly by British exertions Germany was almost completely disarmed; and the whole military caste, that vast vested interest and also type of national virtue which had been the permanent agency of German might must fade in the passage of a generation out of German life. The streams of youth and patriotism, of valour and ability which flow perennially from the German race would henceforward follow new channels, and as in

England or the United States find other forms of national or social service. This was and is a fact of prime importance.

But the French still remained incredulous and inconsolable. How long would all this last? What would happen twenty or thirty or forty years on? No one expected a renewal of war in the lifetime of the generation that had known its horror and its squalors. These disarmament provisions would be effective in the years when there was no danger; they would cease to act at the very time when they were needed. The left bank of the Rhine, reiterated the French, was the only enduring defence.

The second measure of reassurance proposed both by Great Britain and the United States and welcomed by France was the demilitarisation of a broad zone between France and Germany. The Treaty accordingly prescribed that all fortified works and fortresses situated in German territory west of a line traced 50 kilometres east of the Rhine should be disarmed and dismantled. All new fortifications within this zone were forbidden. Inhabitants of this zone would not be permitted to bear arms or receive any military training or be incorporated in any military organisation, voluntary or compulsory; and no depots, establishments, railways or works of any kind adapted to military purposes would be permitted to exist within the area. The permanent enforcement of these conditions would be supervised by such means and by such organs as the Allied and Associated Powers might decide to employ or to create.

The British members of the drafting Committee were impressed with the difficulty of thus disarming Germany while leaving, for instance, Poland free to develop her forces to any extent and while Russia remained entirely outside the scope alike of the Peace Conference and the League of Nations. It was therefore suggested it seems by the British delegation that a preamble should be inserted to these chapters of the Treaty by which the permanent disarmament of Germany was connected with a general process of disarmament throughout the world. This was fathered by President Wilson, and readily adopted. It is from this preamble that the prolonged and, as they have proved, disturbing labours of the Disarmament Commission at Geneva have originated.

The French continued to argue that admirable as these safeguards might be in theory, real as they might be in tranquil periods, they would break and fail in the generation for whose protection they were needed. One final security was therefore sought, and the idea of a British and American guarantee to France against a future German invasion rose and gradually became definite. This was of course, as far as human arrangements extend, an absolute safeguard. It was inconceivable that any German Government would invade France if such an act involved war with both the British Empire and the United States. The strength of the English-speaking world in combination was irresistible, and the experience of the war had proved that that strength could certainly be applied in Europe, or indeed elsewhere, in a military, naval, or economic form to any extent necessary—though only after an uncertain interval of time.

Foch, however, continued irreconcilable; and the choice before Clemenceau was poignant. How could the dwindling, or at best stationary, manhood of France, bled white by the war, hold the Rhine by military force alone, in defiance not only of Germany, but of the English-speaking world? How could he reject the all-sufficing guarantee which the two overseas giants so freely offered? On the other hand, he knew that the abandonment of the Rhine would never be forgiven by the strongest elements in France. Not even his services to France in her mortal peril would avail him. But his courage and wisdom were equal to the ordeal. He accepted the British and American guarantee and the treaty was framed on the basis of the inviolability of the German Rhine-lands subject only to an interval of military occupation, now drawing to its close.

The sequel dwells with us to-day. The British Parliament duly approved their treaty of guarantee. The Senate of the United States repudiated the signature of President Wilson. The joint guarantee was therefore void. The British obligation depended upon the American acceptance and fell simultaneously with the American refusal. Thus France having bound herself by treaty to give up the Rhine was deprived of her compensating security. Isolated and, as they claim, deceived and deserted, the French people have fallen back on their own military force, upon technical equipment, upon African reserves, upon fortifications and military conventions with Poland and other new European States. There will be more to be said on the general question when we come later on to the Treaty of Locarno: but those who deplore these developments and criticise their evil features would do well to study their causes as well as their effects.

*　*　*　*　*

The fierce stresses of the settlement of the German peace terms had exhausted for the time being the energies of the Triumvirate. It was natural that they should shrink from immediately plunging into the less crucial but none the less important and even more complicated problems of the Austro-Hungarian Empire and its fate. Some lassitude was inevitable and perhaps excusable. Numerous Commissions had long been working upon the various aspects. It seemed sufficient at the moment to give a general direction to these Commissions and to the drafting Committee of jurists to apply the principles of the treaty with Germany in framing the treaties with the other defeated States.

But the principle of Self-determination which had preserved Germany as the greatest united branch of the European family was finally fatal to the Empire of the Hapsburgs. Moreover, in this vast scene the decisive events had already taken place. The Austro-Hungarian Empire had in fact shivered into fragments in the last fortnight of the war. On October 28, 1918, Czechoslovakia had proclaimed itself and had been recognised by the Allied and Associate Powers as an independent sovereign state. Strong in the memories of the Czechoslovak army corps and in the influence upon the Allies of Masaryk and Benes, the Czechoslovaks successfully presented themselves at the Peace Conference, not as part of an enemy empire defeated by the Allies, but as a new state technically at war with Germany and Austria and awaiting peace settlements with both these countries. A similar metamorphosis had accompanied the creation on December 1, 1918, of Jugo-Slavia, formed from the union of the victorious Serbians and the defeated Croats and Slovenes into a Southern Slav Kingdom of approximately 13,000,000 souls. This new State was also promptly recognised by Great Britain, France and the United States. Italy, however, demurred. The Croats, they complained, were enemies who had fought hard and well against Italy throughout the war. Whatever might be said of Bohemia and the

Czechoslovaks, the Croats had no right to change sides in the moment of defeat and by a judicious dive emerge among the victors. However the force of events prevailed. The Croats sought, and the Serbians accorded shelter and status as a friendly people forced into war against their will by a defunct and guilty Imperialism. Their claims were recognised by Italy in April, 1919.

Hungary had also seceded from the Empire and proclaimed herself an independent monarchy. Austria isolated with the ancient and cultured capital of Vienna in her midst endeavoured to tread a similar path. The Austrians proclaimed a Republic, declared that they were a new State which had never been at war with the Allies and pleaded that its people ought not to be penalised for the misdeeds of a vanished régime.

These transformations confronted the reunited Council of Four with novel problems. The representatives of Czechoslovakia and Jugo-Slavia were ensconced as friends and in part as allies within the charmed circle of victory. The Austrians and the Hungarians who had fought at their side on the same fronts and in the same armies sat outside under the shadow of defeat and the stigma of war-guilt. Although the ruling class in Austria and Hungary bore an exceptional responsibility, it was absurd to regard the mass of the populations of any of these four States as peculiarly innocent or culpable. All had been drawn by the same currents irresistibly into the vortex. Yet one half were to be cherished and the other half to be smitten.

Two soldiers have served side by side, sharing in a common cause the perils and hardships of the war. The war is ended and they return home to their respective villages. But a frontier line has been drawn between them. One is a guilty wretch lucky to escape with life the conquerors' vengeance. The other appears to be one of the conquerors himself. Alas for these puppets of Fate! It is always unlucky to be born in the central regions of any continent.

It was to this strange and tumultuous scene that the Peace Conference endeavoured to apply the principle of Self-determination which had governed the German Treaty, and thus redraw the map of Central Europe. The word 'Czechoslovakia' was new to British ears; but the ancient kingdom of Bohemia and Moravia, where the Czechs lived, stirred popular memories of King Wenceslas on the Feast of Stephen, of blind King John of Bohemia at the Battle of Crécy, of the Prince of Wales's Feathers with its German motto 'Ich Dien', and perhaps of John Huss of Prague. Here were time-honoured tales. For several hundred years we had lost sight of Bohemia. The personal union of the Crowns of Austria and Bohemia, effected in the sixteenth century, had made the head of the Hapsburgs Austrian Emperor and King of Bohemia. The torment of the Thirty Years War scarred for ever the history of the two countries. Bohemia, persecuted for Protestantism, became partly Catholicised under duress. From 1618, after the total defeat of the Bohemians in the Battle of the White Mountain, the Hapsburgs ruled a conquered kingdom with autocratic power. The Bohemian people were never reconciled. Their national sentiment slumbered during the eighteenth century; but memories were long and tradition powerful. The latter half of the nineteenth century saw the rebirth of Bohemian nationalism embodied in the Czech movement. Popular education revived here as elsewhere a long forgotten national language. The schools became the centres of strife between the Czech population and the Imperial Government. Lingual self-consciousness and national aspirations rose together. The Emperor Francis Joseph had been crowned King of Hungary at Budapest; but the Czech desire that he should come to Prague and be crowned King of Bohemia was obstinately and, as it now seems, insensately, refused.

During the war the Czech movement developed into the demand for autonomy and thence into independence. The Czechs had been accustomed to look to Russia for sympathy. After the Russian Revolution they turned under the guidance of Masaryk to the United States and to the Western Powers. Their independence had been already recognised. It remained to define their frontiers. But here were stubborn complications. Bohemia and Moravia contained at least three millions of German-speaking population, often concentrated, usually in the ascendant, a strong, competent stock holding firmly together like the Ulstermen in Ireland. To exclude the German-speaking population was deeply and perhaps fatally to weaken the new State; to include them was to affront the principle of Self-determination. The Peace Conference in this dilemma decided to adhere to the ancient frontiers of Bohemia, well defined by mountain ranges, and consecrated by five hundred years of tradition. Apart from some vexatious but petty alterations on the frontier towards Austria, this decision became effective.

The Czechs of Bohemia had joined hands with the Slovaks. This tribe dwelt upon the southern slopes of the mountains on the north of Hungary, and stretched some distance into the Danubian plain. The Slovaks had for centuries been under a Magyar rule which they regarded as oppressive. They were a Slav people akin to the Czechs. They spoke a dialect of the same language. They wished to escape from Hungary and join the new State. President Wilson towards the close of the war had agreed with Professor Masaryk that the United States would support the inclusion of the Slovaks in the new Bohemia; and on this Czechoslovakia had, as we have seen, proclaimed itself a sovereign State. The drawing of the frontier between the Slovaks and the Magyars was in any case a task of difficulty. No line could have been drawn to which there were not valid objections. The natural bias of the Commission was in favour of the Slovaks, and in the result about a million Magyars found themselves included against their will within the limits of Czechoslovakia.

The Kingdom of Jugo-Slavia had formed itself by the union of the old Kingdom of Serbia, augmented by the Provinces of Bosnia and Herzegovina, with the Croats and Slovenes. The Croats had for centuries been under the Hungarian crown. They were not down-trodden like the Slovaks, but a home rule movement was in progress among them by constitutional and legal methods before the war. The Dalmatians and the Slovenes, who inhabited the mountainous country north and north-west of Venice and Trieste, were subject to the Austrian crown. Both these populations sought a new allegiance; and the new Serb-Croat-Slovene Kingdom, denoted by the initials S.H.S., entered upon the troubles of existence.

Again the limits of the new State had to be determined. The frontiers of Jugo-Slavia with Hungary presented little difficulty; with Austria they were more difficult, and at least one plebiscite was required to mitigate the sharpness of decisions. The frontiers with Italy were the most difficult of all; and here victorious Allied Governments faced each other in armed menace. The Italian frontiers of Jugo-Slavia were eventually settled by separate negotiations between the two countries.

Roumania, like Serbia, was to gain a great accession of population and territory. The crescent moon of the Roumanian map waxed to full by the incorporation of Transylvania. The problem of Transylvania was insoluble by the principle of Self-determination. It presented the feature of a considerable Hungarian population isolated within a Roumanian border belt. The peoples of the Roumanian zone wished to join Roumania; those of the Magyar nucleus to adhere to their kinsmen in Hungary. Either decision would have conflicted with Self-determination. The issues of principle being thus physically excluded and the integrity of Transylvania being an important factor, the Peace Conference transferred the whole country to Roumania and thus alienated at least another million Magyars from Hungary.

The new limits of Hungary and Austria were the result of these events. Hungary lost Slovakia to Bohemia, Croatia to Serbia, Transylvania to Roumania. She was also required to cede to Austria a considerable German-speaking area near Vienna which was essential to the food supplies of that forlorn capital. It happened unluckily for the Magyars that they had lost command of their own government in the critical period of the Paris Conference. A Communist revolution had erupted in Budapest. Bela Kun, a disciple of Lenin and a paid tool of Moscow, had seized power and had used it with cruel violence and tyranny. The Supreme Council could only expostulate. It therefore expostulated. But the Roumanian army was in Transylvania. Attacked by Communist rabble this army advanced as invaders of Hungary and were at first welcomed in the guise of deliverers by the Hungarian population whom they mercilessly pillaged. The Hungarian people were therefore at their weakest when the crucial issues of their future were to be decided. Not only were the various subject races, which Hungary had in the course of centuries incorporated, liberated from her sway, but more than two and a half million Magyars, a fourth of the entire population, dwell to-day under foreign rule.

Austria is the final remnant. With Hungary she bore the whole blame and burden of the once mighty Hapsburg Empire. Reduced to a community of six millions around Vienna and in the Alpine lands, with the Imperial capital of two millions in its midst, the state of Austria was pitiful indeed. The frontier had still to be drawn between Austria and Italy. The secret Treaty of London had promised Italy the line of the Alps. But in the South Tyrol, the land of Hofer, four hundred thousand German-speaking people of the upper valley of the Adige lived south of the Alps. Italy claimed her Treaty rights, and England and France were bound. President Wilson was free, and his problem was painful. On the one hand stood the principle of Self-determination; on the other, the Alps, the Treaties and the strategic security of Italy. In April President Wilson withdrew the opposition he had hitherto maintained, and the Southern Tyrol passed to Italian sovereignty.

It should be added that in all the treaties constituting the frontiers of the new States precise and elaborate provisions were inserted and accepted providing for the protection of minorities, their good treatment and equal rights before the law. Italy as one of the victorious Great Powers was not called upon to assume a treaty obligation for the protection of minorities. She instead voluntarily declared her solemn resolve to accord them the consideration and fair play which were their due. The inhabitants of the South Tyrol may therefore base themselves directly and in a peculiarly personal sense upon the faith and honour of the Italian nation.

In her miserable plight Austria turned to Germany. A union with the great Teutonic mass would give to Austria a vitality and means of existence from which she was cut off by a circle of resentful neighbours. The new Austrian Government appealing at once to the right of Self-determination and of nationality, claimed to become a part of the German Republic. Theoretically upon Wilsonian principles this demand—the Anschluss, as it is called—was difficult to resist. In practice it was loaded with danger. It would have meant making the new Germany larger in territory and population than the old Germany which had already proved strong enough to fight the world for four years. It would have brought the frontiers of the German realm to the summits of the Alps and made a complete barrier between Eastern and Western Europe. The future of Switzerland and the permanent existence of Czechoslovakia alike appeared to be affected. A clause was therefore inserted both in the German and Austrian Treaties forbidding such a union except with the unanimous consent, presumably unattainable, of the Council of the League of Nations.

The exclusion of this alternative for the gravest reasons of European peace made it the more necessary to improve the conditions in the new Austria. This required a speedy recognition of the Republic, and the greatest care to lighten the financial burden imposed upon it. Notwithstanding the urgent representations made by those Englishmen who were actually in Vienna, the whole Austrian question was for months completely neglected. When at last the drafting of the Austrian Treaty began, the different Commissions endeavoured to apply to it the terms of the German Treaty. This meant that the whole financial burden was to be laid upon the small Austrian Republic, together with Hungary. The Reparation clauses technically imposed the onus of paying reparations for the whole of the former Austro-Hungarian Monarchy upon these two small derelict States. This pure nonsense could of course never be applied. But a needless and dangerous delay arose. The complete financial collapse of Austria followed, and a social collapse was only averted at a later stage by the intervention of the League of Nations at the instance chiefly of Mr. Balfour.

Bulgaria was better treated; she missed the hiatus and inertia which followed the Treaty of Versailles. She profited by the recoil from the decisions of the Treaty of St. Germain. Her population was scarcely at all reduced; her economic and geographical needs were studied; she was assured of commercial access to the Aegean. Yet the griefs of the Allies against the Bulgarians were not light. The cold-blooded entry of Bulgaria into the war; the historic ingratitude which this act involved to Russian liberators and English friends; the stabbing of struggling Serbia in the back; the frightful injury inflicted thereby upon the Allied Cause; the war crimes committed on Serbian soil—all these made a long and dark account. Dr. Temperley states in his History of the Peace Conference that the Bulgarian delegation was surprised on their arrival at Paris by the fact that no one wished to shake hands with them, and a pregnant footnote sets forth

THE NEW MAP OF EUROPE

many gruesome explanations of this coolness. Yet the Bulgarian Treaty was drafted in a far more instructed and careful mood than that which had regulated the fate of Austria and Hungary. The experts were becoming adepts in the work of treaty making; the best and ablest officials were acquiring control. The passions and interests of the Great Powers were not involved; they were indeed benevolently indifferent. The worst complaint of the Bulgarians was that they were forbidden to have a conscript army and that their people would not become professional soldiers. For the rest they were a warrior race, industrious and brave, apt to till and defend their soil or take the soil of others. They sat on the ground-floor of life's edifice, with no great risk of falling further. It was accepted they had been driven into war by King Ferdinand, and with his departure into luxurious exile the wrath of the Allies had been sensibly appeased.

* * * * *

It is with the general aspects of the territorial settlements with the Central Powers, and the principles underlying them, that this chapter is mainly concerned. The Peace with Turkey and the Treaties of Sèvres and Lausanne require separate treatment. The dispute between Jugo-Slavia and Roumania about the Banat of Temesvar; the quarrel between the Poles and Czechs about the Duchy of Teschen, the problem of the Carpathian Ruthenes, and the larger difficulty of Eastern Galicia are complications with which this brief account cannot deal. It is obvious how many points of friction remained to cause heart-burnings to the populations affected, and anxiety to Europe. But a fair judgment upon the whole settlement, a simple explanation of how it arose, cannot leave the authors of the new map of Europe under any serious reproach. To an overwhelming extent the wishes of the various populations prevailed. The fundamental principle which governed the victors was honestly applied within the limits of their waning power. No solution could have been free from hardship and anomaly. More refined solutions in the disputed areas could only have been obtained if Britain, France and the United States had been prepared to provide considerable numbers of troops for lengthy periods to secure a far more elaborate and general adoption of plebiscites, to effect transferences of population such as were afterwards made in Turkey, and meanwhile to supply food and credits to those whose destinies would thus be held in suspense. The exhaustion of the war forbade such toilsome interferences, nor would the scale of the remaining grievances have justified their hazards. The moulds into which Central and Southern Europe has been cast were hastily and in parts roughly shaped, but they conformed for all practical purposes with much exactness to the general design; and according to the lights of the twentieth century that design seems true.

CHAPTER XII
THE RUSSIAN CIVIL WAR

A Ghost War—The Peasants—Their Suitors—Half Policies—Lord Curzon's Criticism—North Russia—The New Brigades—The Rear-guard—Evacuation—A Parting Blow—Obligations Discharged—Collapse of Kolchak—Withdrawal of Aid—The Czechs: The Imperial Treasure—Betrayal of Kolchak—His Execution—Denikin's Effort—Vast and Precarious Conquests—Poland—Denikin's Responsibilities—His Failure—Anti-Semitism—Ruin of Denikin—Allied Responsibility—Lack of Concert—Situation in December, 1919—The Refugees—The Final Horror.

During the year 1919 there was fought over the whole of Russia a strange war[1]; a war in areas so vast that considerable armies, armies indeed of hundreds of thousands of men, were lost—dispersed, melted, evaporated; a war in which there were no real battles, only raids and affrays and massacres, as the result of which countries as large as England or France changed hands to and fro; a war of flags on the map, of picket lines, of cavalry screens advancing or receding by hundreds of miles without solid cause or durable consequence; a war with little valour and no mercy. Whoever could advance found it easy to continue; whoever was forced to retire found it difficult to stop. On paper it looked like the Great War on the Western and Eastern fronts. In fact it was only its ghost: a thin, cold, insubstantial conflict in the Realms of Dis. Kolchak first and then Denikin advanced in what were called offensives over enormous territories. As they advanced they spread their lines ever wider and ever thinner. It seemed that they would go on till they had scarcely one man to the mile. When the moment came the Bolsheviks lying in the centre, equally feeble but at any rate tending willy-nilly constantly towards compression, gave a prick or a punch at this point or that. Thereupon the balloon burst and all the flags moved back and the cities changed hands and found it convenient to change opinions, and horrible vengeances were wrecked on helpless people, vengeances perseveringly paid over months of fine-spun inquisition. Mighty natural or strategic barriers, like the line of the Volga River or the line of the Ural Mountains, were found to be no resting places; no strategic consequences followed from their loss or gain. A war of few casualties and unnumbered executions! The tragedy of each Russian city, of loyal families, of countless humble households might fill libraries of dreary volumes.

But the population of Russia is a village population. The peasant millions dwell in scores of thousands of villages. There was always the land, and Nature brought forth

[1]See map facing page 185.

her fruits. What was the life of these villages in this period? Savinkov gave a convincing account of it when we lunched together one day with Lloyd George. It was in some ways the story of the Indian villages over whose heads the waves of conquest swept and recoiled in bygone ages. They had the land. They had murdered or chased away its former owners. The village society had flowed over into new and well cultivated fields. They now had these long coveted domains for themselves. No more landlords: no more rent. The earth and its fullness—no more—no less. They did not yet understand that under Communism they would have a new landlord, the Soviet State—a landlord who would demand a higher rent to feed his hungry cities. A collective landlord who could not be killed but who could and would without compunction kill them.

Meanwhile they were self-supporting. Their rude existence could be maintained apart altogether from the outer world or modern apparatus. From the skins of beasts they made garments and footwear. The bees gave them honey in place of sugar. They gave them also wax for such lights as might be needed after sundown. There was bread; there was meat; there were roots. They ate and drank and squatted on the land. Not for them the causes of men. Communism, Czarism; the World Revolution, Holy Russia; Empire or Proletariat, civilisation or barbarism, tyranny or freedom—these were all the same to them in theory; but also—whoever won—much the same in fact. There they were and there they stayed; and with hard toil, there they gained their daily bread. One morning arrives a Cossack patrol. 'Christ is risen; the Allies are advancing; Russia is saved; you are free.' 'The Soviet is no more.' And the peasants grunted, and duly elected their Council of Elders, and the Cossack patrol rode off, taking with it what it might require up to the limit of what it could carry. On an afternoon a few weeks later, or it may be a few days later, arrived a Bolshevik in a battered motor-car with half a dozen gunmen, also saying, 'You are free; your chains are broken; Christ is a fraud; religion is the opiate of democracy; Brothers, Comrades, rejoice for the great days that have dawned.' And the peasants grunted. And the Bolshevik said, 'Away with this Council of Elders, exploiters of the poor, the base tools of reaction. Elect in their place your village Soviet, henceforward the sickle and hammer of your Proletarian rights.' So the peasants swept away the Council of Elders and re-elected with rude ceremony the village Soviet. But they chose exactly the same people who had hitherto formed the Council of Elders and the land also remained in their possession. And presently the Bolshevik and his gunmen got their motor-car to to start and throbbed off into the distance, or perhaps into the Cossack patrol.

Moscow held the controls of Russia; and when the cause of the Allies burnt itself out in victory, there were no other controls: just chatter and slaughter on a background of Robinson Crusoe toil. The ancient capital lay at the centre of a web of railroads radiating to every point of the compass. And in the midst a spider! Vain hope to crush the spider by the advance of lines of encircling flies! Still I suppose that twenty or thirty thousand resolute, comprehending, well-armed Europeans could, without any serious difficulty or loss, have made their way very swiftly along any of the great railroads which converged on Moscow; and have brought to the hard ordeal of battle any force that stood against them. But twenty or thirty thousand resolute men did not exist or could not be brought together. Denikin's forces foraged over enormous areas. They boasted a superficial political sway. They lived on the country and by so doing soon alienated the rural population which at first had welcomed them. Had he collected the necessary supplies at one spot in the South for a direct dash to Moscow, and had he seized the psychological moment just before the Siberian armies began to fade away, he would have had a good chance of success. Master of Moscow and its unequalled railway centre with a corps of trustworthy troops, his power and prestige might have been unshakable. But there never was a thrust; no Napoleon eagle-swoop at the mysterious capital; only the long thin lines wending on ever thinner, weaker and more weary. And then finally when the Bolsheviks in the centre of the circle were sufficiently concentrated by the mere fact of retirement, they in their turn advanced and found in front of them—nothing!—nothing but helpless populations and scores of thousands of compromised families and individuals.

The fitful and fluid operations of the Russian armies found a counterpart in the policy, or want of policy, of the Allies. Were they at war with Soviet Russia? Certainly not; but they shot Soviet Russians at sight. They stood as invaders on Russian soil. They armed the enemies of the Soviet Government. They blockaded its ports, and sunk its battleships. They earnestly desired and schemed its downfall. But war—shocking! Interference—shame! It was, they repeated, a matter of indifference to them how Russians settled their own internal affairs. They were impartial—Bang! And then—at the same time—parley and try to trade.

The reader might well have supposed that the decision of the Big Five to support Kolchak, which was finally taken in June, marked the end of doubt and vacillation. They could send no troops; they could not spend much money. But they could give a steady aid in surplus munitions, in moral countenance and in concerted diplomacy. Had they acted together simply and sincerely within these limitations, they might have reached a good result. But their decisions to support Kolchak, and later to support Denikin, represented only half a mind. The other half had always been, and was throughout the summer of 1919, uncertain of itself, sceptical about the prospects of the anti-Bolsheviks, ill-informed about the true nature of the Soviet Government and the Third International, and anxious to see whether the extremists in Moscow would not respond to the exercise of reason and patience.

A draft memorandum of Lord Curzon's, dated August 16, 1919, describes in severe terms the weakness and confusion of Ally proceedings.

'It cannot be said that an altogether consistent policy has been pursued. Even now the principles upon which that policy rests in the last resort are in some respects in dispute. Action is taken sometimes by the representatives of the Allied and Associated Governments sitting in Paris or by the institutions which they have set up, sometimes by the Governments themselves. The situation is so complex, and the difficulties of arriving at a decision which is acceptable to all are so great that, in some instances, it would be no exaggeration to admit that there is no policy at all.

'In these circumstances, the Great Powers when they met—and too often it must be confessed that refuge is taken in inaction—adopt an uncertain line of conduct; the financial burden tends to fall almost exclusively on the shoulders of those who either have the greatest capacity or the least un-willingness to pay; the independent States or groups of communities, with the fortunes of which we have associated ourselves, do not always make the best use of the help which they get, and are constantly clamouring for more; it remains a matter of almost weekly disputation whether recognition shall or shall not be extended to this or that community; Allied Missions despatched in every direction endeavour to produce something like order out of the prevailing chaos; advice is accepted where it is supplemented by substantial material assistance, elsewhere it is apt to be ignored.' . . .

'On the Western Russian front, Poland and the Baltic States of Lithuania, Latvia and Esthonia are conducting military operations against the Russian Soviet Government. So far as the Baltic States are concerned, continuance of their resistance depends largely on the amount of material assistance which they may be able to obtain, as well as upon the attitude which the Allied Governments may decide to adopt in regard to their national aspirations. Politically, the present situation is in the highest degree unsatisfactory. His Majesty's Government have recognised the *de facto* authority of the Provisional Governments of Esthonia and Latvia established at Reval and Libau respectively, and the Allied representatives in Paris have, in the fifth condition attached to the recognition of Admiral Kolchak, laid down that "if a solution of the relations between Esthonia, Latvia, Lithuania, and the Caucasian and Transcaspian territories and Russia is not speedily reached by agreement, the settlement will be made in consultation and co-operation with the League of Nations, and that, until such settlement is made, the Government of Russia agrees to recognise these territories as autonomous and to confirm the relations which may exist between their de facto Governments and the Allied and Associated Governments." Yet no further steps have been taken to endeavour to secure the co-operation of the Border States of Russia in the policy laid down by the Allied Powers, and no communications have been addressed to the representatives of these States in Paris, in spite of their repeated requests to be informed of the intentions of the Allied Governments. Grave dissatisfaction has consequently resulted in Latvia, Lithuania and Esthonia.' . . .

'"The lack of a clear and decisive policy has been not less manifest in the dealings with the Border States on the Caucasian front." . . . "Here as elsewhere, the policy of the Allied Powers has hovered between recognition and polite indifference." . . . "All is in a flux and uncertainty, and with the withdrawal of the only Allied forces to the south of the Caucasus, serious disturbance, if not worse, may be expected to ensue."

'It would perhaps be an unjustifiable deduction from the untoward developments that I have described, to argue that they have been mainly due to lack either of political vision or harmony on the part of the Allied and Associated Powers. But it would not be unfair to attribute the setback in part to the fact that single Powers have, to a considerable extent, dissipated on various theatres such resources as they have been in a position to give to the whole, instead of pursuing an organised policy whereby effort could be concentrated and a due co-ordination established between political, military, and financial measures.' ...

* * * * *

Meanwhile I had a direct and definite duty to perform.

Our first object was to withdraw from Archangel and Murmansk without disaster and without dishonour. This was a military and political problem both difficult and delicate. I gave the following account of it to the House of Commons[2]:—

'Before the German resistance was broken and the Armistice signed, the winter had settled down on the north Russian coast, and the port of Archangel was ice-bound, or practically ice-bound, and our men were forced to spend the whole of the winter in this bleak and gloomy spot in circumstances which caused the greatest anxiety. It was evident that the Bolsheviks with whom they had been in collision, could, if they chose, have concentrated against this particular sector of the circle by which they were invested, a force of indefinite size; and our men were utterly cut off from the outer world except as far as small parties were concerned. Therefore their position was one of much anxiety. They were men mostly of the C3 class, but they had a fine spirit, and once they were promised that they should be brought home before another winter occurred, they discharged their duty with great determination, and maintained the position against some quite serious attacks, and others which might well have become very serious had they been allowed to proceed, and thus the situation has been maintained throughout this dark period. Not only was there considerable unrest amongst these troops throughout their imprisonment on this coast during the winter, but also ... in the exhaustion and prostration of the public mind which followed the triumph in the main struggle ... there was the greatest difficulty in sending out any form of relief or assistance to those troops for several months.'

And again:—

'. . . Whatever may be the policy decided upon by the Allies in Paris, our forces in Archangel and Murmansk which . . . are inter-dependent, will have to stay there until the summer is far advanced. Since they have got to stay, they must be properly supported. They must be sustained with the reinforcements necessary to their safety, which can reach them within the limit I have described, and must be supplied with everything they may require. It is no use people raising prejudice against these expeditions. Everyone knows why they were sent. They were sent as part of our operations against Germany. . . . That reason has passed away, but the

---

[2]July 29, 1919.

troops sent in obedience to it are still on these wild northern coasts, locked in the depth of winter, and we must neglect nothing required for their safety and well-being. . . .

'Further, we have incurred heavy commitments towards the people of these districts who have espoused our cause, and to the Russian armies, which were encouraged and called into being largely by the Allies and largely for our own purposes during the period of the German war. It has been the custom in this country to pay particular attention to matters of this kind and always to endeavour, to the very best of our ability, to do our duty by those who have put their trust in us, and who have run into danger in consequence of action which we have advised them to take.'

In order to secure the safe and respectable withdrawal of the Allied troops from North Russia, it was necessary to reinforce them. All our Allies wished to quit this melancholy scene as quickly as possible, and the British being in command and constituting more than half of the expedition, had in practice to bear the responsibility and form the rearguard. The bulk of our own troops were entitled to be brought home and discharged under the terms of our demobilisation scheme. It was therefore necessary to raise a special volunteer force to relieve the tired and impatient conscripts and to wind up the affair. On March 4 the War Cabinet decided to press the Allied Representatives in Paris to agree to the early evacuation of North Russia by the Allied troops. To prepare for this, and to meet the dangerous situation existing at Archangel, the War Cabinet authorised me to make any necessary arrangements.

In pursuance of this decision I therefore raised two new brigades each of 4,000 men, composed of volunteers from the great armies which were demobilising. The officers and men came forward readily and in a few days the lists were closed. These fine, war-hardened soldiers rapidly assumed coherent formations. They were despatched to Archangel as soon as the port was open. We thus had a strong, efficient, and well-equipped force at this most critical point from which everyone else was making haste to flee. These troops had no sooner arrived and relieved the wornout garrison than a dangerous and widespread mutiny broke out in the friendly Russian force. This treachery was said to be characteristic of the Russians; but the explanation is simple. From the moment when we had been compelled by parliamentary and political pressure to proclaim our intention to withdraw, every friendly Russian knew that he fought under a death sentence, and his safest course was to make terms with his future masters at the expense of his departing Allies. This reaction, however unpleasant, was inherent in the wise, and indeed inevitable, policy of evacuation.

The mutinies, except on the Onega sector which went over bodily to the Bolsheviks, were checked and quelled by the spirited action of a Polish battalion and a company of British infantry; but thenceforward the 25 to 30,000 armed and trained local troops whom the Allies had organised could not be trusted as an aid, and must indeed be reckoned as a peril. Fortunately, veteran volunteers had gone out with this very job clearly explained to them. Totally immune from the general disintegration but comprehending it, and technically superior in every form of warfare, they occupied the wide, depleted front, gripped the treachery in the rear, and easily smote down the attack in front.

We had been bitterly attacked by the Socialist and the Liberal Oppositions, and also in some Conservative newspapers, for sending any fresh troops to North Russia, and had we not been deaf to these irresponsible counsels and strong enough to take unpopular action, no fresh troops would have been sent. But for their timely arrival, a general landslide and disaster of a peculiarly shameful character and on a considerable scale, would certainly have taken place in July. Behind this tempered shield, the withdrawal of the American, French, Italian, and British conscripts, and the removal of masses of stores, proceeded rapidly, without cessation. This was the first phase of our North Russian operations after the Armistice.

The second is at once more complicated and more disputable. Again, I cannot improve upon the account I gave to Parliament on July 29:—

'In the first week of March the War Cabinet decided that Archangel and Murmansk should be evacuated before another winter set in, and they directed the War Office to make arrangements accordingly. But they also prescribed that whatever support, nourishment, succour, reinforcements or aid might be required or needed by our troops for their safe extrication from this position should be used and despatched by the War Office; and, further, that due regard should be had to the obligations which we had inevitably contracted with every class of the population of Archangel and Murmansk, and with the local Russian Army and local Russian Government we had called into being. . . .

'This decision of policy was communicated to the Russian leaders. On April 30, Admiral Kolchak was informed that all the Allied troops would be withdrawn from North Russia before the next winter; but in the meantime we hoped to make it possible for the North Russian Government and the Russian Army to stand alone after the Allied troops had left. It will readily be seen that if such a solution could have been reached, if this local government and local army could have maintained itself or joined up with the main anti-Bolshevik Russian Army, that would have relieved us of the extremely anxious and painful operation of carrying away a portion of the population and troops who were now there, and affording them asylum and refuge, and of settling a most terrible problem for all those loyal Russians who elected to remain on that shore. . . .

'Although to us who sit here at home in England it may seem very easy to say, "Clear out, evacuate, cut the loss, get the troops on board ship and come away"— and to arrive at that intellectual decision, yet on the spot, face to face with the people among whom you have been living, with the troops by the side of whom you have been fighting, with the small Government which has been created by our insistence, with all the apparatus of a small administration with all its branches and services,—when you get our officers and men involved like that on the spot, it is a matter of very great and painful difficulty to sever the ties and quit the scene. I do not disguise from the House that I had most earnestly hoped and trusted that it would be possible in the course of events for the local North Russian Government to have a separate life and existence after our departure; and with the fullest assent of the Cabinet and the Government, and acting strictly on the advice of the General Staff, we have been ready to hold out a left hand, as it were, along the Dvina River to Admiral Kolchak in the hope that he would be able to arrive in this district, and, by joining the local Russian forces, stabilise the situation and enable our affairs there to be wound up in a thoroughly satisfactory manner.'

There was, however, a third phase in the North Russian campaign. When eventually it became certain that the Czech troops had no longer the will nor Admiral Kolchak the power to form any contact with the North Russian area, the final act of evacuation began. So grave was our apprehension of its difficulty and danger that we decided to send a commander of the highest rank to conduct the operation. On August 4 General Lord Rawlinson, the famous Chief of the old Fourth Army, embarked for Archangel. At his disposition were placed: Three additional infantry battalions; one marine battalion; one machine-gun battalion; two batteries of artillery; a field company of engineers, and five tanks. Powerful naval forces, including monitors which could ascend the Dvina river, lay at hand with ample shipping. The North Russian Government, seeing that our decision was irrevocable, resolved with the assent of a substantial proportion both of their army and their people, to continue their resistance to the end. They received imperative orders to this effect from Kolchak. This forlorn hope excited a strong wave of sympathy among the British volunteers, and it was Rawlinson's unpleasant task to repress these chivalrous instincts by a sharp reminder that obedience was the first of military duties.

The evacuation was to be covered by a sudden offensive against the enemy. He was to be given a blow so severe that before he could recover not a British soldier, nor a loyal Russian who claimed asylum, would remain on shore. This operation, elaborately planned, was carried out under General Ironside's orders by the volunteer brigade of Sadleir-Jackson and Russian troops. On August 10 the Bolshevik position astride the Dvina river was attacked. The assault was completely successful. All the objectives were taken, and six enemy battalions annihilated. Over 2,000 prisoners, 18 guns, and many machine guns, were captured. The advance ended with the occupation of the villages of Puchega and Borok, twenty miles from our original position. One may measure the quality of the Red Army by the fact that our losses did not exceed 120 officers and men.

The naval flotilla advancing with the troops mined the river at the furthest point, thus barring it for some time to hostile vessels. The enemy having been temporarily paralysed, a swift and unmolested withdrawal was made, first to the defences at Archangel and thence to the ships. Food and arms were left with the Russian General Miller and his troops. Six thousand five hundred Russians, who elected to go, were removed by sea to the liberated Baltic States and South Russia. By September 27 the evacuation of Archangel was completed; that of Murmansk followed on October 12. The withdrawal was carried out practically without loss, and for the moment the loyal Russian forces were left in so favourable a position that they actually assumed an offensive of their own.

NORTH RUSSIA

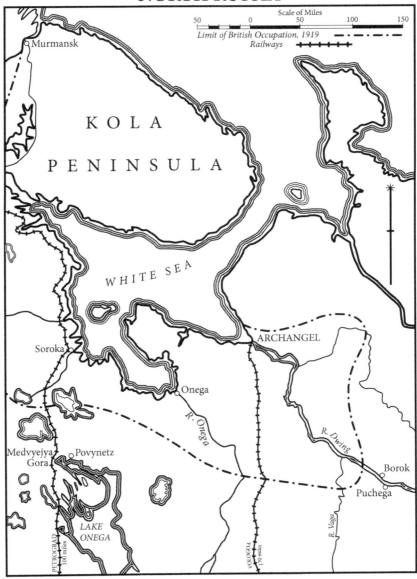

Scale of Miles

50   0   50   100   150

Limit of British Occupation, 1919 ─ ∙ ─ ∙ ─
Railways ┼┼┼┼┼┼

Murmansk

K O L A

P E N I N S U L A

WHITE SEA

Soroka

ARCHANGEL

Onega

R. Onega

R. Dwing

Medvyejya Gora

Povynetz

Borok

Puchega

R. Vaga

PETROGRAD 100 miles

LAKE ONEGA

VOLOGOA 170 miles

The total pre- and post-Armistice casualties, killed, died, wounded and missing, sustained by the British forces in North Russia from the Spring of 1918 to October, 1919, were 106 officers and 877 other ranks, including 41 officers and 286 other ranks killed.

This successful extrication, first of the Allies and secondly of our own troops and the Russian refugees, was only rendered possible by treating with necessary indifference socialist partisanship, opposition mischief making, and newspaper clamour. To the best of their ability the British had discharged their obligations. Safety was provided for every Russian man, woman and child who wished to leave. Those who remained to continue the civil war did so of their own free will. Short of remaining there and waging war indefinitely against the Russian Soviet, no better solution was possible; but nevertheless the sequel was melancholy. In a few weeks General Miller's resistance was extinguished; the Soviet Government re-established its rule on the shores of the White Sea, and mass executions, in one case of 500 officers, quenched the last hope of Russian life and freedom in these regions.

I can see now the pale faces and staring eyes of the deputation of townsfolk from Archangel who visited me at the War Office at the end of July, 1919, to beg for further British protection, to whom I had to return 'a dusty answer.' All these poor workpeople and shopkeepers were soon to face the firing parties. The responsibility for their fate rests upon the mighty and resplendent nations who had won the war, but left their task unfinished.

* * * * *

No sooner had the correspondence between Kolchak and the Big Five terminated satisfactorily on June 12, 1919, than his collapse began. In the early part of June General Gaida's Northern Army made some slight progress round about Glazov. But this did not disguise from our representative, General Knox, that the situation of Kolchak's forces was very unfavourable. The Siberian Western Army had been heavily defeated at the beginning of May in front of Ufa, and at the end of June the Northern Army was involved in its rout. By the end of the month therefore the Western and Northern Armies had fallen back over a hundred and fifty miles to Perm. At the beginning of July the line here ran approximately as follows: East of Perm—Kungar—Krasnoufimsk—Simsk—Sterlitimak—Orenburg. During July the retreat of the Siberian armies continued without interruption; by the end of the month they had evacuated Ekaterinburg and Chelyabinsk, and had lost the line of the Urals. At the beginning of August the Supreme Council decided to give no further help to Kolchak who was evidently fast losing his grip of the situation. General Knox said of the Siberian armies: 'The men are listless and slack, and there is no sign of their officers taking them in hand. The men do not want rest, but hard work and discipline…. The enemy boasts he is going to Omsk, and at the moment I see nothing to stop him. As it retires the army melts, the men desert to their villages or to convey their families to safety.' The retirement of the Siberian army continued throughout August. At the beginning of September they still had a numerical superiority over the Bolsheviks, but having retired since May their morale was very bad. Nevertheless at the beginning of

September General Dietrichs struck back at the enemy and recovered nearly a hundred miles. The success was short-lived, and Petropavlovsk was occupied by the Bolsheviks on October 30. The Southern Army continued to retreat, broke up and ceased to be a factor in the military situation. There was nothing therefore between the Bolsheviks and Omsk, which was evacuated on November 14. The Government moved to Irkutsk on November 17. General Gaida attempted a *coup d'état* at Vladivostok, which appeared for the moment to galvanise the Irkutsk Government into life. Such public opinion as existed in Siberia was however becoming increasingly estranged from Kolchak; and Bolshevik propaganda grew daily more seductive.

While all this was in progress I had done my best in pursuance of the decisions of the Supreme Council to guide and encourage Kolchak. On May 28 I had telegraphed to General Knox, telling him to use his influence in order to get the Admiral to 'accentuate all the broad principles of a constituent assembly and a democratic franchise whose decrees shall settle the future government of Russia.' General Knox was instructed to do his utmost to secure compliance by Kolchak with all the conditions prescribed by the Big Four. Knox was to avail himself of the services of Colonel John Ward in every possible way, for no one could express better the feelings of 'patriotic British Labour men equally opposed to autocracy and anarchy.' Advice was accompanied by aid. British ships with stores continued to arrive at Vladivostok up till October, 1919, and during that year the total amount supplied or carried in British vessels to the Siberian armies amounted to nearly a hundred thousand tons of arms, ammunition, equipment and clothing. In pursuance of the undertaking given to Parliament and the declared policy of the Cabinet, Colonel Ward and his Middle-sex Regiment sailed from Vladivostok for England on September 8, 1919. They were followed by the Hampshires on November 1. Thereafter only the British Military Mission and the Railway Mission represented Great Britain in Siberia.

The withdrawal of the symbols of Allied and British support, and the ceaseless retreat of his forces, consummated the ruin of Kolchak. On December 24 a revolution took place at Irkutsk, and on January 4 the Admiral placed himself under Czech protection.

But what had happened to the Czechs? We have seen them already in October, 1918, 'wearying somewhat in well-doing' and exasperated by White Russian mismanagement. The end of the Great War relaxed the bonds which had made them so serviceable to the Allies. Henceforward their only and most natural wish was to get back to their homes. The Allied victory had liberated Bohemia. The Czech troops were no longer mutineers nor traitors to the Hapsburg Empire. They were the victorious soldiers and pioneers of Czechoslovakia. Home, which might have been forever barred and banned to them, now shone in the lights of freedom and of honour. Very brightly did the beacon gleam to their eyes across the vast snows of Russia.

Early in 1919 the Czech Army Corps began to be a source not of help but of positive danger. The Czechoslovak National Council which the troops had evolved was—no doubt with reason—actively critical of the Omsk Government. Committees were formed in the regiments, not unlike those which rotted the Russian armies after the Revolution. Their discipline and their fighting value deteriorated. In the spring they

163

were withdrawn from the front and put to guard sections of the railways. In June it was settled that they should be repatriated as soon as possible, and appropriate steps were taken to this end.

On Christmas Eve Kolchak, still the nominal Director of Siberia, was in his train at Nijni Udinsk, about 300 miles west of Irkutsk. With him in a second train was the Imperial Russian treasure, consisting first, of gold bricks to the total value of 650 million roubles (sixty-five million pounds), and secondly, about 500 million roubles' worth of valuables and securities, the latter greatly depreciated. Kolchak had been deserted by nearly all his troops and followers. But a 'storm battalion' of Czechs, animated by unfriendly feelings towards the Admiral, remained as the safeguard of his life and treasure. News was received that a Bolshevik force was advancing from the North to capture the gold, and General Janin, a French Officer in command of the Czechs, telegraphed to the 'storm battalion' to retreat upon Irkutsk and leave Kolchak and the gold to their fate. On January 2, however, the Admiral was informed through the Czechs that 'all échelons of the Supreme Ruler will be escorted to a safe zone, and if for any reason it is impossible to escort all échelons, in any case the Admiral . . . is to be safe and escorted to the Far East.' In these circumstances, Kolchak, on January 4, telegraphed to Irkutsk that he surrendered his person to the Czechs. His private car, pasted with the flags of Japan, England, France, America and Czechoslovakia, was attached to one of the trains conveying the 'storm battalion'; and behind followed the train containing the gold. Although they passed through a territory said to be swarming with hostile insurgents, neither Czechs, nor gold, nor Kolchak were molested on their journey to Irkutsk. Here on a railway siding the Admiral and the treasure halted.

General Janin's first duty was the extrication of the Czechs; but he had also become responsible for the safety of Kolchak. Both of these tasks could have been easily discharged but for the gold. Everyone in the dissolving social structure of Siberia, Reds, Social Democrats or banditti wanted to see the backs of the Czechs and would have speeded their departure by every means. Kolchak could have accompanied them without difficulty. But the removal of the gold was a different matter. Russians of all colours were prepared to sink their political differences in order to prevent such an alarming occurrence. General Janin on January 4 had accepted responsibility for the gold and he wasted ten days in parleying and haggling about it. Meanwhile the Bolshevik forces were closing in on Irkutsk and the local Social Democrat Government flushed pinker daily. The situation became definitely menacing. The Red forces spurred on by news of the gold, though poor in quality, were reaching large numbers. Such Allied Commissioners as had any troops of their nationality in tow in Siberia sent peremptory telegrams to General Janin that they would not help him out if he tarried any longer in Irkutsk. There is no reason to suppose that the Czechs, if they had been so disposed, were not strong enough to force their way out with both the Admiral and the gold. But the atmosphere was loaded with panic and intrigue. General Janin on January 14 opened negotiations with the local Irkutsk Government. An agreement was made that the Czechs should be assisted to depart and that the gold and the person of Admiral Kolchak should be left behind.

One of the Admiral's staff, Malinovsky, says in his diary, 'On January 14 at 6 p.m. two Czech Officers stated that they had just received orders from Janin to hand over Kolchak and his staff to the local authorities. The Admiral was always calm, neither by word nor gesture did he allow the Czechs to feel that he was afraid of death. With blazing eyes and a bitter smile the Admiral said "So this is the meaning of the guarantee given me by Janin for an unhindered passage to the East. An international act of treachery. I am ready for anything!" He was then incarcerated with his Prime Minister, M. Pepelaiev, in the jail at Irkutsk.'

These proceedings staggered the High Commissioners further East at Harbin. They were not, however, in a strong position, in view of their recent demands to Janin to retreat from Irkutsk. Their remonstrances now received offensive replies. General Janin said that the Czechs would have been attacked unless they had handed the Admiral over, and that the action of the High Commissioners had never been the slightest help and had always made matters worse, and that he did not recognise their authority. 'I consider myself,' he said, 'under obligation solely to the Czech Government which has ordered the return of its troops to Czechoslovakia, and to the Inter-Allied Council in Paris which has ordered me to carry out this evacuation.' And he is reported to have added, with equal insolence and truth 'Je répète que pour Sa Majesté Nicolas II on a fait moins de cérémonie.'

Every allowance must be made for the difficulties of this officer's position, and it may well be that a more detailed analysis would only reveal those difficulties more clearly.

On January 21 the Social Democrat Government of Irkutsk, already almost vermilion, declared itself Bolshevik. Soviet emissaries entered the town, Red guards replaced the pink around Kolchak. On February 7, before it was light, the Admiral and his Prime Minister were murdered in their cells in the customary Bolshevik manner by the discharging of automatic pistols pressed against the backs of their heads. There was no trial of any kind, but neither does it appear that they were tortured.

The fate of the vast mass of gold and treasure is by no means free from mystery. Undoubtedly the bulk fell into the hands of the Soviet Government. But it is by no means clear that they got it all. Six months later the Finance Minister of General Wrangel's Government began to make inconvenient inquiries about a million dollars in gold reported to be deposited in a bank in San Francisco. He did not last long enough, however, to press this very far.

It is a pity that the magnificent record of the Czechoslovak army corps should have been marred by the surrender of Kolchak. It seems that for a while these legionaries forsook the stage of History on which they had hitherto acted and mingled with the ragged and demoralised Siberian audience.

＊ ＊ ＊ ＊ ＊

The military effort of Denikin was far more serious and sustained. In accordance with the advice of the General Staff, the main British assistance from June onwards was concentrated upon him. A quarter of a million rifles, two hundred guns, thirty tanks and large masses of munitions and equipment were sent through the Dardanelles and the Black Sea to the port of Novorossisk; and several hundred British officers and non-commissioned officers, as advisers, instructors, store-keepers and even a few aviators, furthered the organisation of his armies. Denikin had as a nucleus the survivors of that heroic band who a year before under Alexiev and Kornilov had in the Russian Volunteer Army fought for the Russian cause, while it was still the cause of the Allies. He had therefore at any rate a sprinkling of competent, resolute and faithful officers. He had already, as we have seen, gained great successes; and as the summer wore on his lines advanced rapidly northward till they stretched from the great city of Kieff in the west almost to the Caspian Sea. In his offensive, lasting five months, between April and October, 1919, Denikin took 250,000 prisoners, 700 guns, 1,700 machine guns, and 35 armoured trains; and at the beginning of October he reached Tula, within 220 miles of Moscow, with forces approximately equal to those of his opponents, namely, about 230,000 men. The general survey which I gave to the Cabinet on September 22, 1919, while Kolchak was still in the field, stated:

> General Denikin has under the control of his troops regions which cannot contain less than thirty millions of European Russians, and which include the third, fourth and fifth great cities of Russia. These regions are readily accessible to British and French trade, which is the main need of the population at the present time. They possess a network of railways, which are in comparatively good working order if rolling stock could be obtained. The inhabitants have been thoroughly sickened of Bolshevism, having either tried it of their own free will or experienced its oppression. There is no doubt whatever that the will of these 30,000,000 people, if it could be expressed by plebiscite, would be overwhelmingly against being handed back again to the Bolshevik Government of Lenin and Trotsky. Moreover, General Denikin disposes of an army which, although raised very largely on a voluntary basis, is rapidly growing and at the present time certainly amounts to over 300,000 fighting men. . . . Our policy should continue to be to keep in friendly touch with Denikin, to complete the despatch of the munitions, to help him in his difficulties with other anti-Bolshevik forces, to guide him as far as possible with political counsel, and to prevent him from falling into the hands of the reactionaries. Above all, it seems most important to develop trade and credit in the great regions which have been liberated, in order that the people there may contrast their conditions with the miseries prevailing in Bolshevik Russia. It is to be observed that General Denikin has never asked for men. One British lieutenant in the last nine months has been slightly wounded in a tank. That is the sole British casualty of which we have information. No further large expenditure of money (other than the questionable value of surplus munitions), no assistance of troops, except a very limited establishment of technical personnel, are needed. Countenance, counsel, commerce—these are the means which are alone demanded. . . .

On his western flank, General Denikin is in contact with the rather feeble Ukrainian forces under Petlura. The question at issue between Denikin and Petlura is that of a united Russia *versus* an independent Ukraine. The Roumanians, who feel that they can only take Bessarabia from a weak and defeated Russia, will naturally support Petlura. The duty of the Allies should be to try to reconcile the two conflicting points of view. Why should this be thought impossible? The conception of a Russia consisting of a number of autonomous States, grouped together on a federal basis into a Russian union, is one within which all legitimate aspirations may be comprised. Such a Russian empire would be less of a menace to the future peace of the world than the vast centralised empire of Czarism. And this is the moment when the critical situation of all the Russian parties and forces should make it possible, by a wise exercise of Allied policy, to give such a turn to events. A policy of the partition or dismemberment of Russia, although it might be for the moment successful, cannot have permanent results and could only open up an indefinite succession of wars, out of which in the end, under Bolshevik or reactionary standards, a united militarist Russia would arise. Every effort should therefore be made to guide affairs into the channel which leads into a federalised Russia, without prejudice either to local autonomy or the principle of general unity.

The downfall of Bela Kun amid universal execration, and the ease with which that downfall was accomplished, has been a most heavy blow to the prestige of the Bolshevik system of world-wide revolution. Its influence upon the general situation ought not to be under-rated.

Coming further north, on the left of the Ukrainian forces of Petlura, is the Polish battle front. This has also continuously advanced in the last four or five months, involving the Bolsheviks in continual defeats at the hands of the Polish army and in heavy expenditure in men and munitions. The Polish front now stands in most places on Russian soil. The Poles are now inclined to suggest one of two courses to the Allies:

(a) That the Allies should finance a Polish army of 500,000 men which should advance into the heart of Russia and capture Moscow, or

(b) That the Poles should make a peace with the Bolsheviks.

Either of these courses at the present moment would be injurious. The advance of the hereditary enemy of Russia to Moscow would rouse whatever sense of nationalism is latent in those parts of Russia under the Bolshevik international régime. Moreover, the project is not one for which any of the Allied Powers would be justified by their own public opinion in furnishing funds. On the other hand, if the Poles make a separate and precipitate peace with the Bolsheviks, the Bolshevik army opposite the Polish front, which is the third strongest Bolshevik army now in the field, could swiftly be transferred to the attack of Denikin; and this might fundamentally jeopardise his continued existence. For us to encourage the Poles to make such a precipitate and isolated peace at this juncture, when everything is so critical, would utterly stultify:

(a) The general policy of the Allies in promising support to Admiral Kolchak, and, (*b*)   The special policy of Great Britain in sending great consignments of munitions to Denikin.

We should be undoing with our left hand what we had done with our right, and by pursuing opposite and contradictory policies on different sectors of the common front, we should have done nothing more than prolong useless bloodshed and prevent the establishment of any form of settled authority. It seems therefore clear that our policy at the present moment should be to persuade the Poles to carry on for a few months as they are doing, *i.e.*, fighting and defeating the Bolsheviks on their borders where and when they can, without preparing either for a decisive advance into the heart of Russia or for a separate peace.

In regard to the Baltic States, the policy here is similar to that which suggests itself in regard to Poland, *i.e.*, the taking of no violent action for which the Allies would have to make great sacrifices or become directly responsible, but on the other hand the fostering of the material and moral strength of such anti-Bolshevik forces as exist, and the co-ordination of their action so far as possible in order to prevent an untimely and inopportune collapse on this sector of the front.

But Denikin's dangers grew with his conquests. He became responsible for a large part of Russia without any of the resources—moral, political, or material—needed to restore prosperity and contentment. The population, which welcomed his troops and dreaded the Bolsheviks, were too cowed by the terrible years through which they had passed to make any vigorous rally in his support. The responsibilities for the administrative well-being of great cities and provinces in a time of dearth and confusion, with crumbling railways and arrested commerce, fell upon a blunt, stout-hearted military man with a newly acquired taste for political affairs, who was already overburdened with the organisation of his army and the conduct of the war. The political elements which had gathered around him were weak, mixed, and fiercely divided upon essentials. Some urged him to display the Imperial standards and advance in the name of the Czar. This alone would confront Bolshevism with insignia equally well understood on either side by all. The majority of his advisers and principal officers made it clear that they would not tolerate such a decision. Others urged him to proclaim that the land should be left to the peasants who had seized it. To whom it was replied: 'Are we then no better than the Bolsheviks?' But the worst cleavage arose upon the policy towards the countries or provinces which had broken away from Russia. Denikin stood for the integrity of the Russian Fatherland as he understood it. He was therefore the foe of his own allies in the war against the Soviets. The Baltic States, struggling for life against Bolshevik force and propaganda, could make no common cause with the Russian General who denied their right to independence. The Poles, who provided the largest and strongest army at war with the Soviets, saw that they would have to defend themselves against Denikin on the morrow of a joint victory. The Ukraine was ready to fight the Bolsheviks for independence, but was not attracted by the military government of Denikin.

At every stage these antagonisms presented baffling problems. It was far beyond the power of Denikin to cope with them. But was it beyond the power of the victorious Allies? Could not the statesmen who had assembled at Paris have pursued their task coherently? Could they not have said to Kolchak and Denikin: 'Not another cartridge unless you make terms with the Border States, recognising their independence or autonomy as may be decided.' And having applied this superior compulsion to the Russian leaders, could they not have used their whole influence to combine the operations of all the States at war with Soviet Russia? And if not, would it not have been better at a much earlier stage to have left events to take their course? Surely the Inter-Allied Russian Committee, which I had proposed at Paris in February, was an instrument which it was imperative to call into being, if the declarations of the Big Five to Kolchak in May were ever to be made, or to be made good. But everything was partial, disjointed, half-hearted, inconsistent, and sometimes actually contradictory.

I used what influence I had to prevent excesses and promote concerted action. September 18: 'It is of the very highest consequence that General Denikin should not only do everything in his power to prevent massacres of the Jews in the liberated districts, but should issue a proclamation against Anti-Semitism.' September 20: 'It is very important to bring about an improvement in the relations between the Ukraines and Denikin. . . . It is necessary to avoid a situation which will oblige him to continue to employ troops against Petlura. . . .' 'A report from Moscow states that Green Guards are growing in numbers and organising in many parts of the country, and that if they were not afraid of reprisals from the Whites, they might easily be made use of against the Bolsheviks. Is this point fully realised by Denikin. . . ?' On October 9 I telegraphed to Denikin urging him 'to redouble efforts to restrain Anti-Semitic feeling and to vindicate the honour of the volunteer army [by such restraint].' November 7: 'I have fostered development of a strong Russian and Anglo-Russian group, hoping thereby to develop trade and credit behind Denikin's front.'

The Russian Anti-Bolshevik effort culminated in September. Kolchak was still forming a front in Siberia, and even made a small advance. Yudenitch, with a North-West Russian force based on Reval, was actually at grips with Petrograd. Finland, fully mobilised, awaited only the slightest encouragement from the Great Powers to march also on that city. A flotilla of motor-boats from the British blockading squadron in the Baltic broke into the harbour of Kronstadt, and by a feat of unsurpassed audacity and apparently on the sole initiative and authority of the Admiralty, sank two Russian battleships in the inner basin. The lines of Denikin embraced the whole of South Russia and were moving steadily northward. An arrangement between him and the Ukraine, combined with a steady pressure by Poland, might well have been decisive. But everything fell to pieces. Kolchak petered out. The Finns were chilled and discouraged by the Allies and stood idle. Yudenitch, unsupported, failed. Poland remained inert. Denikin came to blows with Petlura, and his forces had just completely defeated this Ukrainian leader, when his own distended front was pierced by Bolshevik counter-attacks. The immense circle of weak, divided, hesitating and confused armies and States which lapped Soviet Russia, was incapable of exerting a simultaneous pressure. During November Denikin's armies melted away, and his whole front disappeared with the swiftness of pantomime. I cannot describe these disasters and their cause better than in a Memorandum which I wrote on September 15.

Large sums of money and considerable forces have been employed by the Allies against the Bolsheviks during the year. Britain has contributed the nominal value of nearly 100 millions, France between 30 and 40 millions, the United States have maintained, and are still maintaining, over 8 thousand troops in Siberia, Japan has an army of between 30 and 40 thousand strong in Eastern Siberia, which she is now in process of reinforcing. Admiral Kolchak's armies, equipped mainly with British munitions, reached in May a total of nearly 300,000 men. General Denikin's armies aggregate at the present time about a quarter of a million combatants. Besides these, there were the Finns, who could place 100,000 men in the field. There were also the Esthonians, the Letts and the Lithuanians completely maintaining their fronts from the Baltic to Poland. Lastly, there are the powerful Polish forces, and help could also have been obtained from Roumania and, to a lesser extent, from Serbia and Czechoslovakia.

It is obvious from the above that the elements existed which, used in combination, would easily have been successful. They have, however, been dissipated by a total lack of combination, and this has been due to a complete absence of any definite or decided policy among the victorious Allies. Some were in favour of peace and some were in favour of war. In the result they made neither peace nor war. If they made war on one part of the front, they hastened to make peace on another. If they encouraged Kolchak and Denikin and spent both money and men in their support, they gave no encouragement to Finland, to the Baltic States or to Poland. Every proposal to establish a unified system of command and direction of the resistance to the Bolsheviks has been vetoed. In June, Kolchak was promised, on the word of the five plenipotentiaries, continuance of their support in supplies. Since that date, the withdrawal of all support from him has been continuous. Finland at two periods of this year was ready to march, in conjunction with the army of Yudenitch and the Esthonians, and occupy Petrograd. Not the slightest countenance or encouragement was given her in such an enterprise. Poland was prepared to maintain strong pressure against the Bolsheviks: she was actually discouraged. As for the small States, they were told that they could make peace or not, as they liked, and that in any case they would get no help.

All these steps were perfectly compatible with a policy of peace or a policy of strict neutrality. They were certainly not compatible with a policy of war, such as was actually being carried out on other sectors of the immense circle around Bolshevik Russia. Meanwhile the Bolsheviks succeeded in gradually developing their armies. These armies were far weaker than the forces potentially opposed to them; but, as they lay in the centre of the circle, and could, subject to the limits of their transportation, throw their weight from one part of its circumference to the other, they have been able to attack in detail and in many cases to overwhelm the forces opposed to them. Thus, while Denikin was getting on his feet Kolchak was broken and defeated. During the last five months Denikin's power has been steadily growing and great successes have been gained by his armies, but the weight against them has steadily accumulated owing to the defeat of Kolchak and the practical cessation of any serious pressure along the whole Western or European Front. During the last three months the very large numbers of men which the Bolsheviks were able to transfer from in front of Kolchak, from in front of the Poles, and from in front of the Baltic States, and the fact that they were able to throw practically the whole of their reserves on the Southern or Denikin front, have given them a large superiority of numbers over Denikin. His army, which is still the best army, spread out in practically a single line on a front of more than 1,200 miles, has now been thrown back everywhere by these superior forces. Although there are still battles to be fought and the resisting power of his army is still very considerable, he may be overwhelmed and broken up as an effective military factor. The declarations which have been made in public of the withdrawal of support, the lack of any moral support or vigorous concerted action, and the feeling of being abandoned by the great Allied Powers may easily produce conditions in his army which will lead to its complete destruction or disappearance. The destruction of Kolchak's army and Government is practically complete, and the whole vast region of Siberia up to Lake Baikal, east of which the Japanese have taken effectual charge, will be submerged either by the Bolshevik armies or sheer anarchy. Turkestan and the provinces of Central Asia are over-run by the Bolsheviks, who already menace Persia and are intriguing with Afghanistan. Whereas concerted efforts could quite easily have sustained Kolchak, carried Denikin to success and enabled Petrograd to be captured by Yudenitch, with the Esthonians and the Finns, the Bolsheviks are now within measurable distance of complete military triumph on all fronts where they are active.

It is with the situation arising out of these facts that we are now confronted. The inactivity of the Poles has enabled the Bolsheviks to concentrate against Denikin; the destruction of Denikin will enable them, if they choose, to concentrate against the Poles. The growth of Denikin's forces and the efforts of his armies took the pressure off the Baltic States and enabled Finland to remain inert. What is now happening to Denikin has already produced a significant change in the Baltic area. The Bolshevik negotiators have entirely altered their tone towards the small States, as they are quite justified in doing, in consequence of the changed military situation. The alarm of the Esthonians, the Latvians and the Lithuanians is already apparent and will become increasingly apparent as Denikin's fortunes and strength subside. Finland is now reported by the latest telegrams to be mobilising a hundred thousand men as a defensive measure. Half that number two months ago would have sufficed, in conjunction with Yudenitch's effort, to have taken Petrograd. The collapse of Denikin will give the Bolsheviks the command of the Caspian and place them in close and effective relation with the Turkish Nationalists under Enver and Mustapha Kemal and others. The pressure on Persia and the danger in Afghanistan will in that event immediately assume a most direct and formidable character.

We are told that it is idle to speculate about the future, or to indulge in prophecy. But surely certain well-marked and not distant contingencies which will follow upon the destruction of Denikin do require to be thought over in advance. Hitherto it has been a cheap thing to mock at Denikin's efforts and to indulge to the full the easy wisdom of pessimism and indifference. Hitherto the Allies have been fighting Bolshevism mainly with Russian armies. What will happen when these Russian armies are gone? Zinovieff is reported in the latest wireless to have used a most significant expression which reveals clearly the effect upon the minds of the Bolshevik leaders of the intoxicating draught of military success of which they have been made a present. 'The peace,' he is reported to have said, 'which Russia must obtain would not be a Socialist peace but a *bourgeois* peace.' The demands which the Bolsheviks are now to make on Esthonia, the menace which Finland already recognises, and the situation in Central Asia and towards the frontiers of India, are the first illustrations of what is meant by this.

Whereas by taking the proper concerted measures we could, without any large additional employment of men or money, have established an anti-Bolshevik and modernised Russia friendly to the Entente, we are now within measurable distance of a Bolshevik Russia thoroughly militarised, with nothing but its militarism to live on, bitterly hostile to the Entente, ready to work with Germany, and already largely organised by Germany. The idea that Poland will serve as a barrier to such dangers is illusory. The idea that by standing on the defensive on the east until every other anti-Bolshevik force has been destroyed, she will be able to maintain a strong attitude towards Germany in the west, is equally ill-founded. What is the wisdom of a policy which seeks to strengthen Poland by Allied money and munitions and yet calmly acquiesces in the destruction of Denikin and the consequent liberation of the main Bolshevik armies to treble and quadruple the enemies with whom Poland has to contend? What is the justice or logic of recognising every State, and even to a large extent guaranteeing the independence and security of every State which has torn itself away from the Russian Empire, while refusing to recognise and aid in preserving the great territories and populations in the south of Russia from which General Denikin's armies are drawn and which are unquestionably anti-Bolshevik?

It is a delusion to suppose that all this year we have been fighting the battles of the anti-Bolshevik Russians. On the contrary, they have been fighting ours; and this truth will become painfully apparent from the moment that they are exterminated and the Bolshevik armies are supreme over the whole vast territories of the Russian Empire.

As Denikin's failure became pronounced, the fitful countenance which the Great Powers had given him was swiftly withdrawn. On February 3, 1920, it became my duty to instruct General Holman to put the facts plainly before the Russian leader. 'I cannot hold out any expectation that the British Government will give any further aid beyond what has been already promised in the final packet. Neither will they use their influence to make an aggressive combination between the Poles, the Baltic States, Finland, etc., with Denikin against Soviet Russia. Their reason is that they do not possess the resources in men or money sufficient to carry any such enterprise to success, and they do not wish to encourage others without having the power to sustain them. . . . The British Government in general agreement with the French Government are disposed to offer to the Border States a measure of support in case they are attacked by the Soviet Government. . . . It is no good arguing whether this is a wise or a right policy: it is what I believe is going to happen. It is said the Border States are only fighting for their independence, while Denikin is fighting for the control of Russia. We cannot undertake to make further exertions in support of this last objective, although we sympathise with it. . . . The question which must now be faced is how to save as much as possible from the wreck.'

I now pinned my hopes to finding some asylum, however temporary, for the mass of refugees who fled southward from Red vengeance. The Cossack territories of the Don and the Kuban, where the whole population was passionately anti-Bolshevik, might perhaps be constituted an independent or autonomous region. Failing this, there was the Crimea. Into this fertile peninsula the broken fragments of Denikin's armies and several hundred thousand civilian fugitives were soon crowded in every circumstance of misery and want. Their defence was maintained for a few more months after Denikin's supersession, by General Wrangel, a new figure of unusual energy and quality, who thus too late reached the first place in White Russian counsels. Some moral assistance—in the form of gun-fire—was given by the British fleet, officially engaged in rescue work, in preventing the Bolsheviks from invading the Crimea by sea. But in July the marsh defences dried up and the land defences broke down, the Crimea was overrun, and a hideous flight of refugees to Constantinople ensued. There were not enough ships for half of the panic-stricken multitudes. The savage enemy bore down exultingly their last despairing defenders. Smallpox and typhus epidemics made new alliances with sword and famine. Shiploads of destitute and infected persons—sometimes all dead or moribund— arrived continuously in the already overcrowded, impoverished and straitened Turkish capital. A veil has been drawn over the horrors of this final phase. The British troops and sailors, and some British and American philanthropic agencies in Constantinople gave almost all they possessed in local aid; but the 'Allied and Associated Powers' averted their gaze and stopped their ears. They did not wish to know too much, and like Napoleon at the Beresina could only reply 'Voulez-vous ôter mon calme?' After all Death is merciful: it was certainly busy.

Such were the solutions which the victors in the Great War were able to afford to Russian affairs.

CHAPTER XIII
THE MIRACLE OF THE VISTULA

'Our next step on the path to world victory is the destruction of Poland.'

—Trotsky.

The Linch-pin—Poland's Problem—Poland's Dangers—The Bolshevik Concentration—The Polish Advance—The Ukraine—The Invasion of Poland—The Armistice Negotiations—The Deadly Terms—Warsaw: The Miracle—Decisive Results—A Summing-up—Lost Possibilities—A Consolation—An Advantage.

The gates of new perils were now opened on the world. Poland was the linch-pin of the Treaty of Versailles. This ancient State, torn into three pieces by Austria, Prussia and Russia, was at last liberated from its oppressors and reunited in its integrity after 150 years of bondage and partition. The doors of the Bastille had been broken down, its towers and battlements had been overthrown in the supreme convulsion, and from the ruins there emerged this prisoner of the eighteenth century, long cut off from light and air, limbs dislocated by the rack, with a nature as gifted, a heart as proud, and a head as it then seemed as impracticable as ever. Adversity had not broken the spirit of Poland; had it taught her wisdom?

But justice to Poland requires a fair recognition of her extraordinary difficulties. While she was still dazzled by the newly found freedom, before she could brace herself to the atmosphere of this modern age, there rushed upon her a series of perils, perplexities and embarrassments which might well have baffled the sagacity and experience of the most solidly established Government. To the westward lay quivering Germany, half stunned, half chained, but still endowed with those tremendous faculties and qualities which had enabled her almost single-handed to wage an obstinate war against nearly the whole world at once. Eastward, also prostrate, also in dire confusion, lay the huge mass of Russia—not a wounded Russia only, but a poisoned Russia, an infected Russia, a plague-bearing Russia; a Russia of armed hordes not only smiting with bayonet and with cannon, but accompanied and preceded by swarms of typhus-bearing vermin which slew the bodies of men, and political doctrines which destroyed the health and even the soul of nations. And between these two agonised Empires, reacted upon continually by their distresses, stood Poland, comparatively weak, comparatively small, quite inexperienced, without organisation, without structure, short of food, short of weapons, short of money, brandishing her indisputable and newly reaffirmed title-deeds to freedom and independence. A reasonable comprehension of Poland's difficulties was indispensable to a true measuring of Poland's perils.

The intention of those who framed the Treaty of Versailles had been to create in Poland a living, healthy, vigorous organism which should form a serviceable barrier between Germany and Russia and between Russian Bolshevism—as long as it might last—and the rest of Europe. The ruin and collapse of Poland and its incorporation as a whole in the Russian political group would sweep away this barrier and would bring Russia and Germany into direct and immediate contact. The interests of France must be gravely and even vitally affected by the over-running of Poland by the Bolshevik armies, or by the subversion of the Polish State through Bolshevik propaganda and conspiracy. The French had largely themselves to thank for the alarming situation with which they were now to be confronted. They had derided the efforts of Denikin; they had made no attempt to establish good working arrangements between the National Russians on the one hand and Poland and the frontier States on the other. They had in no way taken the lead, as their interests required them to do, in promoting a definite, concerted action between all the anti-Bolshevik forces and States. Their lethargy had made our own half-hearted efforts useless. They had remained impassive and apparently uncomprehending spectators of Denikin's downfall and of the steady concentration of the Russian armies against Poland. They had made no effort to induce Finland, Esthonia, Latvia and Lithuania to combine in common action against the common peril. On the contrary, they, like the British, had encouraged these States to make peace, not a general peace but a piecemeal peace, Poland being left, and even urged, to remain practically isolated, but at war.

Of this new series of dangers I gave the following account on May 21, 1920:

The difficulties of Poland in dealing with a Government like the Soviet Government of Russia should not be underrated. The same difficulties have been experienced by every other country which is in direct contact with Bolshevik Russia. In no case has anything like a satisfactory peace been arranged by such countries with Soviet Russia. The Bolsheviks do not work only by military operations, but, simultaneously or alternatively with these, they employ every device of propaganda in their neighbours' territories to make the soldiers mutiny against their officers, to raise the poor against the bourgeois, to raise the workmen against the employers, to raise the peasants against the landowners, to paralyse the country by general strikes, and generally to destroy every existing form of social order and of democratic government. Thus a state of so-called peace, i.e., a suspension of actual fighting with firearms, may simply mean that the war proceeds in a still more difficult and dangerous form, viz., instead of being attacked by soldiers on the frontier, the country is poisoned internally and every good and democratic institution which it possesses is undermined. For a country like Poland, newly constituted, struggling to get on its feet on being liberated after over a century of foreign oppression, whose finances are in disorder, and whose resources are so greatly impoverished by the horrors of the war, this second form of attack is particularly dangerous.

The Bolsheviks, however, while loudly professing a desire for peace, have, since the end of last year, been preparing for an offensive on the Polish front.

In addition to a steady flow of reinforcements towards the Polish front, there have been numerous indications of an impending attack by the Bolsheviks. The approximate strength of the Bolshevik armies on the Western front has increased from 81,200 in January, 1920, to 99,200 in early March, and to 133,600 by mid-April. These figures are rifles and sabres, i. e. effective fighting strength. The downfall of Denikin liberated a large number of troops. Many statements have been made by Bolshevik leaders to the effect that they would deal with Poland as they have dealt with Denikin and Kolchak, and great anxiety was felt by Poland during the winter as to what the fate of Poland would be if exposed to such an attack.

There is no doubt that the Bolsheviks hoped that, what with their propaganda and their reinforced front, they would be able to beat the Polish troops and overthrow the Government behind them, and, if so, a most difficult situation would have arisen. The reactionary Germans would of course be delighted to see the downfall of Poland at the hands of the Bolsheviks, for they fully understand that a strong Poland standing between Russia and Germany is the one thing that will baulk their plans for [an Imperialist] reconstruction and for revenge.

About two months ago (on March 5) the Bolshevik offensive against the Poles began, the main weight of this attack being between the Pripet and the Dniester, a front of 250 miles. It then however became apparent that the Polish Army, although ill-supplied and ill-clothed, was nevertheless imbued with a strong patriotic spirit. The Bolshevik attack never made any real progress, in spite of being repeatedly renewed during the rest of the month. The Bolsheviks then initiated discussions regarding the opening of peace negotiations, and invited the Polish Government to indicate the time and place for such negotiations.

The Poles offered Borisov, a place a short distance within their lines, and suggested April 10 as a suitable date, at the same time expressing their readiness to order a cessation of hostilities on that portion of the front. The Poles also guaranteed that their Army would abstain from offensive action during the negotiations. The Bolsheviks, however, rejected the Polish proposals, and demanded an armistice on the whole front, and the selection of a place either in the interior of Poland or in a neutral or Allied country for negotiations.

In the meanwhile, fresh Bolshevik reinforcements were being concentrated on the Polish front, and there was every indication that the offensive against the Poles was about to be renewed. The Poles therefore naturally assumed that the Soviet Government was only procrastinating, and was endeavouring to create a delay in which to undermine the morale of the Polish troops and population by propaganda, while preparing for the renewed offensive.

The Polish Government, under Marshal Pilsudski, a former revolutionary against the Czarist regime, of course understand very intimately the Russian political situation, and have shown a profound knowledge of how to tranquillise Russian territory which they are temporarily administering. Their desire is believed to be to have some sort of buffer between them and Bolshevik Russia, at any rate over a portion of their front. Such a buffer state would be constituted by an independent Ukraine.

The Polish Foreign Office, on April 27, issued a communiqué to the effect that Poland acknowledged the right of the Ukraine to independence, and recognised Petlura's Government. Marshal Pilsudski, on the same day, issued a declaration in which he stated that the Polish Army would co-operate with Ukrainian forces, and would only remain in Ukrainian territory long enough to enable the Ukrainian Government to be established. When this government had been established the Polish troops, he said, would withdraw.

Petlura also published a declaration on that day urging the Ukrainian people to do all in their power to facilitate the operations of the Polish and Ukrainian forces.

General Denikin was of course entirely opposed either to a strong Poland or to an independent Ukraine, his idea, to which he was always true, being a united Russia on pre-war lines, although willing to recognise a Polish State, the boundaries of which were to be settled by negotiations sanctioned by the Constituent Assembly. With his disappearance the Ukrainians, under Petlura, have driven the Bolsheviks out of a large part of their territory, and are making an effort to establish an independent Ukraine free from Bolsheviks. Simultaneously with the Polish-Ukrainian advance, great popular risings occurred in the Ukraine against the Bolsheviks, and the liberating forces were shown every sign of welcome. Incidentally one Ukrainian-Galician division (impressed by the Bolsheviks for service with the Red Army) laid down their arms and refused to fight against the Polish-Ukrainian forces.

There could be no greater advantage to the famine areas of Central Europe than the re-establishment of a peaceful state of the Ukraine on a basis which permitted economic and commercial transactions to take place. It is there in the Ukraine, and not in the starving regions of Russia, reduced to destitution under Bolshevik rule, that an addition to the food supply may be hoped for.

It is not possible to say yet what the outcome will be. The Bolsheviks will no doubt make an effort to overwhelm the Poles, and they will certainly get any assistance from the reactionary Germans which can be given unofficially. It will be very difficult for the Ukrainians to establish order in their own country. But on the assumption that Petlura's Government manages to set up and maintain a separate Government of a civilised type capable of liberating the corn supplies of the Ukraine, and with that territory sheltered and assisted in this task by a strong Poland, it ought not to be impossible to arrive at satisfactory conditions of a general peace in the east in the course of the present summer. If on the other hand Poland succumbs to Bolshevik attacks and the Ukraine is again overrun, the anarchy and disorder destroying all productive capacity which invariably accompanies the establishment of the Soviet regime will prevent all effective export of grain from the Ukraine, and the downfall of Poland will directly involve the vital interests of France, and, in a lesser degree, of Great Britain; it will, moreover, materially further the designs for reconstruction on imperialistic lines which the reactionary elements in Germany desire.

Again on June 26, after the Poles had been forced to evacuate Kieff and when the Bolshevik invasion of Poland was clearly imminent:

'Are we looking ahead at all and making up our minds what we shall do if there is a complete Polish collapse and if Poland is over-run by the Bolshevik armies or its government overturned by an internal Bolshevik uprising? Would it be the policy of the British Government to remain impassive in the face of such an event, which may be conceivably near? If so, what would be the policy of the French Government? In the event of the collapse of Poland, what reaction would this situation entail upon the German position? It would clearly not be possible to disarm Germany if her eastern frontiers were in contact with a Bolshevised area. . . . We ought at any rate to consider in advance what our line of action should be.'

By June 30 the situation had become so menacing that a Council for National Defence was formed in Poland, with power to decide all questions concerning war or peace; and the Polish Prime Minister declared to the Diet that the whole nation stood in peril and must realise its responsibilities. At the beginning of July the main Bolshevik advance began on the northern section of the Polish frontier. On the 4th they crossed the Beresina, and on the 5th took Kovno. On the 6th the Polish Government addressed the Supreme Council, which was then sitting at Spa, a note appealing for assistance in Poland's desperate plight. Poland offered to accept a peace based upon the self-determination of the populations between Poland and Russia, and warned the Allies of the consequences if the Polish Army succumbed to Soviet force. On the 14th the Bolsheviks captured Vilna. On the 17th Chicherin refused to admit the intervention of the British Government in his negotiations with the Poles. On the 19th it was reported to us that 'There is now nothing but disorderly rabble between Warsaw and the Bolsheviks, and if they continue their advances at the present rate, they will be in front of Warsaw in ten days' time.' On the 23rd the Poles sued for an armistice.

These events staggered the Supreme Council. The French saw in jeopardy the whole results of the Great War in Eastern Europe. On August 4 Mr. Lloyd George warned Kamenev and Krassin that 'if the Soviet armies advanced further into Poland, a rupture with the Allies would be inevitable.'

On that famous anniversary, as we sat in the Cabinet room upon this serious communication, my mind's eye roamed back over the six years of carnage and horror through which we had struggled. Was there never to be an end? Was even the most absolute victory to afford no basis for just and lasting peace? Out of the unknown there seemed to march a measureless array of toils and perils. Again it was August 4, and this time we were impotent. Public opinion in England and France was prostrate. All forms of military intervention were impossible. There was nothing left but words and gestures.

Over a wide area the Red armies rolled forward through Poland. Behind the receding Polish front the Communist germ-cells and organisations in every town and city emerged from their seclusion and stood ready to welcome the invaders and proclaim a new Soviet Republic. Poland seemed to have escaped from her hundred and fifty years' partition among three military Empires to fall beneath the yoke of Communism. Doom closed in upon the new liberated State. On August 13, the Red bayonets stood before the gates of Warsaw, and the Red propaganda rose in a surge within the city. Where would the tides of social dissolution stop?

Feverish efforts by the Poles and by the Allies to obtain an armistice and a peace had meanwhile continued. These were received by the Bolsheviks with elaborate assurances of their willingness to negotiate coupled with repeated delays in fixing a meeting place. Eventually Minsk was chosen. On the 10th, Kamenev handed to Mr. Lloyd George a forecast of the Russian peace terms, which involved the reduction of Poland to a virtually defenceless condition, but offered her a reasonable frontier. He mentioned significantly that there were some subsidiary clauses. The British Labour Party had developed a violent agitation against any British assistance being given to Poland. Under Communist influences and guidance councils of action were formed in many parts of Great Britain. Nowhere among the public was there the slightest comprehension of the evils which would follow a Polish collapse. Under these pressures Mr. Lloyd George was constrained to advise the Polish Government that the Russian terms 'do no violence to the ethnographical frontiers of Poland as an independent State,' and that if they were rejected, the British Government could not take any action against Russia. The French on the other hand took the opposite view, dissociated themselves from the British and informed the Polish Government that the terms were totally unacceptable. In these circumstances the Poles continued to rally their forces for the defence of Warsaw, and simultaneously tried to open the armistice proceedings at Minsk; while the Bolsheviks advanced their forces and delayed the parleys.

It was not until August 17 that the Conference finally assembled. The Soviet representatives, acting on instructions given them some days earlier, put forward their conditions. They recognised the independence of the Polish Republic. They would not demand any indemnities. They agreed that the Polish frontier should be the line fixed by Lord Curzon in his note of July 11. Nothing could be more reasonable. But by article IV: 'Poland will demobilise her Army to 50,000 men. *For the maintenance of order a citizens' militia of workmen will be formed.*' Article VII: 'The manufacture of arms and war material in Poland is prohibited.' Article XII: '*Poland undertakes to give land for the families of her citizens killed, wounded or incapacitated in the war.*' Thus under a fair-seeming front of paper concessions about independence, frontiers and no indemnities, the Soviets claimed nothing less than the means to carry out a Bolshevik revolution in a disarmed Poland. The scope of these designs, although hidden from simpletons, was equally comprehensible to every anti-Communist and Communist throughout the world. The establishment of the citizens' militia of workmen, combined with the grants of land for the families of Polish citizens killed or wounded in the war, meant a Red Guard under Communist direction to enforce a policy of land nationalisation. Those internal fires were to be lighted, from which the Polish nation would emerge a Communist annex of the Soviet power.

But meanwhile there had come a transformation—sudden, mysterious and decisive. It produced the same sort of impression upon the mind as had the Battle of the Marne, almost exactly six years before. Once again armies were advancing, exulting, seemingly irresistible, carrying with them measureless possibilities of woe and ruin. Once again for no assignable cause they halt, they falter, become disconnected, become disordered, and begin to retreat under a compulsion seemingly as inexorable as that which had carried them forward. Warsaw, like Paris, is saved. The ponderous balances have adjusted themselves to a new decision. Poland, like France, is not to perish but to live. Europe, her liberties and her glory, are not to succumb to Kaiserism or to Communism. On August 13 the battle for Warsaw had begun at Radzimin less than 15 miles from the city: and four days later the Bolshevik armies were in full flight leaving 70,000 surviving prisoners in Polish hands. The Miracle of the Vistula had repeated in a different form the Miracle of the Marne.

What had happened? How was it done? Of course there are explanations. At the head of Marshal Foch's *'famille militaire'* stood a soldier of subtle and commanding military genius veiled under an unaffected modesty. Weygand had arrived in Warsaw. France had nothing to send to the aid of Poland but this one man. He was, it seems, enough. Through the influence and authority of Lord D'Abernon, the British Ambassador at Berlin, who had been sent to Warsaw at the head of the Allied Missions, Weygand was given effective military control. He regrouped the retreating Polish armies and changed their retirement into a concerted counterstroke. The spirit of Poland which had not been quenched through generations of oppression blazed into one last supreme effort for national existence. The Bolsheviks, incapable of withstanding or overcoming any resolute opposition, submitted immediately to a new will-power. There was hardly any fighting. The blatant-feeble Terror, which had marched so confidently to carry world revolution into the West, recoiled with the utmost precipitation across the Polish frontier; while the Polish peasants, urged by Pilsudski in a fierce proclamation to arm themselves with scythes and cudgels and cleanse their land, devoured the stragglers.

Alternatively, other accounts explain that all was part of the deliberate plan of the Polish General Staff, sustained by the rugged personality of Marshal-President Pilsudski himself. They had deliberately fallen back, like Joffre before the Marne, until the moment was ripe for the grand right-about turn. They had allowed the invaders to extend themselves, to overrun their supplies, to gain a false confidence from a pretended weakness in the defence, and then struck with the sureness and vigour of a Galliéni. They now were glad that so competent a military eye as that of General Weygand had been the witness of their successful combinations.

The British observers thought that the result was due to Weygand. Weygand however characteristically declared, both publicly and privately on all occasions, that it was the Polish army which did the work. The reader may choose either explanation, or both together. The more the facts about the Marne are exposed, the more the gap between them and their tremendous consequences is widened. So here now in this petty warfare of raw, ill-organised, dispirited and exhausted levies a study of what happened leaves one still asking: Why?

But anyhow it was all over. The dangers which I had foreseen and feared had come to pass. But their consequences had been averted. The terrible forfeit due to drift and indecision had been remitted at the very moment when it was claimed. A Peace Treaty was signed on October 12 at Riga which secured the independence of Poland and her means of self-defence against Russian invasion or subversion. Russia fell back into Communist barbarism. Millions had perished by war and persecution, and many more in future years were to die of famine. The frontiers of Asia and the conditions of the Dark Ages had advanced from the Urals to the Pripet Marshes. But there it was written: 'So far and no farther.'

* * * * *

It is perhaps worth while to sum up this Russian story. Unsuccessful intervention in the affairs of another country is generally agreed to be a mistake; and accordingly all the efforts made by the Allies in Russia after the Revolution and after the Armistice fall under a common condemnation. But the Allies were bound to intervene in Russia after the Bolshevik Revolution if the Great War was to be won. They had no reason at the end of 1917, nor during the greater part of 1918, to count upon a German collapse in the West. Even in September it was prudent to expect a German retreat to the Meuse or to the Rhine, and every nerve was strained in preparation for a vast campaign in 1919. In such circumstances it would have been criminal negligence to make no effort to reconstruct an anti-German front in the East, and so to deny the vast resources of Russia in food and fuel to the Central Powers. Thus the Allies became committed to the support of the national Russian governments and forces which were struggling against the Bolsheviks and which claimed to have maintained an unbroken steadfastness in the original purpose of the war.

During the Great War too little was done to achieve decisive results in Russia. Any real effort by Japan or the United States, though made with troops which could never have reached the European battlefields, would have made success certain in 1918. As it was, enough foreign troops entered Russia to incur all the objections which were patent against intervention, but not enough to break the then gimcrack structure of the Soviet power. When we observe the amazing exploits of the Czech Army Corps, it seems certain that a resolute effort by a comparatively small number of trustworthy American or Japanese troops would have enabled Moscow to be occupied by National Russian and Allied forces even before the German collapse took place. Divided counsels and cross-purposes among the Allies, American mistrust of Japan, and the personal opposition of President Wilson, reduced Allied intervention in Russia during the war to exactly the point where it did the utmost harm and gained the least advantage. In consequence at the Armistice nothing was finished and the Allies were entangled in feeble action in many parts of Russia. Side by side with them, dependent upon them for moral, even more than material aid, were the loyal Russian organisations. Had the Great War been prolonged into 1919, intervention, which was gathering momentum every week, must have been militarily successful. The Armistice proved to be the death-warrant of the Russian national cause. As long as that cause was interwoven with a world purpose represented by twenty-seven Allied States at war with Germany, victory was certain. But when the Great War suddenly ended and the victors hurried off to mind their own affairs and exhaustion laid its hands on every Government, the tide that would have borne the loyal Russians onwards ebbed swiftly away and left them forlornly stranded.

Nevertheless there seemed perhaps a chance that with their own strength these Russian National forces might yet save themselves and their country. It was never a very good chance. 'These armies of Kolchak and Denikin,' Foch is said to have remarked with much discernment, 'cannot last long because they have no civil governments behind them.' It would not have been right after the Great War was over, even had it been possible, to use British, French or American troops in Russia. Those that were already there must be withdrawn as soon as possible. Intervention after the Armistice could only take the form of money, supplies, munitions, technical instructors, moral countenance and a concerted diplomacy. But even resources thus strictly limited offered a fair chance of success provided they had been skilfully and sincerely applied in good time. Instead, they were frittered away by doubtful or contradictory convictions and disjointed inconsequent actions. The dualism of policy already described was fatal to success either by peaceful or warlike plans. Either the policy of helping all the anti-Bolshevik forces which encircled Soviet Russia should have been straightforwardly pursued, or a peace should have been unitedly made with the Bolsheviks on terms which assured some hopes of life and liberty to the loyal Russians who had been fighting with the Allies in the war, and to whom we were in honour bound. Neither the one nor the other was earnestly attempted. Half-hearted efforts to make peace were companioned by half-hearted attempts to make war. The conflict was thus prolonged without real prospects of peace or victory. The achievements of the National Russians, though inadequate, exceeded what had been expected by Allied statesmen or generals. But deprived of world-wide moral support and separated by antagonistic national aims from the Border States, from Poland and from Roumania, they were one after the other broken up and destroyed.

I have explained the part I played in these events. I had no responsibility either for the original intervention or for the commitments and obligations which it entailed. Neither did it rest with me to decide whether intervention should be continued after the Armistice or brought to an end. It was my duty in a subordinate though important station to try to make good the undertakings which had been entered into by Great Britain, and to protect as far as possible those who had compromised themselves in the common cause of the Allies and of Russia herself. I am glad to think that our country was the last to ignore its obligations or to leave ill-starred comrades to their fate. Painful as is the story of Archangel and Murmansk, we may claim to have wound up our affairs there without weakness or discredit. In Siberia our part was always small. But to Denikin we gave substantial assistance. We provided him with the means of arming and equipping nearly a quarter of a million men. The cost of this effort has been loosely stated at a hundred millions sterling; but this is an absurd exaggeration. The actual expense, apart from munitions, was not a tithe as great. The munitions themselves, though they had been

RUSSIA
SCALE OF MILES
100 50 0   100   200   300   400   500   600

Shewing positions of Anti-Bolshevik Armies
—— May 20 1919 (Date of Kolchaks farthest advance)
—·—· Oct. 13 1919 ("   Denikins   "   )

most costly to produce, were only an unmarketable surplus of the Great War, to which no money value can be assigned. Had they been kept in our hands till they mouldered, they would only have involved additional charges for storage, care and maintenance.

Although intervention failed, there remained two results of our persistency. The first is moral. We can at any rate say that the Russian forces who were loyal to the Allies were not left without the means of self-defence. There were placed in their hands weapons which, had they been a society of higher quality and with greater comprehension of their cause and of their own countrymen, might have enabled them to conquer. Here too, the exploits of the Czechs afford a measure of what was possible in these times in Russia. At least it can be said that the National Russians did not perish for want of arms. It was not the want of material means, but of comradeship, will-power and rugged steadfastness that lost the struggle. Bravery and devotion shone in individuals, ruthlessness was never absent; but the qualities which enable scores of thousands of men to combine and to act for a common purpose even when isolated, were not to be found in the wreckage of the Empire of the Czars. The Ironsides who charged at Marston Moor, the grenadiers who escorted Napoleon back from Elba, the Red-shirts of Garibaldi and the Black-shirts of Mussolini, were held by widely different moral and mental themes. But in them all there burned a flame. There were only sparks in Russia.

But there was also a more practical result of intervention. The Bolsheviks were absorbed during the whole of 1919 in the conflicts with Kolchak and Denikin. Their energy was turned upon the internal struggle. A breathing space of inestimable importance was afforded to the whole line of newly liberated countries which stood along the western borders of Russia. Kolchak and Denikin, and those who followed them, are dead or scattered. Russia has been frozen in an indefinite winter of sub-human doctrine and superhuman tyranny. But Finland, Esthonia, Latvia, Lithuania, and above all Poland, were able during 1919 to establish the structure of civilised States and to organise the strength of patriotic armies. By the end of 1920 the 'Sanitary Cordon' which protected Europe from the Bolshevik infection was formed by living national organisms vigorous in themselves, hostile to the disease and immune through experience against its ravages. In this same period also there first began among the Socialists of France, Great Britain and Italy those disillusionments which have steadily developed into the strong repulsions of the present day.

CHAPTER XIV
THE IRISH SPECTRE[1]

eheu, cicatricum et sceleris pudet
fratrumque. quid nos dura refugimus
aetas? quid intactum nefasti
liquimus? unde manum iuventus
metu deorum continuit? quibus
pepercit aris?

—Horace, *Odes*, I, 35.

O wounds that scarce have ceased to run!
O brothers' blood! O iron time!
What horror have we left undone?
Has conscience shrunk from aught of crime?
What shrine has rapine held in awe?
What altar spared?

—Conington.

Self-Preservation—Changing Proportions—The Irish at Westminster—Ireland at the Outbreak of War—The Conscription Question—The Sinn Fein Members—Their Merciful Boycott—The Beginning of Irish Disorder—The New Home Rule Bill—Its Decisive Importance—The Black and Tans—The Military View—Authorised Reprisals—The Prime Minister's Attitude—Cabinet Divergencies—The Craig-De Valera Interview—Sir Nevil Macready's Report—The King's Speech in Ulster—The Response—A Grave Decision—The Truce—Prolonged Negotiations—Within the Dail—The Irish Conference—Stresses in the Unionist Party—Political Tension—Resignation Inadmissible—Acid Hatreds—The Ultimatum—The Agreement Signed—Lloyd George and Ireland.

Integral communities, like living things, are dominated by the instinct of self-preservation. This principle is expressed in each generation by moral, logical, or sentimental arguments which acquire the authority of doctrine. Children are taught the doctrines which their parents have found useful and which probably were useful in their day. Therefore, the beliefs linger after their need has passed. But though it is not always

---

[1] For this and succeeding chapters see map on page 239.

apparent at the time, in fact at every stage we rely upon the weapons and lessons of a bygone war. The underlying needs are always changing at varying rates and at uneven intervals. Some large outside shock is necessary from time to time to force a revision of the data and a readjustment of the proportion.

The relations of Britain and Ireland were established during centuries when the independence of a hostile Ireland menaced the life of Britain. Every policy, every shift, every oppression used by the stronger island arose from this primordial fact. In the twentieth century it was a fact no longer. When Britain, counting twelve millions, was sandwiched between a France—for a thousand years her hereditary foe and potential invader—of twenty millions on the one hand, and a hostile Ireland of seven millions on the other, the anxieties of these twelve millions may be pardoned and the resulting measures understood. But when France had been far outnumbered by a united Germany, also her secular antagonist; when Ireland had sunk to four and a quarter millions— without Ulster to three; and when Britain, apart from her Empire, had risen to forty-three millions; the situation was transformed.

Meanwhile, however, Parties with their organised structures, interests, prejudices, and passions persisted on the old basis and judged and fought as their fathers had done before them. The shock and overturn of the world war enforced the realisation of the altered statistical scale.

Two other factors, practical and material in character, were also at work. The first was financial. For many years before the war the taxes collected from Ireland were substantially less than the public moneys expended in Ireland by the Exchequer of the United Kingdom. Ireland was in fact continuously a financial gainer from the fact of a joint exchequer. But when, under the undreamed-of expenses of the war and the debts piled up beyond previous imagination, the taxes for Imperial purposes rose out of any relation to the expenses of Irish local administration, the flow of public money from the joint exchequer was no longer westward to the far smaller and poorer island.

The second new factor was not less practical. By the Act of Union Ireland was entitled to send 103 members to the Imperial Parliament. The astonishing changes in the relative populations during the nineteenth century had not affected this quota. The Irish contended that the figure had been fixed by Treaty, and the British with continual grumblings acquiesced in the claim. There were therefore always at the centre of Imperial Government at least eighty Members of Parliament who boasted that they cared nothing for Britain and her institutions; that England's difficulty was Ireland's opportunity; that they would take all they could extort by parliamentary pressure and would give nothing in return; that they would throw their weight mechanically disciplined upon the side of every subversive movement at home and of every foreign antagonism. By such-like declarations the Irish Nationalist Party, at least from Parnell to the Great War, maintained their ascendancy over the forces of actual rebellion and assassination in Ireland.

However, in practice (such is the emollient influence of parliamentary and democratic institutions), the anti-British doctrines of the Irish Nationalist Party were sensibly modified. If they wrecked the ancient free procedure of the House of Commons by obstruction and disorder, they nevertheless adorned and enlivened its debates.

If they declared themselves the sworn foes of British institutions, they played a noteworthy part in the carrying in good time of many of the reforms which were essential to the growth of British social life, and through which these very institutions preserved their perennial vitality. When Irish Nationalist members denounced the jingo character of the South African War, they were none the less thrilled by the gallant conduct of the Irish regiments. Irish manhood enlisted freely, and Irish leaders comforted themselves in their hearts by remembering that after all it was only a small war, and that they could splash about boisterously without endangering the safety of the whole concern.

The deluge of Armageddon swept away all these minor defences and small ways of carrying on. August 4, 1914, stirred the vast majority of the Irish people to its depths with a generous sentiment. The heart of Ireland did not beat with the same rhythm as that of Britain, but the moral and intellectual decision was the same in both islands. The British Nation should never forget, and history will deeply mark the surge of comradeship with the whole British Empire and with the Allies which the news of the invasion of Belgium and the British declaration of war evoked from the mass of the Irish people. Mr. John Redmond, with the assent and in the name of the whole Nationalist Party, pledged Ireland to the conflict in words of noble eloquence. The Irish Members voted the war credits and the taxation they entailed. The quarrels of North and South faded in the glare of the struggle, and throughout the green island Catholics and Protestants alike hastened to the recruiting offices.

Now was the time to strike while the iron was hot. Now was the moment to confer upon Ireland the Constitutional Home Rule she had so long desired. A separate but subordinate Parliament for Ulster could then have been agreed to as a mere incident in the wide and solemn troth plighted among all the peoples of the Empire when for the first time they formed a common line of battle. Such an achievement was not permitted to the Government, nor indeed can we declare it to have been practicable. Few foresaw the long years of jeopardy that lay ahead of us all. All eyes were upon the battlefield. The Liberal Government insisted upon placing the Home Rule Bill upon the Statute Book, but a suspensory clause postponed its application until after the war. Even this was gravely resented by some of those statesmen who afterwards, in circumstances incomparably more disagreeable, signed the Irish Treaty in 1921.

In the building up of the Irish Army other important opportunities were foregone. Irish nationalism sought—and surely it was natural—to emphasise in every way the distinctive Irish characteristics of the swiftly forming battalions and brigades. Banners, badges, uniforms, watchwords of national significance were everywhere in the South of Ireland objects of keen desire, and a bolder indulgence of this wish would have fostered alike recruiting and good will. Lord Kitchener saw these manifestations from a different angle, and no one can deny the substance behind his misgivings. The history of 1798 stared him in the face, and, an Irishman himself, he could feel no assurance that Irish armies raised for one purpose might not be used for another. Beneath him the War Office drew its stiff routine, and much native enthusiasm was affronted or even frozen. Old misunderstandings and imperfect sympathies resumed their sway as the war ploughed heavily onward and its excitements evaporated. The forces of hate in Ireland began to regain their control of the national mind; and with them the desire of youth to dare and suffer—but for something else. There followed the tragedy of Easter week, 1916. The attempted German assistance, the mad revolt, the swift repression, the executions, few but corroding. Well was it said, 'The grass soon grows over a battlefield but never over a scaffold.' The position of the Irish Parliamentary Party was fatally undermined. The keys of Ireland passed into the keeping of those to whom hatred of England was the dominant and almost the only interest.

It was not till this melancholy pass was reached that earnest efforts were made by the Irish national leaders, by Sir Edward Carson and by the British Government, then a Coalition, to reach a settlement between the two parts of Ireland and between Ireland and Great Britain. The Conferences failed not perhaps by so very much. All this time the Irish divisions fought with traditional bravery wherever the war led them. Voluntary recruitment failed to supply their losses. The war deepened and darkened. With every year the contending nations raised their stakes; voluntary service gave place throughout Great Britain to compulsion. Canada and New Zealand passed Conscription Acts. The United States, coming late into the war, sought to hurl her whole military population by rigorous law into the welter. Finally, boys of eighteen and men of forty-five and even fifty, fathers of families and only sons of widows in Great Britain were taken for active service. 'Why,' it was sternly asked, 'should Ireland remain a favoured area full of men in their martial prime?'

The question of Irish Conscription was handled in such a fashion during 1918 that we had the worst of both worlds, all the resentment against compulsion and in the end no law and no men. The English demand for compulsory service in Ireland spread disaffection through the whole Irish people. Sixty thousand Irish soldiers were serving at the front, but 60,000 British troops were simultaneously garrisoning Ireland, and on the balance our resources were not increased.

The victory brought no joy to Southern Ireland. The thoughts of its people were now entirely centred upon their own affairs. At the election of 1918 all who had supported the cause of the Allies were swept away. The Nationalist Party, which had represented the Irish democracy for sixty years, vanished overnight. In their place were elected eighty Sinn Fein Members, entirely ignorant of and unaffected by all those assimilating processes which under the peace-time surface of wordy and voting hostility had in fact produced a great body of latent sympathy and comprehension. Here was the old atavistic hatred, pristine and unassuaged. These were the men of single and local purpose, intellectually at any rate reckless of consequences to themselves or to larger interests. Here was the spirit of the Easter rebellion embodied in eighty Members of the House of Commons. There were some Parliaments in Europe before the war, there are perhaps some to-day, which present this frightful discordance of a minority.

The Parliament which met in January, 1919, was, as has been shown, in its composition overwhelmingly Conservative. The pressure of eighty deadly foes might have destroyed its debates or even have led to violence in the Chamber itself, but it could not have impeded or changed the march of events. But other Parliaments lay ahead. Any thoughtful man looking to the future must count on Parliaments in which British parties would be in equipoise and when the balance would be turned against the main well-being of the State by an implacable minority. The franchise had been extended almost to the widest limits. The anti-German passion which the electors had carried to such unreasonable excess would swiftly fade. In its decline, all those forces which work the undoing of states and civilisations were reviving. Within four years, in fact, a Parliament was to come into being in which eighty Sinn Fein Members would almost have given an absolute majority to an inchoate, half-organised and less than half-instructed Socialist Party. For a long time in our Parliamentary life and Party electioneering, there would be gnawing at the very vitals of the Empire an untamed, untutored band of haters, carrying into English public life a malignity unknown for generations—even for centuries.

Mercifully the Sinn Feiners themselves spared us these squalid-tragic experiences. Their own sense of what was due to Ireland led them to scorn the execrable function of baffling and distracting the British realm. Without hesitation and following a Magyar example, the Sinn Fein Members renounced all representation in the House of Commons. Not for a moment did they weigh or value the immense influence and leverage they could exert, for ill or for good, upon the decisive affairs of the British Empire. 'Sinn Fein,' 'Ourselves alone,' that was the cry, and by an act of self-abnegation, remarkable even when born of hatred, they cut themselves off for ever from an inheritance in the House of Commons which, though invidious, was in a worldly sense inestimable. The two supreme services which Ireland has rendered Britain are her accession to the Allied cause on the outbreak of the Great War, and her withdrawal from the House of Commons at its close.

The reader, prepared by these general but by no means exhaustive observations, must now be recalled to the current of events.

On January 15, 1919, the Sinn Fein Congress met in Dublin and read a Declaration of Independence. On the 22nd a Republican Parliament met at the Dublin Mansion House and elected a Cabinet. When on February 4 the new House of Commons assembled at Westminster, scarcely any representatives of Ireland, except from Ulster, were present. So much was going on all over the world and our own affairs pressed upon us so importunately, that the significance of these demonstrations was hardly noticed. Bringing home the Army; the reconstruction of peace-time industry; the resumption of civil life; the Peace Conference; the eventual Treaty; and the vast confusion of Europe, completely absorbed the thought and energy of the new administration. The scale and speed of world history had to fall by sharp and continuous gradations before the fact that Ireland still existed rose again in British minds. But as the tumult of the whole world gradually and spasmodically subsided with many reverberations, Southern Ireland was perceived to be crying aloud in a strange voice, and the words she cried were presently understood to be 'Independence or Murder.'

During the summer and autumn of 1919 occasional but nationally conceived murders began to be perpetrated upon the humble agents of the British Crown in Ireland, and by the end of the year an organised campaign of assassinations of magistrates, of police and of soldiers when found in twos and three, developed progressively through the three provinces of Southern Ireland. The policy of these outrages was not discountenanced by the Sinn Fein Parliament, but the actual work was done by the secret societies called the

'Irish Republican Army' and the 'Irish Republican Brotherhood.' The form of warfare was repulsive. A constable on his beat in the streets of a town or village is asked some casual question like 'What is the time?' As he takes out his watch to give the information, he is shot dead. The perpetrator, although seen by dozens of persons, walks off unpursued, and no one will give evidence against him. Or again, British soldiers returning from Mass are suddenly fired upon from behind a hedge and three or four are shot down. As the year advanced these murders grew in number and in scale. They culminated in a determined attempt on December 19 to murder Lord French. The Viceroy's motor-car was held up by gunmen and received several volleys of pistol shots. Lord French himself was uninjured; one of the assailants was killed and one of the escort was wounded. All was, however, on a fairly petty scale. Between May and December, 1919, there were about 1,500 political offences, including 18 murders and 77 armed attacks.

Under the pressure of these events Dublin Castle decided in August to proclaim the suppression of Sinn Fein, and in September they banned its Parliament. In December leading Sinn Feiners were arrested and deported, and the *Freeman's Journal* was prohibited. These modest counter-measures were attended only by increasing disorder. The troops and the police bore the strain of the assassinations, for which of course hardly anyone was brought to justice, with exemplary patience for a long time. But at length their distress and indignation led them to take the law into their own hands. Soldiers whose comrades had been murdered wrecked the shops and dwellings of persons in the neighbourhood of the crime, and the police began here and there unauthorised reprisals upon suspected persons. Large numbers of people in England, themselves exposed to no danger, were sincerely shocked by such undisciplined conduct. However, it will always be very difficult to persuade armed bodies of men to endure with impassive good humour for any long period being hunted down and murdered one by one. Reinforcements were sent to Ireland and the Constabulary were largely increased. The unauthorised reprisals grew with the increasing provocation.

Meanwhile the British Cabinet had in September, 1919, decided to introduce a Home Rule Bill. This measure was designed to replace the famous Home Rule Act which had received the Royal Assent but was indefinitely suspended. The Government of Ireland Bill of 1920 was a considerable measure. It gave real and important powers of self-government to Ireland. It came with the authority of a Government and a Parliament based upon an overwhelming Conservative and Unionist majority. Life-long opponents to Home Rule, like Mr. Walter Long, become a Coalition Minister, sponsored the Bill. He could do this because separate Legislatures were proposed for North and South, and because the matters reserved to be dealt with by the Council of Ireland were of a non-controversial character. Irish representation at Westminster was materially reduced.

After prolonged debates this Bill received the Royal Assent in December, 1920. It was accepted under bitter protest by the Protestant North. They bowed to the decision of the Imperial Parliament. They used their option to contract out of the Dublin Parliament and set up their own legislature and Government as prescribed by the Act. Had the powers of this measure been accepted and exercised in a reasonable and friendly spirit by the dominant elements in Southern Ireland there is little doubt that the Irish Nationalist grievance would have been substantially met, and certainly Ireland—escaping a long and painful ordeal—would to-day be more prosperous, more influential and more united. No doubt there had been many occasions since 1886 when such a measure, if it could have been presented by a Conservative Government, would have been accepted with good will. In 1920 it was simply ignored by the ruling Sinn Fein organisations. They refused to put it into operation in Southern Ireland, and the campaign of disorder and systematised murder continued to grow.

Nevertheless the Bill of 1920 was a decisive turning-point in the history of the two islands. In important respects it was tantamount to the repeal of the Act of Union after 120 years of friction. As such it profoundly affected the Unionist Party, whose very name lost its meaning. It had a more practical and irrevocable importance. Ulster, or rather its six predominantly Protestant counties, became a separate entity clothed with constitutional form, possessing all the organs of government and administration, including police and the capacity of self-defence for the purposes of internal order. From that moment the position of Ulster became unassailable. It could never again be said that Ulster Protestants barred the aspirations of their Southern fellow countrymen. They had indeed on the contrary acquiesced in a large disturbance of their own foundations and by their compliance with the decision of the Imperial Parliament exposed themselves to poignant reproaches from the Unionists of Southern Ireland. Every argument of self-determination ranged itself henceforward upon their side. Never again could any British Party contemplate putting pressure upon them to part with the Constitution they had reluctantly accepted. They were masters in their own house, and small though it might be, it was morally and logically founded upon a rock. The Act of 1920 ended for ever this phase of the Irish Problem.

During the whole of 1920 the murder campaign grew and spread in Ireland. The scale of the outrages increased. In one ambush fifteen out of seventeen auxiliary police were killed. On a November morning fourteen officers, believed by the rebels to be engaged in Intelligence work, were shot, unarmed, several in the presence of their wives, in their billets in Dublin. The faithful recital of these deeds would fill a chapter. They must not further darken these pages.

In the same period considerable measures were taken by the British Government. Large numbers of additional troops were sent to Ireland. Armoured cars and motor-cars, forces of police and military were organised upon an important scale, and a special police force was formed entirely of ex-officers and from the wartime armies. These special police, who ultimately amounted to 7,000 men, were nicknamed on account of their dark cap and khaki uniform the 'Black and Tans.' It has become customary to lavish abuse upon the Black and Tans and to treat them as a mob of bravos and terrorists suddenly let loose upon the fair pastures of Ireland. In fact, however, they were selected from a great press of applicants on account of their intelligence, their characters and their records in the war. Originally they were intended to supplement the hard-pressed Royal Irish Constabulary; but in grappling with murder they developed within themselves a very strong counter-terrorist activity. They acted with much the same freedom as the Chicago or New York police permit themselves in dealing with armed gangs. When any of their own men or police or military comrades were murdered they 'beat up' the haunts of well-known malignants, or those whom they conceived to be malignants, and sharply challenged suspected persons at the pistol's point. Obviously there can be no defence for such conduct except the kind of attack to which it was a reply.

Liberals who had always supported Home Rule were on strong ground when they dwelt upon the consequences of its denial. They were reinforced by another school of thought which had much less justice or logic behind it. A certain number of high Tories, while rigidly opposing any effective concession to Irish Nationalist demands, were still more violent in their denunciations of the Black and Tans. They demanded that the Government should strictly and inflexibly maintain order by the regular processes of law, and that it should punish unsparingly any of its agents who, no matter what the provocation, departed a hair's breadth from the orthodox procedure of a civilised state in time of peace. 'Maintain the Union,' they cried, 'and do not give way to violence. Adhere with circumspection to the law of the land. Detect and arrest the criminals and bring them to justice before the Courts.' This was easy to prescribe but impossible to perform. Where no witnesses would give evidence or could give it only at the peril of their lives, where no juries would convict, the ordinary processes of law were non-existent.

From another angle the military authorities contributed unhelpful counsel. Headed by the Chief of the Imperial General Staff, Sir Henry Wilson, they demanded incessantly universal martial law throughout Southern Ireland. How this would have solved the problem was never explained. These military authorities were vehement in repudiating any suggestion of counter-terrorism. They contented themselves with vague assertions that putting rebellious Ireland under martial law 'would show that the Government was in earnest.' I never received during my tenure of the War Office any practical or useful advice on this subject from these quarters. My military advisers also naturally complained continuously of the strain on the troops, the bulk of them post-war recruits, in having to live month after month in the constant expectation of being murdered by some apparently inoffensive member of the civil population. They dwelt with insistence, both in my time and in that of my successor, Sir Laming Worthington-Evans, on the urgent need of reinforcing the army in Ireland and simultaneously relieving the bulk of the existing garrison. By an occult and unstudied combination between the opinions of the Tory legalists and those of the military martial law men—martial law being no law—the decision was induced and announced in Parliament that 'authorised reprisals' such as would have ruled in a war zone, and these only, should be adopted. All unauthorised action on the part of the police or the special police was to be repressed with rigour.

This resolve came with great relief to the Irish secret societies. To do them justice, they were almost the only people in the whole world who were not shocked by the activities of the Black and Tans. They thought it fair that their own measure should be meted out to them. By the end of 1920 they found themselves extremely hard pressed by the activities of the Black and Tans, who, with increasing information and ruthlessness, were striking down in the darkness those who struck from the darkness. Mr. Lloyd George went so far as to say at the Guildhall Banquet on November 9, 'We have murder by the throat.'

The policy of 'authorised reprisals' came into force on New Year's Day, 1921. It speedily proved far less effective than the rough and ready measures of the special police. On the morrow of an outrage the military sallied forth in a brigade to burn a cottage; in the night the Sinn Feiners padded out and burnt a country house.

Meanwhile, the actual power of the British forces to go wherever they wished and do whatever they thought proper never encountered appreciable opposition. Sweeps were made by cavalry and motor-cars on 30- or 40-mile fronts, and every male taken into the net was meticulously examined, often without a single person being found accountable. And perhaps that same night an audacious murder took place on the very ground so thoroughly scoured. It was clear by the early summer of 1921 that Britain was at the parting of the ways. It would have been quite easy to quell the odious and shameful form of warfare by which we were assailed and into which we were being increasingly drawn, by using the ruthlessness which the Russian Communists adopt towards their fellow countrymen. The arrest of large numbers of persons believed by the police to be in sympathy with the rebels and the summary execution of four or five of these hostages (many of whom must certainly have been innocent) for every life taken of a Government servant, might have been a remedy at once sombre and efficacious. It was a course of which the British people in the hour of their deliverance were utterly incapable. Public opinion recoiled with anger and irritation even from the partial measures into which our agents had been gradually drawn. The choice was by now clearly open, 'Crush them with iron and unstinted force, or try to give them what they want.' These were the only alternatives, and though each had ardent advocates, most people were unprepared for either.

Here indeed was the Irish Spectre—horrid and inexorcisable!

* * * * *

No British Government in modern times has ever appeared to make so complete and sudden a reversal of policy as that which ensued. In May the whole power of the State and all the influence of the Coalition were used to 'hunt down the murder gang': in June the goal was 'a lasting reconciliation with the Irish people.' The vivid contrast between these two extremes might well furnish a theme of mockery to superficial judgment. Actually, however, there were only two courses: war with the utmost violence or peace with the utmost patience. Vast argument could be deployed for either course, but nothing in sense or mercy could excuse weak compromises between the two. In ordinary domestic politics these sharp dichotomies are usually inapplicable; but when the sword is bared and the pistol pointed, and blood flows and homes are laid waste, it ought to be one thing or the other.

The legend has obtained some credence that this diametrical change of policy arose from a waning nerve power in the Prime Minister. For instance, Sir Nevil Macready has suggested in his recently published memoirs that he found Mr. Lloyd George concerned about his personal safety. Such insinuations are contrary to fact. Up till the summer of 1921 no one was more resolute or ready to be more ruthless against the Irish rebellion than Mr. Lloyd George. He had constantly to measure the British political situation. This required as a prelude to any form of Home Rule, first the security of Ulster and secondly a clear victory over the gunmen. The first condition was broadly satisfied by the 1920 Act: the second was certainly not yet attained. What then were the causes and incidents which induced him to abandon his policy of repression before it was effective? I shall set them out as I measured them at the time.

By April, 1921, the Irish problem had become the main preoccupation of the Government. The Prime Minister showed himself markedly disposed to fight the matter out at all costs, and to rely for this purpose upon 'the age-long loyalties of the Conservative Party.' The Cabinet were at one with him in this. Upon the method, however, there were two distinct opinions. It was evident to all Ministers that efforts to restore order in Ireland must be made during the rest of the year upon an extraordinary scale. A hundred thousand new special troops and police must be raised; thousands of motor-cars must be armoured and equipped; the three Southern Provinces of Ireland must be closely laced with cordons of blockhouses and barbed wire; a systematic rummaging and questioning of every individual must be put in force. In order to paralyse the activities of a few thousand persons the entire population must when required be made to account for every hour of their time. There was no physical bar to accomplishing all this. It was a matter of men and money, and both would have been supplied in ample measure by a Parliament which still had three years of constitutional life. These were the kind of projects which now came bluntly into view.

Some Ministers, of whom I was one, while ready to undertake the responsibilities and to share the exertions which such a policy involved, held that these drastic processes should be accompanied by the offer of the widest possible measure of self-government to Southern Ireland. 'Let us,' they said, 'lay aside every impediment; let us make it clear that the Irish people are being forced by Sinn Fein to fight not for Home Rule, but for separation; not for an Irish Parliament under the Crown, but for a revolutionary Republic.' An impressive debate in Cabinet took place upon this issue. Personally I wished to see the Irish confronted on the one hand with the realisation of all that they had asked for, and of all that Gladstone had striven for, and upon the other with the most unlimited exercise of rough-handed force. I was therefore on the side of those who wished to couple a tremendous onslaught with the fairest offer. It will be sufficient to say that the division of opinion was almost evenly balanced, but that weight, apart from numbers, inclined to those who preferred the dual policy. The Prime Minister was astonished and indeed startled to find how many Conservatives adhered to this more complicated course. I could see that he was profoundly impressed both by the argument and by the authority behind it. On the question being put 'Would you then allow a Dublin Parliament like any other Dominion to levy a tariff against British goods?' the answer was fiercely made, 'How can this petty matter be weighed against the grievous action we are preparing?' As usual when there is a deep and honest division in a Cabinet united on main issues, nothing was settled at the moment and everyone went home to chew the cud. I must record my opinion that Mr. Lloyd George reached the conclusion that a policy of unmitigated repression in Ireland would not command whole-hearted support even among the Conservatives.

The Prime Minister had on several occasions in the name of the Cabinet offered to negotiate for a settlement, provided the Irish rebels were prepared to accept the Crown and the Imperial connection. Renewed efforts were now made to establish contact. In May of 1921 Lord FitzAlan, one of the leaders of the English Catholics, succeeded Lord French as Viceroy. Devotion to public duty alone inspired him to undertake so melancholy a task. Three days later, Sir James Craig, Prime Minister of Northern Ireland, at the request of Mr. Lloyd George, met Mr. de Valera in his hiding-place. This meeting, which had been the subject of considerable previous negotiation, was certainly a remarkable episode. The Ulster leader, representative of all that had stood against Home Rule, was conducted by the Sinn Fein gunmen through long devious and secret routes to the headquarters of the leader of the Irish rebellion. His robust outlook and single-minded sense of duty to the well-being of the Empire, joined to disdain of personal risks, capital or political, led Sir James Craig to undertake this mission. His conversations with the Sinn Fein leader were abortive. At the end of four hours Mr. de Valera's recital of Irish grievances had only reached the iniquities of Poynings' Act in the days of Henry VII. There were by that time various reasonable excuses for terminating not a discussion, but a lecture. Sir James Craig placed himself again in the hands of his guides and was motored circuitously and erratically back to Dublin. They were three in the little car rattling and bumping over the ill-kept roads—two Sinn Feiners whose lives were probably forfeit, and the Prime Minister of Orange Ulster. Suddenly behind them arrived an armoured lorry filled with Black and Tans. Although Sir James Craig's conductors were not particularly anxious to be scrutinised at close quarters, they judged it prudent to let it pass them. The heavy vehicle ran by within a foot of the little car. When, after inquisitively continuing level for some time, it finally drew ahead and rumbled on, the three Irishmen so differently circumstanced exchanged glances of perfect comprehension.

Although the actual Craig-de Valera conversations were barren, a rope had been flung across the chasm. From that moment British Government agents in Ireland were upon occasion, through one channel or another, in touch with the Sinn Fein Headquarters.

At the end of May Sir Nevil Macready presented a pessimistic report upon the state of Ireland. 'While,' he said, 'I am of opinion that the troops at present in Ireland may be depended upon to continue to do their best under present circumstances through this summer, I am convinced that by October, unless a peaceful solution has been reached, it will not be safe to ask the troops to continue there another winter under the conditions which obtained there during the last. Not only the men for the sake of their morale and training should be removed out of the "Irish atmosphere," but by that time there will be many officers who, although they may not confess it, will in my opinion be quite unfit to continue to serve in Ireland without a release for a very considerable period. . . . Unless I am entirely mistaken, the present state of affairs in Ireland, so far as regards the troops serving there, must be brought to a conclusion by October, or steps must be taken to relieve practically the whole of the troops together with the great majority of the Commanders and their staff.' This report was endorsed by Sir Henry Wilson. There could of course be no question of giving effect to it. These despairing counsels were not justified by the facts; nor in any case was there any possibility of relief. Not relief, but reinforcement on a large scale—all the old forces with new forces added—was the obvious step; and this, though costly and troublesome, was quite practicable. Still, while the Cabinet did not accept, they were bound to weigh these sweeping and alarmist assertions of the Commander-in-Chief in Ireland, endorsed, as they were, by the Chief of the Imperial General Staff.

All these pressures and tendencies might have remained subliminal but for the spark of an event. On June 22 the First Parliament of Northern Ireland was to be inaugurated by the King in person. It would not have been right for Ministers to put in the mouth of the Sovereign words which could only appeal to the people of Northern Ireland. It is well known that the King, acting in harmony not only with the letter but with the spirit of the Constitution, earnestly expressed the wish that language should be used which would appeal to the whole of his Irish subjects, South as well as North, Green as well as Orange. The outlook of the Sovereign lifted high above the strife of Party, above the clash of races and religions, and sectional divergencies of view, necessarily and naturally comprised the general interest of the Empire as a whole—and nothing narrower. The Prime Minister and leading Members of the Government therefore took the responsibility which rested with them, and with them alone, of inserting in the Royal Speech what was in effect a sincere appeal for a common effort to end the odious and disastrous conflict.

'The eyes of the whole Empire,' said the King with evident emotion, 'are on Ireland to-day—that Empire in which so many nations and races have come together in spite of ancient feuds, and in which new nations have come to birth within the lifetime of the youngest in this Hall. I am emboldened by that thought to look beyond the sorrow and the anxiety which have clouded of late My vision of Irish affairs. I speak from a full heart when I pray that My coming to Ireland to-day may prove to be the first step towards an end of strife amongst her people, whatever their race or creed.

'In that hope I appeal to all Irishmen to pause, to stretch out the hand of forbearance and conciliation, to forgive and to forget, and to join in making for the land which they love a new era of peace, contentment, and good will. It is my earnest desire that in Southern Ireland too there may ere long take place a parallel to what is now passing in this Hall; that there a similar occasion may present itself and a similar ceremony be performed.

'For this the Parliament of the United Kingdom has in the fullest measure provided the powers; for this the Parliament of Ulster is pointing the way. The future lies in the hands of My Irish people themselves. May this historic gathering be the prelude of a day in which the Irish people, North and South, under one Parliament or two, as those Parliaments may themselves decide, shall work together in common love for Ireland upon the sure foundation of mutual justice and respect.'

No one responsible for the King's Speech had contemplated immediate results in action. But in such declarations everything depends upon the sounding-board.

The King-Emperor, the embodiment of the common inheritance, discharging his constitutional duty at the peril of his life, had struck a note which rang and reverberated, and which all ears were attuned to hear. The response of public opinion in both islands to that appeal was instant, deep, and widespread, and from that moment events moved forward in unbroken progression to the establishment of the Irish Free State. On June 24 Mr. Lloyd George invited Sir James Craig and Mr. de Valera to a conference in London. On July 11 the invitations were accepted, and a truce, the terms of which had been settled on the 9th, was proclaimed.

No act of British state policy in which I have been concerned aroused more violently conflicting emotions than the Irish Settlement. For a system of human government so vast and so variously composed as the British Empire to compact with open rebellion in the peculiar form in which it was developed in Ireland, was an event which might well have shaken to its foundations that authority upon which the peace and order of hundreds of millions of people of many races and communities were erected. Servants of the Crown in the faithful performance of their duty had been and were being cruelly murdered as a feature in a deliberately adopted method of warfare. It was only possible to say of those responsible for these acts that they were not actuated by selfish or sordid motives; that they were ready to lay down their own lives; and that in the main they were supported by the sentiment of their fellow countrymen. To receive the leaders of such men at the Council Board, and to attempt to form through their agency the government of a civilised state, must be regarded as one of the most questionable and hazardous experiments upon which a great Empire in the plenitude of its power had ever embarked.

On the other hand stood the history of Ireland—an unending quarrel and mutual injuries done to each other by sister countries and close neighbours, generation after generation; and the earnest desire in Britain was to end this hateful feud. During the nineteenth century both England and Ireland had re-stated their cases in forms far superior to those of the dark times of the past. England had lavished remedial measures and conciliatory procedures upon Ireland; Ireland in the main had rested herself upon constitutional action to support her claim. It would have been possible in 1886 to have reached a solution on a basis infinitely less perilous both to Ireland and to Great Britain than that to which we were ultimately drawn. Said Mr. Gladstone in the House of Commons before the fateful division on the Home Rule Bill, 'Ireland stands at your bar expectant, hopeful, almost suppliant. Her words are words of truth and soberness. She asks a blessed oblivion of the past, and in that oblivion our interest is deeper even than hers. . . . Think, I beseech you—think well, think wisely; think not for the moment but for the years that are to come, before you reject this Bill.'

And, after all, we were the victors in the greatest struggle of all time. We did not claim more than our true share in those supreme events, but it was sufficient to make us easy in our own minds about a matter so comparatively small in a material sense as Ireland. No one, for instance, could say that the life of the Empire was in danger when every hostile force in the world, including armies of millions of soldiers had passed out of existence, when the German fleet lay at the bottom of Scapa Flow, and when every armed opponent was prostrate. No one could say we were a cowardly or decadent race. There may be no logical relevance for such thoughts, but they contributed an important factor to the national decision. And what was the alternative? It was to plunge one small corner of the Empire into an iron repression, which could not be carried through without an admixture of murder and counter-murder, terror and counter-terror. Only national self-preservation could have excused such a policy, and no reasonable man could allege that self-preservation was involved.

However, the die was now cast. A truce had been proclaimed. The gunmen emerged from their hiding-places and strode the streets of Dublin as the leaders of a nation as old and as proud as our own. The troops and police and Black and Tans, but yesterday urged on to extirpate the murder gang, now stood relaxed and embarrassed while parleys on equal terms were in full swing. Impossible thereafter to resume the same kind of war! Impossible to refill or heat up again those cauldrons of hatred and contempt on which such quarrels are fed! Other courses remained at our disposal as a last resort. Ports and cities could be held; Dublin could be held; Ulster could be defended; all communication between Sinn Fein Ireland and the outer world could be severed; all trade between the two islands, that is to say the whole of Irish trade except from Ulster, could be stopped—at a price. But from the moment of the truce, the attempt to govern Southern Ireland upon the authority of the Imperial Parliament had come to an end.

It is no part of this tale to record, except in outline, the course of the negotiations or to recite the documents and records in which their public interchange was embodied. The opening contact was, however, notable. On July 14 the first of several interviews took place between Mr. de Valera and Mr. Lloyd George in the Cabinet Room at 10, Downing Street. Mr. de Valera had himself introduced with ceremony by "the representative of the Irish Republic in London" (Mr. Art O'Brien). The Prime Minister, never a greater artist than in the first moments of a fateful interview, received the Irish chieftain cordially as a brother Celt. Mr. de Valera was guarded and formal. He presented a lengthy document in the Irish language, and then for convenience a translation in English. The Prime Minister's literary curiosity was excited by its heading: "Saorstat Eireann." Saorstat, he remarked, did not strike his ear as Irish. What was its literal translation? After a pause Mr. de Valera replied that literally it meant "Free State." "I see," said the Prime Minister, "Saorstat means Free State; then what is your Irish word for Republic?" While the two Irishmen were discussing together in English what answer they should give to this innocent question, the Prime Minister turned to Professor Thomas Jones of the Cabinet Secretariat and conversed with him in Welsh to the evident discomfiture of his English-speaking Sinn Fein visitors. Eventually, as Mr. de Valera could get no further than that Saorstat meant Free State, the Prime Minister observed: "Must we not admit that the Celts never were Republicans and have no native word for such an idea?" A long embarrassed silence followed. This was the first move in a dialogue continued for many hours until, after an exhaustive survey of Irish history in ancient and mediæval times, it became clear that progress could only be made by the British Government tabling its own proposals. These were handed to Mr. de Valera on July 20. They comprised complete Dominion Home Rule involving, of course, autonomous control of finance and taxation, of the police and the military. Six conditions were attached. Four dealt with the naval and military aspects; one prohibited protective duties between the two islands, and the last imposed upon Ireland a share to be fairly determined of the jointly contracted national debt. These proposals were rejected by Mr. de Valera, who proclaimed the principle of complete independence and repudiated the Crown. The Prime Minister in his replies made it plain that the British Government could discuss no settlement 'which involves a refusal on the part of Ireland to accept our invitation to a free, equal, and loyal partnership in the British Commonwealth under one Sovereign.' The correspondence became lengthy and the difficulties no smaller. The Cabinet, at that time scattered in the holiday season, met on September 7 at Inverness. Two courses appeared to be open: to summon Mr. de Valera to a conference conditional on allegiance to the Crown; or to resume the unconditional parleys with him in the presence of other Irish representatives. The reply which was eventually settled asked whether Mr. de Valera was prepared to enter a conference to ascertain 'how the association of Ireland with the community of nations known as the British Empire can best be reconciled with Irish national aspirations.' If the answer was in the affirmative, a conference at Inverness was proposed for the 20th.

On September 12, Mr. de Valera wrote accepting this invitation: but in his letter he stated:—

'Our nation has formally declared its independence and recognises itself as a sovereign State. It is only as the representatives of that State and as its chosen guardians that we have any authority or powers to act on behalf of our people.'

On this the Prime Minister dismissed the two Irish emissaries who bore the message to his retreat at Gairloch, and cancelled the arrangements for the conference.

Nevertheless there was a well-founded feeling that neither side wished to see the whole parley break down, and the letters and telegrams continued to pass backwards and forwards perseveringly. Mr. de Valera would no doubt have gone on indefinitely fighting theoretical points without the slightest regard to the resultant misery and material ruin of his countrymen. But meanwhile, behind the tightly closed doors of the Dail, in almost continuous session at Dublin, and in the central conclaves of the Sinn Fein extremists, a definite and resolute movement of opinion grew up against him. Anarchy, stark, sheer and progressively degenerating might at any moment lay its talons upon Southern Ireland. The genius of the Irish race has a soberly practical side, and men, with forces behind them, stood forth from the confusion, men whose melancholy credentials could not be impugned, but whose aims were sane and whose word was their bond. These men were determined not to throw away what had been gained. No whisper of these divisions in Sinn Fein had yet reached the outer air. But Mr. de Valera's reply to the Prime Minister's cancellation of the conference was appreciably more conciliatory. Eventually he explained that he and his friends had no thought of committing the British Government to any conditions as a prelude to a conference. They could not abandon their national position, but neither did they expect a similar surrender by the British Government. A treaty he suggested between Great Britain and Ireland would end the dispute for ever and enable the two nations, each pursuing its own development, to work together in free and friendly co-operation in affairs of common concern. He invited the Prime Minister to state whether the British Government was demanding a surrender of the Sinn Fein position as a preliminary to conference or whether the conference could open free on both sides. The Cabinet Committee which met at Gairloch on September 21, in these circumstances, after reiterating their fundamental position, drafted a fresh invitation, sent on the 19th, to a conference in London on October 11 where they could meet the delegates of Sinn Fein 'with a view to ascertaining how the association of Ireland with the community of nations known as the British Empire might best be reconciled with Irish aspirations.' This invitation, sufficiently vague in character, was accepted and on the appointed date the Prime Minister, Mr. Chamberlain, Lord Birkenhead, Sir Laming Worthington-Evans, Sir Hamar Greenwood and myself met the Irish representatives, Mr. Griffith, Mr. Michael Collins, Mr. Barton, Mr. Gavan Duffy and Mr. Duggan in the Cabinet Room at Downing Street. It was significant that Mr. de Valera remained in Ireland.

* * * * *

It is not easy to measure the internal stresses set up in the Unionist Party by these events. Although everyone in every Party had been swept from his political socket by the cataract of world events; although human fortunes still ran in rapids all over the world, and men were baffled and bewildered by all that was going on and exhausted by all that had happened, yet the giving up in these ignominious circumstances of life-long convictions was almost intolerable. Resentment gathered all the deeper because those who felt the most keenly and were among the most tenacious elements of the nation knew that they were powerless. Ulster remained deeply agitated and refused to associate with the Government. The 300,000 Loyalists in Southern Ireland, perfectly helpless in the fighting, raised a lamentable cry in the parley.

At this stage much depended upon the action of individual Ministers. It was easy for Liberals and Home Rulers to support the widest form of Irish self-government, but those whose whole political careers had been absorbed in fighting Home Rule had a disagreeable and hazardous task to accomplish. The chief responsibility fell upon the leader of the Unionist Party, Mr. Austen Chamberlain. He had acted throughout in the closest harmony with the Prime Minister, and he was a man prepared to carry his actions to their conclusion and to face any consequences personal to himself.

When a leader takes a course fundamentally divergent from the whole traditions and even character of his Party, it is often open to some other prominent man to acquire great and possibly dominant political power. No one can impugn his motives; he is only carrying on in the old way, in a straightforward, simple and consistent manner. Such a man will find himself sustained by great numbers of persons of the highest integrity. His actions, however favourable to his ambition, will always appear to be sanctioned by duty and conviction. The attitude of Lord Birkenhead, then Lord Chancellor, was therefore at this juncture of the utmost importance. He was prominently and peculiarly connected with the resistance to Home Rule. He had been in comradeship with Sir Edward Carson; he had used to the full those threats of civil war which had played their part in the 1914 phase of the Irish conflict. There was no man who would have gained greater personal advantage by opposing the Irish Settlement; and none who would suffer more reproach by sustaining it. He now appeared, in the teeth alike of his past and his future, as its most aggressive Conservative supporter. The Irish Free Staters have always felt that they owed him their gratitude—and they are right. At this juncture qualities of independent and fearless judgment in the leader of the Unionist Party and in his most powerful lieutenant played their part in history. Political systems can to some extent be appraised by the test of whether their leading representatives are or are not capable of taking decisions in great matters on their merits, in defiance of their own interests and often of their best friends.

In due course, after many delays and much manœuvring, the Irish Delegates arrived in Downing Street, and those Members of the Cabinet who from their offices or from their personalities were deemed to be the chief actors met across the table those whom they had so recently denounced as 'The Murder Gang.' All these Irish Delegates had recently been in prison or had been hunted for their lives, and some in varying degrees had been associated with violent crime. The confrontation was not without its shock, and for some weeks the strictest formalities were observed. Not only were the discussions themselves baffling through their vagueness and uncertainty, but they were cumbered with a bulky mass of intricate and highly explosive detail. The negotiations, private and public, were continued for two months. They were reacted upon at all stages by the internal stresses of the Conservative Party and the convulsions of the newly reassembled Irish Dail. Disorders broke out in Belfast. The Ulster Government declared that they were being betrayed and, although they refused to come to the Conference, complained that they were not even consulted. The political tension was almost as acute as in the months before the war, but without the solvent of catastrophic events. Things merely lagged; the Irish could not say 'yes' or 'no' to anything. The condition of Ireland degenerated daily, and the Conservative Party with two-thirds of the House of Commons in its ranks stirred with anger and distress.

Although I only played at this time a part of second rank in Irish affairs and therefore did not feel the full pressures, I had as a member of the Cabinet Committee a decided opinion. We must go through with the business and persevere until we either were dismissed from power, or reached a settlement, or reopened in a new form hostilities against Southern Ireland. I urged that Ministers could not escape from their miseries by resignation. The desire for release was in the early part of November so general that no one could predict the fortunes of a single day. The degree of the crisis can perhaps in after days be as well measured by the following letter—of no particular consequence—as by any other test.

Mr. Churchill to the Prime Minister.

Nov. 9, 1921.

The criticism will certainly be made that the Government in resigning have abdicated their responsibility. More especially will this charge be made if the reason given is 'we are debarred by honour from coercing the North, and by conviction from coercing the South.' It will be said, 'here are men united in principle, knowing what they ought to do and what the interests of the country require, who are possessed of an overwhelming Parliamentary majority, including a majority of their own followers, who nevertheless without facing Parliament throw down the commission and declare themselves incapable of action in any direction.'

I greatly fear the consequences of such tactics, no matter how lofty may be the motives which prompt them.

2. After this has occurred, Mr. Bonar Law will be invited to form a Government. Why should he not do so? Surely he would be bound in honour to do so, if the members of the present Government have declared themselves inhibited from moving in any direction. Why should he not succeed . . .? In the crisis under consideration, the Conservative Party will have to rally to someone. Obviously they will rally to a Conservative leader, forming a Conservative Government, which has come forward to fill the gap created by the suicide of the Coalition; and which will be entitled to carry the standard forward against Labour at an imminent election, and to receive considerate treatment from ex-Ministers who have just thrown up the sponge. The delusion that an alternative Government cannot be formed is perennial. Mr. Chamberlain thought Sir Henry Campbell-Bannerman would be 'hissed off the stage.' Mr. Asquith was confident that you could not form an administration. But in neither case did the outgoing administration tie its hands in every direction by proclaiming itself honourably bound to do what the situation might require.

On these lines a very great public disaster might easily ensue, in which a reactionary Conservative Government might go forward to the polls against Labour, with the great central mass of England and Scotland remaining without leadership or decisive influence.

3. I wish to put on record that I consider that it is our duty to carry forward the policy about Ireland in which we believe, until we are defeated in the House of Commons, and thus honourably relieved from our duty to the Crown. . . .

From the outset it became of the utmost importance to convince those who were now accepted as the Irish leaders, of the sincerity and good will of the Imperial Government. The issue was too grave for bargaining and haggling. We stated from the very beginning all that we were prepared to give, and that in no circumstances could we go any further. We also made it clear that if our offer were accepted, we would without hesitation carry it through without regard to any political misfortune which might in consequence fall upon the Government or upon its leading Members. On this basis, therefore, and in this spirit the long and critical negotiations were conducted.

We found ourselves confronted in the early days not only with the unpractical and visionary fanaticism and romanticism of the extreme Irish secret societies, but also with those tides of distrust and hatred which had flowed between the two countries for so many centuries. An essential element in dynamite and every other high explosive is some intense acid. These terrible liquids slowly and elaborately prepared unite with perfectly innocent carbon compounds to give that pent-up, concentrated blasting power which shatters the structures and the lives of men. Hatred plays the same part in Government as acids in chemistry. And here in Ireland were hatreds which in Mr. Kipling's phrase would 'eat the live steel from the rifle butt,' hatreds such as, thank God, in Great Britain had not existed for a hundred years. All this we had to overcome.

Mr. Griffith was a writer who had studied deeply European history and the polity of States. He was a man of great firmness of character and of high integrity. He was that unusual figure—a silent Irishman; he hardly ever said a word. But no word that ever issued from his lips in my presence did he ever unsay. Michael Collins had not enjoyed the same advantages in education as his elder colleague. But he had elemental qualities and mother wit which were in many ways remarkable. He stood far nearer to the terrible incidents of the conflict than his leader. His prestige and influence with the extreme parties in Ireland for that reason were far higher, his difficulties in his own heart and with his associates were far greater. The other delegates were overshadowed by the two leaders. Mr. Duggan, however, was a sober minded, resolute man. In the background Mr. Erskine Childers, though not a delegate, pressed extreme counsels.

In the end, after two months of futilities and rigmarole, scarred by outrages in Ireland in breach of the truce, unutterably wearied Ministers faced the Irish Delegates, themselves in actual desperation and knowing well that death stood at their elbows. When we met on the afternoon of December 5, the Prime Minister stated bluntly that we could concede no more and debate no further. They must settle now; they must sign the agreement for a Treaty in the form to which after all these weeks it had attained, or else quit; and further, that both sides would be free to resume whatever warfare they could wage against each other. This was an ultimatum delivered, not through diplomatic channels, but face to face, and all present knew and understood that nothing else was possible. Stiff as our personal relations had been, there was by now a mutual respect between the principals and a very deep comprehension of each other's difficulties.

The Irishmen gulped down the ultimatum phlegmatically. Mr. Griffith said, speaking in his soft voice and with his modest manner, 'I will give the answer of the Irish Delegates at nine to-night; but, Mr. Prime Minister, I personally will sign this agreement and will recommend it to my countrymen.' 'Do I understand, Mr. Griffith,' said Mr. Lloyd George, 'that though everyone else refuses you will nevertheless agree to sign?' 'Yes, that is so, Mr. Prime Minister,' replied this quiet little man of great heart and of great purpose. Michael Collins rose looking as if he was going to shoot someone, preferably himself. In all my life I have never seen so much passion and suffering in restraint.

We then went off and drummed our heels and had some food and smoked, and discussed plans of campaign. No one expected that anyone but Mr. Griffith would agree, and what validity would his solitary signature possess? As for ourselves, we had already ruptured the loyalties of our friends and supporters.

The British Representatives were in their places at nine, but it was not until long after midnight that the Irish Delegation appeared. As before, they were superficially calm and very quiet. There was a long pause, or there seemed to be. Then Mr. Griffith said,

'Mr. Prime Minister, the Delegation is willing to sign the agreements but there are a few points of drafting which perhaps it would be convenient if I mentioned at once.' Thus, by the easiest of gestures he carried the whole matter into the region of minor detail, and everyone concentrated upon these points with overstrained interest so as to drive the main issue into the background for ever.

Soon we were talking busily about technicalities and verbal corrections, and holding firmly to all these lest worse should befall. But underneath this protective chatter a profound change had taken place in the spirit and atmosphere. We had become allies and associates in a common cause—the cause of the Irish Treaty and of peace between two races and two islands. It was nearly three o'clock in the morning before we separated. But the agreement was signed by all. As the Irishmen rose to leave, the British Ministers upon a strong impulse walked round and for the first time shook hands. We shall see in later chapters how many toils and vexations lay in the path of the Irish Settlement, and how many disappointments and anxieties were in store for both sides. But this was the moment, not soon to be forgotten, when the waters were parted and the streams of destiny began to flow down new valleys towards new seas.

The event was fatal to the Prime Minister. Within a year he had been driven from power. Many other causes, some at least of which could have been avoided, contributed to his fall; but the Irish Treaty and its circumstances were unforgivable by the most tenacious elements in the Conservative Party. Even among those who steadfastly supported it there were many who said, 'It must needs be that offences come, but woe to that man by whom the offence cometh.' Yet in so far as Mr. Lloyd George can link his political misfortunes with this Irish story, he may be content. In falling through Irish difficulties he may fall with Essex and with Strafford, with Pitt and with Gladstone; and with a line of sovereigns and statesmen great or small spread across the English history books of 700 years. But Lloyd George falls with this weighty difference, that whereas all these others, however great their efforts and sacrifices, left behind them only a problem, he has achieved—must we not hope it?—a solution.

CHAPTER XV
THE IRISH SETTLEMENT

"Tout savoir, c'est tout comprendre."

De Valera's Repudiation—The Debate in the Dail—I become Responsible for carrying out the Treaty—The Main Objectives—The Defence of Ulster—Irish Leaders—A Preliminary Survey—Craig and Collins—The Irish Free State Bill—The Boundary Question—Passage of the Bill—Limerick and Tipperary—Letter to Mr. Collins—Rory O'Connor seizes the Four Courts—Further Letter to Mr. Collins—A Further Letter.

The relief of the public at the Irish Settlement was manifest. There was a general feeling of awaking from a nightmare. The whole Empire rejoiced, and foreign countries smiled approvingly, if sardonically. The King took the unusual and indeed unprecedented step of receiving the Ministers concerned at Buckingham Palace in the early morning and had a photograph taken with himself in their midst. No one was more delighted than the poor, ordinary people of Ireland who had been so mauled by both sides and who longed for peace and comfort. This, however, they were not to have for some time.

The Sinn Fein Delegates returned to Dublin immediately and presented the result of their labours to Mr. de Valera and the Dail. It would be easy to prove that in logic de Valera was committed by his previous declarations not indeed to the actual form of the agreement but to its scope and principle. Moreover, the Irish Delegates were plenipotentiaries and he was their chief. They had come as his representatives to London. He had been continually kept informed of the whole process of negotiation. They had gained in substance, if not in theory, all that they had striven for and far more than any other Irish leaders had ever demanded. It was therefore generally expected that he would stand by his colleagues, make allowances for their difficulties, and even if not satisfied on this or that theoretical point would throw in his lot with them. After all, Southern Ireland had acquired the whole constitutional position of a Dominion, that is to say, independence under the Crown plus all the good offices of Great Britain.

But we speedily learned that Mr. de Valera was still maundering about Poynings' Act, and that his view of Anglo-Irish relations and of the griefs of Ireland had not yet reached the sixteenth-century part of the story. He now made a passionate endeavour to reopen the conflict, and conceiving himself as head of the only government existing in Ireland, he repudiated the action of the Delegates, who were also his colleagues and had been his fellow-conspirators. These men, reproached as traitors to their cause and to the oaths of their secret societies, were however immediately found to be in possession, even in the ranks of the extremists, of a strong separate power. Two of the Irish signatories out of the five went over to de Valera, but Arthur Griffith, supported by Duggan, acted with energy and conviction, and Michael Collins, carrying with him the principal gunmen and the majority of the inmost circles of the Irish Republican Brotherhood, stood by his friend.

While their territory was still in the utmost confusion the Dail proceeded to debate the Treaty, for weeks at a time. They adjourned at length to celebrate the nativity of the Saviour, and when they resumed in January they were cleft in twain. On January 8 the vote was taken and the Treaty was carried by seven votes—64 against 57. De Valera resigned his Presidency and quitted the Chamber. All the Republicans having walked out, Mr. Arthur Griffith was elected President of the Dail, which then was immediately adjourned.

Shortly after the signing of the Treaty I became a principal in British-Irish affairs. In January, 1921, the Prime Minister had asked me to go from the War Office to the Colonial Office for the purpose of settling our affairs in Palestine and Mesopotamia. This work was now nearly done. The Arabs and Colonel Lawrence were appeased by the enthronement of King Feisal at Bagdad; the British Army in Mesopotamia, which had been costing thirty millions a year, had been brought home; and complete tranquillity was preserved by the Royal Air Force under the guidance of the thrifty Trenchard.[1] Apart from ordinary work I was therefore free. Southern Ireland as a Dominion fell constitutionally into the sphere of the Colonial Office. I took over the task from the Chief Secretary, Sir Hamar Greenwood. He had borne the brunt during the most terrible period, showing the utmost courage as a man, and never losing the hope of a statesmanlike solution. In my capacity as Secretary of State I became Chairman of the Cabinet Committee upon Irish affairs. My colleagues gave me generous aid when I required it and a wide freedom of action at other times. Thenceforward I conducted all the negotiations with the Irish leaders, both North and South, and dealt with all the Parliamentary situations in the House of Commons.

Two objectives stood clearly out from the general confusion and uncertainty. The first was to bring and nurse into being in the South a living and responsible organism of government. This could only be done by investing the Provisional Government which we were about to recognise with the authority of a popular election. From the moment of publication of the Treaty, the Irish people had by every means and method open to them loudly expressed their desire that good and peaceful relations should be established with the British people on the basis of that settlement. We therefore impressed upon the Provisional Government the importance and urgency of an election, which alone could give them the status of a national administration and enable them to govern with native authority. Griffith and Collins were fully persuaded of this; but the difficulties were enormous. Mr. de Valera, knowing himself to be in a minority, and, as it proved, in a small minority, set to work by every means in his power to obstruct, to delay, and if possible to prevent, such an election. For this purpose he had recourse to the Irish

---

[1]Marshal of the Air Force Sir Hugh Trenchard, Chief of the Air Staff. Those who wish for further information on this long and intricate piece of public business will find a memorandum in the Appendix.—W. S. C.

Republican Army. This so-called Army had hitherto existed for the object of organising attacks on the Crown forces ranging from individual murder to ambuscades. It had never been capable of fighting any serious action according to the rules of war. Nevertheless it contained a considerable number of men perfectly ready to suffer imprisonment and execution for what they considered to be their cause. The Irish Republican Army was divided in opinion in the same way and probably in the same proportions as the Dail. Yet it was the only organisation at the disposal of the Provisional Government for the maintenance of their authority. They were therefore forced into a series of weak and unsatisfactory compromises upon the control of the Republican Army and about the date and character of the elections.

They were soon led as a measure of accommodation with Mr. de Valera to postpone the election for three months, relying upon his promise that then the election should be free, that in the meanwhile the army should act unitedly under the orders of the Provisional Government, and that it should not interfere in the election or oppose by force any government returned at the election. But Mr. de Valera had no sooner made this promise to his fellow-countrymen than he proceeded to break it. Everything was done by him and by his friends to weaken and discredit the Provisional Government; to create disorder throughout the country, and to embroil Southern Ireland with Ulster. For this purpose the anti-Free State portion of the Republican Army was always available, and around them and behind them gathered those predatory and criminal elements which in a greater or less degree exist in every society and claim to lead in times of revolution. It was across these difficulties that the British and Irish signatories of the Treaty endeavoured to march to a free election and an Irish national mandate.

The second main objective, equally vital to us, was to sustain the Ulster Government in its indefeasible rights. Two so-called divisions of the Irish Republican Army were located in Ulster and were maintained in intense secret activity in spite of the truce, in spite of the Treaty, and in spite of the fact that the evacuation of the British Army from Southern Ireland was rapidly and steadily proceeding. The Ulster Government therefore found themselves at grips with a conspiracy in their midst the object of which was to make their task of maintaining a separate government impossible, while at the same time from over the border serious raids occurred and hostile forces gathered and threatened.

These menaces to Ulster both internal and from without were met in an equally combative and bellicose manner by the Protestant Orangemen of the North. Every outrage committed by the Irish Republican Army or by the Catholic element was repaid with bloody interest. Reprisals and counter-reprisals soon built up a ghastly score on both sides; the Catholics, being numerically the weaker, suffering during the summer about twice as many casualties as the Protestants. It was no doubt natural that the Sinn Fein extremists, having seen the success which attended their attack on British authority, should expect by a continuance of such methods to break down a much smaller and apparently much weaker organism of government in the North. Having, as they thought, humiliated and beaten the mighty British Empire and forced it to make an accommodation with them, they assumed it would be an easy matter to make the position of a separate Ulster Government impossible; and by shooting public men and burning public buildings to create a continuous terror, and so to weary and impoverish the Government and the citizens of the North that for the sake of a quiet life they would be willing to submit themselves to Sinn Fein rule.

'In the North,' as I said to the House of Commons at a later period, 'the large majority of the people are bitterly opposed to Sinn Fein. They ardently proclaim their loyalty and affection for this country, for its monarchy, for its constitution, and for its empire. Even if they were deserted by Britain they would fight desperately and rightly to preserve their freedom. But they will not be deserted by Britain; on the contrary, they will be aided and strengthened by money, arms, and men to any extent that may be necessary to help them to maintain their Parliamentary and political rights and to defend themselves.'

These were the two separate aims by which I was guided. They appealed very differently to English political Parties. All the strongest elements in the Conservative Party rallied to Ulster, and even while recognising and accepting the Treaty, recoiled with dislike and scorn from Sinn Fein Ireland. Liberals and Labour men on the other hand watched with tender solicitude the fortunes of the Irish Free State, and took little interest in the welfare of the Northern Government, except to denounce it for the reprisals with which the Orangemen repaid every Sinn Fein murder. But if success in undoubted measure attended our policy, it was due to the fact that we pursued both these separate, and in many respects antagonistic, objectives with equal earnestness. Either alone spelt ruin. Both simultaneously pursued led to safety and peace.

Of course the task of helping both sides in some directions, and of restraining both as far as possible in others, was delicate and liable to be misunderstood. It is easy to declare that the balance should be held even; but when people are actually murdering each other and being murdered, when terror stalks the land and anarchy rises about infant administrations; when you are in constant and intimate and honourable relations with the champions of both sides, when you know many of their secrets and when anything done for one excites the resentment or suspicion of the other, an impartial course is easier to prescribe than to steer. Fortunately for Ireland she did not in this time of tribulation lack chiefs of high and firm qualities. In Arthur Griffith and Michael Collins, and also in two new figures who now appeared, Richard Mulcahy and Kevin O'Higgins, were found realists of the first order; men who feared God, who loved their country, and who kept their word. In Ulster Sir James Craig stood solid as a rock. Imperturbable, sagacious, above hate or anger yet not without a lively sentiment; steady, true, and untiring, he brought his own people at length out from the midst of indescribable miseries and difficulties back to daylight and civilisation.

With this general survey of scene and actors, it will be better to tell the tale selectively by contemporary documents rather than by summarised narrative.

I started hopefully on my duties, and endeavoured to outline for the guidance of the Departments concerned the immediate practical steps.

December 21, 1921.

'The Prime Minister having asked me to preside over a Cabinet Committee for the purpose of arranging the details of setting up the Provisional Government in

Dublin should a favourable decision be taken by the Dail, I have put down a few draft headings for consideration.

Should the Dail ratify, the first step should be to get an Irish delegation, comprising Mr. Griffith and Mr. Collins, over here at the earliest moment. We should then tell them that we wish them to form a Provisional Government without delay. This Government should be immediately responsible for the whole internal peace and order of Southern Ireland and would take executive control of the country on the basis arranged. We do not wish to continue responsible one day longer than is absolutely necessary. In my view we should aim at New Year's Day for the definite assumption of power, provided they are willing. When the basis has been worked out, it will be for the Viceroy after consultation in Dublin with such leaders of parties and political personages as he thinks fit, to invite some gentleman to form a Government. Presumably he would invite Mr. Arthur Griffith, and we shall know by then whether this gentleman will accept the commission, and on what basis. Mr. Griffith would then form his Government, his Ministers would sign the declaration prescribed in the Treaty, and take up their duties without delay.

As a general principle we should not seek to alter the existing machinery more than is absolutely necessary, but should place it in the hands of the new Ministers as it now is. If statutory authority to give directions of any kind is required and such authority cannot yet be obtained, the British authority who now has the power to give such directions should be told to act upon instructions received without personal responsibility except for execution.

The following special points occur:—

(1) *The Police.* Every man in the R.I.C., whether English or Irish, should be given the option of resigning on disbandment-terms guaranteed by the Imperial Government. The allocation of expense as between Great Britain and the Irish Free State must be taken into consideration on the general financial settlement which will be made during the present year, so that it is only a question of accounting. All R.I.C. who do not exercise this option will be expected to carry on.

The Auxiliary Division will be disbanded at once at the cost of the Imperial Government, advantage being taken at the same time of the decision provisionally arrived at to raise a gendarmerie for Palestine.

(2) *The Army.* The principle we should proclaim is that the whole of our military forces in Southern Ireland should be withdrawn as quickly as convenient. The Provisional Government will be expected to take over the Guard of the Viceroy and of the seat of Government with uniformed troops of their own as the first step. The routine of salutes, Guards of Honour, etc., due to the King's representative must be arranged with the Sinn Fein leaders. The normal Irish garrisons outside Dublin would, I presume, remain until barrack accommodation can be found for them elsewhere and the Free State Government are prepared to dispense with them. But ostentatious preparations to quit should be begun everywhere. It is quite

possible that in two or three months very insistent demands will be made for some of them to stay permanently. This, I fear, we shall not be able to accede to except as a matter of convenience for the new Government and for a very limited period. All the additional troops in Ireland not accommodated in permanent peace-time barracks should quit at the very earliest moment. All troops remaining in Ireland should, from the date of assumption of office by the Provisional Government, be moved outside their cantonments and immediate stations only in accordance with arrangements agreed upon with the responsible Ministers. They should act in support of the civil power only on requisitions signed by the responsible Ministers. The Provisional Government should be legally authorised to raise forces as may be necessary in the transition period under the Territorial Forces Act. It is not presumed they will wish to raise their full quota until they are definitely established. It is, however, of high importance that there should be at the earliest moment an Irish force uniformed and disciplined and capable of supporting the civil power.

(3) *Justice.* The necessity for Sinn Fein Courts will presumably have disappeared, as all the Courts will become Free State Courts at the earliest moment. Meanwhile, however, it is presumed the existing Courts would function, the Viceroy being advised on the exercise of the prerogative by the Prime Minister or Home Secretary of the Irish Free State. The Attorney-General will, it is hoped, explain how the transition is to be effected in this sphere.

(4) *Finance.* No alteration whatever at present in the taxes, nor in the spending of money on the ordinary internal services of the country. The interceptions which have lately been in force should of course cease at once, the full sum for Irish internal administration being made available. . . .

Funds must also be provided for the raising of the Irish Free State forces for the maintenance of order.

(5) *Education, Agriculture, and internal administrative services generally.* Full responsibility for these should be placed on the shoulders of a Free State Minister at the earliest moment.

(6) *Measures relating to Indemnity and Amnesty.* [Must be prepared.]

The above notes are on the assumption that the Dail ratifies the Treaty. It is possible, however, that they may ratify, but by a majority insufficiently large to afford a lasting basis of settlement. In this case the new Government should still take office, and should themselves ask the Viceroy either for a dissolution or for a plebiscite. A dissolution is infinitely preferable, as it will give a more responsible Dail. The Viceroy would be guided by the advice received from the Ministers on this subject, and in the event of such advice being in favour of a plebiscite, the necessary machinery must be brought into being by the Irish Departments, funds being supplied on the authority of the Treasury in anticipation of Parliamentary sanction. Pending this appeal to the country, all troops and police would stand fast as at present, but otherwise the procedure would be as above, though in a modified form.

A third alternative is the rejection of the Treaty by the Dail. In this case it is presumed that the Parliament of Southern Ireland would be dissolved and a General Election for a new Dail held immediately. We should, however, before deciding get into touch with the leaders of the ratification party in the existing Dail and ascertain their wishes. It is presumed that the Treaty would be re-submitted to the new Dail as soon as it assembled.'

* * * * *

On January 11 I was surprised and glad to receive a letter from Sir James Craig, who had been for some time officially out of touch with His Majesty's Government. He offered to come to see me at any time when the interests of Ulster were affected. He added, 'I am quite ready to attend a conference between you and the delegates of Southern Ireland . . . in fact I would welcome an opportunity of meeting Mr. Griffith, or whoever may be charged with the administration of the Provisional Government, at an early date, so as to ascertain clearly whether the policy of Southern Ireland is to be one of peace or whether the present method of pressure on Northern Ireland is to be continued.'

I lost no time in bringing Craig and Michael Collins together. On January 21 they met in my room at the Colonial Office, which, despite its enormous size, seemed overcharged with electricity. They both glowered magnificently, but after a short, commonplace talk I slipped away upon some excuse and left them together. What these two Irishmen, separated by such gulfs of religion, sentiment, and conduct, said to each other I cannot tell. But it took a long time, and, as I did not wish to disturb them, mutton chops, etc., were tactfully introduced about one o'clock. At four o'clock the Private Secretary reported signs of movement on the All-Ireland front and I ventured to look in. They announced to me complete agreement reduced to writing. They were to help each other in every way; they were to settle outstanding points by personal discussion; they were to stand together within the limits agreed against all disturbers of the peace. We three then joined in the best of all pledges, to wit, 'To try to make things work.'

Alas, it was not to be so easy. When little more than a week had passed, Craig had to give reassurance to the Ulstermen, and Collins back in the Dublin atmosphere was making violent speeches about the Ulster boundary; and the southern boycott of Belfast, which had been 'lifted' on January 24, was soon resumed in full intensity. Early in February Sinn Fein raids took place on the Ulster border, and the simultaneous disturbances which broke out in Belfast left during a single night thirty dead and seventy injured in the streets.

It was therefore upon a considerable disappointment that I had to introduce the Irish Free State Bill implementing the Treaty on February 16. All the Ulster Members, with their strong influence throughout the Conservative Party, openly declared their opposition. Reading the debate again I see how carefully I had to walk. The general feeling was that the Treaty was necessary, but would it be observed? Had we been hoodwinked, or at the best, had we negotiated with men of straw? Had we not given all we had to give and received in return only a grimace? On the other hand, what else was there to do at the moment? I had to appeal to faith, hope and law.

'. . .If you want to see Ireland degenerate into a meaningless welter of lawless chaos and confusion, delay this Bill. If you wish to see increasingly serious bloodshed all along the borders of Ulster, delay this Bill. If you want this House to have on its hands, as it now has, the responsibility for peace and order in Southern Ireland, without the means of enforcing it, if you want to impose those same evil conditions upon the Irish Provisional Government, delay this Bill. If you want to enable dangerous and extreme men, working out schemes of hatred in subterranean secrecy, to undermine and overturn a Government which is faithfully doing its best to keep its word with us and enabling us to keep our word with it, delay this Bill. If you want to proclaim to all the world, week after week, that the British Empire can get on just as well without law as with it, then you will delay this Bill. But if you wish to give a fair chance to a policy to which Parliament has pledged itself, and to Irish Ministers towards whom you are bound in good faith so long as they act faithfully with you to give fair play and a fair chance, if you wish to see Ireland brought back from the confusion of tyranny to a reign of law, if you wish to give logical and coherent effect to the policy and experiment to which we are committed, you will not impede, even for a single unnecessary week, the passage of this Bill.'. . .

'Ought we to regret having made the settlement and signed the Treaty?'. . .

'Contrast the positions. It appears to me as if the tables were turned. Ireland, not Britain, is on her trial before the nations of the world. Six months ago it was we who had to justify ourselves against every form of attack. Now, it is the Irish people who, as they tell us, after 700 years of oppression, have at last an opportunity to show the kind of government that they can give to their country and the position which they can occupy among the nations of the world. An enormous improvement in the situation, as I see it, has been effected in the last six months. Take the position of Ulster. The position of Ulster is one of great and unshakeable strength, not only material strength, but moral strength. There was a time when, as is well known, I and others with whom I was then associated thought that Ulster was not securing her own position, but was barring the way to the rest of Ireland to obtain what they wanted. Those days are gone. Ulster, by a sacrifice and by an effort, has definitely stood out of the path of the rest of Ireland, and claims only those liberties and securities which are her own, and standing on her own rights, supported as she is and as she will be by the whole force and power, if necessary, of the British Empire, I am entitled to say is in a position of great moral and material strength at the present time.

'The position of the Imperial Government has also become greatly improved. It is very desirable that the great affairs of the British Empire should be increasingly detached from the terrible curse of this long internal Irish quarrel, and that the august Imperial authority should stand on a more impartial plane.'. . .

The gravamen of the Ulster complaint was the article of the Treaty which prescribed the future regulation of the boundary between North and South.

'Of course, all this trouble in regard to boundaries surrounds the boundaries of Fermanagh and Tyrone. I remember on the eve of the Great War we were gathered together at a Cabinet Meeting in Downing Street, and for a long time, an hour or an hour and a half, after the failure of the Buckingham Palace Conference, we discussed the boundaries of Fermanagh and Tyrone. Both of the great political parties were at each other's throats. The air was full of talk of civil war. Every effort was made to settle the matter and bring them together. The differences had been narrowed down, not merely to the counties of Fermanagh and Tyrone, but to parishes and groups inside the areas of Fermanagh and Tyrone, and yet, even when the differences had been so narrowed down, the problem appeared to be as insuperable as ever, and neither side would agree to reach any conclusion. Then came the Great War. . . . Every institution, almost, in the world was strained. Great Empires have been overturned. The whole map of Europe has been changed. The position of countries has been violently altered. The mode and thought of men, the whole outlook on affairs, the grouping of parties, all have encountered violent and tremendous changes in the deluge of the world, but as the deluge subsides and the waters fall we see the dreary steeples of Fermanagh and Tyrone emerging once again. The integrity of their quarrel is one of the few institutions that have been unaltered in the cataclysm which has swept the world. That says a lot for the persistency with which Irishmen on the one side or the other are able to pursue their controversies. It says a great deal for the power which Ireland has, both Nationalist and Orange, to lay her hands upon the vital strings of British life and politics and to hold, dominate and convulse, year after year, generation after generation, the politics of this powerful country. . . .'

I concluded after much argument:—

'Ulster must have British comfort and protection. Ireland must have her Treaty, her election, and her constitution. There will be other and better opportunities of dealing with the difficult boundary question. . . . For generations we have been floundering in the Irish bog, but at last we think that in this Treaty we have set our feet upon a pathway, which has already become a causeway—rather narrow, but firm and far-reaching. Let us march along this causeway with determination and circumspection, without losing heart and without losing faith. If Britain continues to march forward along that path, the day may come—it may be distant, but it may not be as distant as we expect—when, turning round, Britain will find at her side Ireland united, a nation and a friend.'

The debate following was worthy of the issue. The general opinion was well expressed by Mr. Neville Chamberlain:—

'I, for one, am not going to be exasperated by outrages into changing my opinion as to the proper course to pursue. I consider in these difficult times that our business is to keep our heads, not to allow ourselves to be flustered into courses we may regret hereafter, but to give all the powers that are necessary to enable the Provisional Government to establish itself securely and to carry out its proper obligations; and that in that way we may at any rate save for ourselves the only hope there is of escaping civil war.'

The majority was overwhelming—302 to 60. But most of the majority were miserable and all the minority were furious.

It took more than a month to pass the Bill. During this time the dissatisfaction and anxieties of Parliament and the public were continually fanned by cruel and treacherous crimes and by the obvious impotence of the only possible Irish Government.

More serious disturbances had occurred early in February. Raids across the Ulster border resulted in the kidnapping of Northerners. A reinforcement of Northern constabulary, despatched from Belfast to Enniskillen, were by an unlucky forgetfulness of the new frontier sent via Clones in the Free State, instead of by the longer, safer route through the Northern territory. On the arrival of the train at Clones these nineteen men, treated as invaders, were ambuscaded. Without warning or challenge four were killed, eight wounded, and seven captured.

At the same time Mr. Collins flooded me with protests about the vendettas and counter-vendettas proceeding nightly in Belfast.

This merciless episode reduced the border to barbaric conditions. Many other outrages occurred throughout Ireland; there would have been more, had it not been that throughout Southern Ireland not only the loyalists but the mass of the population subsided abjectly under the terror. In Belfast a foul kind of warfare was maintained fiercely by the dregs of both religions.

It was a long way to Tipperary, but at last apparently we arrived there.

Mr. Churchill to Mr. Cope.[2]

March 7, 1922.

Personal and Secret.

Many questions are asked me about Limerick and Tipperary. You must let me know what the Provisional Government are really doing, telling me whether the information must be kept secret or not. Do they intend to put down the Limerick revolt, or are they just going to parley and continue to be set at defiance? There

---

[2]Now Sir Alfred Cope, K.C.B. A daring and trustworthy agent of the British Government who was closely involved in all the Treaty negotiations and ardent throughout for settlement.

are reports in the papers that Irish troops have been despatched from Dublin to an unknown destination. Is this true? How many? Are they to be trusted? The position in Cork seems as bad as ever, and it is reported that a notorious man who had been captured has now escaped. Do you think there is any fighting quality in the Free State Government? Will anybody die for it or kill for it? Let me know your view, not your wish.

Mr. Churchill to Mr. Collins.

March 14, 1922.

Private and Personal.

I have read with attention your letter about the Belfast outrages in 1920–21. I note that you are going to send me a statement about more recent events in Belfast. I send you herewith a report from Sir James Craig with which he has furnished me in response to your previous communication of complaints. The state of affairs in Belfast is lamentable. There is an underworld there with deadly feuds of its own, and only the sternest and strictest efforts by leading men on both sides, coupled with ample military and police forces, will produce that tranquillity which is demanded by the interests of Ireland as a whole.

(2) I had long conversations with Sir James Craig before he returned to Ulster, and I am sure that he will do his very utmost to maintain order impartially. He has so far steadily declined to entertain the idea of a further conference with your Government, on the ground that while you are illegally holding the Clones men as hostages he cannot meet you. So here we are at a deadlock for the moment. I am bound to say that Sir James Craig left me with the impression that he would be glad to see the obstacles removed and to have a further parley. I quite see your difficulties, but I have no doubt whatever that, in spite of them, you ought to put yourself in the right by either effecting the release of these men or bringing them to trial in the regular way on a definite charge before lawfully constituted tribunals. Sir James Craig would be quite satisfied if they have a fair trial and are dealt with according to law. This is surely the only line for Heads of Governments to take. It may be that you do not feel able to do this till the Bill is through and you are formally equipped with lawful powers. If so, there is nothing for it but to wait and keep things as calm and as cool as possible in the interval. This hostage business is more suited to the Balkans than to Ireland, and the sooner we get on to a normal footing, the better.

(3) I am very much obliged to you for having speeded up the transfer of the necessary staff to the North of Ireland; and I hear from Sir John Anderson[3] that

---

[3] A Civil Servant of the highest rank; sent to Dublin in 1920 as Under-Secretary to the Lord Lieutenant and Secretary to the Treasury for Ireland; a man of singular capacity and firmness of character, sagacious and imperturbable amid gathering peril and confusion.

the administrative efficiency of your Government is increasing every week, that the Provisional Ministers are getting a good grip, and are appointing good men as their agents, and that in finance particularly systems, the soundness of which has been proved by experience, are being adopted.

(4) I am very glad you are seeing Lord Midleton, representing the Southern Unionists, to-day; and I hope you will be able to reassure him about land purchase. We are pledged to the hilt to do our part in this matter if the Free State call upon us to do so, and the advantage accrues entirely to Ireland as against the larger and more unlucky island.

(5) I hear from quite an independent source that the Provisional Government is gaining ground all over the country, and that one of the principal supporters of De Valera has expressed the opinion that they will do well if they get 40 seats in the new Parliament. I hope this is so.

(6) You seem to have liquidated the Limerick situation in one way or another. No doubt you know your own business best, and thank God *you* have got to manage it and not we. An adverse decision by the convention of the Irish Republican Army (so called) would, however, be a very grave event at the present juncture. I presume you are quite sure there is no danger of this.

(7) I read with great interest the full report of the speech delivered by you in Dublin which Lady Lavery sent me. I wish it had been reported more fully in the English papers. I showed it to the Lord Chancellor, who praised its tone and diction and will possibly quote some passages from it in his defence of the Free State Bill this week.

(8) I am much interested in your visit to Cork, and especially in the fact that you appear to have been welcomed by the Irish ex-Service men, with whom I sympathise so much. I shall do my best to get a further extension in regard to Haulbowline [Dockyard] as I am most anxious that the Cork situation shall adjust itself satisfactorily.

Mr. Churchill to Mr. Collins and Mr. Griffith.

March 21, 1922.

The whole position on the border is undoubtedly becoming more dangerous. An explosion would be disastrous, and even a continuance of the present tension tends to stereotype the border line and make it into a fortified military frontier, which is the last thing in the world you want. I cannot think there is the slightest danger of a raid from the North into the South. If such a raid took place those making it would put themselves in the wrong, and the British Government would take every measure in its power. I am certain that you do not need to be alarmed on this score. Even if it happened it would only do harm to those responsible, just in the same way as the kidnapping raids from Monaghan have done harm to

Southern Irish interests. I am told that I.R.A. (so called) are collecting along the border in increasing numbers. Surely this is not necessary. Statements also appear in the papers that Free State troops are stationed at various points. Pray let me know exactly what is happening.

You must understand that I am at the same time making the strongest representations to Sir James Craig to prevent provocative action on the part of his people.

On April 13 a high-souled fanatic, Rory O'Connor, with a band of adherents and many sympathisers seized the Law Courts in Dublin. In this venerable and massive building he and his friends proclaimed themselves the Republican Government of all Ireland. Three days later Michael Collins was murderously attacked in Dublin. He escaped, but during the rest of the month the murder of Free State troops and police continued, diversified by a general railway strike.

In these pressures a tormented government and its servants rallied somewhat; their troops began to fire back, and even this slight resistance startled their enemies.

Mr. Churchill to Mr. Collins.

April 12, 1922.

On the whole my impression is that public opinion is increasingly mobilising and asserting itself in Ireland, and that you will get very strong national support in defending your just and lawful position. I have been speaking in this sense in the House of Commons. I hope that Easter will not belie these anticipations.

The Cabinet instructed me to send you a formal communication expressing their growing anxiety at the spread of disorder in the 26 Counties. Instead of this, however, I write to you as man to man. Many residents are writing to this country tales of intimidation, disorder, theft and pillage. There is no doubt that capital is taking flight. Credits are shutting up, railways are slowing down, business and enterprise are baffled. The wealth of Ireland is undergoing a woeful shrinkage. Up to a certain point no doubt these facts may have the beneficial effect of rousing all classes to defend their own material interests, and Mr. De Valera may gradually come to personify not a cause but a catastrophe. It is difficult for us over here to measure truly, but it is obvious that in the long run the Government, however patient, must assert itself or perish and be replaced by some other form of control. Surely the moment will come when you can broadly and boldly appeal not to any clique, sect or faction, but to the Irish nation as a whole. They surely have a right to expect you to lead them out of the dark places, and the opportunity is one [the loss of] which history will never forgive. Ought you not to rally round the infant Free State all the elements in Ireland which will whole-heartedly adhere to the Treaty and sign a declaration attaching them to it irrespective of what their former attitudes have been? Would you not find reserves on this basis infinitely more powerful than any you have obtained at the present time? Ought you not to summon your 'far flung people'[4] to your aid? In America, Australia, Canada, New Zealand, there must be hundreds of Irishmen intensely devoted to the welfare and freedom of their native land who would come to see fair play over the Elections and make sure that the people had a free vote.

I am greatly impressed by the courage with which such large numbers of Irishmen have attended public meetings to testify to their opinions in spite of so many deterrents, and I feel at the tips of my fingers the growing national strength that is behind you, ready for use when the moment comes for no cause but your own.

I am going into the question of your claim for an Inquiry into some post-agreement outrages in Belfast. I will have a talk with Sir James Craig and let you know the result. Things are settling down to some extent, both in Belfast and on the frontier, and there is no doubt that the Ulster Government is making a tremendous effort towards appeasement. They will be greatly helped by the release of the Clones Specials, which I am very glad to see you have achieved.

I am glad to see you have arranged a meeting with De Valera; but I hope you will understand that we cannot go any further in any respect. We have run every risk and made every effort and fulfilled every stipulation according to the agreement we signed with you. But that is the end absolutely so far as we are concerned, and every one of us will swing round with every scrap of influence we can command against a Republic or any inroad upon the Treaty structure.

It would seem to me also extremely dangerous to allow any further delay in the Elections to be extorted from you. Every day that the uncertainty continues must be attended by the progressive impoverishment of Ireland. Nobody can invest or make plans for production while the threat of civil war, or of a Republic followed by a state of war with the British Empire, hangs over the country. I trust the end of May or at the very latest the first week in June will see the issue submitted to the Irish people. We really have a moral right to ask that the uncertainty as to whether our offer is accepted or rejected should not be indefinitely prolonged....

Mr. Churchill to Mr. Collins.

April 29, 1922.

It is now three weeks since I wrote to you last, and it may be well to review a little what has passed in the interval. First, let me congratulate you and Mr. Griffith on the spirit and personal courage which you have consistently shown in confronting the enemies of free speech and fair play. I have no doubt that the development of strong, bold, romantic personalities at the head of the Irish Provisional Government and among the leaders of the Treaty party will be of real value in the general situation. I also sustain the impression that the great swing of Irish opinion

---

[4]Mr. Collins had used this phrase about the Irish race in conversation a few weeks earlier. 'We too are a far-flung people.'

is increasingly towards the Free State and the Treaty and those who stand for them; and that for every manly reason large numbers of persons will endeavour to assert their political rights at the poll. From this point of view the delay has not turned out nearly so badly as we in this country feared. You have not lost your hold on public opinion; you have indeed strengthened it. The excesses of the De Valera faction and the consequent inconvenience and impoverishment of Ireland have to a large extent concentrated the discontent, not upon the Government, but upon its opponents.

I read with very great interest in the Irish papers the excellent speeches which are made and the courageous and energetic manner in which the Irish Press defends the essentials of social freedom.

Easter is passed without disaster. Your troops are increasing in numbers and appear to stand to their engagements and obey their officers. . . .

Altogether I see many sober reasons for hope. This makes me wonder all the more why you adopt such a very harsh tone in dealing with Sir James Craig. I am sure he has made a very great effort to fulfil the agreement in the letter and in the spirit, and that he is continuously and will continue striving in that direction. Of course, no one expected that everything could be made right immediately or that the terrible passions which are loose in Ireland would not continue to produce their crop of outrages dishonouring to the island and its people, and naturally you have many grounds of complaint against him. He, too, has furnished me with a long set of counter-complaints, and the Protestants also have suffered heavily in the recent disturbances. Belfast goods of very great value, running into millions, have been destroyed, debts owing to Belfast have been collected illegally and intercepted, and the boycott I am assured is more injurious in fact than ever before. Instead of these rough communications, I should have thought that the Irish leaders, North and South, would have found it much better to meet together, to take stock of the position, to record what has been achieved, to mark what has fallen short in the working of the late agreement, and to decide on new steps to complete its execution.

As I have frequently pointed out, the interest of your opponents, North and South, Orange or Green . . . is to provoke the worst state of feeling between the two parts of Ireland; and they would cheerfully welcome every step and every event which led up to a definite civil war between the two Governments. Your opponents in the North hope to see a Republic in the South because it will bring about *inter alia* such a civil war, in which they know they will have the whole force of the British Empire behind them. Your opponents in the South hope to use antagonism against Ulster as a means of enabling them to snatch the power from the hands of the Provisional Government or else involve them in a series of events so tragical that they will break up under the strain. And on both sides the wreckers dread any approach to the idea of a united Ireland as the one fatal, final blow at their destructive schemes. All this seems perfectly simple to me, and I think these people judge rightly according to their own tactical view. What I do not understand is why you should let yourself be drawn into the quarrel. I know Craig means to play fair and straight with you, and I do not think you will find such another man in the whole of the North; and it perplexes and baffles me when I see you taking up such a very strong, and even aggressive, attitude against him in your public utterances. Although perhaps you get some political advantage for the moment by standing up stiffly against the North, yet every farthing of that advantage is drawn and squandered from the treasure chest of Irish unity. However provoking it may be, I am certain that your interest and that of the cause you serve demands patience and suavity in all that concerns relations with the North. They are your countrymen and require from you at least as careful and diplomatic handling as you bestow on the extremists who defy you in the South. Moreover, they are in a very strong, and in fact inexpugnable, position; and they hold in their hands the key to Irish unity.

When you feel moved to anger by some horrible thing that has happened in Belfast, it may perhaps give you some idea of our feelings in Great Britain when we read of the murder of the helpless, disarmed Royal Irish Constabulary and now, this morning, of what is little less than a massacre of Protestants in and near Cork. Twenty Constabulary men have been shot dead and forty wounded, together with six or seven soldiers, and now these eight Protestant civilians, within the jurisdiction of your Government since the Treaty was signed. All these men were under the safeguard of the Irish nation and were absolutely protected in honour by the Treaty. Their blood calls aloud for justice and will continue to call as the years pass by until some satisfaction is accorded. As far as I know, not a single person has been apprehended, much less punished, for any of these cruel deeds. Yet we on our side have faithfully proceeded step by step to carry out the Treaty, have loyally done our utmost to help your Government in every way, and have not lost confidence in the good faith and goodwill of those with whom we signed the Treaty. But do not suppose that deep feelings do not stir on both sides of the Channel. We, too, are a people not altogether to be treated as negligible in the world. No one can read the history of England without perceiving how very serious some of these matters may easily become. It is the business of statesmen not to let themselves be moved unduly by these feelings, however deep and natural, but to try as far as possible to steer away from these dangerous currents and persevere steadily towards the harbour which they have set out to gain.

At any time when you think it useful to have a further meeting with Sir James Craig, I will endeavour to bring it about. I found him reluctant when I addressed him on the subject this last week, but I know that he sincerely desires a peaceful, decent and Christian solution.

CHAPTER XVI
THE RISE OF THE IRISH FREE STATE

"Tout comprendre, c'est tout pardonner."

The Election Compact—Crumbling Foundations—Reactions in the North—Letter to Sir James Craig—The Whitsuntide Debate—Patience or Credulity? Michael Collins—Pettigo and Belleek—The Irish Constitution: The Election—Murder of Sir Henry Wilson—Critical Parliamentary Situation—Intervention of Mr. Bonar Law—Resolve of the Government—Attack on the Four Courts—A Decisive Effort—Letter to Mr. Collins—Letter to Sir James Craig—Deaths of Griffith and Collins—Cosgrave and O'Higgins—The Corner Turned—The Future.

Up till the end of April we seemed to be ploughing our way heavily but surely through all our difficulties. The Free State Government seemed to be functioning fitfully but increasingly, and the Party and Parliamentary situations in England held. All our hopes and aims were directed towards the free election by the Irish people of a representative assembly. There was no doubt whatever that by an overwhelming majority they were for both the Treaty and for the Free State Government.

Towards the end of May a new, and to me a most disconcerting, development took place. On May 19 Mr. Griffith had told the Republicans in the Dail that in their violent courses they did not represent 2 per cent of the people of Ireland, and that 'the course that they were pursuing placed them on the level of the worst traitors in Ireland, namely, those who by their actions were rendering the return of the English troops inevitable.' The very next day, to the astonishment of all, to the dismay of their friends, and to the joy of every enemy, a compact was signed between De Valera and Michael Collins. The compact dealt with the approaching election. It comprised an agreement that the Republican anti-Treaty men (who Mr. Griffith had declared the day before did not represent 2 per cent of the Irish people) were to have 57 seats in the new Parliament as against 64 for the supporters of the Treaty. They were not to be opposed by the Provisional Government to the extent of 57 seats. In other words, the existing balance on the question of accepting or rejecting the Treaty was to be preserved in the new Parliament and was not to be disturbed by any contest between members of the Sinn Fein Party. Secondly, this compact prescribed that after this so-called election a Coalition Government should be formed consisting of five pro-Treaty Ministers and four anti-Treaty Ministers, with the President of the Assembly and the Minister at the head of the Army additional. On this basis, the two Sinn Fein parties, pro-and anti-Treaty, were to divide the representation and challenge the candidates of every other opinion.

I had received news a few days before of what was in the wind and I wrote immediately to Michael Collins.

Mr. Churchill to Mr. Collins.

May 15, 1922.

I have received information which leads me to believe that among the subjects being discussed between you and the Irregular or Republican party is the proposal that there should be 'an agreed election,' that is to say an election at which there would be no contests but at which Mr. De Valera would be accorded 40 seats and the Provisional Government 80. I think I had better let you know at once that any such arrangement would be received with world-wide ridicule and reprobation. It would not be an election in any sense of the word, but simply a farce, were a handful of men who possess lethal weapons deliberately to dispose of the political rights of the electors by a deal across the table. Such an arrangement would not strengthen your own position in the slightest degree. It would not invest the Provisional Government with any title to sit in the name of the Irish nation. It would be an outrage upon democratic principles and would be universally so denounced. Your Government would soon find itself regarded as a tyrannical junta which having got into office by violence was seeking to maintain itself by a denial of constitutional rights. The enemies of Ireland have been accustomed to say that the Irish people did not care about representative Government, that it was alien to their instincts, and that if they had an opportunity they would return to a despotism or oligarchy in one form or another. If you were to allow yourself to be misled into such an arrangement as is indicated, such action would be immediately proclaimed as justifying to the full this sinister prediction. As far as we are concerned in this country, we should certainly not be able to regard any such arrangement as a basis on which we could build.

I do earnestly hope that you will put me in a position to deny these most injurious reports. At any moment questions may be asked in Parliament on the subject. I see already that the *Daily Chronicle* has referred to it in a leading article.

I beg you will show this letter to Mr. Griffith and to Mr. Duggan, to whom as co-signatories of the Treaty I am bound also to address myself.

So we were not, it seemed, to get any foundation after all. It was common ground between Republicans and Free-Staters, regulars and irregulars in the I.R.A., Catholics and Protestants, landlords and tenants, Unionists and Nationalists, from one end of Ireland to the other, that the dominant wish of the Irish people was to take the Treaty, to work it honourably, and to restore under its ægis the dignity and prosperity of Irish life. But they were not to be allowed to express their opinion. The Irish masses, just like the Russian two or three years before, were not to be allowed a voice in their fate. They were to be led by the nose, by a tiny minority making an immoral deal among themselves and parcelling out the nation as if they were cattle. This was more baffling than any of the raids and outrages. It threatened to reduce the whole situation to a meaningless slush.

We were however on this issue in possession of the ensigns of Democracy. Until you get a certain distance down the slope these count for much. We invited the Free State leaders over to London. They came immediately; Griffith plainly in resolute dissent from what had been done; Collins half defiant, half obviously embarrassed. It was all right, he said; we did not know their difficulties. These were hideous and indescribable. Nothing was stable under their feet. A contested election was physically impossible. It would mean widespread civil war; no one would dare to vote; they had not the strength to keep even the semblance of order. Nevertheless Collins declared himself unchanged in general intention to stand by the Treaty. It looked as if the wounds of Ireland would not react to any treatment known to science, but would just slough away into mortification.

These events produced their immediate reaction in the north. Protestant Ulster was convinced that Southern Ireland would now sink into chaos, and to wall themselves off from this infection was the only thought. Incessant demands were made for troops and arms. Sir James Craig made an uncompromising statement about the boundary.

Mr. Churchill to Sir James Craig.

May 24, 1922.

Londonderry will tell you the results of his discussions with the War Office and the arrangements which we have made for the supply of this great mass of material to you. I must say at once, however, that I do not consider your declaration made without any reference to the Government that in no circumstances would you accept any rectification of the frontier or any Boundary Commission as provided for in the Treaty is compatible with requests for enormous financial aid and heavy issues of arms. While I was actually engaged in procuring the assent of my colleagues to your requests, you were making a declaration which was in effect in one passage little short of a defiance of the Imperial Government whose aid you seek. Several of my colleagues have communicated with me this morning in strong protest against a statement of this kind being made by you when you are asking for and receiving our assistance and especially at so critical a moment in Irish affairs. All I was able to reply was that De Valera and Collins had made statements in the Dail yesterday of an equally unsatisfactory character. The effect of such a statement on your part is to make it far more difficult for the Imperial Government to give you the assistance you need, and also it robs the Ministers who will meet the Provisional Government representatives of any effective reproach against Mr. Collins for the contemptuous manner in which he has spoken of the Treaty. It has enabled many newspapers in England, on whose support we should have to rely if the worst comes to the worst, to treat the whole Irish situation on the basis of six of one and half a dozen of the other. A very strong effort will undoubtedly be made in favour of a policy of Britain disinteresting herself entirely in Irish affairs, leaving them 'to stew in their own juice and fight it out among themselves.' Such a disastrous conclusion is rendered more difficult to combat by a statement of the kind you have made.

I know you will not mind my speaking quite plainly, because I am doing my best to support you in all that is legitimate and legal. We could not have complained, for instance, if you had said that the Collins-De Valera agreement rendered all co-operation between you and the South impossible. I should have regretted such a statement, but it was entirely one within your rights to make. But it is not within your rights to state that you will not submit to the Treaty which the British Government has signed in any circumstances, and at the same time to ask the British Government to bear the overwhelming burden of the whole of your defensive expenses. I cannot understand why it was not possible to communicate with me before making a declaration in this sense. I should have thought it would have been quite possible for you to have made a thoroughly satisfactory declaration to your own people in these critical times without taking ground which seems to show you just as ready as Collins or De Valera to defy the Imperial Government if they take a course you do not like. You ought not to send us a telegram begging for help on the largest possible scale and announce an intention to defy the Imperial Parliament on the same day.

P.S.—I have just received your telegram and am very glad to know that you are relieved by the decisions which I have been able to procure on your behalf.

While not by any means giving up hope, I thought it right to prepare Parliament for a slattern development, and on the motion for the Whitsuntide adjournment I laid the whole story before the House of Commons, repeating the most valid of the explanations which Mr. Collins had offered.

'The Provisional Government could not possibly guarantee the ordinary security of life and property if these securities were challenged by an active, ardent, violent, Republican minority. This Republican minority, it is explained, consists mainly of a comparatively small number of armed men, violent in method, fanatical in temper, but in many cases disinterested or impersonal in motive. But behind these, strengthening these, multiplying these, disgracing these, are a larger number of common, sordid ruffians and brigands, robbing, murdering, pillaging, for their personal gain or for private revenge, or creating disorder and confusion out of pure love for disorder and confusion. These bandits—for they are nothing else— pursue their devastating course under the so-called glamour of the Republic and are inextricably intermingled with bona-fide Republican visionaries.

'The Provisional Government declared that they found themselves unable to deal with these bandits, while at the same time they were engaged in armed struggles with bona-fide Republicans. They declared that the Agreement into which they have entered with the Republicans would isolate the brigands and would enable these brigands to be struck at and suppressed, that a greater measure of liberty and security would immediately be restored, and that such conditions are an indispensable preliminary to any free expression of the political will of the Irish people, to which they look forward at an early date. They say, further, that it is in the power of the extreme minority in Ireland, by murdering British soldiers, or ex-soldiers, or Royal Irish Constabulary men who have retired from the Constabulary, or Protestants in the South, or by disturbing Ulster, to produce a series of episodes which, if prolonged and multiplied would in fact destroy the relationship between Great Britain and Ireland and render the carrying through of the Treaty impossible on both sides.'

I urged the House not to underrate this argument. I added this warning.

'Irish Prosperity has been seriously affected. Banking and business are curtailed; industry and agriculture are languishing; revenue is only coming in with increasingly laggard steps; . . . stagnation and impoverishment are over-taking the productive life of Ireland; the inexorable shadow of famine is already cast on some of its poorer districts. Will the lesson be learned in time, and will the remedies be applied before it is too late? Or will Ireland, amid the stony indifference of the world—for that is what it would be—have to wander down those chasms which have already engulfed the great Russian people? This is the question which the next few months will answer.'

I strove against a silent tide of scepticism.

'I do not believe that the members of the Provisional Government are acting in bad faith. I do not believe, as has been repeatedly suggested, that they are working hand in glove with their Republican opponents with the intent by an act of treachery to betray British confidence and Ireland's good name. I am sure they are not doing that. They may not have taken the wisest course, or the strongest course, or the shortest course, but they, and a majority of Dail Eireann who steadfastly support them and support the Treaty are, I sincerely believe, animated by an earnest desire and resolve to carry out the Treaty. Not only Mr. Griffith and Mr. Collins, the two leading men on whose good faith we took this memorable departure, but the other Ministers who are in this country, Mr. Cosgrave, Mr. Kevin O'Higgins and others have repeatedly declared their adherence to the Treaty and have renewed their personal assurances while they have been here with us in the strongest manner. They have argued vehemently that the course they are taking—questionable and doubtful as it appears to British eyes; as it must necessarily appear to almost any eyes—is the surest way, and indeed the only way open to them of bringing the Treaty into permanent effect. Whether their policy and methods are right may be questioned. Whether they will succeed or not is open to doubt. But that they are still trying to do their best to march forward on that path which alone can save Ireland from hideous disaster we firmly believe. Some here may think us wrong. Some here may think we are being deceived and hoodwinked, and by being deceived ourselves are deceiving others.

'If we are wrong, if we are deceived, the essential strength of the Imperial position will be in no wise diminished, while the honour and reputation of Ireland will be fatally aspersed. Whether you trust or whether you mistrust at this moment, equally you can afford to wait. We have done our part, we are doing our part with the utmost loyalty before all the world. We have disbanded our police. We have withdrawn our armies. We have liberated our prisoners.' (Here there were scornful interruptions.) 'Yes, I say it and I boast it! We have transferred the powers of government and the whole of the revenues of Ireland to the Irish Ministry responsible to the Irish Parliament. We have done this on the faith of the Treaty, solemnly signed by duly accredited plenipotentiaries—for such they were—of the Irish nation, and subsequently endorsed by a majority of the Irish Parliament. This great act of faith on behalf of the stronger power will not, I believe, be brought to mockery by the Irish people. If it were, the strength of the Empire will survive the disappointment, but the Irish name will not soon recover from the disgrace.'

Mr. Asquith, my old Chief, rising equally above Party and above passion, threw the whole weight of his authority upon the side of the Government. Then the House separated in sombre mood.

On that very day, however, a new incident which I duly reported to the House had occurred. The townships of Pettigo and Belleek had been seized and occupied by Irish Republican forces. Pettigo lay astride the border and Belleek was wholly in Northern territory. This military affront brought into play the other side of the dual policy I was endeavouring to apply. It gave me the opportunity of reassuring Ulster that we were not merely sliding with apologies down the slope, but that whatever else went to wreck, the integrity of their territory would be protected. The Secretary of State for War and my other colleagues on the Cabinet Committee were in full agreement.

Immediately after the debate, Michael Collins, who had listened to it, came to my room. I mentioned to him amicably that if any part of the Irish Republican Army, either pro-Treaty or anti-Treaty, invaded Northern soil, we would throw them out. He took it quite coolly, and seemed much more interested in the debate. 'I am glad to have seen it,' he said, 'and how it is all done over here. I do not quarrel with your speech; we have got to make good or go under.' We argued a little about Pettigo and Belleek and about Belfast atrocities. Before he left he said, 'I shall not last long; my life is forfeit, but I shall do my best. After I am gone it will be easier for others. You will find they will be able to do more than I can do.' I repeated the phrase of President Brand which I had learned in the days of the Transvaal Constitutional Bill, 'Alles zal regt kom' (All will come right). I never saw him again.

Here I will record a few thoughts about this man, Michael Collins. He was an Irish patriot, true and fearless. His narrow upbringing and his whole early life had filled him with hatred of England. His hands had touched directly the springs of terrible deeds. We had hunted him for his life, and he had slipped half a dozen times through steel claws. But now he had no hatred of England. Love of Ireland still possessed his soul, but to it was added a wider comprehension. He had come in contact during the Treaty negotiations with men he liked; with men who played the game according to the agreed rules; he had plighted a new faith to act fairly by them. As Griffith seemed to rely especially upon Mr. Austen Chamberlain, so Michael Collins was deeply impressed by the personality of Lord Birkenhead. The transition of his sympathies can be followed in gradations through his speeches by anyone who cares to study them. Whereas he had had only one loyalty, he now had two. He was faithful to both; he died for both. When in future times the Irish Free State is not only the home of culture and of virtue, not only prosperous and happy, but an active, powerful, and annealing force in the British Commonwealth of Nations, regard will be paid by widening circles to his life and to his death.

Large bodies of troops, equipped with all the appliances of war, were now set in motion on the Ulster border. About 7,000 men with cannon and armed launches advanced upon the villages of Pettigo and Belleek. A demonstration was made of overwhelming force in support of indefeasible rights. For more than ten days a British village having every right to claim protection from the Crown had been continually in lawless occupation of Irish Republican forces. After all, there are occasions when one hundred aggrieved, armed men are entitled to expel one wrongdoer in his shirt.

The Prime Minister was disquieted by this development. He feared that we were being manœuvred by the extremists of both sides into giving battle on the very worst ground. 'If the Free Staters insist upon a constitution which repudiated Crown and Empire and practically set up a Republic, we should carry the whole world with us in any action we took; but an issue fought on Ulster would not command united British opinion, still less world-wide support. I understand,' he wrote, 'we are marching against a rotten barracks at Belleek garrisoned by a friendly blacksmith and a handful of his associates . . . but MacKeown [the blacksmith] is a strong Treaty man and has publicly denounced De Valera and the Pact. If he should be killed at Belleek it would be a disaster to the cause of reconciliation with the Irish race. . . .

'Quite frankly, if we force an issue with these facts we shall be hopelessly beaten. There will be a great Die-Hard shout which will last for a very short time, but we shall have no opinion behind us that will enable us to carry through a costly strangling campaign. Let us keep on the high ground of the Treaty, the Crown, the Empire. There we are unassailable. But if you come down from those heights and fight in the swamps of Lough Erne you will be overwhelmed. You have conducted these negotiations with such skill and patience that I beg you not to be tempted into squandering what you have already gained by a precipitate action, however alluring the prospects may be.'

Mr. Churchill to the Prime Minister.

I was in train of answering your letter when it was superseded by events. Belleek village and fort were occupied to-day by strong forces. Pursuant to our orders the village was reconnoitred first by an armoured car, and not until this reconnaissance had been fired upon while in Ulster territory and from points in Ulster territory did the troops advance. About 20 shell and 400 rounds were fired. On one shell bursting near the fort its garrison of 40 fled without loss of any kind. The blacksmith to whom you refer had not left Dublin according to Mr. Griffith. As far as we know the 'battle' has been almost bloodless. One soldier has been slightly wounded and no enemy casualties have been found or prisoners taken. I am issuing a communiqué explaining that the operations are at an end, that our troops will advance no further, that no further fighting will take place unless they are attacked, that communications are being made to the Provisional Government with a view to establishing peaceful conditions on this part of the border, and that as soon as we are assured there will be no further incursions, the British forces will be withdrawn wholly within the Ulster border-line.

It is always difficult to deal with a small urgent local situation without compromising grave general issues, but I do not think the action taken will have evil results. I hope, indeed, it may have had good results and I am quite sure that we could not have met the House of Commons on Monday with the admission that we did not know what was going on in a British village and did not dare go there to find out.

The results of this operation which threaded its way so narrowly between tragedy and ridicule were salutary. Ulster felt that if it came to actual invasion they would certainly be defended. The Irish Republican Army realised that we should not hesitate to levy open war, and the Free State Government knew that at any rate one line was drawn which could not be transgressed. Not the slightest ill will was manifested by those Free State leaders with whom we were in relation. On the contrary, they seemed fortified in spirit for the very serious crisis which was soon to supervene.

Meanwhile the terms of the Irish Constitution were being worked out in detail by the Provisional Government in Dublin. There had been many suggestions, open and covert, that the Constitution would not be within the four walls of the Treaty. Extremists in Ireland looked forward to it as likely to provide the occasion for a breach. In England everyone was at his limit and the fires of wrath were double-banked. Fortunately, though not without hard words and much argument, an instrument which both parties were able to accept was produced and the apostles of violence were once more disappointed. The text of the Irish Free State Constitution was issued on June 15, and the next day the electors of Southern Ireland went to the poll. In spite of the farcical and indecent compact and the absurdities of proportional representation, the voting for the Treaty was heavy. The figures were: Pro-Treaty Sinn Fein, 58; Republicans, 36; Labour, 17; Farmers, 7; Independents, 6; and Unionists, 4. On a plain issue and a free vote hardly any of the opponents of the Treaty would have been returned. The result was masked and confused by the compact, and no sure foundation was established. Nevertheless the form of the Constitution to which the Free State leaders had agreed, was such as to preclude Mr. de Valera and his followers from sharing in the Government. A pernicious duality in the Executive was thus avoided.

A few days later a resounding crime was perpetrated. Sir Henry Wilson, after completing his term as Chief of the Imperial General Staff, had been elected a Member of Parliament for an Ulster constituency. It had also been freely stated in the newspapers that he would act as the military adviser of the Ulster forces. He had not, in fact, taken any part in their executive affairs. Two Irishmen living in London, one of them a messenger in a Government office, regarding him as the commander of the hostile army and personally responsible for the murders in Belfast, waylaid him on his doorstep in Eaton Square and shot him to death with their pistols at three o'clock on the afternoon of June 22. He had just returned from the unveiling of a War Memorial and was in the khaki uniform of a Field-Marshal. He fell, pierced by numerous bullets, on the doorstep of his home. The murderers took to flight, but every human being on the spot, although unarmed, spontaneously pursued them. They retreated for some distance, firing at the gathering crowds. However, there was no escape. Everyone rushed upon them from all sides. They were seized and hurried to gaol to await the certain and speedy doom of British law. The effect of this murder in the heart of London of a man renowned throughout Europe as a strategist, and also of a Member of the House of Commons, was profound. The murderers do not seem, according to our present knowledge, to have been directed by any Irish organisation. They exploded independently; but Great Britain reacted with the same sudden anger as had followed the murders in the Phœnix Park nearly forty years before. The late Field-Marshal was carried to his grave on the following Monday with the highest military honours. All the way to St. Paul's Cathedral dense crowds thronged the streets. I had to face the House of Commons in the afternoon.

I had thought out most carefully the arguments to use, and in spite of the intensity of feeling I was allowed to unfold them fully. I surveyed with extreme plainness the good and bad points in the Irish situation. I paid a tribute to the memory of Sir Henry Wilson, the substance of which is embodied in the third volume of this account. I described the growing strength of the Ulster Government, and our plans for placing a complete cordon of Imperial troops across Ireland to separate the north from the south. I dwelt upon the will of the Irish people as manifested by the election. But all of this would have been futile apart from the following:—

'I should not be dealing honestly and fully with this subject if I left in the minds of the House the impression that all that is required is patience and composure. No, Sir. Firmness is needed in the interests of peace as much as patience. The constitution which we have seen, which has been published, satisfactorily conforms to the Treaty. It has now to be passed through the new Irish Parliament. There is no room for the slightest diminution of the Imperial and Constitutional safeguards and stipulations which it contains. That is not all. Mere paper affirmations, however important, unaccompanied by any effective effort to bring them into action, will not be sufficient. Mere denunciations of murder, however heartfelt, unaccompanied by the apprehension of a single murderer, cannot be accepted. The keeping in being within the Irish Free State by an elaborate process of duality, merging upon duplicity, of the whole apparatus of a Republican Government will not be in accordance either with the will of the Irish people, with the stipulations of the Treaty, or with the maintenance of good relations between the two countries. The resources at the disposal of His Majesty's Government are various and powerful. There are military, economic, and financial sanctions—to use a word with which we frequently meet in Continental affairs—there are sanctions of these kinds which are available, and which are formidable. They have been very closely studied, and the more closely they are studied the more clearly it is seen that those measures will be increasingly effective in proportion as the Irish Government and State become more fully and more solidly organised. . . .

'Hitherto we have been dealing with a Government weak because it had formed no contact with the people. Hitherto we have been anxious to do nothing to compromise the clear expression of Irish opinion. But now this Provisional Government is greatly strengthened. It is armed with the declared will of the Irish electorate. It is supported by an effective Parliamentary majority. It is its duty to give effect to the Treaty in the letter and in the spirit, to give full effect to it, and to give full effect to it without delay. A much stricter reckoning must rule henceforward. The ambiguous position of the so-called Irish Republican Army, intermingled as it is with the Free State troops, is an affront to the Treaty. The presence in Dublin, in violent occupation of the Four Courts, of a band of men styling themselves the Headquarters of the Republican Executive, is a gross breach and defiance of the Treaty. From this nest of anarchy and treason, not only to the British Crown, but to the Irish people, murderous outrages are stimulated and encouraged, not only in the twenty-six Counties, not only in the territory of the Northern Government, but even, it seems most probable, here across the Channel in Great Britain. From this centre, at any rate, an organisation is kept in being which has branches in Ulster, in Scotland, and in England, with the declared purpose of wrecking the Treaty by the vilest processes which human degradation can conceive. The time has come when it is not unfair, not premature, and not impatient for us to make to this strengthened Irish Government, and new Irish Parliament a request, in express terms, that this sort of thing must come to an end. If either from weakness, from want of courage, or for some other even less creditable reasons, it is not brought to an end and a very speedy end, then it is my duty to say, on behalf of His Majesty's Government, that we shall regard the Treaty as having been formally violated, that we shall take no steps to carry out or to legalize its further stages, and that we shall resume full liberty of action in any direction that may seem proper and to any extent that may be necessary to safeguard the interests and the rights that are entrusted to our care.'

The subsequent debate was marked by the intervention of Mr. Bonar Law, who had retired from the Government and from the leadership of the Conservative party in April, 1921, whose health was now restored, and whose political influence was a factor of first importance.

'The Colonial Secretary . . . at the end of his speech did everything which I would say you could ask the Government to do, or any Government to do to-day. . . . His attention was called to what is happening in the Four Courts. I do not think anyone could have read the letter issued from that quarter without the same feeling of abhorrence as was expressed by the Colonial Secretary; but there was something else in it more likely than anything to arouse our horror. The reference to Sir Henry Wilson's death in which they said they did not do it, clearly implied that they found no fault with it. . . . Just think of this. . . . There is in Dublin a body which has seized the Four Courts—to make the irony more complete it is the centre of justice in Ireland—and from these Four Courts, undoubtedly, emissaries are going out, trying to carry out in Ulster precisely the same methods which they think succeeded in the South, and are instigating murder in every direction. Is that tolerable for a moment? Let the Committee think what it means. Suppose we found out that there was a body occupying an important position in Paris, which was openly subsidising murderers to come to this country and upset our Government. What would happen? We should not make representations in Paris, and say, "We must make sure you do not approve of it." We should say, "You must stop this or there is war." Are we to be in a different position, in that respect, towards what appears to me to be one of our own Dominions . . .? I do not think there is any man in this House . . . who does not realize what a terrible thing it would be if we were reduced again to try to secure order in Southern Ireland by that means. . . . Now the position is clear. Much time cannot elapse before these grave matters—to quote a saying of the Colonial Secretary—are brought to the test. I for one say that I believe the Government means to see this through, but if they do not, I will be against them, and I hope the House of Commons will be against them also.'

Later in the evening the Prime Minister and I met Mr. Bonar Law in the Lobby. Although always holding himself in strict restraint, he manifested an intense passion. As far as I can remember he said, 'You have disarmed us to-day. If you act up to your words, well and good, but if not——!!' Here by an obvious effort he pulled himself up and walked away from us abruptly.

The Cabinet, supported by the House of Commons, were resolved that whatever happened Rory O'Connor must be put out of the Four Courts. The only question was when and how; and this must be promptly settled. Orders were actually sent to General Macready. However this officer prudently, and as it turned out fortunately, counselled delay and at this darkest hour in Ireland came daybreak. On June 27 Rory O'Connor's band, ranging cheerfully through the streets of Dublin, kidnapped General O'Connell, Commander-in-Chief of the Free State Army. Michael Collins, under the pressure of this event, and having doubtless learned that if he did not march, we would, determined to attack the Four Courts at dawn. All authority in Dublin was quaking, but he had his own following among the I.R.A. He asked for the loan of two eighteen-pounder guns from General Macready, and upon instructions from London these were delivered. He had one capable, resolute officer, Dalton by name, who had seen much service in France. This man fetched the guns from the British camp, and working them with his own hands and half a dozen untrained men, opened fire at 4 a.m. on June 28. Then followed one of those comic-tragic conflicts which were characteristic of the Free State Civil War. Both sides loved and respected each other as dear comrades in arms; both were ready to die if it could not possibly be avoided, but much more ready to expend ammunition than blood. Lavish rifle fire directed at the walls of buildings broke out, interspersed by expostulations and appeals to the higher nature of man. Commandant Dalton, half of whose gunners were wounded, continued to hurl shell into the Four Courts, and this cannonade was in fact the salute which celebrated the foundation of the Irish Free State.

Two more guns were asked for and supplied during the afternoon, and by evening all the ammunition, modestly limited to 200 rounds, was exhausted. It is surprising that at this crisis General Macready, who had so often shown good sense and comprehension, should have professed himself unable to supply any more. The Provisional Government were told they must wait until a destroyer from Carrickfergus could arrive with further supplies of high-explosive shells. On receiving this news, they very nearly collapsed. Frantic appeals and threats were made to me that night over the telephone, and every resource was used to hasten the supply. It appeared however that the Commander-in-Chief was unwilling to encroach even for a few hours upon the ample supplies of his defended camp. Two or three hundred rounds would have been ample. His sixteen batteries had nearly 10,000 shells of various natures of which half were high explosive.

On the 30th, the Free Staters having with great circumspection gained a footing in a portion of the Four Courts, Rory O'Connor set it on fire and after an explosion, which caused some loss of life, surrendered with his followers. A mass of papers of legal importance and of historical interest, some of them dating from the thirteenth century, were destroyed, and the dome of the building collapsed amid its ruins. Fighting went on for several days in Sackville Street and became fiercer as it progressed; but by July 5 all rebels actually in arms against the Provisional Government had surrendered.

This week's fighting was the decisive event in the birth struggles of the Irish Free State. When reduced to the last gasp that infant organism had reacted timorously but violently, and had gained new strength with every effort. A hard line was now drawn between friend and foe, and mortal hatreds were exchanged. The Provisional Government, menaced by imminent assassination, fortified themselves under trusty guards in Merrion Square. They lived together for some weeks without ever returning to their homes. Mr. Kevin O'Higgins told me some years later how some of them sat one evening in an angle of the roof for a little fresh air; how in lighting a cigarette he inadvertently raised himself for a few moments above the parapet, and how the bullet from a neighbouring house cut the cigarette from his fingers. But these men, although deeply troubled in their souls, were courageous and hot-blooded; and driven as they had been into a corner with their lives at stake—and far more than their lives, the cause they had conducted so far—they hit back with primordial freedom. On July 12 they issued a proclamation threatening drastic reprisals against all attempts at murder; they nominated a War Council under Michael Collins, and set on foot active aggressive operations against their enemies all over Ireland. Thus began the Free State Civil War. It was a very curious war, conducted by a few people who knew each other extremely well; who knew where to find each other and what the other man was likely to do in given circumstances. Collins and his adherents set to work to hunt down and kill those who they knew were compassing their destruction. In this guerrilla most of the best-known gunmen lost their lives.

Mr. Churchill to Mr. Collins.

Private and Personal.

July 7, 1922.

I have not troubled you during these anxious days and have confined my messages to your practical requirements. But the events which have taken place since you opened fire on the Four Courts seem to me to have in them the possibilities of very great hope for the peace and ultimate unity of Ireland, objects both of which are very dear to your British co-signatories. I feel this has been a terrible ordeal for you and your colleagues, having regard to all that has happened in the past. But I believe that the action you have taken with so much resolution and coolness was indispensable if Ireland was to be saved from anarchy and the Treaty from destruction. We had reached the end of our tether over here at the same time as you had in Ireland. I could not have sustained another debate in the House of Commons on the old lines without fatal consequences to the existing governing instrument in Britain, and with us the Treaty would have fallen too. Now all is changed. Ireland will be mistress in her own house, and we over here are in a position to safeguard your Treaty rights and further your legitimate interests effectually.

As soon as you have established the authority of the Irish Free State throughout the 26 Counties, as I do not doubt you will in a short time, and have placed yourself and your colleagues at the head of the great mass of the Irish nation, a new phase will begin far more hopeful than any we have hitherto experienced. In this phase the objective must be the unity of Ireland. How and when this can be achieved I cannot tell, but it is surely the goal towards which we must all look steadfastly. There will be tremendous difficulties, vexations and repulses, and no doubt any premature hope will be disappointed. But I have a strong feeling that the top of the hill has been reached, and that we shall find the road easier in the future than in the past. We must endeavour to use the new strength and advantages which are available to secure broad solutions. Minor irritations, however justifiable, must not be allowed to obstruct us or lead us off the track. Craig and Londonderry are coming over here on the 13th. I have not worried them with the various complaints, some of which are undoubtedly justified, contained in your letter of the 28th June. The Viceroy has reserved the Bill abolishing Proportional Representation in the North for the Royal Assent, which means that we shall have time to talk it all over. Otherwise I wish to keep the ground clear in the hopes of a general return at the right moment to the governing idea of the Collins-Craig pact. You remember how

Mr. Griffith wrote it all over the blotting pad in my room. There is the key to the new situation. We must wait till the right moment comes and not fritter away growing advantages by premature efforts. I will write to you after I have seen Craig and Londonderry again. I think I can get a better result in friendly conversation about your various complaints than by nagging them in official correspondence.

Meanwhile, in the intervals of grappling with revolt and revolution, I think you should turn over in your mind what would be the greatest offer the South could make for Northern co-operation. Of course, from the Imperial point of view there is nothing we should like better than to see North and South join hands in an all-Ireland assembly without prejudice to the existing rights of either. Such ideas would be vehemently denounced in many quarters at the moment, but events in the history of nations sometimes move very quickly. The Union of South Africa, for instance, was achieved on a wave of impulse. The prize is so great that other things should be subordinated to gaining it. The bulk of people are slow to take in what is happening, and prejudices die hard. Plain folk must have time to take things in and adjust their minds to what has happened. Even a month or two may produce enormous changes in public opinion.

Please give my good wishes to Mr. Griffith and show him this letter if you will.

P.S. I hope you are taking good care of yourself and your colleagues. The times are very dangerous.

Mr. Churchill to Sir James Craig.

Private and Personal.

July 7, 1922.

Very great events have taken place in Southern Ireland since we last met, and I am sure you will have been pondering over their consequences. The framing of a satisfactory Constitution for the Irish Free State; the clear wish of the Irish people recorded at the polls in spite of so many difficulties; the determined suppression by force of arms of the Republicans in Dublin and the campaign against them now being launched all over the country, particularly in Donegal; and lastly, the appeal made to Irishmen generally to come forward in support of the Government—all these constitute a series of stepping-stones towards a far better state of affairs than we had any right to hope for a few weeks ago.

I know you and Charlie[1] will be on the look out on your side for anything that can turn these favourable events to the general and lasting profit of Ireland and of the Empire. We want quiet and we want time, in order that the new situation may sink into people's minds and in order that the superior solutions which may now be possible may occur naturally to many people.

I see all your difficulties over the Boundary Commission, and as you know we have on two occasions got Collins to agree to alternative methods of procedure.

---

[1] Lord Londonderry.

It may well be that after he has won his fight in the South he will be in a position to make you a much broader offer which will render the intervention of the Boundary Commission unnecessary, and which will secure the effective co-operation in your Government of all the best of the Catholic elements in Ulster. Meanwhile I trust you will not have to make any references to the subject of the Boundary Commission which might suggest the possibility of a conflict between you and H.M. Government. We really have got to work these things out together, and I feel increasingly hopeful that we shall succeed.

I do not want to hurry you in any way, and I feel that we must see quite clearly what the results of the fighting in the South are going to be. It may carry the Provisional Government very far. Once the position is appreciated and forces are raised with definite aims and principles, people's minds are changed very much: a gulf opens between them and their past. I always live in hopes that we may come back again to your suggestion of the Craig-Collins pact to stand together and settle all the outstanding issues in accord. This seems to me to be all the more possible now that you seem to be getting increasing control of the situation in Ulster and now that Collins has definitely drawn the sword.

I do not bother you with minor matters in this letter, although there are several outstanding which cause me anxiety. These we can discuss when we meet, but I feel that we must be on the look out for an opportunity to deal with the situation on much broader lines than have hitherto been possible.

Death was soon to lay its hands upon the two principal signatories of the Irish Treaty. Arthur Griffith died of heart failure, so it is established, on August 13, and Collins himself, moving audaciously about the country rallying and leading his supporters in every foray, was killed in an ambush on August 22. The presentiment of death had been strong upon him for some days, and he only narrowly escaped several murderous traps. He sent me a valedictory message through a friend for which I am grateful. 'Tell Winston we could never have done anything without him.' His funeral was dignified by the solemn ritual of the Roman Catholic Church and by every manifestation of public sorrow. Then Silence. But his work was done. Successor to a sinister inheritance, reared among fierce conditions and moving through ferocious times, he supplied those qualities of action and personality without which the foundation of Irish nationhood would not have been re-established.

The void left by the deaths of Griffith and Collins was not unfilled. A quiet, potent figure stood in the background sharing, like Griffith, the dangers of the rebel leaders without taking part in all that they had done. In Cosgrave the Irish people found a chief of higher quality than any who had yet appeared. To the courage of Collins he added the matter-of-fact fidelity of Griffith and a knowledge of practical administration and state policy all his own. At his side rose the youthful Kevin O'Higgins, a figure out of antiquity cast in bronze.

These men restored order in Ireland by ancient methods and with no great effusion of blood. The people in their turmoil, confusion, and distress felt the stimulus of a will-power calm, intense, and ruthless. The attempt to break down the Dail by murdering its Members individually was countered in the following way. On two Deputies being shot almost on the steps of the Parliament House, Rory O'Connor and three of his leading associates were awakened and shot without trial on a December morning. They had been residing in easy confinement in Mountjoy Prison since their surrender at the Four Courts. They met their fate with equal astonishment and fortitude. A year before Rory O'Connor had been best man at the wedding of Kevin O'Higgins. It is evident that those who judge these events in future time will have to do so with comprehension of the stresses and strange conditions of this period of convulsion.

Mr. Churchill to Mr. Cope.

August 23.

Following for Cosgrave, Duggan and the Provisional Government:—

I take the earliest opportunity in this hour of tragedy for Ireland and of intense difficulty for the Irish Provisional Government of assuring you of the confidence which is felt by the British Government that the Treaty position will be faithfully and resolutely maintained. The death of the two principal signatories, the retirement of another and the desertion of a fourth, in no way affects the validity and sanctity of the settlement entered into with the plenipotentiaries of the Irish nation. On the contrary we are sure that the Provisional Government and the Irish people will feel it all the more a sacred duty to carry into full effect the act of reconciliation between the two islands which was the life-work of the dead Irish leaders, and with which their names will be imperishably associated. For our part the word of Britain has been passed and is inviolable. We hold ourselves bound on the Treaty basis and will meet good faith with good faith and goodwill with goodwill to the end. You, as acting Chairman of the Provisional Government, and your civil colleagues and your high military officers, may count on the fullest measure of co-operation and support from us in any way that is required.

Another man of distinction, ability and courage fell a victim. Erskine Childers, author of *The Riddle of the Sands*, who had shown daring and ardour against the Germans in the Cuxhaven raid of New Year's Day 1915, had espoused the Irish cause with even more than Irish irreconcilability. He, too, was shot for rebellion against the Free State. Said Kevin O'Higgins in public, with severity, 'If Englishmen come to Ireland looking for excitement, we will see that they get it.' He died with the utmost composure. Kevin O'Higgins himself was also in after years to fall by the bullet.

Before these closing tragedies I had ceased to be connected with Anglo-Irish affairs; but when the Coalition Government resigned at the end of October, 1922, the strength and power of the Irish Free State was firmly erected upon the basis of Treaty. One of the first decisions of Mr. Bonar Law's Cabinet was that the Treaty should be made good in letter and in spirit; and this has guided all later British Administrations. Who cares to

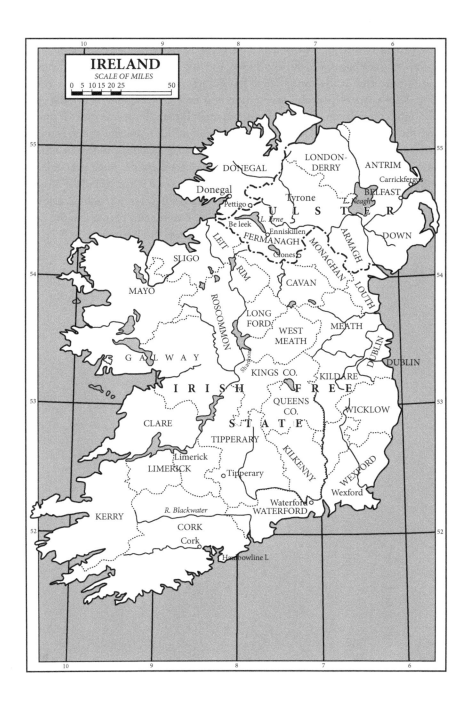

IRELAND

SCALE OF MILES

0 5 10 15 20 25   50

predict the future? Britain is free and Ireland is lonely. Ireland is poor, and Britain is still ploughing through the sombre consequences of Armageddon. Ireland as a Dominion within the British Commonwealth of Nations has much to give to her neighbour and much to withhold from her. No one can expect that the hatred and prejudices of centuries will pass away in the passage of our short lives. But that they will pass away in the merciful oblivion of time and in the recuperative fruitfulness of nature seems to be a good and fair hope. Fifty years of peaceful association and new growth must bring the study of common interests increasingly into prominence. In the undying words of Grattan: 'The Channel forbids union; the Ocean forbids separation.' Two ancient races, founders in great measure of the British Empire and of the United States, intermingled in a thousand ways across the world, and with the old cause of quarrel ended, must gradually try to help and not to harm each other. It may well be that a reward is appointed for all and that an Ireland reconciled within itself and to Great Britain will on some high occasion claim to guide the onward march, and offer to the British Empire and perhaps to the English-speaking world solutions for our problems otherwise beyond our reach.

CHAPTER XVII
TURKEY ALIVE

'Vote it as you please. There is a company of poor men who will shed their last drop of blood, before they see it settled so.'

—Oliver Cromwell.

Turkey before the War—The Offer of the Allies—The Pan-Turks—Enver—German-Turkish Plans—The Requisition of the Turkish Battleships—The *Goeben*—Enver's *Coup d'État:* The Final Crash—After the Armistice—American Criticism—President Wilson's Commission—Insurgence and Paralysis—A Deadly Step—The Greek Descent on Smyrna—Turkey Alive—Justice Changes Camps—A New Turning-point—Headlines—Ferid—The Melting of the Armies—Restrictions and Illusions—Talks about Constantinople—Cabinet Decision—The Treaty of Sèvres—The March of Facts—Attack on the Ismid Peninsula—My Letter of March 24.

No State plunged into the World War so wilfully as Turkey.[1] The Ottoman Empire was in 1914 already moribund. Italy, using sea power, had invaded and annexed Tripoli in 1909, and a desultory warfare was still proceeding in the interior of this province, when the Balkan States in 1912 drew the sword upon their ancient conqueror and tyrant. Important provinces and many islands were ceded by the defeated Turkish Empire in the Treaty of London, and the division of the spoils became a new cause of bloodshed among the Balkan victors. Rich prizes still remained in European Turkey to tempt the ambition or satisfy the claims of Roumania, Bulgaria, Serbia and Greece; and through all Constantinople glittered as the supreme goal. But imminent as were the dangers of the Turkish Empire from the vengeance and ambition of the Balkan States, nothing could supplant in the Turkish mind the fear of Russia. Russia was in contact with Turkey by land and water along a thousand-mile frontier which stretched from the western shores of the Black Sea to the Caspian. England, France and Italy (Sardinia) in the Crimean War, the exceptional power of England under Disraeli in 1878, had preserved the Turkish Empire from ruin and Constantinople from conquest. Although before the Balkan Allies quarrelled among themselves, the Bulgarians had marched to the gates of Constantinople from the West, the sense of peril from the North still outweighed all else in Turkish thoughts.

---

[1] See map of Turkey facing page 301.

To this was added the antagonism of the Arab race in the Yemen, the Hedjas, Palestine, Syria, Mosul, and Iraq. The population of Kurdistan and the widely distributed Armenian race were estranged. From every quarter the nations and races who for five or six hundred years had waged war against the Turkish Empire or had suffered the fate of Turkish captives, turned their gaze in a measureless hatred and hunger upon the dying Empire from which they had endured so much so long. The hour of retribution and restoration was at hand; and the only doubt was how long could the busily spun webs of European diplomacy, and particularly of English diplomacy, postpone the final reckoning. The imminent collapse of the Turkish Empire like the progressive decay and disruption of the Austrian Empire, arising from forces beyond human control, had loosened the whole foundations of Eastern and South-Eastern Europe. Change—violent, vast, incalculable, but irresistible and near, brooded over the hearths and institutions of 120 millions of people.

It was at this hour and on this scene that Germany had launched her army to the invasion of France through Belgium, and all other quarrels had re-aligned themselves in accordance with the supreme struggle. What was to happen to scandalous, crumbling, decrepit and penniless Turkey in this earthquake?

She received what seemed to British eyes the most favourable offer ever made to any government in history. She was guaranteed at the price merely of maintaining her neutrality the absolute integrity of all her dominions. She was guaranteed this upon the authority not only of her friends, France and Britain, but on that of her enemy, Russia. The guarantee of France and England would have protected Turkey from the Balkan States, and especially Greece; the guarantee of Russia suspended to indefinite periods the over-hanging menace from the North. The influence of Britain could largely allay and certainly postpone the long rising movement of the Arabs. Never, thought the Allies, was a fairer proposition made to a weaker and more imperilled State.

But there was another side to the picture. Within the decaying fabric of the Turkish Empire and beneath the surface of its political affairs lay fierce, purposeful forces both in men and ideas. The disaster of the first Balkan War created from these elements a concealed, slow-burning fire of strange intensity unrealised by all the Embassies along the shores of the Bosphorus—all save one. 'During this time' (the years before the Great War), wrote a profoundly informed Turk in 1915, 'the whole future of the Turkish people was examined by Committees down to the smallest details.'[2]

The Pan-Turk Committee accepted the Anglo-Russian Convention of 1907 as a definite alliance between the Power who had been Turkey's strongest and most disinterested supporter and friend with the Power who was her ancient and inexorable enemy. They therefore looked elsewhere for help in the general European war which they were convinced was approaching. Their plan, which seemed in 1913 merely visionary, was based upon the recreation of Turkey on a solely Turkish human foundation: to wit, the Turkish peasantry of Anatolia. It contemplated as a national ideal the uniting of the Moslem areas of Caucasia, the Persian province of Azerbaijan, and the Turkish

[2] *Turkish and Pan-Turkish Ideals, by* 'Tekin Alp.' First published in German, 1915.

Trans-Caspian provinces of Russia (the homeland of the Turkish race) with the Turks of the Anatolian peninsula; and the extension of Turkey into the Caspian Basin. It included the rejection of theocratic government; a radical change of relationship between Church and State; the diversion of the 'Pious Foundations'' endowments to the secular needs of the State, and a rigorous disciplining of the professional religious classes. It included also the startling economic, social and literary changes which have recently been achieved in Turkey. Mustapha Kemal has in fact executed a plan decided upon, and to which he may well have been a party, fifteen years ago. The centre point of all the Pan-Turk schemes was the use of Germany to rid Turkey of the Russian danger. Marschall von Bieberstein, for so many years German Ambassador at Constantinople, nursed these hidden fires with skilful hands.

Pan-Turkish schemes might have remained in dreamland but for the fact that in a fateful hour there stood almost at the head of Turkey a man of action. A would-be Turkish Napoleon, in whose veins surged warrior blood, by his individual will, vanity and fraud was destined to launch the Turkish Empire upon its most audacious adventure. Enver, the German-trained but Turkish-hearted subaltern, had 'thrown his cap over the fence' (to quote himself) as the signal for the Young Turk Revolution in 1909. Together with his handful of Young Turk friends forming the committee of Union and Progress, he had bravely faced all the gathering foes. When Italy had seized Tripoli, it was in the deserts of Tripoli that Enver had fought; when the armies of Balkan Allies were at the lines of Chatalja, it was Enver who had never despaired. 'Adrianople,' said Mr. Asquith, then Prime Minister in 1912, 'will never be restored to Turkey.' But Enver entered Adrianople within a month, and Adrianople is Turkish to-day. The outbreak of the Great War saw Enver with his associate, Talaat, and his skilful and incorruptible Finance Minister, Djavid, in control of Turkish affairs. Above them, an imposing façade, were the Sultan and the Grand Vizier: but these men and their adherents were the unquestioned governing power, and of them Enver in all action was the explosive force.[3]

The Turkish leaders rated the might of Russia for the rough and tumble of a general war far lower than did the Western allies of the Czar. They were convinced that the Germanic group would win the war on land, that Russia would be severely mauled and that a revolution would follow. Turkey would secure in the moment of a German victory gains in territory and population in the Caucasus which would at least ward off the Russian danger for several generations. In the long preliminary discussions Germany promised Turkey territorial satisfaction in the Caucasus in the event of a victory by the Central Powers. This promise was decisive upon Turkish policy.

The policy of the Pan-Turks in every sphere of Turkish life and their territorial ambitions were embodied in a definite war plan. This plan required as its foundation the Turkish command of the Black Sea. Whenever the Great War should come—as come they were sure it must—and Russia was at grips with Germany and Austria, the Pan-Turks intended to invade and conquer the Caucasus. The control of the sea route

---

[3] I happened to know all these men personally. I had met Enver at the German manœuvres in 1910. Talaat and Djavid had been our hosts when, with Lord Birkenhead, I visited Constantinople in 1909.

from Constantinople to Trebizond was indispensable to an advance from Trebizond to Erzerum. Hence Turkey must have a navy. Popular subscriptions opened in 1911 and 1912 throughout Anatolia, and even throughout Islam, provided the money for the building for Turkey in Great Britain of two dreadnoughts. The arrival of one at least of these battleships at Constantinople was the peg upon which the whole Turkish war plan hung. The supreme question in July, 1914, among the Turkish leaders was: Would the ships arrive in time? Obviously the margin was small. The first Turkish dreadnought, the *Reshadieh*, was due for completion in July; the second, a few weeks later. Already Turkish agents in Russian territory round Olti, Ardahan and Kars were busy arranging for the hoarding of corn crops by the Moslem Turkish peasantry who formed the bulk of the population, in order to make possible the advance of the Turkish columns down the valley of the Chorukh and against the Russian rear. On July 27 a secret defensive and offensive alliance between Germany and Turkey against Russia was proposed by Turkey, accepted forthwith by Germany, and signed on August 2. The mobilisation of the Turkish Army was ordered on July 31.

But now came a surprise. England suddenly assumed an attitude of definite resistance to Germany. The British fleets had put to sea in battle order. On July 28 I requisitioned both the Turkish dreadnoughts for the Royal Navy. A Turkish transport with five hundred Turkish sailors on board lay in the Tyne ready to take over the first. The Turkish Captain demanded delivery of the vessel, and threatened to board her and hoist the Turkish flag. In these tremendous days (July 31) I gave orders on my own responsibility that this was to be prevented, and that any attempt at seizure by the Turks should be resisted if necessary by armed force. I took this action solely for British naval purposes. The addition of the two Turkish dreadnoughts to the British Fleet seemed vital to national safety. No one in the Admiralty, nor so far as I know in England, had any knowledge of the Turkish designs or of the part these ships were to play in them. We built better than we knew. I was later in the year criticised in some quarters for having requisitioned the Turkish ships. The rage and disappointment excited thereby throughout Turkey was said to have turned the scale and provoked Turkey into war against us. We now know the inner explanation of this disappointment. The requisitioning of these ships, so far from making Turkey an enemy, nearly made her an Ally.

But there still remained to the Turks one hope: the *Goeben*. This fast German battle cruiser was in the western Mediterranean under peace time orders to refit at Pola in the Adriatic. She was in herself sufficient to dominate the Russian squadron in the Black Sea. Would the Germans send the *Goeben* back to Constantinople? Would she get there? It was at this moment that the news of the British ultimatum to Germany, carrying with it the certainty of the British declaration of war, reached Constantinople. The Turkish realists had never counted on such an event. It transformed the naval situation in the Mediterranean. Could the *Goeben* escape the numerous British flotillas and cruiser squadrons and the three more powerful though less speedy British battle cruisers which lay between her and the sea? When on the night of August 3 Enver learned that the *Goeben* was under orders to escape up the Adriatic to Pola, his anxiety knew no bounds. He immediately sought the Russian military attaché, General Leontev, and casting all previous schemes to the wind, including the agreement he had signed with Germany the day before, proposed to this astonished officer an alliance between Turkey and Russia on various conditions, including Turkish compensations in Western Thrace. Whether the Germans realised that they would never be forgiven by the Pan-Turks unless the *Goeben* made an effort to reach Constantinople, or whether it was already part of their war plan, fresh orders to go to Constantinople were at this moment (August 3) being sent by Admiral Tirpitz to the *Goeben* then about to coal at Messina; and after events which are well known she reached the Dardanelles on the 10th and was after some parley admitted to the Sea of Marmora.

Enver's confidence was now restored, for the command of the Black Sea rested potentially with the Turks. But the certain hostility of Great Britain was serious, in view of her naval supremacy and the undefended conditions of the Dardanelles. Moreover Italy had unexpectedly separated herself from the Triple Alliance. It might therefore perhaps be prudent for Turkey to see how the impending great battles on land, and especially those upon the Russian front, were decided. Meanwhile the mobilisation of the Turkish Army could proceed unostentatiously and be justified as a precautionary measure. Thus there followed a period lasting for about three months of Turkish hesitation and delay, having the effect of consummate duplicity. I can recall no great sphere of policy about which the British Government was less completely informed than the Turkish. It is strange to read the telegrams we received through all channels from Constantinople during this period in the light of our present knowledge. But all the Allies, now encouraged by the friendly assurances of the Grand Vizier and the respectable-effete section of the Cabinet, now indignant at the refusal to intern and disarm the *Goeben* and generally mystified by many contradictory voices, believed that Turkey had no policy and might still be won or lost. This period was ended when Enver in November, acting as the agent of all the Pan-Turk forces, delivered the unprovoked attack by the *Goeben* and the Turkish Fleet upon the Russian Black Sea ports, and thus plunged Turkey brutally into the war.

What followed has been to some extent recounted in these volumes.

Turkey was animated, guided, and upheld during the struggle for four years by the German military and intellectual power. She contended with varying success against Russia in the Caucasus, but the British Empire became her greatest foe. The main strength of the Turkish Army was broken on the Gallipoli Peninsula by British and Australasian forces. The British invasion of Mesopotamia, though marked by notable Turkish victories, advanced remorselessly up the Tigris. Lawrence raised and led the Arab revolt in the desert. Allenby, with an Anglo-Indian Army of a quarter of a million, conquered Palestine and entered Syria. Although the French had commanded on the Salonikan Front, and a French General presided over the advance upon Constantinople from the west, the conviction of the Turks at the Armistice was that they had been destroyed by England. Certainly three-quarters of the Turks killed in the Great War had fallen to the bullets and bayonets of the British Empire, and well they knew the slaughter they had inflicted upon this old friend and misjudged antagonist without mitigating his hostile energy.

When the Hindenburg Line and Germany broke, all Turkish resistance fell flat on the ground. Turkey, prostrate, looked up and saw with relief that her conquerors were British. 'We have made a great mistake; we have chosen the wrong side; we were forced into it by Enver and Talaat, but they have now fled. We sincerely regret what has occurred. How could we tell that the United States would go to war with Germany; or that Great Britain would become a first-class military Power? Such prodigies are beyond human foresight. No one ought to blame us for being so misled. Of course we must be punished, but let us be chastised by our old friend, England.' Such was the mood of Turkey for two or three months after the armistice of Mudros on October 30, which ended the Great War in the East.

In Lord Curzon's words:—

'At the time the Peace Conference assembled, the Allied Powers were in possession of Constantinople, where the Turkish Government, if not cowed, was subservient. Our military power in the occupied Turkish regions of Asia was sufficient to enable us to enforce not merely the agreed terms of the Armistice but also any supplementary terms that were found necessary. The British were in secure possession of Mesopotamia up to and including Mosul. . . . The British position in Persia was, both in a military and political sense, extraordinarily strong. We were still in Trans-Caspia, but were contemplating an immediate retirement, since accomplished. The Caspian was in our hands and was being made the base of naval action against Bolshevik forces. British divisions occupied the entire Caucasus, from the Black Sea to the Caspian, and provided the only guarantees for peace . . . between the rival peoples: Georgians, Armenians, Tartars, Daghastanis, and Russians. . . . In Asia Minor (outside the region of British military occupation) no Allied forces had appeared. The fate of Armenia was undecided, the bulk of the Armenians being fugitives from their country. Apart from Armenia, and possibly Cilicia, the partition of Asia Minor was not even contemplated. In Syria a more critical condition existed, owing to the difficulty of reconciling the aspirations of the French with the hard facts of the Arab situation and the insistence of the French on the letter of the unfortunate Sykes-Picot Agreement. In Palestine the interests of the Arab population and the Zionist immigrants appeared to be capable of reconciliation and everything pointed to an early mandate for Great Britain with the consent of both. Egypt was still quiet.'

In a situation of this kind, broad, clear, and above all, swift decisions were needful. Every day's delay in these loosely knit but inflammable communities was loaded with danger. There had already been two months' delay; and all over this immense area, once the seat of ancient wealth and civilisations, and now filled with fierce and fanatical peoples largely armed, everyone was asking 'What has happened and what have we got to do?' But the victorious statesmen in Paris had for them no answer. They had to come to grips and understanding with each other. They had to explain to America what, as far as they knew, was happening in Europe. They had to face the vehement demands of France that once her armies had reached the Rhine, they should never have to give it up. They had to mete out what they considered justice and judgment to Germany, and stand on guard with their armies to enforce what they might prescribe. And around them welled and mounted the flood of confusion.

President Wilson and the American Peace Delegation and Staffs were all under the impression of the Secret Treaties, and of their superior virtue in not being a party to any of them. In the Middle East they were indeed 'the only disinterested Power.' This fact was undoubtedly helpful, for much of the Secret Treaties made, as has been described, in the pangs of war, had to be swept out of the way. The influence of President Wilson and the United States, uncompromised and at the same time most weighty, was just the new element needed to make a good and practical review and settlement possible. It was a tragedy that President Wilson in action did not keep a closer grip upon the realities. He rendered valuable, he had it in his power to render invaluable services.

So President Wilson said that,

'The point of view of the United States of America was indifferent to the claims both of Great Britain and of France over peoples unless those peoples wanted them. One of the fundamental principles to which the United States of America adhered was the consent of the governed. This was ingrained in the thought of the United States of America. Hence . . . the United States wanted to know whether France would be agreeable to the Syrians. The same applied as to whether Great Britain would be agreeable to the inhabitants of Mesopotamia. It might not be his business, but if the question was made his business owing to the fact that it was brought before the Conference, the only way to deal with it was to discover the desire of the population of these regions.

'He therefore suggested a Commission of Inquiry in Turkey and he gave his opinion of what they should do.'[4]

'Their object should be to elucidate the state of opinion and the soil to be worked on by any mandatory. They should be asked to come back and tell the Conference what they found in this matter. . . . It would . . . convince the world that the Conference had tried to find the most scientific basis of settlement. . . . The Commission should be composed of an equal number of French, British, Italian and American representatives. They would be sent out with *carte blanche* to tell the facts as they found them.'

'The President,' says Mr. Baker, 'was most enthusiastic and urgent in pressing this idea.'

Now nothing could be more plausible than this request. In fact, we know in domestic politics that when matters are complicated and tempers are rising, the usual household remedy is to appoint a committee or a Royal Commission. And this remedy is very

---

[4] *Woodrow Wilson and the World Settlement*, by Ray Stannard Baker, Vol. I, p. 76.

often efficacious. Although the problem is not solved by the Commission, although the Commission are probably less competent to solve it than the responsible Ministers, in a great many cases a long delay, the patient taking of evidence and the resulting ponderous Blue Book, make it probable that the problem will be presented in a different and peradventure a less acute form. It was natural that President Wilson should propose this device, and inevitable that the sharply divided Powers should acquiesce in it. Certainly no blame can attach to either party.

But the nations concerned would not stand so long at the footstool of undecided power, and of all the processes likely to rouse their passion, none was more apt than the peripatetic Commission of Inquiry making a roving progress in search of truth through all the powder magazines of the Middle East with a notebook in one hand and a lighted cigarette in the other. Anyone could see how sensible and right President Wilson was, and how well his proposal would have suited a political difficulty in the United States or in Great Britain. But of course in the circumstances and the atmosphere it was simply a means of preparing explosions. Statesmen in a crisis, like generals or admirals in war, have often to take fateful decisions without knowing a very large proportion of the essential facts. It is hard to do this, but anything is better than not taking decisions at all. To stroll around among masses of disorganised, infuriated people, asking them what they think about it and what they would like, is the most sure and certain method of breeding strife. When one is helping in affairs which one does not understand and in which one is scarcely at all interested, a mood of elevated and airy detachment easily dominates the mind. 'Let us have all the facts unfolded before we take our decision. Let us know where we are. Let us ascertain the wishes of the population.' How prudent and correct it all sounds! But before the Commission, on which in the end only America was represented, had gone a third of the way through the sphere of their studies, almost all the peoples concerned were in armed revolt and almost all the Allied troops had gone home.

However, from the date of the appointment of the Commission the whole of the Middle East was placed under an indefinite decree of hesitancy and investigation. When from day to day a dozen harsh local problems, all expressed in terms of people shooting one another, were presented to the British Public Departments concerned, the only Minute which could be written by any official was, 'These matters must wait until the Inter-Allied Commission has completed its inquiry.' So the friendly elements kept on marking time and asking questions, and the unfriendly elements loaded their rifles and made plans.

But all this might have subsided and come back into hand but for one act, positive, aggressive, and by every standard of statecraft wrong. The claims and ambitions of Italy to lay hands upon the Turkish Empire outstripped the boldest imagination. And Italy lost no time in startling Paris with proof that she would back her aims with deeds. The decision to send a commission to the East to which Italy was a party had scarcely been taken, when the Italians, on the pretext of a local riot, seized Adalia and at the some time officially complained that the Greeks were making preparations for a descent upon Smyrna. The Greeks on their side cried out that the Italian action at Adalia was only a prelude to an encroachment upon the sphere of Greek aspirations. Towards the end of April it was reported that the Italians had landed small parties of troops at Budrum, Makri, and Alaya. At the same time the Triumvirate, attracted by the prestige and personality of Venizelos, was moving steadily towards assigning Smyrna with the Aidin Province to the Greeks. Smyrna and portions of its littoral had been populated extensively by Greeks for thousands of years. Its prosperity was largely attributable to their intelligence and to their industry and agriculture. As early as 1915 Mr. Asquith's Government had resolved that in any partition of Turkey, Greece if she took part in the war ought to have Smyrna. The Territorial Commission on Greece at the Peace Conference had by a majority, including British, French and American members, newly decided in favour of the Greek claim. President Wilson had definitely accepted that conclusion. The rumour of this intention had however roused the protests of the Smyrna European colony, and the American missionaries in Smyrna vied with the British High Commissioner at Constantinople in their separate simultaneous warnings against the perils of such a step.

The complete breach between President Wilson and the Italian delegation had at this moment led to the temporary withdrawal of Italy from the conference. In the ardour of his encounter with Signor Orlando it was natural that Wilson should lean to Greece. Here he found an only too eager sympathiser in the British Prime Minister. Clemenceau, preoccupied with the Rhine and the future of France, moved amicably with these two. Events now precipitated action. The reports that the Italians were going to seize Smyrna forcibly, combined with stories of Turkish maltreatment of the Greek population, provoked a deadly step. On May 5 the Triumvirate entertained the project that the Greeks should be allowed to occupy Smyrna forthwith for the purpose of protecting their compatriots there. Mr. Lloyd George asked for a decision that M. Venizelos might be authorised to send troops to be kept on board ship at Smyrna ready for landing in case of necessity. President Wilson asked why the troops should not be landed at once as the men did not keep in good condition on board ship. Mr. Lloyd George did not demur.

The subject was dealt with again on May 10. The principle of the landing was however assumed to be settled and only practical details were discussed. Sir Henry Wilson was present on both occasions but confined himself to the technical aspects. On the 12th a third meeting was held. Signor Orlando had now returned to the fold. He was assured that the future destination of Smyrna would not be prejudiced by a Greek occupation. It was an emergency measure for the protection of the Greek population. In accordance with Armistice conditions notice must be given to Turkey to surrender the Smyrna forts to British, French and Italian detachments. Signor Orlando, after consideration, made no objection in principle to the landing but urged that the British, French and Italian detachments should not be withdrawn pending a final settlement. The decision of the Council of Four was that the Greek forces should start from Kavalla as soon as ready and that the Italian detachment should take part in the operations of the allied forces.

Venizelos is entitled to plead that in going to Smyrna he acted as mandatory for the four greatest Powers. But he went as readily as a duck will swim. Whatever the responsibilities of the Four or rather of the Triumvirate, for they were the moving force, his own are ineffaceable. He alone possessed the means of action. There could never have been any question of sending British, French or American troops except in symbolic detachments on such a mission. But Greek divisions were within swift and easy striking distance; and were straining at the leash. On May 15, in spite of serious warning and protests from the British Foreign Office and War Office, twenty thousand Greek troops, covered by the fire of their warships, landed at Smyrna, killed a large number of Turks, occupied the city, advanced rapidly up the Smyrna-Aidin railway, had a bloody fight with Turkish troops and irregulars and the Turkish population of Aidin, and set up their standards of invasion and conquest in Asia Minor.

I well remember the bewilderment and alarm with which I heard on a lovely afternoon in Paris of this fatal event. No doubt my personal views were affected by the consternation it produced upon the British General Staff. Making every allowance for the pro-Turk inclinations of the British military mind, it was impossible to excuse the imprudence of this violent act, which opened so many new perils when our resources were shrivelling. At the War Office we were not long in feeling its consequences. Our officers in twos and threes were all over Asia Minor supervising the surrender of armies and munitions as prescribed by the Armistice. They rode about freely and unarmed from place to place, and with their finger indicated what should be done. They were almost mechanically obeyed. Important 'dumps' of rifles, machine guns, cannon and shells were being submissively piled up; Turkey was under the spell of defeat, and of deserved defeat. 'Let us be punished by our old friend England.' So the arms were stacked and the guns were parked and the shells were arranged in massive heaps as the accepted result of stricken fields and of conventions signed.

But from the moment that the Turkish nation—and, though Paris did not seem to know it, there was a nation—realised that it was not Britain and India and Allenby that they had to endure and for the time obey, but Greece, the hated and despised foe of generations—to their eyes a revolted province, certainly a frequently defeated opponent; from that moment, Turkey became uncontrollable. The British officers supervising the execution of the Armistice terms were first ignored, then insulted, then chased for their lives or flung into arduous captivity.[5] The 'dumps' in which the equipment of considerable armies was already gathered passed in a week from British to Turkish control; and Mustapha Kemal, the Man of Destiny whom we have met in these volumes on the Gallipoli Peninsula in April and in August, 1915—till then almost a rebel against the Turkish Government at Constantinople,—was furnished with the power, as he already possessed the qualities, of a Warrior Prince.

But more important than the recapture of arms and munitions were the moral advantages which flowed to his cause. We have explained how cold-blooded and malignant Turkish policy in the Great War had been, and how well founded were the grievances of the Allies against her. The ghastly fate of the Armenians has yet to be

---

[5]Colonel Sir Alfred Rawlinson, brother of the renowned Commander of the Fourth Army, suffered the worst experiences. His personal account of a long bondage which shattered his health and nearly cost him his life is well worth reading.

recorded. Nevertheless the whole attitude of the Peace Conference towards Turkey was so harsh that Right had now changed sides. Justice, that eternal fugitive from the councils of conquerors, had gone over to the opposite camp. Defeat, thought the Turks, must be accepted and its consequences must be borne: but the loosing of the Greek army into Asia Minor, at the very moment when Turkey was being disarmed, boded the destruction and death of the Turkish nation and their suppression and subjugation as a race among men. On June 9 in the little town of Kharas near Amasia, Mustapha Kemal publicly expounded his plans for the salvation of Turkey. All the half raked-out fires of Pan-Turkism began to glow again. That Greeks should conquer Turks was not a decree of Fate which any Turk would recognise. Loaded with follies, stained with crimes, rotted with misgovernment, shattered by battle, worn down by long disastrous wars, his Empire falling to pieces around him, the Turk was still alive. In his breast was beating the heart of a race that had challenged the world, and for centuries had contended victoriously against all comers. In his hands was once again the equipment of a modern army, and at his head a Captain, who with all that is learned of him, ranks with the four or five outstanding figures of the cataclysm. In the tapestried and gilded chambers of Paris were assembled the law-givers of the world. In Constantinople, under the guns of the Allied Fleets there functioned a puppet Government of Turkey. But among the stern hills and valleys of 'the Turkish Homelands' in Anatolia, there dwelt that company of poor men . . . who would not see it settled so; and at their bivouac fires at this moment sate in the rags of a refugee the august Spirit of Fair Play.

I cannot understand to this day how these eminent statesmen in Paris, Wilson, Lloyd George, Clemenceau and Venizelos, whose wisdom, prudence, and address had raised them under the severest tests so much above their fellows, could have been betrayed into so rash and fatal a step.

Many will be surprised at the prominence which I give to the episode of the Greek invasion of Smyrna at the behest of the Allies. It has been my endeavour in these volumes to show the stepping-stones of fate. Out of an incomprehensible fecundity of violent and interesting facts and combinations of facts, I try to choose those that really mattered. Here then we have reached a new turning-point in the history of the peoples of the Middle East.

However, the meaning of Smyrna was obscured at the time from the public eye. There was so much to talk about, so many exciting and important things to do, so many rough and disagreeable episodes to record, so many high ideals to strive for, that the mere sending of a couple of Greek divisions to Smyrna and the shooting of a few hundred Turks at the landing did not seem to make any impression upon public opinion of the principal Allied countries. The five hundred exceptionally able correspondents and writers who beset the purlieus of the Conference, pumped out their eighty thousand words a night, and there were always plenty of headlines in all the leading newspapers with the largest circulations. No doubt among these headlines, 'GREEK DIVISIONS LAND IN SMYRNA: *Turkish resistance overpowered*,' found its place. But next day there was something else. There have to be headlines for every day. It was not the fault of the newspapers or of the public. Both were surfeited with sensation, and the public, though it read the newspapers, was busy building up its homes and businesses. They may well be granted 'leave of absence on urgent private affairs.'

We must now record chronologically a few events. The Young Turk leaders who had ruled Turkey from the revolution of 1910 to the end of the Great War were scattered and in exile. Enver, after desperate adventures and exploits in Turkestan, was to perish in the field. Talaat was to be shot dead in Berlin by an Armenian, who certainly had public cause for his revenge. Djavid was to be executed in 1926 by the triumphant Mustapha Kemal and to mount the scaffold 'repeating the stanzas of an old Turkish poem.' A new figure, fleeting but recognisable, now appears in Turkish politics. Ferid Pasha had taken office on March 4, 1919 with a submissive policy and in close alliance with the Sultan. All around him in Constantinople were the warships and bayonets of the Allies. Out in the mountains of Asia Minor in sombre mood and half-mutinous attitude were the survivors and rank and file of the leaderless Committee of Union and Progress. Between these two sets of compulsions Ferid held his balance precariously. He bowed and expostulated to the Allies and kept himself in friendly touch with the Nationalists. In protest against the occupation of Smyrna he resigned; he resumed office the same day. On June 7 he led a Peace Delegation to Paris to appeal for the lenient treatment of Turkey. He received a scathing reply from the Conference. On July 1 he appointed Mustapha Kemal Inspector-General to Northern Asia Minor. In August and September Mustapha Kemal convened congresses of Eastern delegates at Erzeroum and Sivas. On September 11 the Sivas Congress published a manifesto of Turkish rights which subsequently formed the 'National Pact,' or solemn covenant of the new Turkey. By the end of September the authority of Constantinople did not extend beyond the shores of the Bosphorus and the Sea of Marmora. Even Brusa, an hour by rail from the Marmora shore, seceded to the Angora Government in October. Ferid resigned again to make way for a Government half-way between the Sultan in the grip of the Allies, and Mustapha Kemal and his National Pact at Angora.

Meanwhile our armies were melting fast. In January, 1919, the War Office had still nearly three million men abroad under its orders. In March it had two, and these in a rapid process of demobilisation. By mid-summer, 1919, apart from the forces on the Rhine, we had hardly any troops at all. The conscript and war-enrolled forces had to be sent home; the new permanent army was forming; and volunteers for professional military service were only gradually forthcoming. A year after the Armistice we counted in battalions of five or six hundred men, where we had previously disposed of divisions of fifteen or twenty thousand complete in every detail. It was very strange to watch the vast shrinkage of our military power, while at the same time the increase of danger and hostility in almost every quarter could be so plainly discerned. In December, 1919, I circulated to the Cabinet a General Staff memorandum explaining how far our power had diminished and pointing out the disproportion between our policy and our strength.

Para. 3. (i) 'It seems scarcely necessary to mention that the situation has changed considerably since the commencement of the Turkish Armistice on 31st October,

1918, both as regards the armed resources of His Majesty's Government and the political situation within the pre-War Turkish Empire. The British military contribution now available for enforcing peace terms, otherwise than in Palestine and Mesopotamia, is as follows:—

One division plus army troops (including garrison of Batum), comprising: British, 13,000; Indian, 18,000; a total of 31,000 combatants.

The striking power of this force would be practically limited to the railway system. And here the General Staff wish to observe that without resorting to the raising of fresh troops by conscription or other means no British reinforcements will be available for Turkey.'

The General Staff proceed to express the hope that:—

'Only such terms will be seriously considered by His Majesty's Government, in the first place, as may be reasonably compatible with the resources which exist or which it may be intended to provide for their execution.

Without going into detail or the political pros and cons of the various questions, the General Staff wish to record the following list of measures which may be advocated for various reasons, but the enforcement of which, according to their information, might call for reinforcement of the Army of the Black Sea, either by our Allies or further British levies:—

(i)   The creation of a Greater Armenia, linking up Cilicia with the Erivan Republic.

(ii)   The creation of an independent Kurdistan.

(iii) Acquisition by Greece of any portion of the Pontus (*sic*).

(iv)   Permanent occupation by Greece of any part of the Aidin Vilayet.

(v)   Permanent occupation of any part of Southern Anatolia or Konia by Italy, though it is doubtful whether this would cause such resentment to the Turks as any other of the above causes.

In addition to the above measures, which would call for immediate reinforcements, the adoption of either of the following would call for the retention of a permanent garrison for a period which it is impossible to estimate:—

(vi)   Acquisition by Greece of Eastern Thrace.

(vii) Expulsion of the Turks from Constantinople.'

But so far from coming to any decision, the Allies were content in the presence of their differences to let matters slide. While the American Commission roamed disturbingly around the Middle East, the most fantastic plans for the partition of Turkey were indulged in. There were to be no annexations, but 'mandates' were to be granted to the principal Powers which would give them the necessary excuses for control. France was to take Syria and Cilicia; Italy blithely undertook to occupy the whole of the Caucasus as well as the province of Adalia in the Asia-Minor Promontory; England seemed anxious to take over Mesopotamia and Palestine which our armies already held; and there was a lively expectation that the United States would accept a mandate for Armenia. In January, 1920, Greece, which was bearing the brunt of these protracted financial, military and political uncertainties, began to show signs of strain.

In these seductive delusions the year 1919 ebbed away. Slowly, fitfully, laboriously, with frequent disputes and exhausting argument, the future of the Middle East was mapped out in Paris and a draft of the Treaty of Peace with Turkey prepared. Several exciting questions awaited the decision of the various Governments. December, 1919, and January, 1920, saw the British Cabinet deeply moved upon whether the Sultan in his capacity as Caliph should, under innumerable restrictions, be allowed to remain at Constantinople; or whether on the other hand the Turks should be expelled 'bag and baggage' from Europe. A secondary issue was whether the mosque of San Sophia should be reconsecrated a Christian Church. In these controversies Lord Curzon, mounted upon the Foreign Office, rode full tilt against Mr. Edwin Montagu, whose chariot was drawn by the public opinion of India, the sensibilities of the Mohammedan world, the pro-Turkish propensities of the Conservative Party, and the voluminous memoranda of the India Office.

The combat was well sustained. According to Mr. Montagu, the expulsion of the Turks and the Caliph from Constantinople with the assent or even with the connivance of England, would strike a last fatal blow at the diminishing loyalties of the two or three hundred peoples and religious sects who inhabit the Indian Peninsula. According to Lord Curzon they would not mind at all. Some would rather like it; most would be indifferent; while the Mohammedans, who were alone concerned, had not hesitated to fight with vigour and courage in various theatres of war against the armies of the said Caliph. On the question of the reconsecration of San Sophia, Mr. Montagu urged that it had been a Mohammedan Mosque of great sanctity for upwards of 469 years. We were all much swayed by this, until Lord Curzon rejoined that it had been previously a Christian Church for 915 years. Then the argument seemed very nicely balanced; a substantial modern title as against twice as lengthy an original prescription! This was one of those questions the rights and wrongs of which might well be debated by the university students of almost any country.

On the main issue of Constantinople Mr. Lloyd George was whole-heartedly with Lord Curzon. Indeed, on this he was himself a prime-mover. The War Office intervened with their dreary drone, voiced by Field-Marshal Wilson and me, that we had not got any soldiers, and how could you drive and keep the Turks out of Constantinople without soldiers? We continued with the India Office to ingeminate a Turkish peace, real, final, and above all, prompt. As long as the Dardanelles could be kept open for the free passage of the ships, including the warships, of all nations, we were content. That would entail the permanent occupation of both sides of the Straits by international forces, for which, within our limited means, our quota could be provided. Such an arrangement might in a few years become only an unchallenged formality.

These issues as they were fought out in the British Cabinet have already been made public quite as far as is proper in the *Life of Lord Curzon*.[6] It is not necessary to elaborate them here. An Anglo-French Conference was held in London at the Foreign Office at Christmas [1919] to settle the many thorny difficulties between the two Governments upon the Turkish and Arab problems. Mr. Lloyd George, so patient and good tempered a Chief, had a habit of picking his colleagues for any preliminary discussions so as to have a working majority of those who were favourable to his view. One set for one phase of a question and another for its complementary part! This was perhaps evil constitutional practice; but again it may have been the only way in these crowded times to get things done. When, however, the completed work came before the Cabinet on January 9, every Minister having a right to be present, an overwhelming majority decided after a far more spirited debate than is usually heard in the House of Commons, that the Turks should stay at Constantinople. The Prime Minister accepted in good part the decision of his colleagues, and the next day announced it to Parliament in a speech of convincing power.

The Treaty of Sèvres accordingly prescribed that Constantinople should remain the Turkish capital. For the rest the Bosphorus, the Marmora, and the Dardanelles were to be an open waterway under international guardianship for all vessels. Besides Western Thrace and Eastern Thrace almost up to the line of Chatalja, Greece should possess the Gallipoli Peninsula, the majority of the Ægean Islands, and should administer Smyrna and its hinterland until a plebiscite could be held there. Turkey must re-establish the capitulations and submit her armaments and finances to stringent Allied control. She should undertake to enforce the conventional safeguards for racial and religious minorities. The French were to have Syria, then in frantic ebullition; England would shoulder the costly and troublesome mandate of Palestine and Mesopotamia; and the Armenians were left to sit on the doorstep of the United States. Coincident with the signature of the Treaty of Sèvres and conditional upon its ratification, Great Britain, France and Italy put their names to a tripartite treaty which gave them as spheres of influence those territories which had been assigned to each of these Powers in the Sykes-Picot arrangement and at the conference of St. Jean de Maurienne.

While all these decrees were for the moment unannounced, we must observe the march of Facts. Over stony roads, through the defiles of thorny and rock-clad hills, across ochre deserts baking in the sun, the weary, sullen caravan of Facts kept pertinaciously jogging along. Let us return for a moment to them.

On January 12, 1920, the new Chamber of Turkish Deputies met in Constantinople. The Allies were loyal to the principle of representative government; accordingly the Turks had voted. Unhappily, they had almost all of them voted the wrong way. The new Chamber was preponderantly Nationalist, or, it might be said, Kemalist. So awkward was this that on January 21 the Allies required, as a measure of practical day to day security, the resignation of the Turkish Minister of War and of the Chief of the General Staff.

---

[6] By Lord Ronaldshay.

On the 28th the new Chamber approved and signed the 'National Pact.' Confronted by imminent revolt in Constantinople itself and with shocking possibilities of massacre, the European Allies were forced to united action. On March 16 Constantinople was occupied by British, French and Italian forces. Ferid was induced once again to brew the thinnest government he had yet attempted. At the end of April the Turkish National Assembly met at Angora far beyond the reach of Allied fleets and armies. On May 13—a bad date—Venizelos made public in Athens the terms of the Treaty of Sèvres. In June the British outpost line across the Ismid Peninsula was attacked by Kemalist forces. The attack was not serious. The troops were ordered to fire without hesitation; the Navy hurled shells from the Sea of Marmora, and the assailants withdrew out of range. But there they remained, and we were once again, this time with scanty forces, 'in the presence of the enemy.' At the same time the French, who, after driving Emir Feisal from his throne at Damascus, had encountered heavy fighting in Cilicia (and on the same day that the forthcoming terms of the Treaty of Sèvres were announced in Athens) thought well to ask the local Turks for an armistice.

Venizelos now presented himself as the good fairy. The Greek Army would come to the rescue. Two divisions of the five already in Smyrna would march northward, and passing to the east of the Marmora through difficult country (which, however, they declared they understood) would fall upon the Turks menacing the Ismid Peninsula and drive them away. Marshal Foch, carrying with him the opinion of the British General Staff, declared that the operation was dangerous and would probably be unsuccessful. Mr. Lloyd George, however, accepted the offer, and the Greek advance began on June 22. It was immediately successful. The Greek columns trailed along the country roads passing safely through many ugly defiles, and at their approach the Turks, under strong and sagacious leadership, vanished into the recesses of Anatolia. At the beginning of July the Greeks entered Brusa. In the same month another Greek army swiftly overran eastern Thrace, broke down a feeble Turkish resistance, and occupied Adrianople.

The remarkable and unexpected manifestations of Greek power were hailed by the Ally statesmen; the Ally generals rubbed their eyes; Mr. Lloyd George became enthusiastic. He was right again, it seemed, and the military men wrong, as they so often had been— *vide* Armageddon.

The events sealed the Treaty of Sèvres. Ferid dutifully constructed a Ministry of marionettes, and on August 10, 1920, with due solemnity, the Treaty of Peace with Turkey was signed at Sèvres. This instrument, which had taken eighteen months to fashion, was obsolete before it was ready. All its main clauses depended for their effect upon one thing only: the Greek Army. If Venizelos and his soldiers would clear up the situation and reduce Mustapha Kemal to law and order, all would be well. If not, some other form of words in closer conformity with the actual facts would have to be devised. At last peace with Turkey: and to ratify it, War with Turkey! However, so far as the Great Allies were concerned the war was to be fought by proxy. Wars when fought thus by great nations are often very dangerous for the proxy.

Although this chapter has dealt solely with Turkish affairs, it must be brought into relation with the general situation of Europe. I cannot do this better than by reprinting a letter which I wrote to Mr. Lloyd George on starting for a brief Easter holiday in France.

Mr. Churchill to the Prime Minister.

March 29, 1920.

I write this as I am crossing the Channel to tell you what is in my mind. Since the Armistice my policy would have been 'Peace with the German people, war on the Bolshevik tyranny.' Willingly or unavoidably, you have followed something very near the reverse. Knowing the difficulties, and also your great skill and personal force—so much greater than mine—I do not judge your policy and action as if I could have done better, or as if anyone could have done better. But we are now face to face with the results. They are terrible. We may well be within measurable distance of universal collapse and anarchy throughout Europe and Asia. Russia has gone into ruin. What is left of her is in the power of these deadly snakes. But Germany may perhaps still be saved. I have felt with a great sense of relief that we may be able to think and act together in harmony about Germany: that you are inclined to make an effort to rescue Germany from her frightful fate—which if it overtakes her may well overtake others. If so, time is short and action must be simple. You ought to tell France that we will make a defensive alliance with her against Germany if, *and only if*, she entirely alters her treatment of Germany and loyally accepts a British policy of help and friendship towards Germany. Next you should send a great man to Berlin to help consolidate the anti-Spartacist anti-Ludendorff elements into a strong left centre block. For this task you have two levers: firstly, food and credit, which must be generously accorded in spite of our own difficulties (which otherwise will worsen); secondly, early revision of the Peace Treaty by a Conference to which New Germany shall be invited as an equal partner in the rebuilding of Europe.[7] Using these levers it ought to be possible to rally all that is good and stable in the German nation to their own redemption and to the salvation of Europe. I pray that we may not be 'too late.'

Surely this is a matter far more worth while taking your political life in your hands for than our party combinations at home, important though they be. Surely also it is a matter which once on the move would dominate the whole world situation at home and abroad. My suggestion involves open resolute action by Britain under your guidance, and if necessary *independent* action. In such a course I would gladly at your side face political misfortune. But I believe there would be no misfortune, and that for a few months longer Britain still holds the title-deeds of Europe.

As a part of such a policy I should be prepared to make peace with Soviet Russia on the best terms available to appease the general situation, while safeguarding us from being poisoned by them. I do not of course believe that any real harmony is

---

[7]This of course referred to the economic and financial clauses.—W.S.C.

possible between Bolshevism and present civilisation. But in view of the existing facts a cessation of arms and a promotion of material prosperity are inevitable: and we must trust for better or for worse to peaceful influences to bring about the disappearance of this awful tyranny and peril.

Compared to Germany, Russia is minor: compared to Russia, Turkey is petty. But I am also very anxious about your policy towards Turkey. With military resources which the Cabinet have cut to the most weak and slender proportions, we are leading the Allies in an attempt to enforce a peace on Turkey which would require great and powerful armies and long, costly operations and occupations. On this world so torn with strife I dread to see you let loose the Greek armies— for all sakes and certainly for their sakes. Yet the Greek armies are your only effective fighting force. How are you going to feed Constantinople if the railways in Asia Minor are cut and supplies do not arrive? Who is going to pay? From what denuded market is the food to come? I fear you will have this great city lolling helplessly on your hands, while all around will be guerilla and blockade. Here again I counsel prudence and appeasement. Try to secure a really representative Turkish governing authority, and come to terms with it. As at present couched the Turkish Treaty means indefinite anarchy.

CHAPTER XVIII
GREEK TRAGEDY

A Retrospect—The Rise of Venizelos—Greece in the Great War—Constantine's Divine Right—The General Victory—Commitments in Thrace and Smyrna—The Young King—The Monkey's Bite—The Greek Election—Fall of Venizelos: Its Reactions—Return of Constantine—Isolation of Greece—Mr. Lloyd George's View—Curzon and Montagu—Unofficial Encouragement—My Own Position, February 22, June 11, and June 25—The Greek Advance—The Battle of Eskishehr—The Battle of the Sakaria—A Further Opportunity—Armenia and the Pan-Turks—The 1915 Massacres—The Turkish Conquest—The Friends of Armenia—Obliteration Once More.

This story carries us back to classic times. It is true Greek tragedy, with Chance as the ever ready hand-maid of Fate. However the Greek race might have altered in blood and quality, their characteristics were found unchanged since the days of Alcibiades. As of old, they preferred faction above all other interests, and as of old in their crisis they had at their head one of the greatest of men. The interplay between the Greek love of party politics and the influence exercised over them by Venizelos constitutes the action of the piece. The scene and the lighting are the Great War; and the theme, 'How Greece gained the Empire of her dreams in spite of herself, and threw it away when she awoke.' A prologue must be provided in the form of a retrospect.

In 1908 the Greek Monarchy was in dire straits. Ever since the King and the Princes had commanded in the disastrous war against Turkey in 1897, their situation had been uncomfortable. They were bitterly attacked by the officers of the Greek army, and there was a strong anti-Monarchical movement. It was proposed that they should not be allowed to hold any military command in case a war between the Balkan States and Turkey should break out. Many other similar humiliations were inflicted upon the reigning house. However, there arose in Crete a remarkable man moulded on classic scale and design. He effected the liberation of Crete from Turkey by a rebellion in which he gained the support of the Great Powers. By his energies and their aid Crete threw off the Turkish yoke, and as a stepping-stone to reunion with Greece, gained autonomy under a Greek Prince. In 1909 Venizelos passed from Crete to Greece; in 1910 he became Prime Minister. He purged and reformed the administration in all its branches. He reorganised the Fleet under British, and the Army under French guidance. He restored the King to the head of the army.

The Sovereign, having at his side this great Constable, swiftly regained popularity among the people. Greece enjoyed for some years the strongest of all political combinations for a small country, a constitutional monarch and a national leader, each working in his proper sphere, and rendering loyalty and honour to the other. Venizelos formed the Balkan League and prepared and inspired the war upon Turkey which followed in 1912. The Greeks, Serbs, and Bulgarians, helped greatly by the fighting quality of the last, defeated Turkey, took Adrianople and Salonika, and nearly took Constantinople itself. Great extensions of territory had already been gained by these allies. The Bulgarians, demanding too much and ever forward in quarrels, were fallen upon by their confederates on the one hand and by Roumania on the other. They were speedily overwhelmed by this combination, and were not only cut out of all territorial gains, but actually despoiled of their native province of the Dobrudja. In two years the kingdom of Greece was nearly doubled in extent and population. Crete was reunited with the Motherland, and not only Salonika, but Kavalla, was added to the Greek domain. Thus Constantine saw himself and his kingdom carried by an enormous stride towards the Greek dream of empire. At this point Armageddon began.

Earlier volumes have briefly described the attitude of Greece during the Great War. We may however display the claims of Venizelos upon the loyalty of the Allies. Constantine, married to the Kaiser's sister, and under a profound impression of German military prestige and efficiency, believed throughout that Germany would win. His convictions were shared by the Greek General Staff. But Venizelos judged by other standards. He proclaimed that right lay with the Allies; he discerned their future victory. 'England in all her wars,' he said in a dark hour, 'has always gained one battle—the last!' He acted upon these opinions. He so far persuaded and over-persuaded Constantine and his generals, that late in August 1914, *after* the French had lost the Battles of the Frontiers and before the victory of the Marne, when it seemed that the Germans were marching on irresistibly to the capture of Paris—at this very moment he offered the naval and military forces of Greece to the Allies from the time when Great Britain should judge it expedient to call upon them. He took this step in the face of the implacable resentment of Bulgaria for the Balkan war, and before Turkey had attacked the Allies. Such a resolve, taken with sureness and deliberation in the teeth of such hazards by an experienced and established statesman, proves a prevision beyond compare.

The story of the Dardanelles shows that Venizelos would always have been ready to participate in a well-planned attack by land and sea upon the Gallipoli Peninsula. British diplomacy, influenced to some extent by Russian misgivings, had rejected the Greek offer of assistance in the preceding autumn, and unless Constantine had been irrevocably committed to war against Germany, it seemed impossible to make the Greek Government a party to our plans. The melancholy course of events at the Dardanelles and the incapacity which they revealed did not weaken the fidelity of Venizelos to the Allies. When the peril of Serbia by Bulgarian invasion drew nearer in the summer of 1915, he invoked the Treaty binding Greece to come to the aid of Serbia and thus join in the general war. Constantine resisted. Venizelos resigned. As a result of a general election held in June he was returned to power on August 23. He obtained from the King authority for general mobilisation. Further than this Constantine would not go; he refused definitely to enter the war. According to Venizelos, he explained this overriding of his Prime Minister newly fortified by a national mandate as follows: 'I recognise that I am bound to obey the popular verdict when it is a question of internal affairs; but when it is a question of foreign affairs my view is that so long as I consider a thing right or wrong I must insist that it shall or shall not be done, because I feel responsible before God.' This would seem strange Constitutional doctrine, and it is also doubtful whether the Almighty draws a distinction between domestic and external affairs as such. Confronted with the Royal refusal Venizelos wished to resign, but he withdrew his resignation under pressure from the King, and at the same time invited the Allies to send troops to the rescue of Serbia through Salonika. Ever afterwards Venizelos swore that Constantine had consented to this, and ever afterwards Constantine swore to the contrary. The Allied troops arrived at Salonika, and Venizelos in his struggle with the King was forced to protest against their disembarkation. Simultaneously, however, he made a speech to the Chamber claiming publicly for the first time that the Greco-Serbian Treaty imposed an absolute obligation upon Greece to make war on Bulgaria and Turkey. Though still supported by a majority in the Chamber, he was dismissed from office by the King.

The third phase of the dispute between King and Minister was armed revolt. Venizelos in September 1916 quitted Greece for Crete, where he set up a Provisional Government. Thence he descended upon Salonika, where a Revolutionary government had already been instituted. Here he raised a Greek army in support of the Allies. The accession of the United States to the Allied cause produced a strong effect upon Greek public opinion. There was less dread even in Royalist circles of being left at the end of the war on the side of a beaten England in the face of a triumphant and remorseless Germany and revengeful Bulgaria. In June 1917, everyone being desperate, and the Greek situation increasingly favourable, the French, with keen British approval, occupied Athens and drove Constantine into exile. From that moment Venizelos controlled again the fortunes of Greece, and from that moment Greece shared the fortunes of the Allies. Greek divisions fought on the Salonika front; Greek war-ships joined the Allied Fleet; Allied munitions and credits flowed into Greece during the war, and Venizelos carried his country to the Council Board of the victors after the Armistice. His personal qualities, his prestige, the famous services he had rendered the Allies, secured him a position almost of equality with the heads of the greatest victorious states; and with him his country mounted to dizzy heights and surveyed dazzling horizons.

Meanwhile Constantine brooded in exile, and the Greek politicians, who, if they had had their way, would have kept their country out of all share in the victory or indeed involved it in defeat, awaited morosely the hour of revenge.

* * * * *

It had seemed in Paris that the policy of Britain, France, and the United States would be to develop substantially the power and extent of Greece. They certainly showed themselves ready to use her. We have seen how Greek divisions were called upon to accompany the French in their ignominious incursion into the Ukraine; how they were authorized and encouraged to overrun and occupy Thrace; and above all, how they were launched into the fatal descent upon Smyrna. Venizelos had shown himself more than apt to obey these high commands; and although the Greek armies had been mobilised almost continuously for ten years, they seemed at this time to be the only troops who would go anywhere or do anything. Thus by the summer of 1919 the Greek forces were widely spread and deeply committed on Turkish soil. Venizelos returning to Athens in December was received with enthusiasm; but signs of strain—social, military, and economic—were already to be discerned in the structure of this small State and people.

When in 1920, in the advent of the Treaty of Sèvres, Sir Henry Wilson and I expressed the British military view upon the Greek situation, the Prime Minister asked us to see Venizelos ourselves and to lay before him our misgivings. This we did with candour, asking such questions as: How much is it costing you a day? How long have the soldiers been away from their families? What prospect is there of a real peace with Turkey? and so on. We pointed out that though, or even if, the Greek troops could beat the Turks in their present condition in battle, this would mean for him no extrication from his danger. The Kemalist Turks, a handful of ragged warriors fighting under barbaric conditions, could compel the maintenance of very large numbers of organised troops on a war footing overseas at heavy expense for an indefinite period. 'It is costing *them* nothing, but how long can *you* keep it up?' Venizelos rejoined that the Greek troops stood where they were in response to the requests of Lloyd George, Clemenceau and President Wilson. He admitted the inequality of the warfare, but professed his confidence that with the support of the three greatest Powers he would reach a satisfactory and final conclusion. Almost immediately after this discussion he occupied Thrace, capturing or dispersing the two weak Turkish divisions which were still in the province, and entered Adrianople. We were agreeably surprised by these events, but by no means relieved from our general anxieties. There followed the Treaty of Sèvres.

A similar swift success had attended the northward advance of the Greek forces from the Smyrna Province to drive away the Turks who were molesting the French and British lines across the Ismid Peninsula. Although both Foch and Wilson had advised against it, this operation was executed by two Greek divisions with ease and celerity, and with results extremely gratifying to the British, French, and American political chiefs. There is no doubt that these episodes aroused in Mr. Lloyd George's mind a confidence in Greek military power agreeable to his inclinations. The result however was only to spread the Greek forces over wider areas and burden them with heavier responsibilities. So long as Greece was acting as the capable and willing assistant and informal mandatory of the three greatest Powers, there was a solid and, if need be, an ample backing behind her far-spread lines. But now there occurred one of those apparitions of the unexpected without which no Greek tragedy could unfold itself.

The Treaty of Sèvres was signed on August 10, 1920. Venizelos arrived in Athens in September, bringing home with him for the fourth time in his career the immense gains of triumphant war and policy. The admiration of the welcoming crowds was stimulated by his narrow escape a few weeks before from murder in a Paris railway station. He had carried his country, largely in spite of herself, to the highest pinnacle she has ever scaled in modern times. Great stakes were still on the board, entangling commitments still gripped the armies and finances of Greece; but there seemed no reason why, sustained by the aid of the mightiest nations and their renowned leaders, the problems of the future should prove more formidable than those Venizelos had already successfully surmounted in the past.

When in June, 1917, King Constantine had been driven into exile by the imperious finger of M. Jonnart, the French High Commissioner, supported by French Marines and Allied naval power, his second son Alexander had been set up in his stead. This amiable youth, the victim of fate as well as of policy, had reigned for more than three years. Before the world storm swept him to the throne he had fallen in love with an attractive young lady, Mlle Mânos, the daughter of a small Court official whose family history was by regal standards not particularly impressive. King Alexander would never have hesitated for a moment in a choice between his love and his throne; and since his morganatic marriage with Mlle Mânos in November, 1919, Venizelos had had to face a series of delicate and embarrassing political issues on this account. However, the statesman sympathised profoundly with the young couple, and amid the labours and excitements of treaty-making and the dark but distant clouds that lowered upon the Greek fronts, he made skilful exertions on their behalf. Constitutional niceties were in a fair way to adjustment, and at the time of Venizelos' home-coming it seemed that within the widened boundaries of the new Greek Empire there might well be room for a royal romance.

On October 2, 1920, King Alexander, walking in the garden accompanied by his spaniel, paused to watch the antics of a pair of monkeys comprised among the less disciplined pets of the royal Palace. The spaniel attacked the female monkey, and the male in retaliation attacked the King. It bit him in the leg. The wound, though peculiarly painful, was not judged serious by the physicians. But the bite festered, inflammation became acute, more dangerous symptoms supervened, and after three weeks of agony King Alexander expired in the arms of his bride who might soon have become his Consort.

We have already seen how the escape of a single capital ship, the *Goeben*, spread measureless desolation through the south-east of Europe and through Asia Minor. It is perhaps no exaggeration to remark that a quarter of a million persons died of this monkey's bite.

The Greek Constitution did not specifically prescribe that a General Election should follow a demise of the Crown; but the question of a successor was embarrassing. Venizelos seems to have toyed with the idea of crowning the infant son of Mme Mânos, with a consequential prolonged regency. It was however eventually decided to offer the throne to Prince Paul of Greece. Paul was living in Switzerland under the roof of his exiled father, and no doubt was inspired to reply that he could only accept after the Greek people had at an election definitely decided against, both his father and his elder brother, Prince George. This forced a General Election.

Venizelos in no way shirked the issue. Buoyed by the evidences of his popularity and by the conviction that he had deserved well of the Greek people, he was willing that the issue should be put crudely to the electorate: Were they for the restoration of Constantine or not? It followed from this that all the supporters of the ex-King were free to return from exile or retirement and take an active part in the election. It might well have seemed that there could not be much doubt about the public choice upon the issue 'Constantine *versus* Venizelos' at a moment when the former was stultified and the latter vindicated by world events. But the imperious Cretan did not make sufficient allowances for the strain to which his small country had been put; for the resentments which the Allied Blockade to make Greece enter the war had deeply planted; for the many discontents which arise under prolonged war conditions; for the oppressive conduct of many of his agents; for the complete absorption of his political opponents in party politics and for their intense desire for office and revenge. During his enforced and continuous absence in Paris and London, the Greek people had lacked his personal inspiration and had felt the heavy hands of his subordinates. No one of authority in Greece or out of it seemed to doubt that a substantial Venizelist majority would be returned. But the election results which came in during the evening of November 14 were a staggering surprise for all. Venizelos himself was unseated, and his followers commanded only 114 seats against an opposition of 250. Greek Party Politics are conducted in a high-pitched key. Venizelos at once announced that he would resign and leave the country; and he remained unmoved even by the poignant argument that he would be accused of running away and leaving his friends to be massacred. He declared that his presence could only be a cause of unrest and disorder. He placed his resignation in the hands of his old friend Admiral Condouriotis, indicated his successor, and quitted Greece for Italy on November 17 in a friend's yacht. Thus incontinently did the Greek people at the moment of their greatest hopes and fears deprive themselves of the commanding personality who had created the situation and by whom alone it might have been carried to success.

I happened to be with Mr. Lloyd George in the Cabinet Room at the time the telegram announcing the results of the Greek election and Venizelos's decision arrived. He was very much shocked, and still more puzzled. But with his natural buoyancy and hardened by the experiences we had all passed through in the Great War, he contented himself with remarking, with a grin, 'Now I am the only one left.'[1]

The reactions of the fall of Venizelos must be closely studied by those who wish to follow the chain of events. Greece, though only a small state beset with difficulties and foes, indulged the dangerous luxury of a dual nature. There was the pro-Ally Greece of Venizelos and the pro-German Greece of Constantine. All the loyalties of the Allies began and ended with the Greece of Venizelos. All their resentments centred upon the Greece of Constantine. The ex-King was a bugbear second only to the Kaiser himself in the eyes of the British and French people, and he ranked in Allied estimation with the so-called 'Foxy' Ferdinand of Bulgaria. Here was a potentate who, against the wishes and the interests of his people,—as we saw it—had for personal and family reasons thrown his country, or tried to throw it, on the enemy side, which had also turned out to be the losing side. It would be absurd to ask the British or French democracy to make sacrifices or efforts for a people whose real spirit was shown by their choice of such

---

[1] President Wilson had been struck down by illness, Clemenceau had retired, and Orlando had been defeated.

a man. The return of Constantine therefore dissolved all Allied loyalties to Greece and cancelled all but legal obligations. In England, the feeling was not resentment, but a total extinction of sympathy or even interest. In France, a stronger displeasure was reinforced by other practical considerations. We have seen how the French were involved in difficulties with the Arabs in Syria and with the Turks in Cilicia. For the sake of Venizelos much had to be endured, but for Constantine less than nothing. Indeed, after the first astonishment had worn off an air of relief became manifest in controlling circles. There was no need any more to pursue an anti-Turkish policy. On the contrary, good relations with Turkey would be most conducive to French interests. The situation in the Levant could be relieved, and other positive advantages presented themselves. If Greece was free, everyone was free. Greece had in fact become a liberator. Just at the moment when her needs were greatest and her commitments were becoming most embarrassing to herself and to others, she had of her own free will sponged the slate. It is not every day that moral creditors are so accommodating.

Lord Curzon, voicing the cool and dispassionate view of the Foreign Office, proposed a conditional support of Greece and even the recognition of Constantine; but the Allied Conference which met in Paris on December 3 brushed such plans aside. The three Great Powers informed the Greek Government that 'although they had not wished to interfere in the internal affairs of Greece, the restoration to the throne of a King whose disloyal attitude and conduct towards the Allies during the War caused them great embarrassment and loss, could only be regarded by them as a ratification by Greece of his hostile acts'; that 'this step would create a new and unfavourable situation in the relations between Greece and the Allies'; and that 'the three Governments reserved to themselves in that case complete liberty in dealing with the situation thus created.' And on the next day they declared in a second note that 'if Constantine returned to the throne, Greece would receive no further financial assistance of any kind from the Allies.'

In the teeth of this declaration, but much intimidated by the victorious monarchists, the Greeks by an almost unanimous plebiscite voted for the recall of Constantine. At the end of December King Constantine and Queen Sophie and their children re-entered Athens, amid the same demonstrative rejoicings of the populace as had recently saluted Venizelos. Meanwhile the new Government busied themselves in expelling from every form of public employment all Venizelist officials, from Bishops, judges, university professors, and schoolmasters, down even to the charwomen in the public offices. The Allied Ministers remained in Athens under instructions to carry on formal relations with the Government, but to ignore the King, the Royal Family, and the Court. Henceforward Greece, riven internally, was to face her perils alone.

The only rational object in expelling Venizelos and the only sane policy arising from it would have been to reduce promptly and ruthlessly the Greek commitments in Asia Minor. It was arguable that the great Cretan had ridden his small country too hard; certainly it had thrown him during the triumphal procession. Now, stripped of British support and confronted by Italian rivalries, and by what was soon to become marked French antagonism, one course alone was open to Constantine and his Ministers. Peace with Turkey on the best terms obtainable; the swift abandonment of every position in

Asia Minor; the repatriation and demobilisation of the armies; and the most drastic financial economies, were the logical and inevitable consequences of the decision which the Greek people had been invited to take and which they had taken. But these were the very decisions which the new régime was least inclined to take. They were in temper more expansionist than Venizelos himself. The military and political circles which rallied round the Court pulsated with ambition. They would now show Greece how little Venizelos had had to do with her successes. The idea that they should give up what he had so surprisingly gained was intolerable to their pride as it would have been fatal to their popularity. They proposed on the contrary to secure extensions of Greek territory in Asia Minor beyond anything Venizelos had deemed possible: they adopted the cry of "To Constantinople" to express their ultimate goal. Thus, when the Allies met in Paris on February 21, 1921, with timely if harsh resolve to revise the Treaty of Sèvres, particularly in respect of Smyrna and Thrace, the new Greek Government rejected their proposals and declared that Greece was herself capable of holding unaided the territories awarded her by the Treaty. At this moment, Greece was maintaining 200,000 troops in Asia Minor at a cost of at least a quarter of a million a week. The Turks, in friendly negotiation with the French and encouraged by a Treaty with Moscow, were growing constantly and rapidly in numbers and fighting power.

Only pity must be felt for the mass of the Greek people at this point in their history. They were set tasks beyond their strength; they were asked questions which they were not competent to answer; they had no knowledge of the consequences inherent in the decisions they were led to take. They had endured a longer strain of war, mobilisation, and war-government than almost any other people in a war-wearied world. They were torn and baffled by faction; there were two hostile nations in the bosom of one small harassed state; and even under these distracting conditions their armies maintained for a long period remarkable discipline and constancy. They were now to be launched upon an adventure at once more ambitious and more forlorn than any which we have yet described.

* * * * *

The third act of the Greek Tragedy must begin with a description of the attitude of some personalities in British politics. Being in complete disagreement with Mr. Lloyd George on Turco-Greek affairs, but preserving always an intimate and free intercourse with him, I on more than one occasion during these years invited him to state the foundations of his policy. He declared them, with his usual good humour and tolerance of the opinion of a colleague, in these terms, and more or less in these words. 'The Greeks are the people of the future in the Eastern Mediterranean. They are prolific and full of energy. They represent Christian civilisation against Turkish barbarism. Their fighting power is grotesquely underrated by our generals. A greater Greece will be an invaluable advantage to the British Empire. The Greeks by tradition, inclination, and interest are friendly to us; they are now a nation of five or six millions, and in fifty years, if they can hold the territories which have been assigned to them, they will be a nation of twenty millions. They are good sailors; they will develop a naval power; they will possess all the most important islands in the Eastern Mediterranean. These islands are the potential submarine bases of the future; they lie on the flank of our communications through the Suez Canal with India, the Far East, and Australasia. The Greeks have a strong sense of gratitude, and if we are the staunch friends of Greece at the period of her national expansion she will become one of the guarantees by which the main inter-communications of the British Empire can be preserved. One day the mouse may gnaw the cords that bind the lion.' To which I replied in effect and at suitable intervals, 'If this is so, what are you going to do about it? You have no armies which can be sent; you are always saying there is no money which can be spared; you have no public opinion which will support you. The Conservative party is the traditional friend of Turkey. The bias of your majority is pro-Turk; the bias of your Cabinet is pro-Turk; the bias of your generals is pro-Turk. We are the greatest Mohammedan power in the world. Very deep oppositions will arise to any prolonged anti-Turkish or pro-Greek policy. Moreover, the Turks are very dangerous, because they are both fierce and unget-at-able. If the Greeks try to conquer Turkey they will be ruined, and now that Constantine has come back you will never be allowed to help them effectively.' I cannot pretend that this records the dialogue, but it is in my opinion a fair representation of two different points of view.

Lord Curzon's line was broadly that a very cool, circumspect, but not unhelpful policy should be adopted towards the Greeks; that a friendly peace should be made with Turkey; but that at all costs the Turks should be expelled from Europe and Constantinople. Mr. Montagu, supported by all the forces which represent India, was for peace with Turkey on almost any terms; England should be the friend and head of the Moslem world; and above all, Constantinople should be restored to the Turks. The Cabinet, as has been described, resolved against the Prime Minister and Lord Curzon upon Constantinople, and both these Ministers accepted the decision. But upon action, either to help the Greeks or to pacify the Turks, no coherent policy could be formulated, except the purely negative one of using neither British troops nor money and waiting upon events. This stagnation and arrest lasted for nearly two years, from the fall of Venizelos to the crisis of Chanak.

But we are here concerned with the fortunes of the Greeks. There is no doubt that under the restored Constantine they made an intense and persevering national effort. Had they enjoyed the support in credit, munitions, and goodwill of the Great Powers, no one can say for certain that they could not have enforced a peace upon the Kemalist Turks, which would have secured them Thrace and a footing in Smyrna. Without any of these aids they now proceeded to seek this peace at Angora with the sword.

The question from which so many heartburnings and reproaches have arisen, is whether the British Prime Minister gave them personal and unwarranted encouragement in this enterprise. It is quite certain that according to all the canons of official diplomacy they received no encouragement from His Majesty's Government. They assuredly were warned and discouraged on every opportunity and through every available channel by the British War Office and General Staff. But of course they knew that the Prime Minister's heart was with them and that he ardently desired their victory. Lloyd George was the only Englishman known in Greece, and he appeared to their eyes as the successor of

Canning and Gladstone. His achievements in the Great War, his prestige in Europe, his unquestioned mastery at the time in England, his own resourcefulness and will power, his known and evident partisanship, created in Greek minds a sense of vague but potent confidence. Although, thought they, nothing definite has been said and no agreement has been made, the great man is with us, and in his own way and in his own time and by his own wizardry he will bring us the vital aid we need.

Now this was the worst of all possible situations. The Greeks deserved at the least either to be backed up through thick and thin with the moral, diplomatic and financial support of a united British Government, or to be chilled to the bone with repeated douches of cold water. But all sorts of other things, Ireland, for instance, and British party disturbances, were in progress at the same time. So much was going on in the world, and difficulties so abounded, that the affairs of one small country about which such differences of opinion arose were only considered spasmodically as events happened, and even then without any clear decision emerging. After all, Constantine and his Government had acted on their own responsibility. They were entitled to form their own view of what the eventual action of any of the Great Powers towards their enterprise would be; but they alone were the party who had to decide, and it was their skins in the first place that were at stake. The sentimental support of an eminent man may be a powerful encouragement, but it is no substitute for treaties, agreements, or formal diplomatic communications.

However, on June 11 King Constantine in person assumed the command at Smyrna, and in July the fourth Greek attack upon the Turks in Asia Minor began.

* * * * *

I feel entitled at this point to set forth my own view and action. I have been freely represented as the advocate of violent policies in every quarter and on every occasion, and so far I have never attempted any detailed explanation of my course. Lord Curzon's able biographer, with the fullest knowledge of the official archives and much freedom in their use, has suggested not obscurely that the words 'firebrand' and 'warmonger' may be justly applied to me in this connexion. I shall therefore make the facts plain.

I must begin by reminding the reader of the general statement of policy set forth by the General Staff upon my authority in December, 1919, which has been summarised in Chapter XVII; and secondly, to my letter to the Prime Minister of March, 1920, printed on page 257. The following are the views which I put on record on February 22, 1921, at the time of the Allied Conference upon the revision of the Treaty of Sèvres, and again on June 11, 1921, before the Greeks started their march to Angora:—

Mr. Churchill to the Prime Minister

Feb. 22, 1921.

I did not want to renew the argument about policy this morning. You have the power to decide the British policy, and I can only wait anxiously for the results. The kind of people whose opinions on the questions at issue ought to weigh with you are the following: The Viceroy and Government of India: George Lloyd, the

Governor of Bombay: the Viceroy-Designate of India: Ld Allenby and Sir Percy Cox: the officials of the new Middle-Eastern Department, Mr. Shuckburgh, Col. Lawrence, Major Young: the General Staff, in all its branches and representatives: the High Commissioner at Constantinople and Gen. Harington: Montagu, with his special position and knowledge: true and proved friends of Britain like the Aga Khan. I have yet to meet a British official personage who does not think that our Eastern and Middle Eastern affairs would be enormously eased and helped by arriving at a peace with Turkey. The alternative of the renewal of war causes me the deepest misgivings. I dare say the Greeks may scatter the Turkish Nationalists on their immediate front, and may penetrate some distance into Turkey; but the more country they hold, and the longer they remain in it, the more costly to them. The reactions from this state of affairs fall mainly upon us, and to a lesser extent on the French. They are all unfavourable. The Turks will be thrown into the arms of the Bolsheviks; Mesopotamia will be disturbed at the critical period of the reduction of the Army there; it will probably be quite impossible to hold Mosul and Bagdad without a powerful and expensive army; the general alienation of Mohammedan sentiment from Great Britain will continue to work evil consequences in every direction; the French and Italians will make their own explanations; and we shall be everywhere represented as the chief enemy of Islam. Further misfortunes will fall upon the Armenians.

In these circumstances it seems to me a fearful responsibility to let loose the Greeks and to reopen the war. I am deeply grieved at the prospect, and at finding myself so utterly without power to influence your mind even in regard to matters with which my duties are specially concerned. All the more am I distressed because of my desire to aid you in any way open to me in the many matters in which we are agreed, and because of our long friendship and my admiration for your genius and work.

In the early part of June the Prime Minister held a conference at Chequers, at which we agreed in principle upon putting pressure equally upon both sides to come to a settlement.

Mr. Churchill to the Prime Minister

June 11, 1921.

I have had a talk this morning with Venizelos. I explained to him the conclusions of our conference at Chequers, and he was in agreement with them. I agree with you that we should say to Constantine—'Here are the terms which we think should be offered to Kemal now. If you accept them we will put them before Kemal, if possible in conjunction with France. We should tell Kemal that if he refuses them, we shall help the Greeks in every possible way, and that if the Greeks gain a success the terms will have to be altered proportionately to Kemal's disadvantage.' We should further tell Constantine that he should delay his offensive until he has reorganised his army by the reinstatement of competent Venizelist Generals. If he agrees with all that we ask of him, both in the matter of the terms to the Turks and in the matter of reorganising the army, and if Kemal continues obdurate so that the arrangements with Constantine actually come into effect, we should not hesitate to recognise him. If unhappily we are forced to work with this man and with the Greeks, there is no sense in not doing everything possible to secure success. Half-measures and half-hearted support have been the bane of all the policy we have pursued, whether towards Russia or Turkey, since the Armistice, and they have conducted us to our present disastrous position.

As to the terms, I think they must include the evacuation of Smyrna by the Greek Army. I do not think anything less than that gives a fair chance of winning French co-operation or of procuring Kemalist agreement. The question of the guarantees to be taken either by a local force or by an international force for the protection of the lives of the Christians need not be finally decided at this stage, but I agree with you that effective guarantees must be obtained to prevent massacre.

I do not think there is any time to lose. If the Greeks go off on another half-cock offensive, the last card will have been played and lost and we shall neither have a Turkish peace nor a Greek army.

In taking the line I am now doing on the Greco-Turkish problem, I am sure you will understand that my view as to the objective at which we are aiming has never altered. It has always been and it is still, the making of a peace with Turkey which shall be a real peace and one achieved at the earliest possible moment. I entirely disagree, as you know and as I have repeatedly placed on record, with the whole policy of the Treaty of Sèvres, and the results which have arisen from it have been those which I have again and again ventured to predict. But in the difficult situation in which we now stand I am doing my utmost to find a way out of our embarrassments which will not leave us absolutely defenceless before an exultant and unreasonable antagonist.

And again by official minute of June 25, 1921:—

Prime Minister.
Lord Curzon.

June 25, 1921.

If it be true, as seems probable from the newspapers, that the Greeks are going to refuse our offer of mediation, I do earnestly hope we shall not hesitate to make our policy effective. If they go on against the wishes of England and France and without any moral support, and get beaten or at the very best entangled, our affairs will suffer terribly, as we shall have an absolutely unreasonable Kemal to deal with. I am sure the path of courage is the path of safety. The Prime Minister said the other day at Cabinet that he would agree to any even-handed policy as regards the two sides. I think we should ask the French whether they will join with us in letting the Greeks know that unless they put themselves in our hands as we suggested, we shall definitely intervene to stop the war by blockading Smyrna to Greek ships. This threat is bound to be decisive, as what can they do? Nor will it cost us anything, as the Mediterranean Fleet is overwhelmingly strong and is in the Mediterranean already. I think everybody here would approve of our stopping the war. As the counterpart to this, we should make it clear to the Greeks that if they do put themselves in our hands and Kemal is unreasonable we will give them effective support, including the full use of the naval blockade weapon against the Turks.

I am deeply alarmed at the idea of the Greeks starting off in a disheartened manner on this new offensive. It may produce irretrievable disaster if it fails. It simply means that all the policy we agreed upon at Chequers comes to nought. I may add that if the French decline to participate in the naval blockade, either of Greece or Turkey as the case may be, I should still be in favour of our going on alone, as we are fully possessed of the means to do all that is necessary and to do it quite quickly.

However, the Greek Army was already marching steadily forward through harsh and difficult country to engage in the greatest campaign undertaken by Greece since classic times. This episode deserves a more detailed description than it has usually received.

Before the initial movements the Greeks were assembled in two groups.[2] The right or southern, consisting of seven divisions and a cavalry brigade (32,000 rifles and 1,000 sabres), concentrated near Ushak on the railway; the left or northern, of four divisions (about 18,000 rifles) gathered at Brusa. The interval of about forty miles between these two important forces was covered by a line of posts which stretched from the coast of the Marmora to the south of Smyrna. The Turks were also arranged in two groups: the Northern of six divisions and three cavalry divisions, comprising 23,000 rifles (the cavalry being mounted infantry) between Eskishehr on the railway and the Marmora; and the Southern group of ten divisions and two cavalry divisions, comprising 25,000 rifles, the greater part around Kutaya on the railway but extending as far as Afium Karahissar and beyond. The Greeks were slightly superior in numbers—51,000 against 48,000. They had also an advantage of three to two in guns and eight to three in machine guns, and were better provided with aeroplanes and technical stores. The Turks had however another three divisions (8,000 rifles) in reserve behind Angora, and two divisions (5,000 rifles) to the south-east in Cilicia, and three more divisions and two cavalry divisions (6,500 rifles) 170 miles east of Angora in the Amasia area.

The Greek object was to destroy the Turkish Army and to occupy Angora, but as the Smyrna-Angora railway, which was the only railway line available for the campaign, departing from its general east and west direction, ran roughly north and south behind the Turkish front between Afium Karahissar and Eskishehr, it was necessary as a first step to drive the Turks from this sector, annihilating them if possible, before the advance on Angora could be executed. The operations were begun by a feint.

---

[2] See plan on page 256 and the general map of Turkey facing p. 301.

On July 9 the Greek left group moved 2 divisions eastward from Brusa to hold the Turkish northern group to its position, whilst the other 2 marched south-eastward towards Kutaya to co-operate with the right wing of the army. Three days later 3 divisions of the Greek right group attacked the Turks at Afium Karahissar and defeated them. The clearing of the railway to Eskishehr was now begun. Leaving one division at Afium Karahissar, the rest of the right group and the 2 divisions of the left which had come southward closed on Kutaya, drove off the Turks and entered it on the 17th. The Turks retreated on and beyond Eskishehr, which the Greeks occupied on the 20th. King Constantine reached the front on this day from Athens to take command in person. On the 21st the Turks made a general attack. They were counter-attacked and repulsed all along the line, and retired 30 miles on a position behind the Sakaria river, 50 miles from Angora and covering the approach to their capital.

The Greeks had gained a strategic and tactical success; they had gained possession of the railway for the further advance; but they had not destroyed the Turkish army or any part of it. The losses on both sides in killed and wounded were about the same, 7,000 to 8,000; but the Turks had in addition lost 4,000 prisoners.

A short pause followed during which both armies reorganised and prepared themselves for the next phase. The Greeks improved their rail and road communications. They repaired their rolling-stock and strengthened their road transport by collecting about 500 lorries, 2,000 camels and 3,000 ox carts. Mustapha Kemal, poorer at all points than his opponents in transports and supply, called upon the wives and daughters of his soldiers to do the work of the camels and oxen which he lacked. During the lull files of Turkish women carried food and water and other supplies from innumerable villages, and concentrated them to the east of the great bend in the Sakaria river on which their national guide and ruler had resolved to stand.

The Greeks resumed the advance on August 10, after detaching a second division to the Afium Karahissar front. They had now a total force of 73,000 rifles of which 50,000 were available for the offensive. The Turks had 70,000 rifles of which 44,000 were assembled on the Sakaria river, but 8,000 more from Cilicia were approaching by rail and march. Unmoved by the Greek success at Eskishehr, the Allies at Paris decided on the 14th to maintain neutrality.

Battle was joined on the 24th. The Greek plan had originally been to turn the Turkish position from the south, but at the last moment as the Turks were shifting men from their right to the left, a change was made and it was decided to break the Turkish centre in the direction of Yapan Hammam. Nevertheless it was on the southern flank that the first and most progress was made, and this enabled the centre and left to get forward. In ten days of fighting, during which their line of communications was raided by the Turks, and they suffered from want of ammunition, food, and even water, the Greeks gradually pressed back the Turks some ten miles, and but for the failure of the administrative arrangements would probably have inflicted on them the signal defeat which was confidently expected. But by September 4 their effort was exhausted; both sides indeed had fought practically to a standstill and had used up all their reserves. The fighting had been fierce and bloody. The Greeks had lost 18,000 men, the Turks not quite so many but again many prisoners.

BATTLE OF ESKISHEHR–JULY 9th to 20th 1921.

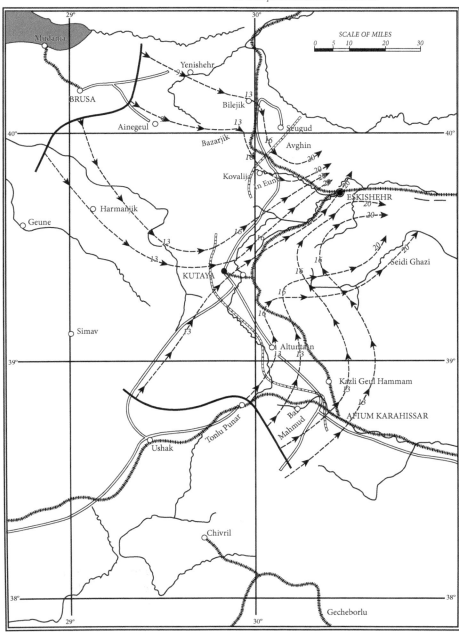

Both armies were in being, nearly equal in numbers, and after rest fit to continue the contest. But the Greeks had involved themselves in a politico-strategic situation where anything short of decisive victory was defeat: and the Turks were in a position where anything short of overwhelming defeat was victory. No aspect of this was hidden from the warrior-chief who led the Turks.

Until September 9 both sides were busy reorganising; but on that day Kemal after being in doubt as to whether the Greeks were merely resting, preparing for a fresh attack, or retiring, came to the conclusion that their offensive had come to an end, and ordered a general counter-attack.

The Greeks resisted stubbornly with success, but the strategic situation was too perilous and on the evening of September 11 King Constantine decided to retire to the west of the Sakaria river. The withdrawal was skilfully executed; but it proclaimed the failure of the Greek campaign. The armies remained in presence astride the railway on a line running south from Eskishehr.

* * * * *

Now again there was a chance for intervention. I circulated the following printed Memorandum:—

GREECE AND TURKEY

September 26, 1921.

The serious reverse which the Greeks have sustained in their attempt to take Angora should add another to the long series of opportunities which have occurred for making a good settlement in the East. It will indeed be disgraceful if we do not make a real effort now to secure such a settlement. The waste and ruin by which the whole of this part of the East is ravaged and its reaction upon the general impoverishment of the world is in itself a sufficient reason.

Is it not, therefore, the very moment now for decided intervention to secure a settlement, whether for the sake of Greece or for the sake of Turkey? It may well be that this further spell of bloody and disappointing fighting may have induced the wish for peace on both sides. Mustapha Kemal may no longer be in the unreasonable mood in which the Bekir Sami negotiations were conducted, and the Greeks must be getting nearer and nearer to bankruptcy and revolution. Now is the time to address ourselves to both sides in the mood which we had reached before the Greek resumption of the offensive. No doubt the terms proposed would have to be remodelled. But having decided ourselves what we think is reasonable, we ought to press upon both sides to the utmost limit of our force, not excluding a blockade of the Piræus if Greece is unreasonable, or direct assistance in money and supplies to her if Turkey is unreasonable. We seem to have done absolutely nothing during the last three months but watch the progress of this disastrous conflict, and if we continue in this attitude we shall certainly find ourselves formidably disturbed in Mesopotamia.

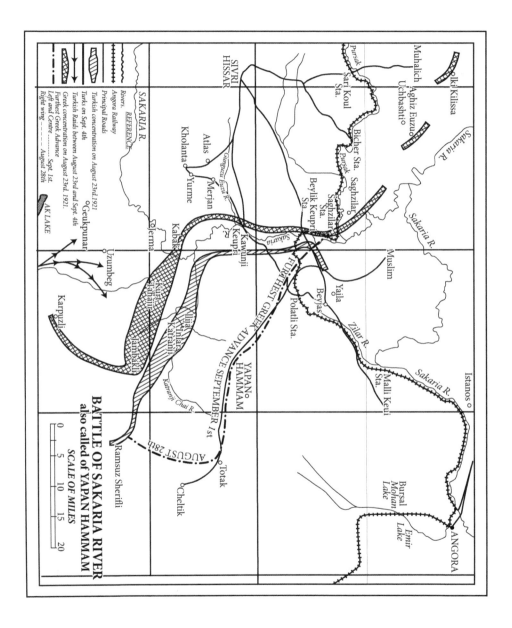

BATTLE OF SAKARIA RIVER
also called of YAPAN HAMMAM

SCALE OF MILES

0   5   10   15   20

REFERENCE

Rivers.
Angora Railway
Principal Roads
Turkish concentration on August 23rd 1921.
Turks on Sept. 4th
Turkish Raids between August 23rd and Sept. 4th
Greek concentration on August 23rd 1921.
Furthest Greek Advance
Left and Centre — — — — Sept. 1st.
Right wing — — — August 28th

SAKARIA R.

But nothing was done, and for a while nothing happened. We entered a period of false calm. There was a pause in the march of events; an interlude in discussion; a gap in policy. The next chapter will explain how the gap was filled: but before the final blows are struck, it will be convenient to outline however briefly the subsidiary Armenian Tragedy which accompanied the revival of the Turkish power.

* * * * *

The events which have been described in Russia and in Turkey, and which were soon to be ratified by new disasters, were fatal to the Armenian people. The Great War had carried them through hideous slaughters to the fairest and broadest hope they had ever known; and then abruptly laid them—it may well be for ever—in the dust. The age-long misfortunes of the Armenian race have arisen mainly from the physical structure of their home. Upon the lofty tableland of Armenia, stretching across the base of the Asia Minor Peninsula, are imposed a series of mountain ranges having a general direction east and west. The valleys between these mountains have from time immemorial been the pathways of every invasion or counter-attack between Asia Minor in the west and Persia and Central Asia in the east. In antiquity the Medes, the Persians, the Romans; in the early centuries of the Christian Era the Persian Sassanids and Eastern Roman Emperors; and in the Middle Ages successive waves of Mongols and Turks—Seljukli and Osmanli—invaded, conquered, partitioned, yielded and reconquered the rugged regions in which an ill-starred race strove ceaselessly for life and independence. And after the rise of Russia to power the struggle for possession of the Armenian regions, as containing the natural frontiers of their own domains, was continued by Russia, Persia, and the Ottoman Empire.

At the moment when the Great War began Armenia, divided between Russia and Turkey, repressed by force or actual massacre, had no defence but secret societies and no weapons but intrigue and assassination. The War drew upon them a new train of evils. After the Balkan Wars the Pan-Turks cast away both 'Ottomanisation' and 'Turkification' as means for recreating the State. They attributed the disasters which the Turkish Empire had sustained in part to the opposition of the non-Turkish races in their midst. In blunt but significant language they concluded that these races 'were not worth considering; they were worse than encumbrances; they could go to the devil.' The recreated State for which patriotic Turks hoped must be formed by Turks alone. The goal, if attainable, could be reached only by a long road and a hard. The sooner therefore the Turkish people set out upon it in deadly earnest, the better. The Turks took this road from 1912 onwards; and the fact that they had done so went long unrecognised in Europe. The Armenians were however better informed. They saw that the incorporation of the Moslem areas of Caucasia in a great Turkish State would, if carried to achievement, place the Armenian plateau, including Russian Armenia, under Turkish sovereignty and jeopardise the whole future of their race. The outbreak of the Great War brought these issues to a head. The Turkish Government in furtherance of their own aims tried to secure Armenian support against Russia, particularly the support of Russian Armenians. A grim alternative was presented to the Armenian leaders. Should they throw their national weight as far as it lay in their power on the side of Russia or of Turkey, or should they let their people be divided and driven into battle against each other? They took the remarkable decision that if war should come, their people in Turkey and in Russia should do their duty to their respective Governments. They thought it better to face fratricidal strife in the quarrels of others than to stake their existence upon the victory of either side.

When Turkey attacked Russian Armenia, the Czar's Government, fearing that a successful defence of Caucasia by Armenians would dangerously inflame the Nationalist aspirations of the race, conveyed a hundred and fifty thousand Armenian conscripts to the Polish and Galician fronts and brought other Russian troops to defend Armenian hearths and homes in Caucasia. Few of these hundred and fifty thousand Armenian soldiers survived the European battles or were able to return to Caucasia before the end of the War. This was hard measure. But worse remained. The Turkish war plan failed. Their offensive against Caucasia in December, 1914 and January, 1915 was defeated. They recoiled in deep resentment. They accused the Armenians of the Turkish eastern districts of having acted as spies and agents on behalf of Russia, and of having assailed the Turkish lines of communication. These charges were probably true; but true or false, they provoked a vengeance which was also in accord with deliberate policy. In 1915 the Turkish Government began, and ruthlessly carried out, the infamous general massacre and deportation of Armenians in Asia Minor. Three or four hundred thousand men, women, and children escaped into Russian territory and others into Persia or Mesopotamia; but the clearance of the race from Asia Minor was about as complete as such an act, on a scale so great, could well be. It is supposed that about one and a quarter millions of Armenians were involved, of whom more than half perished. There is no reasonable doubt that this crime was planned and executed for political reasons. The opportunity presented itself for clearing Turkish soil of a Christian race opposed to all Turkish ambitions, cherishing National ambitions that could only be satisfied at the expense of Turkey and planted geographically between Turkish and Caucasian Moslems. It may well be that the British attack on the Gallipoli Peninsula stimulated the merciless fury of the Turkish Government. Even, thought the Pan-Turks, if Constantinople were to fall and Turkey lost the war, the clearance would have been effected and a permanent advantage for the future of the Turkish race would be gained.

The arrival of the Grand Duke Nicholas in the Caucasus at the beginning of 1916, his masterly capture of Erzeroum in February, 1916, and his conquests of Turkish territory in North-Eastern Asia Minor revived Armenian hopes. The entry of the United States raised them higher. But the Russian Revolution quenched this flicker. It is not possible here to follow the tangled conflicts of the Georgians, Armenians and Tartars which followed. Early in 1918 the Russian Army of the Caucasus abandoned the front in Asia Minor and dissolved into an armed rabble struggling to entrain for home. The Russians had gone. The Turks had not yet come. A desperate effort was made by the remaining Armenian manhood to defend their country. The Armenian elements of the Russian Army therefore held together, and with the help of volunteers succeeded for a time in holding back the Turkish advance. Their hundred and fifty thousand soldiers were already dead or scattered, and they could never muster more than 35,000 men. The Treaty of

Brest-Litovsk in February, 1918, was the signal for a general Turkish advance eastward. The Armenian line was overwhelmed; and by May not only had the Turks recovered the districts occupied by the Grand Duke, but they had taken the districts of Batum, Kars and Ardahan and were preparing to advance to the Caspian. Meanwhile the great Allies strode forward. British, French, and United States troops beat down the German armies in France. The Anglo-Indian armies conquered Mesopotamia, Palestine and Syria. At the very moment when the Turks had reached the goal in Caucasia for which they had run such risks and to which they had waded through crime and slaughter, their whole State and structure fell prostrate. The Armenian people emerged from the Great War scattered, extirpated in many districts and reduced through massacre, losses of war and enforced deportations adopted as an easy system of killing, by at least a third. Out of a community of about two and a half millions, three-quarters of a million men, women, and children had perished. But surely this was the end.

The earlier miseries and massacres of the Armenians have been made familiar to the British people, and indeed to the Liberal world, by the fame and eloquence of Mr. Gladstone. Opinions about them differed, one school dwelling upon their sufferings and the other upon their failings. But at any rate in contrast to the general indifference with which the fortunes of Eastern and Middle-Eastern peoples were followed by the Western democracies, the Armenians and their tribulations were well known throughout England and the United States. This field of interest was lighted by the lamps of religion, philanthropy, and politics. Atrocities perpetrated upon Armenians stirred the ire of simple and chivalrous men and women spread widely about the English-speaking world. Now was the moment when at last the Armenians would receive justice and the right to live in peace in their national home. Their persecutors and tyrants had been laid low by war or revolution. The greatest nations in the hour of their victory were their friends and would see them righted.

It seemed inconceivable that the five great Allies would not be able to make their will effective. The reader of these pages will however be under no illusions. By the time the conquerors in Paris reached the Armenian question their unity was dissolved, their armies had disappeared and their resolves commanded naught but empty words. No power would take a mandate for Armenia. Britain, Italy, America, France looked at it and shook their heads. On March 12, 1920, the Supreme Council offered the mandate to the League of Nations. But the League, unsupported by men or money, promptly and with prudence declined. There remained the Treaty of Sèvres. On August 10 the Powers compelled the Constantinople Government to recognise and as yet undetermined Armenia as a free and independent State. Article 89 prescribed that Turkey must submit to 'the arbitration of the President of the United States of America the question of the frontier to be fixed between Turkey and Armenia in the *vilayets* of Erzeroum, Trebizond, Van, and Bitlis, and to accept his decision thereupon, as well as any stipulation he may prescribe as to access of Armenia to the sea. It was not until December, 1920, that President Wilson completed the discharge of this high function. The frontier he defined gave Armenia virtually all the Turkish territory which had been occupied by Russian troops until they disbanded themselves under the influence of the Revolution; an area which, added to the Republic of Erivan, made an Armenian national homeland of nearly sixty thousand square miles.

So generous was the recognition in theory of Armenian claims that the Armenian and Greek population of the new State was actually outnumbered by Moslem inhabitants. Here was justice and much more. It existed however upon paper only. Already nearly a year before, in January, 1920, the Turks had attacked the French in Cilicia, driven them out of the Marash district and massacred nearly fifty thousand Armenian inhabitants. In May Bolshevik troops invaded and subjugated the Republic of Erivan. In September, by collusion between the Bolsheviks and Turks, Erivan was delivered to the Turkish Nationalists; and as in Cilicia, another extensive massacre of Armenians accompanied the military operations. Even the hope that a small autonomous Armenian province might eventually be established in Cilicia under French protection was destroyed. In October France, by the Agreement of Angora, undertook to evacuate Cilicia completely. In the Treaty of Lausanne, which registered the final peace between Turkey and the Great Powers, history will search in vain for the word 'Armenia.'

CHAPTER XIX
CHANAK

The Greek Soldier—The Silent Strain—British Indifference: French Antagonism—America Absent—The Appeals of Gounaris—An Exhausted Lloyd George—The Agreement with Russia—Turkish Atrocities—The Greek designs Upon Constantinople—The Decisive Battle: Afium Karahissar—Destruction of the Greek Army—A Grave Situation—The Reckoning—The Neutral Zone—A Personal View—Alarm and Despondency—The British Fleet—The Telegram to the Dominions—The Official Communiqué: September 16—The Issue Explained—The Telegram Overtaken—Response of the Dominions—French and Italian Retirement—Military Measures—The Chanak Position—Strategic Reassurance—My Memorandum of September 30—Kemal's Alternative—Mudania—The Crisis ended.

The final act of the Greek Tragedy now begins. It lasted for nearly a year. The Greeks had failed to reach Angora or to crush Kemalist Turkey. Unsuccessful at the Sakaria River in September, 1921, their armies fell back on intermediate entrenched positions covering the Smyrna-Aidin Province. Here they remained disconsolately, but stubbornly, month after month. Justice must be done to the Greek soldier, so often the butt of ignorance and prejudice. Imagine an army of two hundred thousand men, the product of a small state mobilised or at war for ten years, stranded in the centre of Asia Minor with a divided nation behind them; with party dissensions in every rank; far from home, and bereft of effectual political guidance; conscious that they were abandoned by the great Powers of Europe and by the United States; with scanty food and decaying equipment; without tea, without sugar, without cigarettes, and without hope or even a plan of despair; while before them and around them and behind them preyed and prowled a sturdy, relentless and ever more confident foe. Hard as are the tests of battle, the armies of all nations have withstood them. But here was the long gnawing strain of suffering much and talking more, of having little and doing nothing.

> 'All's quiet along the Potomac to-night
>   Except now and then a stray picket
> Is shot, as he walks on his beat to and fro,
>   By a rifleman hid in the thicket.'

The army of the Potomac had a mighty nation behind it; had a clear world cause to light its bayonets; was fed and clothed and reinforced. The soldiers knew what they had come for and they were certain they would get what they sought. But over the Greek Army in Asia Minor there stole an ever-growing sense of isolation; of lines of communication in jeopardy, of a crumbling base, of a divided homeland, and of an indifferent world. Nevertheless they remained in martial posture for upwards of nine months.

It is one of the proofs of Mustapha Kemal's military qualities that he also was able and indeed content to wait and capable of compelling others to wait with him. He saw that time and petty harassing would ripen the fruits he now felt sure of gathering. Nine months is a long time in this quick-moving age; but during nine months the Turks waited and the Greeks endured.

Meanwhile many efforts were made by the British Government to bring about a Turkish settlement and a Greek withdrawal. But they were all made half-heartedly, and with a lack of collective vigour and conviction unworthy of a government whose leading men had been schooled in the greatest of wars. This feebleness can only be explained by the general mental exhaustion of war-worn Ministers, by divergencies of sentiment, and by growing domestic preoccupations. Of these last something will be said later. This was a period when the East seemed in a trance; nothing seemed to be happening there; and with an ever-roughening political breeze at home, it was soothing to the public to see at any rate one spot where the situation was at least stagnant. But all the time a bankrupt Greece was spending a quarter of a million pounds a week in Asia Minor alone; the Venizelists and monarchists of Greece were eyeing each other in deadly rivalry; and an army as large as Britain sent to the South African War was wilting and wasting across the sea.

There are cases in which strong measures are the only form of prudence and mercy. Use firmly the power of Britain—it is still considerable; compel Greece to concede and Turkey to forbear; knock their heads together until they settle. Such was my counsel. 'But,' they said, 'who is going to do the knocking? We have no troops to spare. We cannot embroil ourselves in foreign wars.' But surely this might have been thought of earlier? And so the months sped by—drip, drip, drip; rot, rot, rot.

Meanwhile, Party Politics began to crackle cheerfully on the hearth; and Liberals said, 'Our turn will soon come'; and Labour said, 'What about the unemployed?'; and Conservatives said, 'Isn't it time we had a government of our own?' and everybody said, 'It seems to be settling down out there, and anyhow it is none of our business. Haven't we had enough?'

But the French took a different line. Once Venizelos had quitted Athens they wiped Greece off their ledger. A few months passed and their envoys were at Angora. The new Turkey had much to offer France. She could give France peace in Cilicia. She could mitigate the discontents of Syria. Then there were important commercial openings in Anatolia. A Turkish Government which had marched from Angora to Constantinople with the goodwill of France would have much to give. M. Franklin-Bouillon, voluble, plausible, ardent, ambitious, was already at Angora. On October 20, 1921 he signed a mutually profitable agreement between France and Nationalist Turkey. Mustapha Kemal needed munitions—France had plenty of munitions; he lacked cannon—who makes better guns than Creusot? As for aeroplanes, a few at any rate are necessary to any modern army. It would be a pity that he should not have them. Divergencies of policy and personal incompatibilities had produced at this time an astonishing separation between France and Britain. These days are over; new and more comprehensive unities have been established; but events must be recorded.

Where was America? She was at the other side of the Atlantic Ocean. All the domestic stresses which stirred British politics and politicians reproduced themselves with far greater vehemence in the United States. The Presidential Election of 1920 had swept Wilson and the Democratic Party for the time completely off the stage. Their ill-used and infuriated opponents were in the saddle. Their policy was to find out exactly what President Wilson had wished or had promised and to do the opposite. So the Government of the United States, which had at one time played with the idea of becoming a mandatory for Constantinople and for Armenia and which had definitely undertaken to define the boundaries of Armenia, shrugged its shoulders and moralised upon the quarrels and muddles of the benighted Old World, and fervently thanked Providence that except for some useful souvenirs they were out of it, and back home.

These are not perhaps complimentary accounts of the attitude of the three Great Powers at whose request the Greeks had originally invaded Smyrna. But it would be wrong to impute weakness or turpitude or callousness to any of them. Modern forces are so ponderous and individual leaders relatively so small, so precariously balanced, so frequently changed; the collective life moves forward so irresistibly, that too much vitality or perseverance or coherent policy should not be counted on from large communities. There are moments when each is grand and noble; there are moments when all are expressionless slabs. King Constantine and his Prime Minister Gounaris ought to have thought of this before they broke the links of obligation.

Our brief chronicle of military events ceased with the failure of the Greek Army in September, 1921, to reach Angora and with their retreat from the Sakaria River to winter positions east of the line Eskishehr and Afium Karahissar. Here they remained for nearly a year. Meanwhile the ill-fated Gounaris flitted to and fro between Athens and London begging for money and arms to carry on the war and still more for help to get out of it. He was confronted by Lord Curzon, who soused him in sonorous correctitudes. At these interviews the main effort of Gounaris was to throw the agonised fortunes of Greece into the sole hands of Great Britain; the main object of Lord Curzon was to avoid incurring in any form or sense this ugly responsibility, but at the same time to persuade Greece to accept Allied mediation. On the whole Lord Curzon was successful. Gounaris was made to feel that England would do nothing, and that his only chance lay in inter-Allied good offices. But even this chance was, it seemed, a poor one, because France was now ardently backing and rearming the Turks, and England had no intention of becoming embroiled for the sake of pro-Constantine Greece. On the one hand, the cries of a drowning man; on the other, good advice from one who had no intention of going into the water!

This attitude was justifiable in Lord Curzon, who had throughout, under the guidance of the Foreign Office, played an uncompromised, circumspect and ineffectual part, and who certainly felt no obligation and equally no desire to run any risks either personal or national for the Greeks. It was Lord Curzon's failing, as his biographer has revealed, that he loved to state a case, and lost interest in it once it had flowed from his lips or his pen. He realised and deplored the plight of Greece; he hated the Turks, and feared their growing strength. He was scandalised by the suddenness with which the French had not only washed their hands of all Greek obligations, but had actually thrown their weight upon the Turkish side; but he was not often capable of producing real action in any sense. In deeds he rarely dinted the surface of events; but his diplomatic conversations were extremely well conducted and there was no lack of lucid and eloquent State papers. He did not, for instance, say to Gounaris, 'Evacuate Asia Minor at once or the British Fleet will blockade the Piræus.' Or to the French, 'Act with more comradeship in this matter or we will disinterest ourselves in Europe and withdraw our troops from the Rhine.' He could not be reproached for not taking either or both of these courses or doing anything else, because he had never at any time done anything in this theatre either good or bad which deflected the march of events.

But with the Prime Minister it was different. Yearning as he did for Greek success and still more for Greek extrication; being himself an exemplar of audacious and resourceful action, it was surprising that he did not, having gone so far, on this issue take his own fate in his hands. After all, here again was the occasion he had so often sincerely sought to quit the dimming scene. The forces that sustained the Coalition were swiftly decomposing; he had been flouted and defied by officials of the Conservative organisation; his own followers were cut from their party roots and lived politically like flowers in a vase. In the fierce duress of the war and its consequences he had run through all the parties and many of the friendships. But he was still—and none could strip him of his fame—the 'pilot who weathered the storm'; he was still the great Lloyd George, the best-known human being in the cottages of Britain; he was still armed with the decisive power of a Prime Minister to terminate the life of his Government by resignation. Surely he might have said, 'Either there is a living policy about Greece and Turkey, or I go.' But he was exhausted by all he had gone through, and worse still, he was loaded with day-to-day affairs and the routine of high command. Actually he was negotiating with the Bolsheviks at Genoa and being deceived by them. So nothing happened, and Gounaris, who had pulled down Venizelos, went back from his last London visit to reap where he had sown.

Mr. Churchill to Lord Curzon

April 26, 1922.

Like you I am deeply concerned about this Genoa business.[1] I have long foreseen the danger of Germany and Russia making common cause, and have frequently referred to it in public speeches. The policy which I had thought best calculated to prevent or at least modify and delay such an evil orientation was to secure the confidence of France, and armed with that to bring about a tripartite understanding between England, France, and Germany for mutual help and security, thus making it plain to Germany that she had good hopes of a bright future with England and

---

[1] The Russo-German Agreement had just been disclosed to the Genoa conference.

France, and that she would lose these prospects by exclusive dealings with the Soviets. . . . The foundation of this policy was always the guarantee to France, [of aid against aggression] on the basis of which I believed, and still believe, it is possible to secure so great a measure of French confidence as to enable better relations to be established with Germany both by Britain and by France. . . . However Utopian these aspirations may be, they appear to be capable of simple explanation and to be the lines along which we could have safely worked, not only for a month but for a year, and not only for a year but for several years.

However, an entirely different course has been taken by the Prime Minister, in which the Foreign Office has, it seems to me, had very little chance of bringing its special aptitudes into play. The great objective of the Prime Minister's policy has been Moscow, to make Great Britain the nation in the closest possible relations with the Bolsheviks, and to be their protectors and sponsors before Europe. I have been unable to discern any British interest, however slight, in this. . . . Of trade advantages there are none that will bear fruit for many years. However, we have been led, drawn or dragged steadily along this road. We have separated ourselves in our attitude towards Russia from both the great democracies with which we are most intimately connected, viz., the United States and France. In our anxiety to placate the Bolsheviks we have lost so much French confidence and goodwill that very little influence is left to us now to restrain France from any harsh action against Germany. We ought, on the contrary, to have kept all our strength for this most important development. I am sure that if we had been good friends with them and had kept their goodwill, we should have been in a position very greatly to influence and modify their action. As it is, on what is largely a Russian issue we are being drawn into something perilously near a complete break with France. I am not prepared to contemplate this. I fear that the results would be bad in every sense, that France and the Little Entente will defend their position by strong and drastic action, that Germany and Russia will close their ranks, and that we shall be left a sort of universal marplot without a friend and without a policy.

Another set of misunderstandings has arisen with France about Turkey, and I can well understand the many reasons you have for complaint against them there. At the same time the policy which has been imposed upon us in regard to Turkey has been a policy contrary not only to the interests of France, but to those of Great Britain. Our continued bolstering up of the Greeks and hostility towards the Turks has been incomprehensible to the French, who have been unable in their minds to discern any British interest behind it, and consequently have continually suspected all sorts of extraordinary motives. This has added a long string of difficulties to the relations between the two countries. I greatly admired your efforts in Paris to retrieve a situation already fatally compromised.

To return to our tale; there followed a series of superficial diplomatic movements. Briand had fallen after the Cannes Conference and golf match of January, 1922, and Poincaré, in this phase a bristling partisan scarcely recognisable in the great figure which has since emerged, ruled in his stead. Marching in triumphantly from Opposition, he only thought of Reparations, of the Rhine and of the Ruhr. If the Turks could help France at the moment, so much the better for them. If King Constantine suffered, it served him right. If the Greeks suffered for having chosen King Constantine, that was their affair. 'Vous l'avez voulu, Georges Dandin.' The reader must understand that all this was expressed in the most seemly language, which would have brought no blush to the cheeks of the League of Nations, and our paraphrase is only intended to convey its consequential meaning.

Very sluggishly England, France, and Italy, embarked on simultaneous negotiations with the Turks and Greeks. Technically war continued, but actually from the end of March to the end of May (1922) there was a suspension of arms in Asia Minor. The Allied Conference which eventually met in Paris on March 22–26 proposed an Armistice together with peace terms which would have entailed the Greek evacuation of Asia Minor. Greece accepted the Armistice and made no reply regarding the terms. Angora refused even the Armistice unless it was preceded by the Greek evacuation. For a space the deadlock continued. But in May the belated news of bloody events in Anatolia began to trickle into the subsidiary columns of the newspapers. Reports of massacres of the Christian population appeared daily. The details of the atrocities committed by the Turks in the Caucasus during the winter of 1920 when the fifty thousand Armenians had perished, and the appalling deportations of Greeks from the Trebizond and Samsun districts which had occurred in the autumn of 1921, were now for the first time reaching Europe. During June, 1922, the methodical extermination of Greeks in Western Anatolia was in full swing. In spite of French efforts to minimise these horrors and to prove similar atrocities on a minor scale against the Greeks, public opinion so far as it existed turned sternly against the Turks.

In July Constantine and his Prime Minister Gounaris in their desperation played a shrewd stroke. Swiftly recalling two divisions from Asia Minor to join their army in Thrace, they demanded permission from the Allies to enter Constantinople. There was no reason to doubt their power to occupy the city, and the mere threat when it became known startled the Angora Turks. It is quite possible that under cover of a temporary Greek occupation of Constantinople with Allied approval, the escape of the Greek armies from Asia Minor might have been honourably and comparatively painlessly merged in negotiations for peace. Certainly after the Greek army had failed on the Sakaria, nothing but the occupation of Constantinople could have restored the fortunes of the Royal Family and the Royalists in Greece. At least it could be argued against the Allies that if they would not help the Greeks in their military operations they ought not to hamper them; and if on general grounds they felt compelled to hamper, they ought at least loyally and actively to help them to their ships. However, here again all ended in futility. The Greeks were forbidden by the deployment of the armed forces of England, France, and Italy to enter Constantinople, and the only lasting result of an exceedingly well-conceived means of covering their retirement from Anatolia was a weakening of their army on the threatened front. This was the final move before the catastrophe.

The moment for which Mustapha Kemal had waited so stolidly had now arrived. He knew that the Greeks had withdrawn the two divisions from his front to Thrace.

He knew that this transference had equalised the Greek and Turkish forces. He understood that the Greek troops before him were aware that anyhow they would have to leave Asia Minor. He was now fairly well equipped, thanks to the assistance of at least one Great Power, with arms and war material, and he also enjoyed on a small scale superiority in the air. His operations were complicated and masterly. By threatening the Ismid Peninsula and Brusa, he drew Greek forces to the north; by a cavalry sweep to the east of Aidin in the valley of the Meander, he lured half another Greek division to the south. He concentrated for his main battle on the Afium Karahissar position about eighty thousand rifles and sabres and one hundred and eighty guns. The Greeks mustered about seventy-five thousand men with three hundred and fifty guns. On the morning of August 26 the Turks attacked with three corps on a fifteen-mile front south-west of Afium Karahissar. By the afternoon of the next day the Greek line had been decisively pierced by the First Turkish Corps and a Greek general retreat began. This soon became a rout. The main Greek army fled towards Smyrna. By August 31 their flight was so rapid that the pursuing Turks had lost all touch with them. General Tricoupis, the latest Commander-in-Chief, and his Staff were captured on September 2. They had endeavoured to lead a counter-attack, but not being followed by their men fell into the hands of a Turkish cavalry squadron. Although the Turkish main body marched one hundred miles in three days, they never caught up the Greeks until they reached Smyrna on September 9. Large numbers of refugees and forty thousand Greeks had already embarked when the Turks entered the city. But fifty thousand prisoners were taken by the Turks.

The Third Greek Corps retreated to their base on the Sea of Marmora. As they approached Mudania, hotly pursued, a French officer informed them that they were in the neutral zone and must surrender. The Commanders of the two leading regiments, knowing that Mudania was not in the neutral zone, refused to surrender and led their regiments successfully by hill paths to Panderma. Part of the main body, however, surrendered to the French and were handed over to the Kemalists; the remainder found shipping at Panderma after abandoning their guns. Thus within a fortnight from August 26 the Greek army which had entered Anatolia at the request of Great Britain, the United States and France, which had been for three years the foundation of Allied policy against Turkey and the object of inter-Allied intrigues, was destroyed or driven into the sea. Turkey became once again the sole master of Asia Minor, and Mustapha Kemal's Army, having celebrated their triumph by the burning of Smyrna to ashes and by a vast massacre of its Christian population, turned the heads of their columns hopefully towards Constantinople and the Straits.

The catastrophe which Greek recklessness and Allied procrastination, division and intrigue had long prepared now broke upon Europe. The signatories of the Treaty of Sèvres had only been preserved in their world of illusion by the shield of Greece. That shield was now shattered. Nothing but a dozen battalions of disunited British, French, and Italian troops stood between the returning war and Europe; the flames of Smyrna and its hideous massacres were a foretaste of what the fate of Constantinople might be. The consequences of a new Turkish invasion of Europe were incalculable. A struggle of Kemal's armies, reinforced by the resources and man-power of Constantinople, with the Greeks in Thrace must raise every Balkan danger. The re-entry of the Turks into Europe, as conquerors untrammelled and untamed, reeking with the blood of helpless Christian populations must, after all that had happened in the war, signalise the worst humiliation of the Allies. Nowhere had their victory been more complete than over Turkey; nowhere had the conqueror's power been flaunted more arrogantly than in Turkey; and now, in the end, all the fruits of successful war, all the laurels for which so many scores of thousands had died on the Gallipoli Peninsula, in the deserts of Palestine and Mesopotamia, in the marshes of the Salonika front, in the ships which fed these vast expeditions; all the diversions of allied resources in men, in arms, in treasure which they had required; all was to end in shame. Victory over Turkey absolute and unchallenged had been laid by the armies upon the council table of the Peace Conference. Four years had passed, and the talkers had turned it into defeat. Four years had passed, darkened by a purposeless carnage, not only on fields of battle, but even more of women and children, the old, the weak, the unarmed. All the fine pretensions of Europe and the United States, all the eloquence of their statesmen, all the hiving and burrowing committees and commissions, had led the erstwhile masters of overwhelming power to this bitter and ignominious finish.

But surely the last word had not yet been spoken; surely there was still time, not indeed to retrieve the disaster, but at least to bring about a peace which would leave the Allies some vestiges of respect and would protect Europe from a new conflagration. And here obligation took a precise form. The area around Constantinople from the lines of Chatalja to those of Ismid, from the Black Sea to the Straits of the Dardanelles, had been declared a neutral zone. The Kemalists had agreed to respect it; it had been delimited with their officers; it was plainly marked. We have seen how only a few months before when Greece sought to repair her desperate fortunes by entering Constantinople, these same allies had proclaimed the sanctity of the neutral zone and British, French, and Italian troops had actually marched out in war array and displayed their standards in its defence. If it was right to deprive the Greeks by united allied action of what was perhaps their sole means of saving their armies in Asia Minor, was it not equally a duty to prevent the Turks from passing through this same neutral zone to attack and destroy the remnants of the Greek armies in Thrace? If England, despite the Greek sympathies of her Prime Minister, had marched with France and Italy to arrest the Greek advance upon Constantinople, was it not an equal obligation upon these Powers to stand with us in defence of the limit which the three Powers had jointly prescribed and engaged themselves to maintain?

Were we really going to be chased out of Constantinople to our ships, leaving the Sultan, his Ministers, and every person who had followed our instructions in carrying out the conditions of the Armistice, to be punished as traitors to their country? Were three Great Nations, with the screams of Smyrna in their ears, really to scuttle at the approach of armed men? Would they abandon the city on which they had laid their hands, for which they had assumed so direct a responsibility, to a ruthless vengeance, and still worse to a blind anarchy? But if this was not to be, something more was needed than bluff and blather; unless everything was to clatter down, someone must stand firm.

Not much was to be expected from the Italians. They knew the Greeks had been sent to Asia Minor to forestall what they considered their rightful claims. Now the Greeks had been driven into the sea, and with the Greek dreams there fell also or at least subsided Italian ambitions. But France, the warrior nation, captain of the Allies in Armageddon, the France of Foch and Clemenceau—was France to be found unwilling to discharge her trust? Many allowances may be made for the peccadilloes of which Franklin-Bouillon was the agent. The breach of sentiment and understanding between Lloyd George and Poincaré was complete. Every form of mutual repulsion operated between them. The Lloyd-Georgian policy of building up a great Greek empire had little concern with the interests of France, and a standing quarrel with the Turks exposed France to peculiar difficulties in the Syrian territories she had so recently acquired by force. Indeed, this policy was deemed by dominant British opinion contrary to a long view of the interests of the British Empire. It was a personal policy, pursued moreover by its author only with limited liability. The French could not understand what the British were after. Other divergences had arisen about Reparations and the Peace Treaty; and the shadow of a French invasion of the Ruhr hung darkly over the feeble revival of Europe. Anglo-French relations were at their worst; it was hard to believe that two peoples who had gone through so much and achieved so much together and buried so many dead in common and saved their souls alive from the fiery furnace in good comradeship, should so swiftly have fallen apart. But after all, these had been only superficial difficulties, like bad manners between good friends. Suddenly the situation had become formidable. Fundamental issues rose like granite rocks above the froth and slime.

We had a right to expect that France would stand to her engagements to maintain the neutral zone; and it is always pleasing to remember that this was the spontaneous instinct of the French High Command in Constantinople. On September 11 Mustapha Kemal was notified by the High Commissioners of the Three Powers that he must not transgress the neutral zone. The slender British forces making a front on the Ismid Peninsula and at Chanak on the Asiatic shore of the Dardanelles were reinforced by detachments from the French and Italian armies. In order to avoid the firing of a shot, the three Great Powers had only to act together and thus convince Mustapha Kemal that while he could have a satisfactory peace if he halted beyond the boundary line, he would encounter unlimited resources by its violation. But if we were all three to shuffle off in a 'devil take the hindmost' mood, then blood would flow and fire would burn, and none could tell how peace might be restored. In any quarrel among men, if one side proclaims its complete impotence of will and hand, there are no bounds to the evils that may ensue.

I come down to the personal thread on which this narrative of large events is strung. The reader is perhaps convinced that I tried my best to prevent this hateful and fearful situation from coming into being. But here it was. The resuscitated Turk was marching upon the Dardanelles and Constantinople, and beyond them, upon Europe. I thought he ought to be stopped. If, indeed, unhappily he re-entered Europe it should be by Treaty, and not by violence. Defeat is a nauseating draught; and that the victors in the greatest of all wars should gulp it down, was not readily to be accepted. When one knew that a single gesture would immediately restore to them full control of the event, it was surely worth making an effort. So having done my utmost for three years to procure a friendly peace with Mustapha Kemal and the withdrawal of the Greeks from Asia Minor, and having consistently opposed my friend the Prime Minister upon this issue, I now found myself whole-heartedly upon his side in resisting the consequences of the policy which I had condemned. I found myself in this business with a small group of resolute men: the Prime Minister, Lord Balfour, Mr. Austen Chamberlain, Lord Birkenhead, Sir Laming Worthington-Evans, with the technical assistance, willingly proffered, of the three Chiefs of Staff, Beatty, Cavan, and Trenchard. We made common cause. The Government might break up and we might be relieved of our burden. The nation might not support us: they could find others to advise them. The Press might howl, the Allies might bolt. We intended to force the Turk to a negotiated peace before he should set foot in Europe. The aim was modest, but the forces were small; and events had been so much mismanaged during these last three years that public opinion at home and throughout the Empire was ill-prepared to support, and indeed prejudiced against, the necessary minor but rough measures which had to be taken.

How to stop the Turk, and how, after stopping him, bring the Turk to parley? That was the problem. The days were passing; the long columns of ragged, valiant Ottoman soldiery who, their cruelties apart, deserved the salutes due to those who do not despair of their country, were streaming northward towards Constantinople and the Dardanelles. Would they halt at the neutral zone?

It seemed to many people who woke up suddenly to find an exciting crisis that we had no means of resistance. The forces of the opponent were wildly exaggerated. Mustapha Kemal, we were told, had one hundred and fifty thousand well-armed men, organised in as many divisions as would have held a million in the Great War; behind these were another one hundred and fifty thousand; and again, still further in the rear, all the Moslems in the world. Both the French and Italians had sold them arms and had sought their favours; so it was unlikely that these Powers would give much help. Still one hoped that they would at any rate preserve the decencies. But if it were left to England alone to stop the Turk re-entering Europe, was it a task 'within the compass of her stride'?

Here it is worth while considering the peculiar strategic position which we enjoyed in virtue of our hold upon the Gallipoli Peninsula and of our undisputed command of the sea. The British Mediterranean Fleet lay in the Marmora, and its flotillas swept to and fro through the Dardanelles and the Bosphorus. No army could pass from Asia into Europe except piecemeal and clandestinely, at night. But, it was said, the Turks will bring cannon to the Asiatic shores of both these Straits and fire on the flotillas and supply-vessels. To which we said, what cannon? It was found that they had no cannon that could destroy even small warships, and ours were large ones. Still, they would fire at them. But Beatty said the Navy would put up with that; also that they would fire back. As long as the British Fleet held this line of deep salt water between Europe and Asia the war could not be carried into Thrace.

On September 15, the British Cabinet met in prolonged session. Sir Charles Harington commanded for the Allies at Constantinople. Lord Plumer, his old chief of Second Army days, had arrived there on a visit. He had telegraphed saying that he was sure General Harington's arrangements had been correct and sound. The situation was in his opinion serious and required firm and decided action without delay. It was quite clear to him that the Kemalists meant to try to impose their conditions on the Allies, preferably by threatening force, but actually by force if no result was produced by threats. If things were allowed to drift further, it was absolutely certain that we should be driven into a corner militarily and politically. Such was his view. On this and all other information the Cabinet came, without dissension if not unitedly to serious resolves. I was instructed by minute to draft a telegram for the Prime Minister to send to the Dominions informing them of the critical situation and inviting their aid. I accordingly prepared a message stating that a decision had been taken by the Cabinet to resist aggression upon Europe by the Turks and to make exertions to prevent Mustapha Kemal driving the Allies out of Constantinople, and in particular and above all to secure firmly the Gallipoli Peninsula in order to maintain the freedom of the Straits. We had received a notification from the French Government that they were in agreement with us in informing Mustapha Kemal that he must not violate the neutral zone which protected Constantinople and the Straits. The Italians also were acting in concert with us. We hoped to secure the military participation of Greece, Roumania, and Serbia in defence of the deep-water line between Europe and Asia, and were addressing them accordingly. All the powers were being notified of our intention to make exertions, and a British division was under orders to reinforce the Allied Commander-in-Chief, Sir Charles Harington. The Navy would co-operate to the fullest extent necessary.

The object of these arrangements, the message continued, was to cover the period which must elapse before it was possible to secure a stable peace with Turkey. Proposals were being made to hold a Conference for this purpose probably in Venice, or possibly in Paris. Meanwhile it was essential that we should have sufficient strength to maintain our position around the Straits and in Constantinople until this peace had been achieved. It seemed improbable that if a firm front was shown by a large number of Powers acting together, the forces of Mustapha Kemal would attack. The Prime Minister's message ran:—'These armies, which have so far not had any serious resistance to encounter from disheartened Greeks, are estimated at between sixty and seventy thousand men, but timely precautions are imperative. Grave consequences in India and among other Mohammedan populations for which we are responsible might result from a defeat or from a humiliating exodus of the Allies from Constantinople. . . . I should be glad to know whether the Governments of the [various Dominions] are willing to associate themselves with our action and whether they desire to be represented by a contingent. . . . The announcement of an offer from all or any of the Dominions to send a contingent even of moderate size would undoubtedly exercise in itself a most favourable influence on the situation.'

I also drafted the next morning (Saturday) at the request of the Prime Minister and his principal colleagues (except Lord Curzon, who was at his country seat), a communiqué for publication. We felt that the public ought not to be left longer in ignorance of the situation and its gravity. This statement has been censured for being alarmist and provocative in tone, and certainly it was ill-received in important quarters. I am content to reproduce it so that it can be judged here in retrospect.

'. . . The approach of the Kemalist forces to Constantinople and the Dardanelles and the demands put forward by the Angora Government . . . if assented to, involve nothing less than the loss of the whole results of the victory over Turkey in the late war. The channel of deep salt water that separates Europe from Asia and unites the Mediterranean and the Black Sea affects world interests, European interests, and British interests of the first order.

'The British Government regard the effective and permanent freedom of the Straits as a vital necessity for the sake of which they are prepared to make exertions. They have learnt with great satisfaction that in this respect their views are shared by France and Italy, the other two Great Powers principally concerned.

'The question of Constantinople stands somewhat differently. For more than two years it has been decided that the Turks should not be deprived of Constantinople, and in January of last year at the Conference in London the representatives of the Constantinople and Angora Turkish Governments were informed of the intention of the Allies to restore Constantinople to the Turks, subject to other matters being satisfactorily adjusted.

'The wish of the British Cabinet is that a Conference should be held as speedily as possible in any place generally acceptable to the other Powers involved, at which a resolute and sustained effort should be made to secure a stable peace with Turkey. But such a Conference cannot embark upon its labours, still less carry them through with the slightest prospect of success, while there is any question of the Kemalist forces attacking the neutral zones by which Constantinople, the Bosphorus, and the Dardanelles are now protected.

'The British and French Governments have instructed their High Commissioners at Constantinople to notify Mustapha Kemal and the Angora Government that these neutral zones established under the flags of the three Great Powers must be respected.

'However, it would be futile and dangerous, in view of the excited mood and extravagant claims of the Kemalists, to trust simply to diplomatic action. Adequate force must be available to guard the freedom of the Straits and defend the deep-water line between Europe and Asia against a violent and hostile Turkish aggression. That the Allies should be driven out of Constantinople by the forces of Mustapha Kemal would be an event of the most disastrous character, producing, no doubt, far-reaching reactions throughout all Moslem countries, and not only through all Moslem countries but through all the States defeated in the late war, who would be profoundly encouraged by the spectacle of the undreamed-of successes that have attended the efforts of the comparatively weak Turkish forces.

'Moreover, the reappearance of the victorious Turk on the European shore would provoke a situation of the gravest character throughout the Balkans, and very likely lead to bloodshed on a large scale in regions already cruelly devastated. It is the duty of the Allies of the late war to prevent this great danger, and to secure the orderly and peaceful conditions in and around the Straits which will allow a conference to conduct its deliberations with dignity and efficiency and so alone reach a permanent settlement.

'His Majesty's Government are prepared to bear their part in this matter and to make every possible effort for a satisfactory solution. They have addressed themselves in this sense to the other Great Powers with whom they have been acting, and who jointly with them are associated in the defence of Constantinople and the neutral zones.

'It is clear, however, that the other Ally Powers of the Balkan Peninsula are also deeply and vitally affected. Roumania was brought to her ruin in the Great War by the strangulation of the Straits. The union of Turkey and Bulgaria would be productive of deadly consequences to Serbia in particular and to Yugo-Slavia as a whole. The whole trade of the Danube flowing into the Black Sea is likewise subject to strangulation if the Straits are closed. The engagement of Greek interests in these issues is also self-evident.

'His Majesty's Government are therefore addressing themselves to all these three Balkan Powers with a view to their taking a part in the effective defence of the neutral zones. His Majesty's Government have also communicated with the Dominions, placing them in possession of the facts and inviting them to be represented by contingents in the defence of interests for which they have already made enormous sacrifices and of soil which is hallowed by immortal memories of the Anzacs.

'It is the intention of His Majesty's Government to reinforce immediately, and if necessary to a considerable extent, the troops at the disposal of Sir Charles Harington, the Allied Commander-in-Chief at Constantinople, and orders have also been given to the British Fleet in the Mediterranean to oppose by every means any infraction of the neutral zones by the Turks or any attempt by them to cross the European shore.'

The Prime Minister approved his telegram to the Dominions before 7 p.m. on September 15 and it was ciphered and despatched by 11.30 p.m. It had then to be transmitted, deciphered, and delivered in the various Governments. This process was not completed until the afternoon of the 16th. By that time the communiqué had already been flashed *en clair* by the Press all over the world, and had actually reached Canadian and Australian newspaper offices before the responsible Ministers had received the Government despatch. These Ministers therefore found themselves beset by anxious inquirers and also by eager volunteers for service, before they themselves had received any official information. This was vexatious to all concerned. None of the British Ministers had foreseen that the official telegram approved seventeen hours earlier and with at least twelve hours' start, would be overtaken and forestalled by the newspaper messages. In any case, however, the issue of the communiqué was a separate decision taken in consequence of the growing seriousness of the situation and of the duty of the British Government to warn the public.

The Dominion Ministers were in consequence placed in a false position and were naturally incensed. They protested vigorously against the procedure. The doubts, and on the whole preponderating disapproval which had been felt in the Mother Country of Mr. Lloyd George's pro-Greek policy and the general dissatisfaction at inter-allied handling of the Eastern problem since the Armistice, were reflected in the Governments and peoples of Canada and Australia. Like the British public, they had not been conscious of the protective influence of the Greek Armies behind which we had all lived in peaceful futility for three years. Like the British public, they could not readily comprehend the vast change which the destruction of these armies had wrought in our affairs. Nevertheless, all the Dominions responded to the call and declared their readiness if a great emergency arose to bear their part, subject of course to the consent of their Parliaments. By the night of September 16 the Government of New Zealand telegraphed that 'they wished to associate themselves with the action which is being taken and will send a contingent'; and on the 20th, that 'the House of Representatives had unanimously endorsed the action of their Government; and that over five thousand volunteers had already registered their names for active service.' In a few days these numbers had grown to twelve thousand from a community of fourteen hundred thousand souls whose military manhood had already been more than decimated in the great struggle. Similar manifestations took place in Canada and in Australia, and both these Dominion Governments were embarrassed until long after the actual crisis had passed by the press of war-experienced men answering to the appeal. We attached, of course, special importance to the responses of Australia and New Zealand on account of the knowledge which the Turks, and above all others, Mustapha Kemal, had acquired during the Great War when in contact with the Anzacs. There could be no greater deterrent upon violent Turkish action than the possibility of again facing the formidable volunteers of the Antipodes. It is beyond question that this knowledge, which we took good care to convey, was a definite factor in the eventual avoidance of war.

Meanwhile, the divergence between Britain and France had led to a lamentable episode. On September 18 orders from Paris withdrew the French detachments from the side of their British comrades at Chanak and on the Ismid Peninsula. The French troops were accompanied in their retirement by the Italians, and the British Empire was left alone to face the advancing Turkish armies. The advertised departure of the soldiers of these two Great Powers was likely to inflame the wildest ambitions of the Turks. What, they might ask, could Britain, herself by no means convinced of the issue at this time— Britain, the war-worn, the impoverished, the demobilised—achieve alone? Henceforth the Turks knew that only one Power stood in front of them. Luckily they had at their head a leader who understood a good many things.

We shall deliberately ignore and obliterate the scandalous recriminations which took place when Lord Curzon went to Paris on September 23. These were the worst years of Anglo-French relations which the twentieth century with all its stresses has seen; and this was the worst moment. We have run through this bad weather into better days. It is enough in epitome that the French said, 'We will stop the Turk by diplomacy'; and the British replied, 'Your diplomacy would be worth nothing without our bayonets. These are fixed.'

Meanwhile matters had passed for a space into the military sphere. The control of the Straits would obviously be facilitated if the fateful narrows of the Dardanelles were occupied on both sides by our troops. This made it desirable to hold Chanak on the Asiatic shore. It was a valuable though, as I believe, not an indispensable outwork. Originally the War Office had not contemplated holding Chanak and on the 11th General Harington had been told that he might evacuate at his discretion. He appealed against this decision on account of the importance of the place as an advanced defence of the Gallipoli peninsula. He was then told that he might hold it as if he were a rear-guard.

Availing himself of this permission, General Harington sent on the 19th the following order to the officer commanding Chanak, Major-General Marden: 'You should hold Chanak as long as possible with the forces I have available. I am communicating the decision to the Government. In my opinion in view of the French withdrawing from Chanak, Kemal will challenge British policy there. In all probability he will stop to reflect, if you stop him there with naval support. Your stand there may avert further trouble.'

And on the 20th he telegraphed to the War Office: 'If we continue to show our determination, I am of opinion that the British will be able to carry through the task without them [i.e., the French and Italians], so that I do not consider you need feel concern for their action. According to my information his [Kemal's] ministers are being summoned to Smyrna to-morrow for a conference. Evidently this is to decide whether he will take England on with her Dominions. My own opinion is they will not dare to do so.'

On the same day [September 20], the Cabinet faced the position created by the withdrawal of the French and Italians, and were advised upon the military aspect by the chiefs of the staffs. Sound decisions were taken. General Harington was informed that the defence of Chanak was his first duty; that the defence of Constantinople itself was secondary, and the defence of the Ismid Peninsula, minor. On September 22 General Harington apprised Mustapha Kemal through the Kemalist representative at Constantinople that he was instructed to defend the neutral zone. On the 23rd, eleven hundred Turkish cavalry entered the neutral zone and moved to Eren-Keui. The British general at Chanak warned the Turkish commander that in entering the neutral zone he had committed an act of war, and that he would be obliged to fire upon them if they failed to retire. The attitude of the Turkish officer was correct and reasonable, and the Turkish cavalry withdrew beyond the neutral zone on the morning of the 24th. On September 25 they returned to Eren-Keui two thousand strong, with machine guns. Here they remained, contumaciously and encroachingly, but with much politeness and parleying; and in undoubted violation of the neutral zone.

Both sides had an interest in gaining time, for the Turks had only horsemen without artillery, and we were hurrying reinforcements, artillery, and aeroplanes to the scene as fast as ships could carry them. At the outset Chanak was defended on a four-mile front by only three and a half battalions and by two field batteries, supported, of course, by the almost measureless gun-power of the Fleet. Naval fire against land positions had made remarkable progress since 1915. The most powerful battleships of the Navy lay in the stream supported by numerous cruisers and flotillas. All objectives had been registered, and fire could be regulated by unchallenged air observation. The infantry was therefore supported throughout by an artillery certainly equal to that of a whole army corps and possibly far above it. By the 28th Chanak was defended by six battalions, and three new howitzer batteries were planted on the Gallipoli Peninsula. Thirty-six guns of medium calibre were on the way; sixteen eight-inch howitzers were embarking. The growth of the air force was also substantial. The *Pegasus* with her five seaplanes was joined on the 27th by the *Argus* with six seaplanes and four fighters, and on the 28th by thirteen machines of the 209th Squadron. Three additional squadrons with thirty-six machines were due on October 9 and 10.

The Prime Minister asked me to preside over a Cabinet Committee for the proper concerting of naval, military, and air force movements. The week from the 20th to the 28th was one of anxiety. Information about the Turks was cloudy. So far nothing but cavalry forces, quite incapable of attacking entrenched positions, had appeared. But we did not know where the heads of their infantry columns marching from Smyrna to Constantinople actually were; or whether they would turn aside to assault Chanak, and what artillery and ammunition they could provide for that purpose. We only knew that we had a rather restricted but well-entrenched and well-wired position, air ascendancy, and great artillery superiority, and that the Turks had neither Tanks nor poison gas. This was already a good deal. But from the 28th onward, when our air supremacy became marked and the howitzers came into line from Gallipoli, it was quite certain that the British force could be dislodged from Chanak only by a major operation of war. Certainly on the western front in 1917 and 1918 no one would have attempted to attack such a position without at least equal artillery and air power in the zone of action, and with probably two or three rifles to one on the actual fighting front engaged. All experience shows that unless the artillery of the attack has mastered that of the defence, and further, has pulverised their infantry positions, the mere pushing forward of masses of infantry against machine guns and well-trained riflemen and barbed wire, means only a greater slaughter the longer it is persisted in. And even when the artillery has mastered the defence, it has been bloodily proved upon a large scale a hundred times that without tanks or gas the prospects of an assault are doubtful.

I had particularly in mind the repulse by the Anzacs of the Turks on May 19, 1915, after the first landing on the Gallipoli Peninsula. Here the Anzacs with far less powerful artillery and practically no air help had faced the best-trained troops of the Turkish Regular Army at odds of more than three to one. But the Turks, charging with the utmost bravery, withered before the fire, leaving so many thousands of corpses between the lines that the only truce of the Gallipoli campaign had to be arranged by mutual consent for sanitary purposes. After September 28 therefore there seemed no reason to be uncomfortable about the tactical situation at Chanak.

But it was the strategic situation which gave the real reassurance. Why should a skilful and experienced soldier and able man like Mustapha Kemal turn aside from his march towards Constantinople and lead his worn and sorely tried army against a British entrenched position? What would he gain in politics by driving the British Empire into war against him? What would he gain in tactics by squandering his men and scanty ammunition upon a local cock-fight of this kind? What would he gain in strategy by delaying his march to the Ismid Peninsula and close contact with his adherents in Constantinople? Every day's delay in arriving before Constantinople was perilous to him. He knew that there was a Greek army in Thrace almost the equal of his own. A military revolution in Athens had followed the disasters in Asia Minor. Constantine had been expelled, and the Greek military authorities had declared their resolve to defend Eastern Thrace. Every day they could gain for the reorganisation of their forces and for taking up advanced positions before the Chatalja lines was injurious to Kemal. And there, all the time lay Constantinople, full of Kemalist adherents, with very little but the blandishments and expostulations of M. Franklin-Bouillon to defend it. In fact, Mustapha Kemal never diverted his march a yard from his road. Like a wise man, he hurried on as fast as he could towards the main and easy goal, and used his flank guard of cavalry to give an appearance of strength and aggressiveness towards the British at Chanak. His cavalry officers had the strictest orders to avoid conflict, and above all to get into friendly parley. Their unabashed good humour was proof against the severest and most formal frowns. They made every effort to fraternise, and even ventured requests for camp-equipment and the minor conveniences of campaigning. There never was any danger to the British forces at Chanak. The menace was to Constantinople; but the defence of Constantinople in the absence of the other two Great Powers was not primarily a British responsibility.

I made a note for our small group on September 30 which may so far as it is relevant be reprinted.

CHANAK

Sept. 30, 1922.

We have hitherto prudently considered our position at Chanak as if we were likely to be exposed to attack by the whole of the Kemalist armies. It seems however unlikely that this will occur. The Kemalists are already at war with Greece, and their paramount object is to cross into Thrace and defeat the Greek armies there. It is no use their trying to get across the Dardanelles or the Sea of Marmora. Their only practicable road into Europe is across the Bosphorus or possibly across the Black Sea. It seems probable that they are at the present moment, and have been ever since the fall of Smyrna, steadily re-forming the main body of their troops towards the Ismid Peninsula with a view to crossing the Bosphorus, and that all they have done on the Chanak Peninsula is to send cavalry and minor forces to net in the British and to plant a certain number of guns on the unoccupied shores of the Dardanelles.

In any case it is clear that Kemal will have to choose between marching into Thrace by the Bosphorus and coming to grips with the Greek Army on the one hand, or trying to overwhelm the British at Chanak on the other. He would surely make a great mistake to adopt half-measures, namely, weak attacks on the British at Chanak and insufficient forces to defeat the Greeks in Thrace. Let us examine these two alternatives seriatim, taking the least probable first.

If Kemal attacks Chanak with the main strength of his army, of his artillery and limited ammunition, ample time will be afforded to the Greeks to get their army in Thrace thoroughly reorganised and reinforced to the utmost extent. . . .

If then he takes the second alternative, as he is probably doing, he might in about three weeks be in contact with the Greeks beyond the Chatalja lines. In this case he would no doubt leave sufficient forces around Chanak to close us in, but would not make any serious or costly attack. Nor would he unduly use his ammunition from the Asiatic shore of the Dardanelles upon ships passing the Straits. From about the end of October he will become deeply involved in Thrace. If we have taken the proper measures from the moment that hostilities have commenced, our position will then be a very strong one. The command of the Sea of Marmora and our naval strength will enable us to move our forces in many directions with the utmost rapidity. One cannot conceive a more wonderful system of interior lines and of water communications than will be at our disposal. . . . The position of the Kemalist army, heavily engaged with the Greeks in Thrace, with its line of communications stretching along the Ismid Peninsula, and a strong, compact British army crouched at Gallipoli and Chanak ready with the help of the Navy to cut those communications—such a position would indeed be forlorn. . . .

The more the situation is surveyed, the more the strategic advantages of the British position at Chanak and Gallipoli will become patent. The dilemma which faces Kemal will be painful in the extreme. He has either to break his teeth against the British at Chanak while the Greek armies grow stronger every day, or else to hurry into what is virtually a death-trap in Thrace. . . .

There remains, as there nearly always does, a third hypothesis, namely, that Kemal, if he recognises the futility from his point of view of a serious and prolonged effort against the British at Chanak and the peril of becoming embroiled in Thrace with the hostile British on his communications, will recoil from both projects. In this case we shall have attained our present objects without serious hostilities. Negotiations will be resumed, but in a very different atmosphere from those undertaken in Paris. If as the result of these negotiations the Turks are allowed to come back to Constantinople and Thrace, it need only be upon such conditions as we may judge to be most likely to secure a lasting peace. I trust the strength of our position will be realised before we take any steps that would barter it away.

The climax at Chanak was reached on September 28, when General Harington reported that the Turks were collecting in considerable numbers round the British position, 'grinning through the barbed wire,' that they were clearly acting under orders, that everything possible had been done to avoid conflict, but that the position was becoming impossible. He also reported that the British position at Chanak was 'strong, well wired, and well sited.' The Cabinet thereupon instructed the General to present an ultimatum to the Turks to quit the neutral zone and sheer off Chanak within a brief time-limit, and authorised him to use all the forces at his disposal at its expiration. The General was able, however, to tide over his difficulties without availing himself of the formidable warrant with which he had been armed. The tact, coolness and patience of General Harington were exemplary. It so chanced that from the moment the Cabinet sent the stern telegram, the Turkish provocation which had given rise to it began to subside. On the 30th the commander at Chanak (General Marden) reported that there were no signs of Kemalist guns or infantry being brought against him; and that his force was not in danger. And as every day's delay made the British position stronger, General Harington did not consider it necessary to send the Turks an ultimatum, nor did any incidents occur which required the opening of fire. The Cabinet, relieved by this favourable development, on October 1 approved their commander's forbearance.

Meanwhile after difficult discussions with the French, a joint invitation had been sent to Mustapha Kemal on September 23 to a Conference on the shores of the Marmora at Mudania. The invitation was accompanied by far-reaching offers, mainly at the expense of Greece. The three Allied Governments promised to restore to Turkey Thrace as far as the Maritza and Adrianople, to withdraw from Constantinople as soon as peace was made, and to support the admission of Turkey to the League of Nations. Mustapha accepted the invitation and fixed October 3. To Mudania also proceeded the ineffable M. Franklin-Bouillon, whose efforts were directed towards leading the Turks to hope for more than they would ever get from Great Britain, and to believe that the British were unable or unwilling in the last resort to fight. Largely as a result of his activities a deadlock was soon reached, and the Allied representatives returned to Constantinople on October 5. The French and Italian High Commissioners, appalled by the prospect of war, favoured unconditional surrender. Sir Horace Rumbold, however, stood firmly to the proposals of September 23; and General Harington was instructed from London to make no further concessions. The news that the British were preparing an ultimatum became known to the Turks through French or Italian sources. The continued arrival of British troops, artillery, and aeroplanes in the Dardanelles was evident. When the Conference was resumed at Mudania on October 10, the Turks were found ready after protracted discussion to sign an armistice convention. This provided that the Greeks should retire behind the Maritza and that Greek civil authorities should evacuate Eastern Thrace. On the other hand, the Turks agreed to recognise the neutral zone and undertook not to raise an army in Eastern Thrace until the ratification of the Treaty.

The story of Chanak is instructive in several ways. It reflects high credit upon General Harington, who emphasised the value and significance of the Chanak position and tenaciously held to it, and who knew how to combine a cool and tactful diplomacy with military firmness. There is no doubt that the attitude of the British Government and of the Dominions, particularly Australia and New Zealand, prevented the renewal of the war in Europe and enabled all the Allies to escape without utter shame from the consequences of their lamentable and divided policies. Considering the limited resources available, the public fatigue, the precarious position of the Administration and its declining authority at home and abroad, the achievement of 'Peace with Honour' was

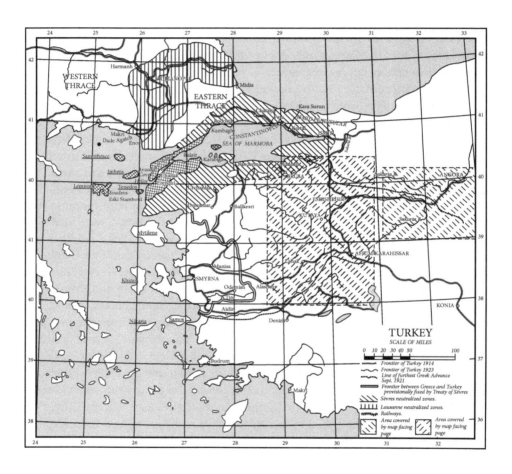

WESTERN
THRACE
Harmanh

EASTERN
THRACE
Midia

Kara Surun

BULAIR PENINSULAR

Makri
Dade Agatch
Eno

Samothrace

Imbros

Lemnos
Moudros
Eski Stamboul
Tenedos

Mytilene

Kumbagh
CONSTANTINOPLE
SEA OF MARMORA
SMYRNA

Bulair
Karabiga
Panderma

ESKISHEHIR
KUTAYA
Sakaria R.
ANGORA
Sukaria R.

AFIUM KARAHISSAR

Rhino

Manisa
SMYRNA
Odemish
Tire
Aidin

Ushakular
Balikesri

Alashehr

Ishak

KONIA
Nikaria
Samos
Denizli

Budrum

Makri

TURKEY
SCALE OF MILES

0 10 20 30 40 50   100

Frontier of Turkey 1914
Frontier of Turkey 1923
Line of furthest Greek Advance
Sept. 1921
Frontier between Greece and Turkey
provisionally fixed by Treaty of Sèvres
Sèvres neutralized zones.
Lausanne neutralized zones.
Railways.
Area covered   Area covered
by map facing   by map facing
page   page

memorable. It formed the basis upon which a peace of mutual respect could subsequently be negotiated with the Turks at Lausanne. The strong action taken by Britain, so far from drawing upon us the lasting enmity of the Turks, aroused a sentiment of admiration and even of goodwill, and will make easier rather than harder our future relationship with modern Turkey.

* * * * *

The Treaty of Lausanne followed in due course. It was a surprising contrast to the Treaty of Sèvres. The Great Powers who had been so ready to dictate terms, not only of peace but of national destruction, to the Turks now found themselves obliged to negotiate on far less than even terms. The Turk was re-established at Constantinople. He regained a large portion of Eastern Thrace. Every form of foreign guidance and control was swept away. The capitulations which for so many hundred years had protected the traders and subjects of western nations in Turkey against Oriental misgovernment or injustice were abolished. The control of the fateful Straits reverted to the Turk under the thinnest of disguises. Mustapha Kemal with prudence resigned the Arab provinces of the Ottoman Empire to the various mandatory powers, the fate of Mosul being remitted to the decision of the League of Nations. By an extraordinary series of provisions all the Greek inhabitants of Turkey, and a still large but smaller number of Turkish inhabitants of Greece, were reciprocally combed out and transported to their natural sovereignties. Turkey lost a great mass of citizens who had for centuries played a vital part in the economic life of every Turkish village and township. Greece, impoverished and downcast, received an accession of nearly one and a quarter million refugees who, under the pressure of misfortune and privation, have already become a new element of national strength. Even these conditions were not obtained by Great Britain, France, and Italy without prolonged parley. They would not have been obtained at all but for the skilful and persevering use made by Lord Curzon of the prestige which Great Britain had preserved through her stubborn attitude at Chanak.

The unhappy M. Gounaris, together with some other Ministers and defeated Generals, was shot in Athens as an expression of Greek disappointment at the results which had flowed from the decision of the Greek electorate in 1921.

CHAPTER XX
THE END OF THE WORLD CRISIS

A General Survey—The Decisive Act—The German War-plan—Mobilisation and
War—The Emperor's Test—The Deadly Current—The Frontiers and the Marne—
The Yser and the Deadlock—The *Goeben* and Turkey—The Dardanelles—
Defensive *versus* Offensive—The Rhythms of History—President Wilson's Part—
War without Glamour—Ancient Limitations—Modern Destructive Power—Only
a Prelude—Universal Suicide—Is it the End? France and Germany—British
Policy—Locarno—The Twin Pyramids—The Urgent Task.

It may be well in conclusion to pass in review the story of the World Crisis to which these
volumes have made their contribution. Time has given its perspective and every year has
brought a fuller knowledge. The proportion of events becomes apparent and it is easier
to discern the hinges of Fate.

I have already, in the opening Chapter of Volume I, summarised the causes by which
Europe was brought to the threshold of Armageddon. I have described as I saw them the
events which preceded and produced the catastrophe. Nothing that has since transpired
from the exposed archives of so many States has modified the conclusions which Volume
I has already recorded. There could have been no Great War if the rulers of Germany
had not first declared war against Russia and immediately launched their armies upon
the invasion and destruction of France, trampling through Belgium on the way. The
attempt to gain the swift and decisive military triumph which then seemed sure, was
a definite conscious act and impulse transcending all other events. The only test by
which human beings can judge war responsibility is Aggression; and the supreme proof
of Aggression is Invasion. Capacity to invade a neighbour implies superior capacity to
defend the native soil. The past has many instances of invasions for the purpose of fore-
stalling a counter-invasion. Disputes as to responsibility for bringing about conditions
which led to various wars are endless. But mankind will be wise in the future to take as
the paramount criterion of war guilt the sending of the main armies of any State across
its frontier line, and to declare that whoever does this puts himself irretrievably in the
wrong. The violation of Luxemburg and Belgium by the German armies marching upon
France will stare through the centuries from the pages of History.

The execution of this vast, elaborate war-plan was believed by the German leaders
to be necessary not only to the victory of Germany but to her safety, not only to her
safety but to her life. They therefore conceived themselves bound to carry it out from the
moment that the Russian mobilisation and the terms of the Russian alliance with France
compelled them to face the long-examined war on two fronts against superior but more

slowly gathering forces. That this belief was sincerely held need not be questioned. It was not, however, well grounded. No one would have dared attack the Central Powers. The strength of the German armies was so enormous, and the conditions of modern war at that time so favourable to the defensive, that Germany could—as events have proved—have afforded to await with iron composure all attack upon her frontiers. Such an attack would never have taken place. If it had, it would have been dashed to pieces by the German armies, and the whole force of world opinion would have been turned against Russia and France. There was in fact no need of self-preservation for the awful plunge which Germany took in consequence of the Russian mobilisation. Let it never be admitted that mobilisation involves war or justifies the other side in declaring war. Mobilisation justifies only counter-mobilisation and further parley.

Was this too high a test for the moral fibre of any Government, of any General Staff, of any military nation? Would it not have required superhuman restraint for Germany not to have put her whole war-plan into operation after the Russian mobilisation had been ordered? The answer is not in doubt. It ought not to have been beyond the virtue and courage of so strong a State and so great a people. But on the assumption—which we dispute—that mobilisation meant war, and—which we also dispute—that war meant the execution of the German war-plan for invading France through Belgium, with all its terrible implications, was not this all the greater reason for prudence and patience while events still rested in the regions of diplomacy? What can be said of the levity with which Germany gave Austria a free hand to take what action she wished against Serbia and promised German support without conditions, without even any warning of the danger to European peace? What can be said for the German rejection of Sir Edward Grey's proposal of July 26—before the Russian mobilisation had begun—for a European Conference? If the next step led inexorably, as we are told, to Germany feeling herself forced in self-preservation to 'hack her way through Belgium,' was it not all the more important to prevent that step from being taken? And here in a European Conference was a simple and sure measure of preventing, or at the very least of delaying, the fatal exodus from the diplomatic field.

The German Emperor was surprised and alarmed, and his military advisers were fiercely excited, by the unyielding spirit which Germany encountered from the Triple Entente in the final ten days. This unyielding spirit had grown up over many years, during which the sense of German preponderance and the fear of German aggression upon land and sea had increasingly dominated the directing minds in France, Russia and Great Britain. The shadow had lain darkly over Europe since the beginning of the century. These three Powers did not mean to be separated and mastered one by one. France was bound by her treaty to Russia. Britain under the growth of the German Navy, though legally free, was morally committed to stand by France, if France were the victim of aggression. The Triple Entente could never have attacked the Central Powers. It would have fallen to pieces at the first aggressive move by any one of its members; but its resisting power in the face of attack was real and solidly founded. If Germany would come to conference, there was no doubt that the Austro-Serbian quarrel could be settled. If Germany did not attack, there would be no war. She had no right to attack. If she did, it would only show what sort of neighbour we had in the world and how wise we had been to stand together.

The convulsive forces surging around the German Emperor, rigidly departmentalised, awkwardly connected or even largely independent of one another, became in the crisis impersonal and uncontrollable. Rational processes departed and the machine took charge. Through the confusion marched the ordered phalanx of the General Staff bearing the Great Design. All was ready, and all would be well—provided there was no hesitation at the top. The deepening of the Kiel Canal was finished, and the Fleet could move freely between the Baltic and the North Sea. The fifty million pound capital levy of 1913–14 had filled the arsenals with ammunition. The supplies of explosives were assured by the new process of extracting nitrogen from the air. The German armies were incomparable, and the *Schlieffen* war-plan sure. By a coincidence the *Goeben* too was in the Mediterranean.

* * * * *

William the Second was not the man to stand against this assault. Those who have wished to judge him should first of all thank God they were not placed in his position.

* * * * *

The question arises whether apart from the European conference proposed by Sir Edward Grey on July 26, there was any means of averting the war? We frequently read statements to the effect that if he had only shown courage and decision and had told Germany plainly at the end of July that to attack France would mean war with England, there would have been no war. Lord Morley's posthumous revelations of the Cabinet situation should be convincing on this point. Such a declaration by Sir Edward Grey at that date would have resulted only in his complete disavowal by four-fifths of the Cabinet and three-quarters of the House of Commons. Mr. Asquith would have resigned, his Government split into fragments, and the four or five tremendous days that remained, in every hour of which indispensable precautions were being taken, would instead have been filled by utter chaos from which no doubt a war decision would have emerged too late for every purpose. A British threat to intervene, if unwarranted by national authority, could only have convinced Germany that we were impotent and out of it.

To divert the deadly current it was necessary to go back along the stream for months and years. If, for instance, Germany had accepted the British proposals of 1911 for a naval holiday, much might have been possible. A European conference on land armaments and the maintenance of peace would in such circumstances have found England a sympathetic listener to all that Germany might have urged about the growth of the Russian army and the perfecting of Russian strategic railways with French money. The marshalling of Europe into two armed leagues might have given place, temporarily at any rate, to a much more relaxed and easy attitude. But at the end, in the final crisis, the British Foreign Secretary could do nothing but what he did. To abandon France and Russia diplomatically in the face of the German threat would have been to break up for years all counterpoise against the ever more assertive German power. To threaten war upon Germany would have been repudiated by Cabinet, Parliament and People. But no words of English Ministers were required to plead the policy of Sir Edward Grey. Hour by hour as the German armies marched through treaties and across frontiers upon defenceless Belgium towards an agonised and cornered France, arguments resounded far above the feeble voice of man. The cannon gained by its first salvo on Belgian soil a verdict for which all the statesmen and soldiers of the British Empire would have pleaded in vain.

When we consider the character of the German Government before the War, as now so fully revealed in all the published records and descriptions of the Emperor's Court, we almost feel that we may leave the issue to the long justice of the German people. Let them never overlook that if France, deserting Russia and false to her Treaty obligations, had declared neutrality, the German Ambassador in Paris had instructions to demand the surrender to German garrisons of the fortresses of Toul and Verdun, as guarantee that that neutrality would be observed.

* * * * *

Carnage and cannonade! All Europe on the march! Fifteen million bayonets seeking the breasts of an equal number of faithful, valiant, pitiful, puzzled mortals! We have passed into the military sphere. Where are the stepping-stones? The incomprehension by the French General Staff of the conditions of modern war; the mad rush forward in blue and red uniforms against the fire of machine guns and magazine rifles: the German invader advancing, yet accorded all the advantages of the defence! The flower of the French Army and its best regimental officers shorn away in the Battles of the Frontier! The worst of all cases on the largest scale—defending your own country by charging the invading bullets! Purblindness to conditions already made bloodily plain among the kopjes of Natal and in the millet fields of Manchuria! No General in all History ever had the chance of Joffre. He had only to say 'Let the attackers attack; let them learn that bullets kill men, and that earth stops bullets.' In martial quality, in every attribute that preserves an iron race, the French soldier of 1914 was at least the equal of the best troops who marched against him.

And then the noble constancy of the French Army, rising superior to defeat and misdirection, fighting as if they were following Napoleon in his greatest days. Bloody defeats all along the line, eight marches to the rear; obvious complete miscalculation! Never a reproach, never a murmur, never a 'Nous sommes trahis!' Determination to conquer or die; conviction that one or the other would be accorded.

So we come to the Marne. This will ever remain the Mystery Battle of all time. We can see more clearly across the mists of Time how Hannibal conquered at Cannae, than why Joffre won at the Marne. No great acquisition of strength to either side—except that usually invaders outrun their supplies and defenders fall back upon their reserves—important, but not decisive. Not much real fighting, comparatively few casualties, no decisive episode in any part of the immense field; fifty explanations, all well documented, five hundred volumes of narrative and comment—but the mystery remains. What was the cause which turned retreat into victory and gave the world time to come to the succour of France? Where vast issues are so nicely balanced every single fact or factor may be called decisive. Some say it was the generous onslaught of Russia and the withdrawal by an inadequate German Staff decision of two army corps from their wheeling flank; some say Gallieni and his leopard-spring from Paris, or Joffre with his phlegm and steadfast spirit. We British naturally dwell on the part played by Sir John French and his five divisions: and there are several other important claims. But if under all reserve I am to choose the agate point on which the balance turned, I select the visits of Colonel Hentsch of the German General Staff on the night of the 8th and the morning of the 9th of September to the Army Headquarters of von Bülow and Kluck, either ordering by an excess of authority, or lending the sanction of supreme authority to, the retirement of these armies. There was no need for such a retreat. Speaking broadly, the Germans could have dug themselves in where they stood, or even in places continued to advance. It was only a continued effort of will that was needed then and a readiness to risk all, where all had been already risked.

The desperate battle of the Yser lies on a lower level of crisis and decision. Both sides were exhausted, but both were reinforced. A long grapple of weakened antagonists, five times as bloody as the Marne, but never presenting the supreme issue. And by this time the defenders have learned to dig, they have learned that even a few hundred resolute well-armed, well-trained infantry or dismounted cavalry may stop ten thousand and kill half of them with bullets. This trick of infantry on the defensive of digging holes in the ground and firing rifles, a curious, newly discovered plan, is going to become a habit in this all-probing war, and now in 1914 there are no technical means by artillery, gas, or tanks of overcoming it. Thus we reach trench warfare, and Christmas, and a breathing space.

Here was the time for Peace. The explosion was over. The invaders of France had been brought to a standstill, the defenders were not strong enough to attack them. Deadlock along the fighting lines, bankruptcy of ideas in the General Staffs. Far away on the Eastern front the Germans had destroyed the Russian offensive, and further South the Russians had beaten the Austrians. Peace now, before the world is ruined, before its capital is consumed, before the whole life force of nations is melted down! Peace now at Christmas, 1914! Here was the first and best American opportunity. But no one would hear of it. The Press and public opinion advanced together. The cup must be drained.

Break away then, Allies. Seek new theatres. Use the sea power of Britain. Find the flanks of your enemy even if you have to travel a thousand miles. . . . Use Surprise, use Mobility, attack where none is ready to resist. Vain to sit glowering at each other in ditches; mad to crawl out of them only to be shot down!

* * * * *

But meanwhile, in another part of the world, at present apparently lapped in peace, a momentous event has occurred. The German battle cruiser *Goeben* has arrived at Constantinople. We need not retell by what chances she got there. There she is; and the Turks in consequence have against the Russians the naval command of the Black Sea. They are therefore able to join the Central Powers and to carry out their long-prepared plan of invading the Caucasus and wresting it from Russia. Collision therefore of Turkey against Russia and entry of Turkey into the general war!

But the arrival of this new enemy brings with it opportunities as well as dangers. It opens a vulnerable flank. The opportunities are greater than the burdens. Swift, then, the Allies. Leave the great armies scowling at each other in the trenches and the great navies hating each other in strict routine from widely separated harbours. Break in upon this new weak opponent before he is on his feet, beat him down by land and sea; force the Dardanelles by fleets and armies, seize Constantinople, join hands with Russia, rally the Balkans, draw Italy to your cause; and then all together hew your way into the naked belly of Austria. Again very simple; again very difficult.

The politicians are attracted, the Generals and Admirals mutter 'To break away from a first-class war, the sort of war that only comes once in a hundred years, for an amphibious strategic-political manœuvre of this kind is nothing less than unprofessional.' Divided councils, half-hearted measures, grudged resources, makeshift plans, no real control or guidance.

However, events move forward. On March 18, 1915, Admiral de Robeck engages the forts of the Dardanelles, seeking to force the passage. And here again we reach an agate point. The Turks have very few mines, they have sown all they have; if these are swept up they have none left—not a dozen. But luckily for them twenty of these mines have been laid in an unexpected quarter. The sweeping flotillas newly and feebly organised have overlooked them. Two or three ships are blown up. The Admiral sustains a sinister impression, he breaks off the attack; he will never renew it. Nothing will induce him to re-enter this area of mysterious danger. Although a fortnight later he is equipped with mine-sweeping flotillas which in a few hours could have cleared with certainty the whole area from which he could engage the forts decisively, he will never allow these flotillas to act. They remain courageous, efficient and useless, and so does his fleet and so does he. They all remain the spectators of a military tragedy. We were condemned to the army attack upon the Gallipoli peninsula. Now we know that not only were there no more mines, but that the big guns of the forts, the only ones that could stop armoured ships, had only a few score shells remaining. A night's sweeping by the flotillas, a morning's bombardment, must have revealed the bankruptcy of the defence. However, it was otherwise decreed. The Fleet recoils from all idea of forcing the passage of the Dardanelles; the Army, after heroic efforts, fails to capture the key points of the Gallipoli peninsula. So the flank attack is over; it has failed, and we all return heavily to the battle-front in France, where nothing but useless slaughter has in the meanwhile occurred.

* * * * *

We have seen how important and possibly decisive was the opportunity open to Germany at the beginning of 1916. If Falkenhayn had left the Allies to break their teeth on the German entrenchments in the West, selling where necessary the conquered territory for a sufficient price in blood, and had marched against Russia in full strength, he might well have compelled Roumania to join the Central Powers and have gained the vast food and fuel regions which stretched from Galicia to the Caspian Sea. He would thus have broken the naval blockade by continental conquest, and gained from the land much that the British Navy denied upon the sea. Instead, in approved professional spirit he chose to gnaw the iron hills of Verdun and their steel defenders. Thus were the Allies delivered from the penalties which their strategic follies in 1915 had deserved, and the equipoise of the war preserved for another bloody year.

During the whole of 1915 and 1916 the defence maintained an immense advantage over the attack and the losses of the assailants nearly always exceeded threefold those of the defenders. But gradually the methods and resources of the offensive improved. The whole front became so heavily packed with guns and so laced by railways and lateral communications that an increasing number of alternative offensives were simultaneously open. The art of camouflage made great progress; almost unlimited ammunition was available. The artillery discovered first the creeping barrage system, and secondly the power of opening a correct fire without previously disclosing their concentration by trial shots. The use of artificial fog, and above all the invention of the Tanks and their employment in great numbers, all restored to the attacking armies the vital element of surprise. Already in 1917 the sudden 'set-piece' attack began to achieve profitable results in its first stages and the gradual diminution of the advantages of the defence was increasingly apparent. 1918 witnessed the definite recovery by the stronger armies of their prerogative to advance at the cost of superior losses. The war of movement was resumed by both sides in cumbrous fashion on a gigantic scale.

* * * * *

The third great climax of the war, successor to the Marne and the failure at the Dardanelles, came at the beginning of 1917. Russia collapsed in revolution. But while this awful event was still among the secrets of the future, the German General and Naval Staffs had forced their Civil Government to sanction the unlimited submarine campaign, and thus dragged the United States into the combination against them. We have seen by what strange fortune the struggling Allies gained in the nick of time a new giant in the West to replace the dying titan of the East. Three months' less resistance by Russia, three months' more patience by the German General Staff, three months' delay in launching the submarine campaign, and that fateful challenge would never have been flung. Russia would have been out without America being in. There are few conjunctures in history more worthy than this of the attention of the strategist, the statesman, the moralist or the philosopher.

But what should inspire the British people with wonder and awe, is that this fortunate double event had occurred in a different combination almost exactly one hundred years before. In 1811 the supreme question was whether the pressure of the British blockade would force Napoleon's allies and especially Russia to break away from him and his continental system, before it provoked the United States to enter the war upon his side. Here also by a few months events followed a favourable sequence. Russia fell out of the hostile combination before America entered it. Napoleon was already marching all his armies upon Moscow before the war of 1812 was declared between England and the United States. Thus twice, and in two successive centuries, England was not left in the worst possible situation. Such mysterious rhythms of history will dim to the eyes of future generations the hazards and drama of the Punic wars.

* * * * *

It is not necessary here to examine the important moral and material contribution of the United States to the general victory. But in the Peace Conference—to European eyes—President Wilson sought to play a part out of all proportion to any stake which his country had contributed or intended to contribute to European affairs. Actuated by the noblest motives he went far beyond any commission which the American Senate or people were willing to accord him, and armed with this inflation of his own constitutional power he sought to bend the world—no doubt for its own good—to his personal views. This was a grave misfortune; for his opportunity, though narrower than his ambition, was nevertheless as great as has ever been given to a statesman. The influence of mighty, detached and well-meaning America upon the European settlement was a precious agency of hope. It was largely squandered in sterile conflicts and half-instructed and half-pursued interferences. If President Wilson had set himself from the beginning to make common cause with Lloyd George and Clemenceau, the whole force of these three great men, the heads of the dominant nations, might have played with plenary and beneficent power over the wide scene of European tragedy. He consumed his own strength and theirs in conflicts in which he was always worsted. He gained as an antagonist and corrector results which were pitifully poor compared to those which would have rewarded comradeship. He might have made everything swift and easy. He made everything slower and more difficult. He might have carried a settlement at the time when leadership was strong. He acquiesced in second-rate solutions when the phase of exhaustion and dispersion had supervened.

However as Captain he went down with his ship.

* * * * *

But all this lies in the past. It is a tale that is told, from which we may draw the knowledge and comprehension needed for the future. The disproportion between the quarrels of nations and the suffering which fighting out those quarrels involves; the poor and barren prizes which reward sublime endeavour on the battlefield; the fleeting triumphs of war; the long, slow rebuilding; the awful risks so hardily run; the doom missed by a hair's breadth, by the spin of a coin, by the accident of an accident—all this should make the prevention of another great war the main preoccupation of mankind. It has at least been stripped of glitter and glamour. No more may Alexander, Cæsar and Napoleon lead armies to victory, ride their horses on the field of battle sharing the perils of their soldiers and deciding the fate of empires by the resolves and gestures of a few intense hours. For the future they will sit surrounded by clerks in offices, as safe, as quiet and as dreary as Government departments, while the fighting men in scores of thousands are slaughtered or stifled over the telephone by machinery. We have seen the last of the great Commanders. Perhaps they were extinct before Armageddon began. Next time the competition may be to kill women and children, and the civil population generally, and victory will give herself in sorry nuptials to the diligent hero who organises it on the largest scale.

* * * * *

The story of the human race is War. Except for brief and precarious interludes there has never been peace in the world; and before history began murderous strife was universal and unending. But the modern developments surely require severe and active attention.

Up to the present time the means of destruction at the disposal of man have not kept pace with his ferocity. Reciprocal extermination was impossible in the Stone Age. One cannot do much with a clumsy club. Besides, men were so scarce and hid so well that they were hard to find. They fled so fast that they were hard to catch. Human legs could only cover a certain distance each day. With the best will in the world to destroy his species, each man was restricted to a very limited area of activity. It was impossible to make any effective progress on these lines. Meanwhile one had to live and hunt and sleep. So on the balance the life-forces kept a steady lead over the forces of death, and gradually tribes, villages, and Governments were evolved.

The effort at destruction then entered upon a new phase. War became a collective enterprise. Roads were made which facilitated the movement of large numbers of men. Armies were organised. Many improvements in the apparatus of slaughter were devised. In particular the use of metal, and above all, steel, for piercing and cutting human flesh, opened out a promising field. Bows and arrows, slings, chariots, horses, and elephants lent a valuable assistance. But here again another set of checks began to operate. The Governments were not sufficiently secure. The Armies were liable to violent internal disagreements. It was extremely difficult to feed large numbers of men once they were concentrated, and consequently the efficiency of the efforts at destruction became fitful and was tremendously hampered by defective organisation. Thus again there was a balance on the credit side of life. The world rolled forward, and human society entered upon a vaster and more complex age.

It was not until the dawn of the twentieth century of the Christian era that War really began to enter into its kingdom as the potential destroyer of the human race. The organisation of mankind into great States and Empires and the rise of nations to full collective consciousness enabled enterprises of slaughter to be planned and executed upon a scale, with a perseverance, never before imagined. All the noblest virtues of individuals were gathered together to strengthen the destructive capacity of the mass. Good finances, the resources of world-wide credit and trade, the accumulation of large capital reserves, made it possible to divert for considerable periods the energies of whole peoples to the task of Devastation. Democratic institutions gave expression to the will-power of millions. Education not only brought the course of the conflict within the comprehension of every one, but rendered each person serviceable in a high degree for the purpose in hand. The Press afforded a means of unification and of mutual encouragement; Religion, having discreetly avoided conflict on the fundamental issues, offered its encouragements and consolations, through all its forms, impartially to all the combatants. Lastly, Science unfolded her treasures and her secrets to the desperate demands of men and placed in their hands agencies and apparatus almost decisive in their character.

In consequence many novel features presented themselves. Instead of merely starving fortified towns, whole nations were methodically subjected, or sought to be subjected, to the process of reduction by famine. The entire population in one capacity or another took part in the War; all were equally the object of attack. The Air opened paths along which death and terror could be carried far behind the lines of the actual armies, to women, children, the aged, the sick, who in earlier struggles would perforce have been left untouched. Marvellous organisations of railroads, steamships, and motor vehicles placed and maintained tens of millions of men continuously in action. Healing and surgery in their exquisite developments returned them again and again to the shambles. Nothing was wasted that could contribute to the process of waste. The last dying kick was brought into military utility.

But all that happened in the four years of the Great War was only a prelude to what was preparing for the fifth year. The campaign of the year 1919 would have witnessed an immense accession to the power of destruction. Had the Germans retained the morale to make good their retreat to the Rhine, they would have been assaulted in the summer of 1919 with forces and by methods incomparably more prodigious than any yet employed. Thousands of aeroplanes would have shattered their cities. Scores of thousands of cannon would have blasted their front. Arrangements were being made to carry simultaneously a quarter of a million men, together with all their requirements, continuously forward across country in mechanical vehicles moving ten or fifteen miles each day. Poison gases of incredible malignity, against which only a secret mask (which the Germans could not obtain in time) was proof, would have stifled all resistance and paralysed all life on the hostile front subjected to attack. No doubt the Germans too had their plans. But the hour of wrath had passed. The signal of relief was given, and the horrors of 1919 remained buried in the archives of the great antagonists.

The War stopped as suddenly and as universally as it had begun. The world lifted its head, surveyed the scene of ruin, and victors and vanquished alike drew breath. In a hundred laboratories, in a thousand arsenals, factories, and bureaux, men pulled themselves up with a jerk, turned from the task in which they had been absorbed. Their projects were put aside unfinished, unexecuted; but their knowledge was preserved; their data, calculations, and discoveries were hastily bundled together and docketed 'for future reference' by the War Offices in every country. The campaign of 1919 was never fought; but its ideas go marching along. In every Army they are being explored, elaborated, refined under the surface of peace, and should war come again to the world it is not with the weapons and agencies prepared for 1919 that it will be fought, but with developments and extensions of these which will be incomparably more formidable and fatal.

It is in these circumstances that we entered upon that period of Exhaustion which has been described as Peace. It gives us at any rate an opportunity to consider the general situation. Certain sombre facts emerge solid, inexorable, like the shapes of mountains from drifting mist. It is established that henceforward whole populations will take part in war, all doing their utmost, all subjected to the fury of the enemy. It is established that nations who believe their life is at stake will not be restrained from using any means to secure their existence. It is probable—nay, certain—that among the means which will next time be at their disposal will be agencies and processes of destruction wholesale, unlimited, and perhaps, once launched, uncontrollable.

Mankind has never been in this position before. Without having improved appreciably in virtue or enjoying wiser guidance, it has got into its hands for the first time the tools by which it can unfailingly accomplish its own extermination. That is the point in human destinies to which all the glories and toils of men have at last led them. They would do well to pause and ponder upon their new responsibilities. Death stands at attention, obedient, expectant, ready to serve, ready to shear away the peoples *en masse*; ready, if called on, to pulverise, without hope of repair, what is left of civilisation. He awaits only the word of command. He awaits it from a frail, bewildered being, long his victim, now—for one occasion only—his Master.

* * * * *

It is not without self-questioning and cherishing of hope that I have chosen the title of this chapter: The End of the World Crisis. Certainly the story ended with 1922 in universal gloom. No peace had been made acceptable to Germany or giving security to France. Central and Southern Europe had broken into intensely nationalistic fragments sundered from each other by enmities and jealousies, by particularist tariffs and local armaments. Russia was, as she is still, beyond the pale. Her people lie prostrate under the hardest tyranny yet seen in Asia. Her rulers, mocked by natural and economic facts, are condemned by their creed to an indefinite process of self-impoverishment and self-torture. The United States in 1922 had shaken the dust of the Old World off her feet and dwelt in opulent, exacting and strongly arming seclusion beyond the ocean. Turkey, resuscitated in a new fierce form, re-established in Constantinople and Europe, freed from her capitulations and foreign guidance, reigns henceforth with untrammelled sway over such Christian and non-Moslem inhabitants as have not been destroyed or expelled. The League of Nations, not yet reinforced by Germany, under the derision of Soviet Russia, abandoned by her mighty trans-Atlantic parent, raised a frail and unsure bulwark against stormy seas and sullen clouds. The Parliaments erected so hopefully by the nineteenth century were already, over a large part of Europe, being demolished in the twentieth. Democracy, for which the world was to be made safe by the greatest of struggles, incontinently lets slip or casts aside the instruments of freedom and progress fashioned for its protection by rugged ancestors. England, bowed by debt and taxation, could only plod forward under her load. And at this dark moment new misfortunes approached. China dissolved into a sanguinary confusion. France sundered from England stood mobilised upon the threshold of the Ruhr. No end to the World Crisis in 1922!

Mercifully our knowledge extends beyond the limits of our tale, and the years that have followed have been lighted by a series of efforts to consolidate world peace. Although these efforts are partial and at present disconnected, each has made a contribution to the supreme cause, and all have aided the process of appeasement.

The Peace Conference had proposed to solve the problem of French security in the face of a united and preponderant Germany lying on both banks of the Rhine, by the joint promise of the British Empire and the United States to come to the aid of France if she were the victim of unprovoked aggression. The French assent to the Peace Treaty had been obtained upon this basis. A tripartite agreement between the three Powers concerned had accordingly been signed by their plenipotentiaries, subject to Parliamentary confirmations. The Imperial Parliament in due course accepted the undertaking entered into by its representative on its behalf. The Senate of the United States repudiated President Wilson's signature. The joint agreement therefore lapsed. The balance of the arrangement to which France had consented was upset, and a situation tense with fear and danger arose. The Prime Ministers of Australia and New Zealand, at the Imperial Conference of 1921, declared that they would advise their Parliaments to stand, together with the Imperial Government, to their engagement to come to the aid of France, although the United States had dropped out. The growing divergencies between French and British policy and sentiment at this time left the issue in suspense. Meanwhile, France, sundered from England, abandoned by the United States, isolated and in the deepest alarm, yielded herself to military influences and trusted to her unquestionable armed superiority. We may take the entry of France into the Ruhr in 1923, and the consequent arrest of German economic revival, as the darkest moment for Europe since the fighting stopped.

The central problem was therefore at this time quite untouched. First and foremost stood the overpowering issue between France and Germany. Deep in the soul of France, and the mainspring of her policy and of almost her every action, lay the fear of German revenge. Sombre and intense in the heart of the powerful classes in Germany brooded the resolve that their national history should not be finally determined in accordance with the Treaty of Versailles; and in the pulses of her multiplying and abounding youth throbbed the hope that they might live to see, or die in advancing, a day when victory should once again light the standards of the Fatherland. On the one hand was displayed the armed and organised strength of France, her overflowing arsenals, her mechanical and technical apparatus, her African reserves, her innate undying military genius—all based upon a dwindling population and the surprises of an ever-changing science of destruction. On the other rose the mighty German nation, sixty millions against forty, with its lusty generations, its sense of injury, its laboratories, its industry and its highly disciplined orderly intelligence. Cruel had been the experiences which Germany had tasted in the Great War. But among all its lessons no facts could be found which would justify despair of future military successes. Almost single-handed the German armies had fought the world, sustaining or driving into battle her allies whose weakness or inefficiency were from the outset patent; and before France could be saved from the ruin which was prepared for her, all the life energy of Russia, of the British Empire, of Italy, and much of the power of the United States had had to be consumed or exerted in an intense degree. But would those conditions ever return? Need Germany contemplate a situation in which once again all the greatest nations and empires of the world would march successively to the aid of her ancient adversary? There then, on both sides of the Rhine, was the root of the matter; and in 1923 no one could feel assured that a future generation would not see Europe laid in dust and ashes as it had been in this same quarrel more than once before.

The policy of Britain in the face of such potentialities was fortunately understood by all parties in the State. Great Britain could have no other object but to use her whole influence and resources consistently over a long period of years to weave France and Germany so closely together economically, socially and morally, as to prevent the occasion of quarrels and make their causes die in a realisation of mutual prosperity and interdependence. The supreme interest of the British people lay in the assuagement of the great feud; and they had no other interest comparable or contrary to that.

The Labour Government under Mr. Ramsay Macdonald in 1924, by the London Convention and the Dawes Agreement, paved the way for the memorable event of 1925. Mr. Baldwin's administration enjoyed, not only unquestioned power, but the assurance of a prolonged period for its exercise. In these conditions of national strength and stability a Foreign Secretary was found with the vision and the courage to run greater risks for peace than the Ministers of any other nation had yet dared. Discarding all ideas of a dual arrangement between Great Britain and France to counteract the power of Germany, Mr. Austen Chamberlain embarked resolutely upon the policy suggested by Herr Stresemann of a threefold pact of mutual security between France, Germany and Great Britain, in which Great Britain would be solemnly pledged to come to the aid of whichever of the other two States was the object of unprovoked aggression. The histories may be searched for a parallel for such an undertaking. Nevertheless, it was from the outset steadfastly endorsed by all classes and parties in Great Britain. The great enterprise was pressed forward by the experience and skill of M. Briand, and by the astonishing civic courage of Herr Stresemann and other leaders. It received at the culminating point the reinforcement of the whole strength of Italy, wielded by the far-seeing realism of Mussolini. Innumerable difficulties were overcome. Processes of agreement which might well have required a decade of perseverance were accomplished in the negotiations of a few months. The co-operation of the smaller Powers was procured; and in October, 1925, by the waters of a calm lake, the four great Western democracies plighted their solemn troth to keep the peace among themselves in all circumstances, and to stand united against any one of their number who broke the compact and marched in aggression upon a brother land. The eventual Treaty of Locarno was signed, as was fitting, in London where the main impulse of the policy had originated, and was duly ratified by all the Parliaments concerned. It had been throughout conceived in harmonious accord with the Covenant of the League of Nations, to the Council of which Germany as a consequence now brought her mighty power. Thus was achieved the greatest measure of self-preservation yet taken by Europeans.

The Treaty of Locarno may be regarded as the Old World counterpart of the Treaty of Washington between the United States, Great Britain and Japan, which in 1921 had regulated and ensured the peace of the Pacific. These two august instruments give assurance to civilisation. They are the twin pyramids of peace rising solid and unshakable on either side of the Atlantic, commanding the allegiance of the leading nations of the world and of all their fleets and armies. They form the cores around which the wider conceptions of the League of Nations and the idealism of the Kellogg Pact can rear the more spacious and more unified structures of the future.

The task is not done. The greatest exertions must continue to be made over a long period of years. The danger of war has by no means passed from the world. Old antagonisms are sleeping, and the drum-beat of new antagonisms is already heard. The anxieties of France and the resentments of Germany are only partly removed. Over the broad plains of Eastern and Central Europe, with their numerous new and highly nationalistic States, brood the offended shades of Peter and Frederick the Great and the memories of the wars they waged. Russia, self-outcast, sharpens her bayonets in her Arctic night, and mechanically proclaims through self-starved lips her philosophy of hatred and death. But since Locarno, Hope rests on a surer foundation. The period of repulsion from the horrors of war will be long-lasting; and in this blessed interval the great nations may take their forward steps to world organisation with the conviction that the difficulties they have yet to master will not be greater than those they have already overcome.

APPENDIX

A MEMORANDUM UPON THE PACIFICATION

OF THE MIDDLE EAST

The situation that confronted His Majesty's Government in Iraq at the beginning of 1921 was a most unsatisfactory one. The system of direct British administration, which had been maintained since the Armistice, had broken down in the previous summer when a local rising on the Euphrates developed into a serious rebellion which was suppressed with much difficulty and with the aid of reinforcements sent from India. A large and costly military garrison still remained in the country. Order had been restored but the future was dubious in the extreme. The events of 1920 had brought the Iraq question strongly into the limelight and a violent agitation had been started in the Press and elsewhere against the whole policy of the British Government. Criticism was directed mainly against the heavy expenditure entailed upon the British taxpayer, already staggering under the financial burden left by the war; but in some quarters it took another line and represented that our troubles were due to our failure to give effect to war-time promises of independence for the Arabs.

After the rising of 1920 it became evident that there must be some change of policy. In the autumn of that year Sir Percy Cox had been sent out to Baghdad as the first British High Commissioner and had lost no time in setting up a provisional Arab Government under the presidency of the Naqib of Baghdad, a venerable figure, who commanded great respect not only in Iraq itself but in the Mohammedan world outside its borders.

Prior to 1921 different departments of His Majesty's Government had dealt with the different Middle Eastern areas conquered during the war. The affairs of Palestine and Trans-Jordan were in the charge of the Foreign Office; those of Iraq in that of the India Office. Early in 1921 the Government decided to place these matters under a single Department, viz., the Colonial Office, to which I had recently been appointed as Secretary of State. A new Middle East Department was accordingly established at the Colonial Office and came formally into existence on March 1, 1921.

My first step was to summon a conference at Cairo, over which I presided personally and which was attended by all the principal officers concerned in the administration of Middle Eastern affairs. The main upshot, so far as Iraq was concerned, was that the Emir Feisal was invited to proceed to Baghdad as a candidate for the throne of Iraq. Though not of Iraqi origin, he had very special qualifications for the post. He came of the Sherifian family which, as guardians of the Holy Places at Mecca, commanded wide veneration throughout the Islamic world. His father, Sherif Hussein (afterwards for a time King of the Hejaz), had organised the Arab revolt against the Turks during the war. He himself had fought gallantly on our side and had taken part in the various exploits of desert warfare with which the name of Colonel Lawrence will always be associated.

The Emir Feisal set out for Iraq in June, 1921. At the same time I announced in the House of Commons that his candidature had the approval of the British Government. On the Emir's arrival it was decided, on a resolution by the existing Council of Ministers, that a referendum should be held throughout the country on the question of his election to the throne. The referendum was duly carried out throughout Iraq, with the exception of one purely Kurdish area, which preferred to hold aloof. The result was that 96 per cent. of the votes cast were in Feisal's favour, and he was crowned King at Baghdad on August 23, 1921. He at once entrusted the Naqib with the formation of his first Cabinet.

In this way direct British administration in Iraq definitely ceased. It was replaced by an Arab Government, acting indeed on British advice, but acting on its own responsibility and not under external dictation. A large number of British officers were retained in the country, but they were retained either in an advisory capacity or as technical officers subordinate to the Iraq Government.

The next task that lay before the British Government was to regularise the whole position. We had agreed, at the San Remo Conference of April, 1920, to assume the position of Mandatory for Iraq under the League of Nations. The draft of a formal 'mandate' was submitted to the League in December, 1920, but owing to various difficulties this draft had never been formally approved. In October, 1921, we obtained a kind of *ad interim* authority from the League in the shape of a letter from the President of the Council inviting us to continue to carry on the administration of Iraq in the spirit of the draft mandate until such time as the position should have been regularised. But while the League hesitated, the local situation did not. Iraq advanced rapidly under our guidance. The term 'mandate' acquired an unpopular significance in the country. It was held to imply a degree of tutelage which the new State considered that it did not require. It was a case of the 'protectorate' in Egypt over again. As a way out of the difficulty, it was decided to conclude a treaty with the King of Iraq, ostensibly as between equals, which would (1) define in detail the relations between the two countries and (2) place the British Government in a position to discharge towards the League of Nations those obligations which it would have incurred under a formal 'mandate.' This treaty was duly signed at Baghdad on October 10, 1922. Shortly after its signature the Coalition Government in England went out of office and I ceased to be Secretary of State for the Colonies. The treaty of October, 1922, left various matters of detail to be dealt with subsequently in a number of subsidiary Agreements. These subsidiary Agreements (Military, Financial, Judicial, etc.) were eventually concluded in March, 1924. In September, 1924, the Treaty and Agreements were laid before the Council of the League of Nations and were accepted by them, with the addition of certain other assurances given by the British Government, as giving adequate effect in respect of Iraq to the mandatory principle as defined in the Covenant of the League. By this means the whole position was eventually placed on a regular juridical basis.

Internally, the progress of the Iraq State has been marked by successive constitutional steps. The first step was the election of a Constituent Assembly, whose business was to frame a constitution for the country. This was done in the form of an Organic Law passed by the Assembly on July 10, 1924. Having discharged its functions the Assembly was dissolved and was replaced in due course by the first Iraq Parliament which came into being in 1926.

A question which long caused much trouble both externally and internally was that of the Turco-Iraq frontier. The Turks claimed the retrocession of the whole of the Mosul vilayet, i.e., about one-third of the whole country, including the most fertile areas. The Treaty of Lausanne (1923) left the question open. Much controversy raged over the matter and at one time there was serious danger of hostilities with the Turks. Ultimately the matter was referred to the League of Nations and a frontier was laid down which maintained the rights of Iraq over practically the whole vilayet. The Turks accepted the *fait accompli*. The frontier was delimited by a mixed Commission without serious friction and friendly relations have not since been impaired.

Of the other matters dealt with by the Cairo Conference it is not perhaps necessary to say much. As regards Palestine, the Conference did little more than confirm the policy previously adopted and still maintained. In Trans-Jordan there have been developments. The Amir Abdullah, a brother of King Feisal of Iraq, was permitted to establish himself as ruler of the country. The experiment has on the whole been a success. The Amir's Government, though it left a good deal to be desired in its early stages, has shown marked improvement of recent years. Public security and public contentment have definitely improved. We have during the past year concluded a Treaty with the Amir very much on the lines of that with King Feisal, providing for a constitutional régime in Trans-Jordan. This Treaty awaits ratification.

Turning again to Iraq, it is necessary to mention one further change of the highest importance that was introduced in 1922. In October of that year military control in the country was transferred from the War Office to the Air Ministry. It may safely be claimed that the change has proved an immense success. It has resulted in a progressive reduction in the cost of the garrison and consequently in the burden imposed on the British taxpayer. At the beginning of 1921 the strength of the British garrison in Iraq stood at 32 battalions plus Artillery, Engineers, etc. By July, 1921, the number had been reduced to 23 battalions, and a further reduction to 12 battalions was started in

October of that year. In the year 1922–23 provision was made for 9 battalions (*plus* other services) for the first half of the year and for 6 battalions during the second half. The process of reduction was continued until in the year 1928 provision was made for no more than one Indian battalion and one Sapper and Miner Company, both of which were withdrawn on the 1st November last. There are now (apart from the R.A.F.) no regular military units, British or Indian, in the whole country. In order to accelerate the programme for relieving Imperial troops a force of native Levies, under British command, and paid for by the British Treasury, was raised in 1921–22. These Levies at one time reached a strength of 4 Infantry Battalions, 3 Cavalry Regiments, 1 Pack Battery and ancillaries. The force has now been reduced to 2 Battalions.

The cost of the British Garrison in Iraq during the past seven years has been as follows:—

1921/2	£20,097,684
1922/3	£6,610,554
1923/4	£5,033,790
1924/5	£3,847,224
1925/6	£3,314,813
1926/7	£2,753,775
1927/8	£1,648,038

In 1928 it was decided to show the normal cost of defence, exclusive of the cost of the Levies and of the 'extra' cost of the British garrison, in the War Office and Air Ministry Estimates with the exception of Indian troops; consequently, figures are not available beyond 1927/8.

The Air Force in Iraq in 1921 consisted of 6 Squadrons which, in the following year, were raised to 8 Squadrons plus armoured car Companies. By April, 1928, the strength had been reduced to 5 Squadrons *plus* 6 sections of Armoured Cars.

It is worth recording that this striking reduction of military strength (with corresponding financial retrenchment) has been carried through without a hitch and without any resultant disturbance in Iraq. When the nature of the country is considered, its vast distances, the unsettled nature of many of its inhabitants and its huge desert frontier, over which really effective control is impossible, it may fairly be claimed that the results achieved have been astonishing. It must be remembered, moreover, that the difficulty with the Turks was not finally resolved until the end of 1925. All the plans made in the earlier stages were based on the assumption that there would be an early settlement with Turkey. This assumption was falsified for nearly five years. Yet the plans were duly carried out and no disorder or mishap resulted. There has, in fact, been nothing in the nature of serious disturbance since the rising of 1920. There have been difficulties from time to time in outlying Kurdish areas and there have been serious raids (particularly last winter) by the Wahabi tribesmen who owe allegiance to Ibn Sa'ud. But these are conditions that have always to be reckoned with and must be taken as they come. There is no reason to suppose that they cannot be dealt with in future as effectively as in the past.

To sum up, the policy inaugurated in 1921 has been continued up to the present time. Like other policies, it has had its ups and downs. There have been moments of difficulty and of danger. In spite of these, however, it has been steadily pursued, often in face of fierce and unscrupulous press criticism at home, and has achieved a measure of success which few of us thought at all probable eight years ago.

INDEX

Index